YO-ASV-793

Linn's

UNITED STATES STAMPS 1922-26

GARY GRIFFITH

Published by *Linn's Stamp News*, the largest and most informative stamp newspaper in the world. *Linn's* is owned by Amos Press Inc., 911 Vandemark Road, Sidney, Ohio 45365. Amos Press also publishes *Scott Stamp Monthly* and the Scott line of catalogs. Illustrated on the cover of this book is the $5 America stamp (Scott 573) of the Series of 1922. This book and its cover were designed by Veronica Schreiber.

Copyright Linn's Stamp News, 1997

For Barbara Gay

Contents

Introduction vii
Acknowledgments ix
Chapter 1: The Harding Postal Administration 1
Chapter 2: The Bureau of Engraving and Printing in 1922 9
Chapter 3: Motorcycle Special Delivery 15
Chapter 4: Planning the Series of 1922 23
Chapter 5: The Series of 1922 37
    1¢ Benjamin Franklin 38
    2¢ George Washington 40
    3¢ Abraham Lincoln 43
    4¢ Martha Washington 45
    5¢ Theodore Roosevelt 48
    6¢ James A. Garfield 51
    7¢ William McKinley 55
    8¢ Ulysses S. Grant 57
    9¢ Thomas Jefferson 59
    10¢ James Monroe 61
    11¢ Rutherford B. Hayes 65
    12¢ Grover Cleveland 70
    14¢ American Indian 73
    15¢ Statue of Liberty 78
    20¢ Golden Gate 81
    25¢ Niagara 84
    30¢ Buffalo 87
    50¢ Arlington Amphitheatre 90
    $1 Lincoln Memorial 92
    $2 U.S. Capitol 94
    $5 America 96
Chapter 6: The Rotary Press 107
Chapter 7: The Sidewise Coils 115
    1¢ Side Coil 118
    2¢ Side Coil 119
    3¢ Side Coil 122

  4¢ Side Coil 123
  5¢ Side Coil 124
  10¢ Side Coil 125
Chapter 8: Coil Waste 127
  2¢ Coil Waste, Perforated 11 x 10 129
  2¢ Coil Waste, Perforated 11 x 11 131
  1¢ Coil Waste, Perforated 11 x 10 132
  1¢ Coil Waste, Perforated 11 x 11 133
Chapter 9: The Imperforates 137
  1¢ Imperforate 138
  2¢ Imperforate 140
Chapter 10: Flat-Plate Booklets 143
  Combination Booklets 143
  1¢ Booklets 144
  2¢ Booklets 144
  1¢ Booklet Pane 147
  2¢ Booklet Pane 148
Chapter 11: A New Sheet Rotary 151
Chapter 12: Death of Harding and Accession of Coolidge 157
Chapter 13: Night Flying and the Transcontinental Airmails 159
  8¢ Propeller and Radiator 165
  16¢ Air Service Emblem 166
  24¢ De Havilland Biplane 168
Chapter 14: The Black Hardings 171
  2¢ Black Harding 173
  2¢ Rotary Black Harding 177
  2¢ Imperforate Black Harding 179
Chapter 15: The Sheet Rotary Rarities 183
  1¢ Sheet Rotary, Perforated 11 187
  2¢ Rotary Black Harding, Perforated 11 190
Chapter 16: The Endwise Coils 193
  1¢ End Coil 194
  2¢ End Coil 195
Chapter 17: Huguenot–Walloon Issue 199
  1¢ Ship Nieu Nederland 201

v

 2¢ Walloons Landing at Fort Orange 205
 5¢ Jean Ribault Monument 207
Chapter 18: Another Rotary Experiment: 213
 2¢ Washington Rotary 216
Chapter 19: The Election of 1924; New Postal Rates of 1925 221
Chapter 20: The 1½¢ Harding 225
 1½¢ Harding Flat Plate 227
 1½¢ Harding Rotary, Perf 10 229
 1½¢ Harding Side Coil 231
 1½¢ Harding Flat-Plate Imperforate 232
 1½¢ Harding End Coil 234
Chapter 21: The ½¢ Hale 237
Chapter 22: Lexington-Concord Issue 243
 1¢ Washington at Cambridge 245
 2¢ Birth of Liberty 249
 5¢ Minuteman Statue 251
Chapter 23: The Star Plates 257
 2¢ Star Plates, Scott 554 260
 2¢ Star Plate, Scott 577 260
 8¢ Star Plate, Scott 560 260
 12¢ Star Plates, Scott 564 261
 15¢ Star Plates, Scott 565 261
 20¢ Star Plates, Scott 567 261
Chapter 24: The Perforation 10 Rotaries 263
 3¢ Lincoln Rotary 264
 4¢ Martha Washington Rotary 265
 5¢ Roosevelt Rotary 266
 6¢ Garfield Rotary 267
 7¢ McKinley Rotary 268
 8¢ Grant Rotary 269
 9¢ Jefferson Rotary 270
 10¢ Monroe Rotary 271
Chapter 25: The Special Handling Stamp 273
Chapter 26: The 15¢ Special Delivery 279
Chapter 27: The ½¢ Due 281

Chapter 28: The 20¢ Special Delivery 285
Chapter 29: The Norse-American Issue 289
    2¢ Sloop Restaurationen 291
    5¢ Viking Ship 294
Chapter 30: Administrative Changes 299
Chapter 31: The 17¢ Wilson 303
Chapter 32: The 13¢ Harrison 313
Chapter 33: Contract Airmail 319
Chapter 34: The Map Airmails 325
    10¢ Map Airmail 325
    15¢ Map Airmail 329
    20¢ Map Airmail 331
Chapter 35: The Sesquicentennial Exposition Issue 335
Chapter 36: The Ericsson Memorial Issue 345
Chapter 37: The 1½¢ Rotary Imperforate 351
Chapter 38: The First Rotary Booklet Stamps 355
Chapter 39: The Battle of White Plains Issue 359
Chapter 40: The First U.S. Souvenir Sheet 367
Epilogue 373
Photo Credits 375
Index 376
About the Author 390

Introduction

Stamps don't just happen. They are issued for historical and political reasons, and in most times, it is the political reasons that prevail. The election of President Warren G. Harding in 1920, which marked a change from a Democratic to a Republican administration, resulted in a new era in American political history.

Harding was not a great president. In fact, most historians rank him at or near the bottom of the list of our chief executives. But his election caused great changes in the nation's stamp program, and that is our subject here. The Post Office Department management that came in with Harding stayed on after his death, and set the tone, if not the policy, for United States stamps during the Coolidge and Hoover administrations that followed. It gave us not only a new series of definitive stamps, but also an important expansion of production by high-speed rotary presses and an enormous expansion of airmail.

In preparing this book, I have sought out a number of primary sources, the most important of which is the Post Office Department's original correspondence file, which has only recently become available to researchers at the Smithsonian Institution Library at the National Postal Museum. Another important batch of correspondence was discovered in the attic of the Bureau of Engraving and Printing in 1993. These files, together with the Bureau's correspondence files at the National Archives, give us a more complete — and sometimes corrected view — of the stamp production of the period. There is much new information here, particularly about the initial requests for the stamps and the political considerations behind the decisions to issue them.

Like anyone else who has studied the stamps of this period, I am deeply indebted to the work of Max Johl and Beverly King, who first published their *United States Stamps of the Twentieth Century* in 1934. King concentrated on the history of the stamps and their designs while Johl concentrated on stamp production and varieties. While their work has stood up well over time, much new information has come to light since 1934, and there is much information here that was not available to King and Johl when they published.

One of the shortcomings of their work, and of many other philatelic books and catalogs, is that they separate stamp material into regular issues, commemoratives, airmails, special deliveries, postage dues and so on. This takes stamps out of their real chronology. The first ½¢ postage due stamp, for example, was issued because the first fractional-value postage stamps were issued at the same time. They belong together. I have tried to put all the stamps of this period back into their real chronology again. Regular issues, commemoratives, airmails and special service stamps are all treated here together.

The Scott *Specialized Catalogue of United States Stamps* is a fine book, and I have used its numbering system here with the permission of the publishers. But Scott over the years has created some real problems in understanding the stamps of this period in their proper sequence. Scott 610, for example, was produced about two years before Scott 553, and Scott 553 was based on the design of 610. It is hard to see the relationship when Scott catalogs and albums have them separated so widely.

This year, 1997, marks the 75th anniversary of the Series of 1922. When the great scholars of our hobby were studying the U.S. stamps we now regard as "classics," the stamps were not as old. John Luff, for example, published his book on U.S. stamps in 1902, when the first adhesives had been with us for only 55 years. Carol Chase published on the 3¢ stamp of 1851 in 1909. Elliot Perry published on the 1857 issue in 1922.

Clearly, the time has come for the Series of 1922 and the other stamps of its era to be considered worthy subjects of a book of their own.

A Note on the Notes

Footnotes are included at the end of each chapter, not only to provide documentation for quotations and factual material, but to guide the reader to the original sources and to more complete treatments of matter that must be treated briefly here.

References to the Scott *Specialized Catalogue of United States Stamps* are not included in the note section at the end of each chapter, but are described by year of the edition in the text.

Similarly, in discussions of the shades and colors, where Max Johl almost always found more shades than Scott did, the references to Johl that are not specifically noted are taken from *The United States Postage Stamps of the Twentieth Century*, Volume III, published by H.L. Lindquist in 1935, or from *The United States Commemorative Stamps of the Twentieth Century*, published by H.L. Lindquist in 1947.

In referring to double-transfer listings and other plate varieties, references to Cloudy French, where not specifically noted, are taken from his *Encyclopedia of Plate Varieties on U.S. Bureau-Printed Postage Stamps*, published by the Bureau Issues Association in 1979.

Acknowledgments

A book on the Series of 1922 stamps was originally suggested to me by Donna O'Keefe Houseman of *Linn's Stamp News* in 1992. She has been a patient and capable editor over the last five years as the subject matter expanded to include all of the stamps of the period.

Research on this project was aided greatly by Cecilia Wertheimer, the curator of the Historical Resource Center at the Bureau of Engraving and Printing, who provided access to original documents, models and source material, as well as to data on Bureau personnel and production. It was she who found the production orders and correspondence that had not been previously available to researchers. She herself, in my experience, has been one of the great resources of the Bureau.

Timothy Carr, the librarian at the Smithsonian Institution Library at the National Postal Museum, provided extensive access to the Post Office Department manuscripts that contain much of the political background on the stamps.

Gini Horn and the staff at the American Philatelic Research Library provided much of the bibliographical material that aided in finding previously published work.

Several experts on United States stamps of this period made corrections and suggestions that have improved this work and kept the inevitable number of errors and mistakes down. Although I alone am responsible for those that remain, George Brett and Wallace Cleland were extremely helpful and diligent in their reading of the manuscript. Their deep knowledge of stamp production, and their willingness to share it, were invaluable to me. Larry Weiss made a number of important suggestions for improvements, including a greater emphasis on first-day material. Jay Stotts and Tony Callendrello, my friends and fellow enthusiasts for the Series of 1922, aided my research over a number of years and also made many suggestions for improvements in the manuscript.

Lastly, Katherine Werner, my friend and partner, helped me in innumerable ways to see the book to completion.

Chapter 1

The Harding Postal Administration

The presidential election of 1920 produced a change in parties in the White House, a change in personnel in the Post Office Department, and within 14 months, a change in the nation's postage stamps.

At the time of the election of Warren G. Harding to the presidency, the stamps that were used on the nation's letters, postcards and packages were the stamps that we now know as the Washington-Franklin series. It was a European-influenced series, copying the style of British stamps, which showed only a portrait of the sovereign on all denominations. The American interpretation of this style employed only the portraits of two men: George Washington, the nation's first president, and Benjamin Franklin, the founder of the nation's postal system.

The Washington-Franklin series was initiated late in 1908, near the end of the Theodore Roosevelt administration. Although it was altered a bit over the years, it remained in use through the four years of the Taft administration and the eight years of the Wilson administration.

A long-standing view is that the Washington-Franklin series came to an end because the designs and colors were so similar that postal workers could not tell them apart. As a result, the story went, the government was losing money on short-paid matter.

In truth, however, postal clerks had been working with these stamps for a dozen years, and could certainly tell the difference between them. The colors had been made more distinguishable in early 1912, and the stamps in use in 1920 were actually not that hard to tell apart. The 1¢ stamps were green. The 2¢ stamps were red, and the 5¢ stamps were blue. These were the most commonly used denominations, and their colors were set by international treaty. Even postal clerks in foreign lands were able to tell them apart. The 10¢ stamps were yellow. The $2 and $5 stamps were a different shape. Of the many things the Post Office Department might do to save money at this period, changing the design of the stamps would have been low on the list of choices.

In reality, a new series of designs came about because there were new people in office who had the desire — and the power — to make changes. In the tradition of American politics, the new Republican administration swept all the Democrats it could from positions of influence after the election, and installed its own party loyalists in their places. In the Post Office Department, it was no coincidence that Republican campaign officials were appointed to the executive positions, and it was no coincidence, when the new stamps were designed the following year, that many of the portraits would be those of former Republican presidents. There was, it seemed, patronage for the living and patronage for the dead.

Partisan politics was anything but foreign to the Post Office Department. It had become the most political of the ten cabinet departments in the executive branch, due in large part to the number of jobs, particularly city and town postmaster positions, that could be doled out to the party faithful. Thus, it had also become something of a tradition for the winning president to appoint his campaign manager as postmaster general.

Warren Harding did not depart significantly from this practice. While he appointed his nominal campaign manager, Harry Daugherty, to the cabinet position of attorney general, he awarded the post office job to Will Hays, the chairman of the Republican National Committee. Hays, an Indiana lawyer of considerable ability, had been the key strategist behind Harding's successful "front porch" campaign. Hays did what he was appointed to do: During the first twelve months after the March 1921 inauguration, he made some 23,000 new postmaster appointments around the country.

The official in charge of stamps was by tradition the third assistant postmaster general, and that job, too, went to an active Republican politician, W. Irving Glover. Glover was a well-to-do businessman and New Jersey legislator. He first became involved in Republican politics in 1898, at the age of 19, when he worked on Theodore Roosevelt's campaign for governor of New York. Glover made his fortune in New York real estate and moved to suburban New Jersey, where he ran for office on his own for the first time. After a term on the Bergen County board of freeholders he was elected to the New Jersey Assembly in 1916, and rose quickly to the powerful position of speaker in 1920.

Figure 1. Warren Harding on the presidential yacht Mayflower. *His election brought a new postal administration with the power and desire to change the nation's stamps.*

Not only did Glover work on behalf of the Republican ticket during the campaign, but he also had the good fortune to do the president-elect a personal favor shortly after the election. Both men and their wives were booked on the same cruise ship for a vacation to Central America and the Panama Canal, but the Glovers had had the foresight to book the best accommodations. Learning that the Hardings were to be traveling on the same ship, the Glovers gave them their stateroom. Irving Glover and Warren Harding became acquainted and struck up a friendship during the cruise. Afterward, the Glovers, an attractive and successful couple, would become frequent guests at the White House. On May 19, 1921, two months after the Harding inauguration, Glover became third assistant postmaster general.

Whether Irving Glover was a stamp collector before he took the job has not been established, but his wife Anna, the daughter of a New York shipbuilder, was known to have an extensive worldwide collection. Glover's children remember his own "ardent collecting interests,"[1] but he never admitted to being a collector during his term in office. In December 1922, for example, when he addressed a meeting of the Collectors Club of New York, he ended his speech to laughter and applause by saying, "I am not a collector, but my wife is." After he left the Post Office Department, however, he applied for membership in the American Philatelic Society, and was admitted on May 1, 1932.

As the Harding administration got under way in 1921, Glover not only took a professional interest in the stamps his department was producing, but also became an advocate for the nation's collectors. The previous post office department had been relatively uninterested in stamps, and Albert Burleson, the postmaster general during the entire Wilson administration, was anything but popular with collectors.

"The eight years that Burleson was the ogre of the Postal Service," one philatelic writer complained, "will long be remembered by postmasters and their clerks as well as carriers and all P.O. workers, as the poorest misfit ever at the head of the P.O. Department."[2]

While that opinion may be a bit severe, it is clear that stamp collectors were longing for a change. Philip Ward, the most informed writer about new issues at the time, wrote gleefully in April 1921 about the rumor — which proved to be true — that the postmaster of Washington, D.C., was about to lose his job with many other outgoing Democrats. "It is rumored," Ward wrote, "that the Postmaster of Washington, one who considers all stamp collectors as cranks, one who refuses to fill stamp collectors' requisitions, one who discontinued the special window at Washington where the stamp collector was catered to, is slated to move."[3]

Glover certainly did not share the opinion that stamp collectors were cranks, and set out to change the attitude within the department. Whether he was aware of this column by Ward is not known, but he soon acted on a suggestion from one of his clerks[3] and established exactly the kind of stamp window

3

that Ward had complained had been discontinued. Formalized as the Philatelic Stamp Agency in December 1921, it started out as a window at the City Post Office that sold all U.S. issues to collectors, including older stamps that had been held in the vaults. New issues were specially selected for centering. Collectors could buy in person or order by mail.

Within the Post Office Department, Glover argued that the new agency would make money, as most of the stamps would be kept in albums and never used for postage. Information, would also become more available. "Detailed statements concerning the desirable stamps and new issues will be furnished to all persons requesting them," the press release announced.

Figure 2. Third Assistant PMG W. Irving Glover (left) and Bureau of Engraving and Printing director Louis A. Hill examining the first printing of the 5¢ Theodore Roosevelt stamp in 1922. A flat-plate press is in the foreground.

The "desirable stamps" that became available at the agency included the Victory issue of 1919, the Pilgrim Tercentenary issue of 1920, some leftover airmail issues of 1918 and a batch of 1911 registry stamps.

But there had been few new issues. Although a few perforation varieties of the Washington-Franklin series had been released, the new postal administration had not ordered any new stamp designs during the ten months of 1921 that it had been in office. But Glover and his staff were making plans for an extensive revamping of the nation's stamp program.

The Priority of Airmail

As Glover himself would realize before long, the real interest of the Harding postal administration, and the first priority of Postmaster General Hays, was airmail.

Airmail was still in its infancy, having been launched in 1918 under the administration of President Wilson and Postmaster General Burleson. The first route was established between New York and Washington, D.C., in May 1918, but it was not really much of a success, due to its high cost and its lack of reliability. One year later, the first leg of what was to be the Transcontinental Route across the United States was opened between Cleveland and Chicago.

The Harding Postal Administration

By the time the Harding administration took office in March 1921, the Transcontinental had been completed between New York and San Francisco, and two spurs or lateral routes were being flown. One lateral connected Chicago and Minneapolis and the other connected Chicago and St. Louis.

During the campaign year of 1920, there had been a number of well-publicized airmail crashes and a disturbing 17 fatalities. Harding said almost nothing about the situation during the campaign, but his administration let it be known that it was committed not only to making aviation more safe but also to getting the government out of the airmail business and turning it over to private enterprise.

The second assistant postmaster general was the official in charge of mail transportation, including airmail, and to this position Hays appointed Edward H. Shaughnessy, a former Army colonel whose expertise and military experience was in rail transportation. Shaughnessy, like Hays, believed the rapid expansion of the airmail system under the previous administration had not only been dangerous, but inefficient and expensive. He almost immediately began shutting down routes.

On May 31, 1921, he shut down the Washington-to-New York route, which had been the nation's first airmail route. The airplanes only flew during the day and in good weather. Trains ran night and day, in foul weather and fair, and often delivered the mail faster over this relatively short route. The Department's official statement about the shutdown was harsh. "This route has been kept in operation for a considerable length of time," it said, "without serving any particular usefulness. ..."[5] Flying on this route was characterized as "experimental" and the new administration believed that all available resources should be shifted to the Transcontinental route.

In the following month, Shaughnessy shut down the other "lateral" routes between Minneapolis and Chicago and St. Louis and Chicago. The staff of the Air Mail Service was cut severely, with 39 pilots laid off or fired. Aircraft were also standardized. The single-engine De Havilland DH-4 would be, after June 1921, the only plane used by the government service.

By January 6, 1922, when Shaughnessy would speak to the Society of

Figure 3. The De Havilland DH-4 became the standard airmail plane in 1921 as the new administration took a businesslike approach to making the airmail service smaller, safer and more efficient.

Automotive Engineers in Washington, he was able to claim that fatalities had been reduced to only one during the previous six months. "In my opinion," he said, "This very much improved showing comes principally from putting into effect a sensible, businesslike program, using trustworthy men and material, leaving the experimenting and stunting to those who are not entrusted with the United States mails."

He also told them he envisioned the time when private airmail contractors would fly the mail, just as private trains and steamships carried it at present. How soon that day would come, Shaughnessy said he didn't know. But he added, in the Republican philosophy of the day, "The department does not feel that it should operate an Air Mail Service any more than it should operate a steamboat service or a railway service."[6]

A few days later, Shaughnessy was dead. He was one of 96 people killed on January 28, when the roof of the Knickerbocker Theater collapsed during a Washington snow storm. His wife Myrtle, who was with him in the theater, survived and was given the position of assistant philatelic agent in Glover's Philatelic Stamp Agency.

A Second Postmaster General

Will Hays, too, would be gone shortly. On the first anniversary of Harding's inauguration, he left the administration to become the chairman of the Motion Picture Producers and Distributors of America. This essentially made him the first censor of the American film industry, a position for which he ultimately became more famous than as postmaster general.

Taking Hay's place was Hubert Work, a dignified and mature physician who had become one of the most prominent Republican activists in Colorado. Born in Pennsylvania in 1860, Work completed his medical studies in the East, then went to Colorado to seek his fortune. He established a hospital in Pueblo in 1896 and chaired the state Republican party by 1908. During the war, he served in the Army Medical Corps, and was elected president of the American Medical Association afterward.

During the 1920 campaign he was recruited by Hays to organize ranchers and farmers for the Republican ticket. After the election, Hays appointed him as first assistant postmaster general. He proved to be a capable manager and was the logical choice within the Department to succeed Hays. Like Hays he appeared to have little interest in stamps. And also like Hays, he would not stay long in the position.

Notes

1. Conversation with Randolph Charrington, grandson of W. Irving Glover, June

30, 1990.

2. William W. Randall, "Washington Notes," *A.C. Roessler's Stamp News*, March 1921.

3. Philip H. Ward Jr., "Chronicle of New Issues and Varieties," *Mekeel's Weekly Stamp News*, Vol. 35, No. 17 (April 23, 1921).

4. W.J. Barrows, chief clerk in the third assistant's office, forwarded to Glover on September 28, 1921 a memorandum from William E. Buffington, of the Post Office Department's Division of Finance, making the suggestion that his division take over the sale of stamps to collectors, "collectors desiring better service and postmaster complaining that collectors were too exacting and required too much time of the stamp clerk in handling the business." The memorandum is quoted in George Brett, "The Philatelic Agency," *Bureau Specialist*, Vol. 28, No. 6 (June 1957), p. 174.

5. Quoted in Thomas J. O'Sullivan and Karl B. Weber, *History of the United States Pioneer and Government-Operated Air Mail Service, 1910-1928* (American Air Mail Society, 1973) p. 142.

6. Post Office Department, *Press Releases*, release dated January 7, 1921. These volumes are located in the library of the U.S. Postal Service in Washington, D.C.

United States Stamps 1922-26

Chapter 2

The Bureau of Engraving and Printing in 1922

The Bureau of Engraving and Printing had printed all United States stamps from 1894, and would also print the new stamps that would soon be ordered by the Harding administration. But it too, like the Post Office Department, was undergoing significant changes as a result of the 1920 election. The Bureau, in fact, would soon be turned topsy-turvy by a so-called scandal and mass firings and layoffs.

Just as the Air Mail Service was being trimmed and reorganized, the new secretary of the treasury, Andrew Mellon, was also streamlining the Bureau, which fell under his direction. Six hundred employees were dropped from the rolls on July 3, 1921, and by September there were 1,200 fewer workers than there were a year before.

Some employees who thought they had been dismissed unfairly convinced congressional investigators that there had been a scandal a few years earlier involving the issuing of duplicate Liberty Loan bonds. Those bonds had been issued in part to fund the country's participation in the war, and the claim was that the government had been defrauded of "hundreds of millions of dollars."[1]

Criminal charges were not leveled against any Bureau employees, but some members of Congress were convinced that there had been mismanagement and misconduct. On March 31, 1922, President Harding issued an executive order dismissing the director of the Bureau, James Wilmeth, and 24 other supervisors. The presidential order wiped out the entire management team at the Bureau.

Among those who were dismissed were Benjamin Stickney, the mechanical expert who had designed the rotary press; George Rose Jr., the chief of the engraving division; and George F.C. Smillie, the superintendent of picture engravers.

Smillie was a somewhat legendary figure at the Bureau, and the most imposing and powerful figure in the engraving department. While director Wilmeth was making an annual salary of $6,000, Smillie was paid $7,500. He, rather than the Bureau's designer, had also chosen much of the vignette artwork that was used for stamps and currency on the theory that he, as the master engraver, could best determine what designs could be engraved to the best effect.

The Liberty Bond scandal was soon found to be baseless, and some former supervisors, including Stickney, returned to their jobs. But Smillie and

9

Figure 4. Designer C. Aubrey Huston at his desk, about 1920. One of the few important Bureau employees to survive the 1921 firings, he would design all of the stamps requested by the new administration.

Rose did not. In their absence, a younger group of engravers rose to the forefront, and the Bureau's designer, Clair Aubrey Huston, became an even more powerful force in stamp design.

Although he was an important individual at the Bureau, Huston reported to the director of the engraving department. Since he was not a department head, he had not been fired with the other top people. Huston had started at the Bureau in 1902 and soon replaced the former designer, R. Ostrander Smith. With only one exception (that of the "Merry Widow" special delivery stamp of 1908), Huston had designed all of the stamps issued since 1904. And he would design most of the stamps for the next ten years as well, including all of the stamps that the new postal administration was about to request.

Huston's style was neoclassical. His frame designs are almost always symmetrical, and often contain arches, ovals and acanthus leaves. He generally used the same typeface for lettering, which was known as Banknote Roman. By using these classical elements, he gave a unified look to the stamps and currency he designed over a number of years.

While he had not been called on for many new designs during the eight years of the Woodrow Wilson administration, he was about to get busy again. And now, without Smillie's presence, his authority in the design area would be unchallenged. He would have a new freedom in approaching the stamps of a new administration.

Intaglio Printing and the Flat-Plate Press

As the year 1922 began, most of the postage stamp printing at the Bureau of Engraving and Printing was accomplished using flat plates and the intaglio printing method. Steel was the major material used in the engraving division.

After the designs were approved, craftsmen at the Bureau engraved the design in reverse on a die, or small piece of soft steel, usually about 3 inches x 3½ inches. Almost always, more than one engraver worked on each die. The

The Bureau of Engraving and Printing in 1922

most highly paid engravers were called picture engravers. They worked on scenes, portraits and ornaments. Most of their work was done by hand, using a metal tool called a graver. Letter engravers were paid less. They laid out the frames and engraved letters, numerals and straight lines, often with the use of a mechanical device called a ruling machine.

A proof, or die proof, was made directly from the engraved dies and sent back to the Post Office Department for final approval. Often these were made in a number of colors to help in the decision of the final color for the stamp. Die proofs in colors that differ from the color of the issued stamp are known as trial color proofs.

Once approved, the die was hardened or tempered by heating and cooling. To transfer the master design from the die to the plates, a transfer roll was used. It employed a thick disk of soft steel that was rocked back and forth, under high pressure, into the engraved lines of the die. This resulted in a positive design, or relief in raised soft steel that was then hardened.

Each plate, like the die and the transfer roll, started off as soft steel. Plates usually were laid out to hold 400 or 200 stamp subjects, depending on the size of the stamp. Before using the transfer roll, the siderographer, the craftsman who transferred the stamp images, laid out the plate with dots and lightly scribed lines.

Using the transfer roll in a transfer press that exerted heavy pressure, the stamp images were impressed into the soft steel one by one until the plate was completed. After he transferred the designs, he engraved an identifying number onto the plate and scribed guidelines, separating it into quarters, usually representing the panes that would sold at the post office. After all the subjects were transferred, he used the transfer press again to impress his initials at the bottom left of the plate.[2]

Figure 5. The die for the 2¢ value of the 1922 series. Engraving on the steel dies was always a negative or reverse image of the printed stamp.

Other craftsmen, known as plate finishers, then cleaned up any scratches or layout lines that remained on the plate. When they were done, they stamped their initials at the lower right of the plate, using a punch, and a proof was pulled of the plate. Often, some touch-ups were made. Then the plate was hardened.

Although it could operate with a single plate, the flat-plate press usually used four plates at a time, so plates were usually made in sets of four. Not only were the plates them-

11

United States Stamps 1922-26

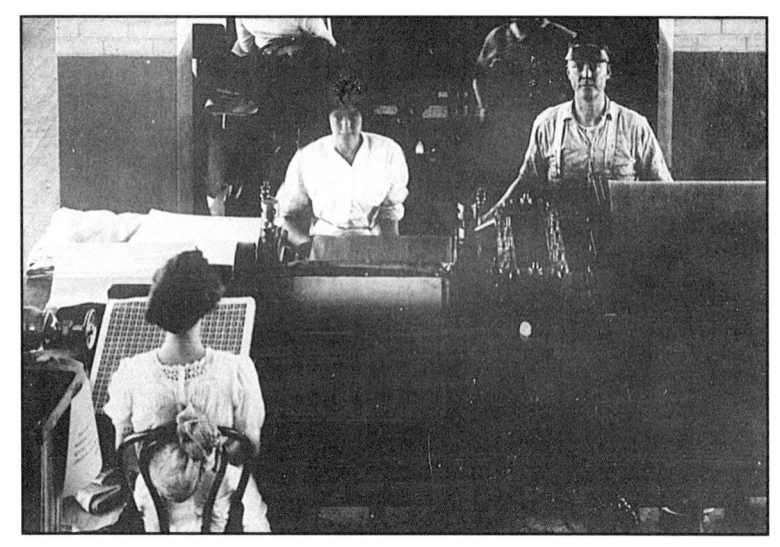

Figure 6. The flat-bed press usually operated with four plates, moving in a counter-clockwise direction. The male plate printer hand-polishes the machine-inked plate for uniformity. The woman at center places a sheet of paper on the inked plate. The woman at left takes the printed sheets off the plate. She has just removed a sheet of 400 stamps.

selves flat, but the bed of the press was also flat, like a table. Sometimes this press is called the flat-bed press. The four plates traveled around the press in a counter-clockwise direction, driven by an electric motor.

Much of the inking, wiping and impression were mechanical, but three operators were needed to work each press. The plate printer, who was always male, polished the inked plate by hand to assure that the ink was properly distributed and wiped. As the plate moved to the next position, one female assistant put sheets of stamp paper on top of the inked plates. She was known in the Bureau jargon as the "putter-on-er." An impression roller mechanically forced the dampened paper down onto the inked plate. Ink in the recessed areas of the plate adhered to the paper, providing the printed image on the paper.

As the plate moved to the next position on the press, another female assistant removed the printed sheet from the plate, examined it briefly, and put a sheet of interleaving tissue paper on top of the freshly printed sheets as she stacked them. This person was known in the jargon as the "taker-offer."

The printing process was then complete, but the stamps had not yet been gummed, perforated or cut into the proper size for sale at post offices. That was the next process, which is also important for collectors to understand.

Gumming and Perforating Flat-plate Stamps

After being printed, the sheets of stamps were sent to a drying room and allowed to dry overnight. The interleaving tissues were removed, and the sheets of stamps were then pressed in a hydraulic press under 500 tons of pressure. It was during this pressing process that an offset of the ink from the front of one sheet of stamps would usually be transferred to the back of another sheet. Many flat-plate stamps show some degree of ink offset on the back.

Next the sheets of stamps were gummed by being passed under a glass roller bathed in a solution of dextrine. The dextrine was made from the root of the cassava or manioc plant, native to South America, which also yields tapioca. In cold weather, glucose, made from corn, was added to the dextrine to keep the gum soft.

A drying chamber attached to the gumming equipment dried the gum "in less than 30 seconds." A device was also employed to break the gum into "innumerable cracks" to prevent subsequent curling."[3] Employees in the gumming division also "worked" stacks of gummed sheets by hand to crack or break the gum. This helped to make the gummed sheets lie flat.

After gumming, the stamps were sent to the perforating division where the stamps were not only perforated, but cut into panes for distribution to post offices.

The perforating technology in use in 1922 was not very different from what was used in 1894 when the Bureau first began making stamps. The perforating machines perforated only in one direction at a time, using wheels set

Figure 7. The perforating room about 1920, showing a rotary perforator in use on flat-plate stamps. The operators are perforating half-sheets of 200 with vertical perforations. The center wheel cuts the half-sheets into two panes of 100. The horizontal perforations have already been made on a different perforator.

13

with pins. While these machines were called rotary perforators, they were mostly used with flat-plate stamps.

Each wheel set with pins rotated on a shaft. Each had a corresponding wheel, on a separate shaft, which was drilled with holes to accept the pins. These sets of pin wheels and die wheels could be adjusted from side to side to accommodate stamps of different sizes.

To cut the sheets of 400 in half, the center wheel did not have pins but was fitted with a rotary knife and became a cutting wheel. One pass through the "straight" perforating machine applied the vertical perforations and cut the sheet of 400 into two half-sheets of 200. These half-sheets were then sent through the "cross" perforating machine, which applied the horizontal perforations and cut the half-sheets of 200 into panes of 100 for packaging and sale in post offices. Stamps of this period were usually shipped in packages or decks of 100 panes.

In both the gumming and perforating departments, women were usually the operators of the equipment. In the perforating process, one operator fed the sheets or half-sheets into the machine, and another woman inspected and stacked.

At different times, the cross perforator was used first, then the straight perforator. Since the perforating and cutting wheels could be moved from side to side, or removed entirely, these machines could be set up to accommodate different sizes of stamps, and different plate layouts.

Notes

1. Treasury Department, *History of the Bureau of Engraving and Printing, 1862-1962* (U.S. Government Printing Office, 1963), p. 104.

2. For a more complete and well-illustrated explanation of the intaglio process, see James H. Baxter, *Printing Postage Stamps by Line Engraving* (American Philatelic Society, 1939).

3. Treasury Department, *Historical Sketch of the Bureau of Engraving and Printing and Its Work*, (U.S. Government Printing Office, 1921), p. 9.

Chapter 3

Motorcycle Special Delivery

10¢ Motorcycle Delivery

Scott Number:	E12
First Day of Issue:	July 12, 1922
Perforation:	11
Scott Color:	Gray violet
Designer:	Clair Aubrey Huston
Engravers:	Louis S. Schofield (vignette and frame)
	Edward M. Hall, (lettering)
	Edward M. Weeks (numerals and lettering "Ten Cents")
Press:	Flat plate
Plate Layout:	200 subjects cut into panes of 50
Quantity Issued:	332,299,906
Plate Numbers:	Total of 69; lowest, 13916; highest 18686
Scott Varieties:	a. Deep ultramarine
	Double transfer

The Political Background

This was the first stamp ordered by the new Harding postal administration, early in its second year. Hubert Work was the postmaster general, and Third Assistant Postmaster General W. Irving Glover ordered the work started on March 13, 1922. It would mark the beginning of a revamping of all of the nation's postage stamps.

There was no practical need for a new stamp. The special delivery rate remained at 10¢, and postal clerks certainly had no difficulty recognizing the current stamp, the design of which had been in use on and off since 1902. The oblong shape of the existing stamp was distinctive, as was its deep blue color.

Changing the special delivery stamp was symbolic, as the existing stamp showed a bicycle messenger, and the new design would show a motorcycle

15

Figure 8. Postmaster General Hubert Work buys the first copy of the Motorcycle Special Delivery stamp, which he later presented to President Harding. The person behind him in line is W. Irving Glover, the third assistant postmaster general who orchestrated the publicity for this first stamp issued under the new administration.

messenger. America and the post office were mechanizing and motorizing, and this stamp would represent it. In ordering the new stamp, Glover was quite specific. He wrote to the Bureau: "The messenger boy might be shown at the door of a house about to deliver a letter with his motorcycle resting against the curb, similar to the subject of the 2¢ parcel post stamp, which shows a city carrier delivering mail. ..."[1]

This letter not only demonstrates the specific nature of Glover's instructions, but also his familiarity with the stamps of the past. The parcel post stamp to which he referred was in use for only a few months, between November 1912 and July 1913. While Glover might well have remembered these stamps, or have referred to proofs on file at the Post Office Department, it also seems likely that he was familiar with them in his own or his wife's collection.

The unusual publicity for this new issue was an indication of change as well. Both the stamp and the newly formed Philatelic Stamp Agency were touted in press releases, which noted that the new design was a representation of "more prompt and efficient service."[2]

For this first new stamp of the Harding administration, Glover arranged to have Postmaster General Hubert Work partake in the publicity, by becoming the first person in line at the Philatelic Stamp Agency to buy one of the new stamps. Another release was prepared for afternoon papers on July 12, relating that Work bought the first stamp and that he "will present the stamp he bought to the President along with a die-proof prepared from the master die."

Glover was not shy about his own role in the matter. He was the second person in line, or at least he appeared that way in the press photographs that were taken. In the press releases he was reported as having "direct supervision over the design, manufacture, and issuing of postage stamps." One release also noted that he had purchased the second stamp "for Mrs. Glover, who is an enthusiastic stamp collector." A successful politician in New Jersey, he was introducing himself as a personality to the stamp collectors of the day. We find more information about Glover and his thoughts and family life in the press information of this period than we find about any of the three postmasters general under which he would serve.

This same long release for afternoon papers noted that Glover himself, Bureau director Hill and Michael L. Eidsness, superintendent of the Division of Stamps, had been present at the printing of the stamps and had signed "the first 24 sheets" in the margin. This was in actuality not 24 sheets of 200, but 24 panes of 50, which were sent to the Philatelic Stamp Agency for sale to collectors. This practice of signing the first stamps off the press, while not entirely new, became consistent.

It was also in this same press release of July 12 that Glover made the announcement that there were more stamps to come: "It is the intention of the Department to prepare future issues of postage stamps in such designs and colors that will be easily distinguishable and memorized by postal clerks as well as of interest to stamp collectors. Further new issues are contemplated and are being given consideration at this time. However, the subjects and denominations have not as yet been settled on."[3]

This was the first time that the new issue of stamps would be described as being more distinguishable by postal clerks, but it was a feature of the new stamps that would be emphasized again and again. The new special delivery stamp, it should be noted, was not any more distinguishable than the previous issue. Both were oblong and blue, and quite different than any other stamp in the Post Office Department's inventory.

The Subject and Design

According to the Post Office Department, "The central design is the front of a private residence, showing a motorcycle parked against the curb, with the special-delivery messenger delivering a letter." The design is an original illustration by C. Aubrey Huston, but no original artwork or reference remains in the Bureau files. One preliminary drawing exists, showing a less symmetrical design, and a stone rather than a brick house.

A comparison with the 2¢ parcel post stamp of 1913, which had also been designed by Huston, shows the influence of Glover's letter of instruction on Huston's new design. Although the doorway is not identical, it is of the same federal or neoclassical architecture. The brickwork and foliage are also similar.

Although a great deal of special delivery mail went to businesses, the special nature of immediately delivered mail seems to be captured rather well, if in miniature, by the smiling woman who is being handed a letter at her home.

Not all special delivery messengers used motorcycles, as many were teenage boys or other casual employees. The minimum age for messengers had been raised to 16 from 13 in 1913. They received 8¢ of the 10¢ fee that the special stamp paid. Not all wore uniforms like the neat and seemingly polite chap depicted on the stamp. The regulations stated that "special delivery messengers need not be uniformed ... but they should be decently and comfortably clad."

The motorcycle shown was a specific one. Huston, like most commercial artists, worked from reference, and he no doubt used a photograph or drawing of a current 1920 Indian Chief, produced by the Hendee Manufacturing Company of Springfield, Massachusetts. In 1923, a year later, Hendee woud change its name to Indian Motorcycle Manufacturing Company. Indian motorcycles of this period had a distinctive leaf-spring fork, which the motorcycle on the stamp clearly displays. Some of the features, particularly the shape of the tank, seem to have been changed a bit, but others, like the tail lamps, are definitely Indian.

Steven Rich, writing in 1954, also identified the motorcycle as "beyond any mistake an Indian."[4]

While there were more than twenty motorcycle manufacturers in the United States at one time, only Indian and Harley Davidson survived the Great Depression. Indian did not change the basic profile of the Chief very much until after World War II.

Like the motorcycle, the brick house with its Federal-period facade and Palladian fan window was a classic piece of miniature architecture. This stamp, so modern in 1922, proved timeless. With several changes in the denomination, this design remained in use from 1922 to 1951. It had one of the longest lifetimes of any U.S. postage stamp.

The wording on the stamp, "At Any United States Post Office," was something of a throwback to the wording that appeared on earlier special delivery stamps, but it also served to reinforce that this was a domestic service only. Special delivery, or so-called Express service in Europe, was not universal. Many countries did not offer it at all, and where it did exist, the fees varied.

Figure 9. A special delivery stamp issued by the Dominican Republic plagiarizes the U.S. stamp, but demonstrates the appeal and usefulness of the design.

Perhaps as a mark of its appeal, this stamp's design was copied by another country. The Dominican Republic issued special delivery stamps in the late 1920s that plagiarized this design (see Figure 9).

Philatelic Aspects and Varieties

First-day covers. This stamp marked an important change in the way the Post Office Department notified the public of new issues. Although some commemorative stamps had been issued on specific dates in the past, the Department had not previously made a practice of notifying collectors of a stamp's issue date. The practice of releasing new stamps on a specific day and at a specific place began with this stamp.

The announcement that the new motorcycle special delivery stamp would go on sale on July 12 was not made until July 7, but this was sufficient time to allow several collectors to prepare covers. By far the most numerous were serviced by Edward C. Worden, the wealthy first-day enthusiast from Millburn, New Jersey.

According to Robert Markovits, a specialist in this stamp, Henry Hammelman, a pioneer servicer from Washington, D.C., also serviced "not more than ten of this issue."[5] No printed cachets are known, as the practice of preparing cachets had not quite begun, and was about a year away.

Plate layout and plate number blocks. The 200-subject plate layout was a standard one for special delivery stamps. It was 10 stamps wide by 20 stamps deep. There were eight plate numbers on the sheet, and two on each pane. Plate number blocks were traditionally saved in blocks of six. Five positions are generally recognized: left, right, bottom, top left and top right. While the two bottom plate numbers are not easily distinguished from one another, the right top plate number is usually preceded by a stamped letter "F" indicating the plate was approved and ready for hardening.

The complete list of the numbers of the 69 different plates used for printing this stamp can be found in the current *Durland Standard Plate Number Catalog*, published by the Bureau Issues Association.

E12a. Scott lists this one small-letter variety, a deep ultramarine shade with a slight premium over the gray violet given as the primary shade. Shades and color always present problems, as no two people see them exactly the same, and without reference material it is often hard to determine what is indicated by Scott's listings. The Post Office Department described this stamp only as blue when it was issued.

The Scott *Specialized* did not list special delivery issues until 1926, and when it did (as in 1901) deep ultramarine was the only shade. The blocks signed by Post Office and Bureau officials on the first day are very good reference sources for this original or deep ultramarine shade.

More on shades. Philip Ward, the new issues columnist for *Mekeel's Weekly Stamp News* and unquestionably the best chronicler of the new stamps of this period, noted in September 1925 that this stamp could be found in "three very distinct shades, two of the shades being well worthy of catalog rank." Here is his discussion:

"We have the blue which is the normal stamp and also a distinct violet blue or some may designate it as ultramarine. These shades stood out so clearly that one of the postal clerks brought them to my attention, for although he is not interested in stamps, the difference was immediately noticed and he inquired if there had been a change of color. Whether one shade will turn out rarer than the other I cannot say but in those that I have had an opportunity of examining, I find the deep indigo seems to be the scarcer variety. They are certainly different printings."[6]

Scott took note of the existence of a second shade and listed gray violet as a secondary shade to deep ultramarine in the 1928 edition of the *Specialized Catalogue*. Later that same year, the *American Philatelist* also remarked on the two shades of this stamp saying "the comparison between the two is really striking."[7]

Gray violet was given a small-letter listing, as 1901a in the 1932 edition of the *Specialized*. In the 1969 edition, as Scott decided to make the more common shade the major shade, gray violet became the major shade and deep ultramarine became E12a.

Double transfer. Scott first listed a double transfer for this stamp in the 1932 edition of the *Specialized,* and the listing remains today without any information about its source, appearance or location. W.L. Babcock took note of the lack of information about this double transfer in 1933, writing, "It is listed but unpriced in Scott's and is seldom brought to light."[8] Although this listing is now priced, it still has not seen much light.

Johl, in 1946, reported a double transfer on a copy of this stamp with a straight edge at the top, "plate number and position otherwise unknown," which he described as having "an added line below the bottom frameline which extends beyond the lower left hand corner."[9]

There are no doubt several double transfers on this stamp, but none of them seem to be very well known. Loran French, in his *Encyclopedia*, lists seven double transfers, but illustrates none of them.

Notes

1. W. Irving Glover to Louis A. Hill, March 13, 1922. Historical Resource Center, Bureau of Engraving and Printing.

2. Post Office Department press release, "For Sunday Papers, July 9," July 7, 1922. Library, U.S. Postal Service.

3. Post Office Department press release, "Released For Afternoon Papers July 12," July 12, 1922. Library, U.S. Postal Service.

4. Steven G. Rich, *Weekly Philatelic Gossip*, October 23, 1954.

5. Robert Markovits, *First Days*, Vol. 13, No. 6.

6. Philip H. Ward Jr., "Chronicle of New Issues and Varieties," *Mekeel's Weekly Stamp News*, Vol. 39, No. 8 (September 21, 1925), p. 444.

7. "Some Wandering Thoughts," *American Philatelist*, Vol. 43, No. 3 (December 1928), p. 154

8. M.L. Babcock, "Notes on U.S. Stamps, *Mekeel's Weekly Stamp News*, Vol. 47, No. 10 (March 6, 1933), p. 110.

9. Max Johl, "Max G. Johl Reports on 20th Century United States," *Stamps*, Vol. 54, No. 9 (March 2, 1946), p. 388.

United States Stamps 1922-26

Chapter 4

Planning the Series of 1922

Exactly a week after approving the final model for the new Motorcycle special delivery stamp on April 17, 1922, Third Assistant Postmaster General W. Irving Glover wrote to the director of the Bureau and asked for a new series of stamps.

As with the Motorcycle stamp, Glover had a fairly specific idea of what he wanted, and he demonstrated his familiarity with previous stamp issues. In his letter of April 24, he stated that he wanted the denominations up to and including 12¢ to have "portraits of Washington, Franklin, Roosevelt, and others." The frame was to be "similar to the border design of the 1894 issue, except that the outer edge of the design should be sharp horizontal lines similar to the approved design for the new special delivery stamp."

His letter went on: "Above the oval, which will contain the portrait, should appear, in a curved line, the words 'United States Postage' and in both lower corners of the stamps the numerals indicating the denomination would appear with the word 'cents' between, and directly under the portrait a space should be provided for the surname of the subject."

This did not give the designer a great deal of leeway, but Glover's directions were compatible with the designs that Bureau designer C. Aubrey Huston had been producing for several years.

Glover asked for models of the frames first, noting that "upon the approval of the border design a list of the subjects for the different denominations will be furnished." And he also noted that "as the subject for the model or design to be prepared for the 5¢ denomination, the portrait of Roosevelt might be used. ..."

Theodore Roosevelt was the most recently deceased Republican president, having died in 1919. No stamp was issued in his honor by the Woodrow Wilson administration, and the new Harding administration was about to correct the situation. Glover himself had begun his own political career by working for Roosevelt in his 1898 campaign for governor of New York. President Harding was also a Roosevelt fan, and the son and daughter of the former president were frequent guests at the White House.

Glover wanted Roosevelt's portrait to be used for the 5¢ because it was the most frequently used stamp other than the 1¢ and 2¢ values, which were reserved, by long tradition, for Benjamin Franklin and George Washington.

While Roosevelt was the only subject he suggested for the lower values, he suggested that the higher values "will probably require a different bor-

United States Stamps 1922-26

der design," and "a picture of the United States Capitol, the Goddess of Liberty, Niagara Falls, or similar views as subjects."[1]

Although Glover had a firm idea of what he wanted for the border and some of the subjects, the others were left unstated. In responding to his request for designs, the Bureau responded in June with two sets of designs.

One set of 15 models was prepared by Clair Aubrey Huston, the Bureau's designer, and another set of eight models by John Stevenson, an engraver who had been at the Bureau for only a short time. Both of these sets followed Glover's directions to a large degree and are shown in Figures 10 and 11.

Max Johl and Beverly King were provided photographs of most, but not all of these models for illustrations in their 1934 book, *The United States*

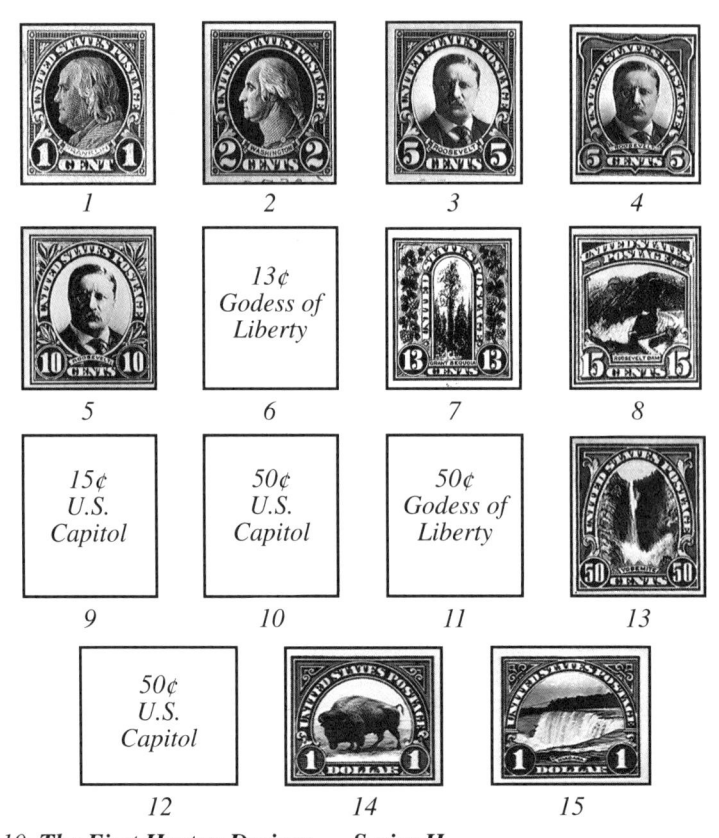

Figure 10. The First Huston Designs — Series H
In response to a request by the Post Office Department, Bureau designer C. Aubrey Huston prepared 15 models to show potential frame designs. Ten of these can be illustrated today. Huston prepared three different frame designs for low value stamps, which he demonstrated with the same Roosevelt portrait. He also prepared at least four different frame designs for higher value stamps.

24

Planning the Series of 1922

Postage Stamps of the Twentieth Century. But they were not aware of the place of these models in the chronology of the design process. In many cases this led to mistaken conclusions. The correspondence that explained when and why these models were produced did not come to light until 1994.[2]

A letter of June 2, 1922, lists the 23 models being sent to the Post Office Department on that date and lists the title of each.[3] One set was called Series H, and each of these was a Huston design. The other set was called Series S; each of these was a Stevenson design. These were listed as follows:

	Series H		**Series S**
1	1¢ Franklin head	1	2¢ Washington head
2	2¢ Washington head	2	3¢ Harrison head
3	5¢ Roosevelt head	3	5¢ Roosevelt head
4	5¢ Roosevelt head	4	5¢ Roosevelt head
5	10¢ Roosevelt head		(with eagle in mosaic)
6	13¢ Goddess of Liberty	5	15¢ Yellowstone Falls
7	13¢ Grant Sequoia	6	20¢ Niagara Falls
8	15¢ Roosevelt Dam	7	50¢ U.S. Capitol
9	50¢ U.S. Capitol (square)		(horizontal oval)
10	50¢ U.S. Capitol (vertical)	8	$1 Goddess of Liberty
11	50¢ Goddess of Liberty (¾ length)		
12	50¢ U.S. Capitol (horizontal)		
13	50¢ Yosemite		
14	$1 Buffalo (horizontal)		
15	$1 Niagara Falls (horizontal)		

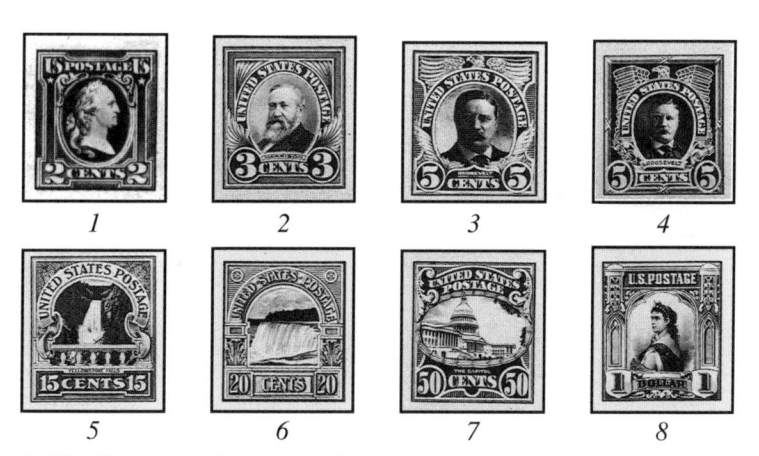

*Figure 11. **The Stevenson Designs — Series S***
The Bureau also sent to the Post Office Department eight designs by engraver John Stevenson. While none of the Stevenson designs were accepted, they also followed the specifications set by the Post Office Department, including denominations in both bottom corners and the words "United States Postage" at the top.

Not all of Huston's designs have survived with these denominations, probably because some of the models were altered to make additional models. In some cases Huston may simply have painted over the denominations to change them. In others, he may have disassembled the listed models to construct new ones, as he generally made his working models in two pieces consisting of a frame placed over a vignette. Photographs of 10 of the 15 Series H models have been located.

Huston produced a frame design for the portrait stamps that conformed closely to Glover's request, and he used it on at least three values, the 1¢, 2¢, and one of the two 5¢ models that used a Theodore Roosevelt portrait. For good measure, it seems, he also provided a Roosevelt model with two additional frame designs.

For the higher values he provided at least four different frame designs. One, which was demonstrated with Roosevelt Dam as the subject, had a somewhat square vignette area. The others had vignette areas oriented either for horizontal subject matter or for vertical subject matter.

Huston seems to have interpreted the "Goddess of Liberty" as Bartholdi's *Liberty Englightening the World*, which is familiar to us today as the Statue of Liberty. But what Glover no doubt meant was Crawford's *Statue of Freedom*, which surmounts the U.S. Capitol. Crawford's *Freedom* was used on the newspaper stamps of 1875 and is called the "Goddess of Liberty" in some Post Office Department records.

All eight of the Stevenson designs still survive in one form or another, but none were approved. For his series he used some of the same vignette art as Huston had, particularly Niagara Falls, the U.S. Capitol and Theodore Roosevelt. For the "Goddess of Liberty," he used an old engraving of an allegorical figure of "Columbia."

More Models

Unfortunately, we do not know Glover's reaction to the models that were submitted, but he and Postmaster General Hubert Work must have liked much of what they saw. They chose the portrait frame that most closely followed the specifications that Glover had provided, and it is the frame that is familiar to us today. Glover's letter requesting the stamp had requested that the border have "sharp horizontal lines" like the Motorcycle special delivery stamp that had already been issued. These lines served to tie the special delivery stamp and the new series together, although they are seldom if ever shown as a series in modern stamp albums or catalogs.

For the higher values, the Post Office Department chose both a vertical and a horizontal frame. The vertical frame, which we call the horseshoe frame today, was eventually approved for the 15¢ and 20¢ values, although only the

Planning the Series of 1922

15¢ value went into production. The horizontal frame was eventually used for the 20¢ and all higher values.

Perhaps Glover's office provided a list of subjects for the stamps, but it seems that the Bureau had some strong ideas as well. On July 12 the first batch of 12 models for approval were sent to the Post Office Department. These were in denominations of 1¢, 2¢, 3¢, 5¢, 6¢, 7¢, 8¢, 9¢, 10¢, 12¢, 13¢ and 15¢.

Glover wrote back the next day, saying that he had received the models and commenting, "they certainly look very fine to me." He noted however, "We are going to defer action on them until we are in receipt of the entire set and will then get at it very quickly and let you have our decision so that you can get to the work and the issue may be in service during the present year."[4]

Bureau director Hill sent another batch of eight models on July 14, which included the denominations of 4¢, 11¢, 20¢, 30¢, 50¢, $1, $2 and $5. This completed the set of 20 values. However, it differed substantially from the set of 21 values that would be issued. There was no 25¢ value yet, and several of the designs submitted had denominations that are unfamiliar today. Included in this set, and shown in Figure 12, were the following models that were later changed to different denominations:

13¢ Hollow Horn Bear   15¢ Yosemite   20¢ Statue of Liberty
30¢ Niagara Falls   50¢ Buffalo

Figure 12. **Familiar Designs with Unfamiliar Denominations**
These four models were sent to the Post Office Department as part of the new series, but each had its denomination changed. On the 13¢ model, the name in the ribbon, "Hollow Horn Bear," was changed to "American Indian."

Hollow Horn Bear was the name of the American Indian whose portrait was submitted on the 13¢ value, which was later given a 14¢ denomination. On the 13¢ model, his name was printed in the ribbon under the design, and Glover telephoned Hill on July 17 to ask if the Sioux chief was still alive. Hill assured Glover in a letter of July 19 that "this man died March 13, 1913."[5] This is the strongest indication, and a convincing one, that the Bureau had chosen the subjects for this design and probably several of the others.

Over the next few weeks, Glover requested a few changes. He wanted the $5 stamp in a horizontal rather than the vertical format. We know that in the original Series H the Goddess of Liberty had been modeled in a 13¢ and 50¢ denomination. One of these, probably the 50¢ denomination, which had been

United States Stamps 1922-26

described as "¾ length," had the denomination changed to $5 for resubmission. Figure 13 is a photograph of the known model with the $5 Statue of Freedom in a vertical format. Although this design, which was essentially a portrait, lent itself to a vertical format, the other high denominations were in a horizontal format. This change made the higher denominations uniform.

Figure 13. "Godess" in ¾ Frame. The head is from an allegorical statue of Freedom, not of Liberty, and not America, although it would get that label.

Also requested was a new stamp in a 40¢ denomination, "the subject to contain a reproduction of the Arlington Amphitheatre, showing the Unknown Soldier's tomb."[6] Before models were submitted however, the request was changed to a stamp with a 25¢ denomination. Four different models were made at the Bureau for the Arlington stamp and are shown in Figure 14. It seems that only one was submitted. This model had its denomination changed later to 50¢.

Figure 14. Arlington Amphitheatre Designs
First requested as a 40¢ denomination, but quickly changed to a 25¢ denomination, the Arlington stamp had four known models, but only the one on the far right, showing the Tomb of the Unknown Soldier in the foreground, may have actually been submitted to the Post Office Department.

Politics and Controversy

Originally planned as a series of 20 values, the new 25¢ stamp brought the total to 21 values. On August 16, Glover returned all the models, with some of the denominations changed, and a listing so there would be no confusion. This list was nearly identical to the denominations and subjects that we know today, with the exception of the 20¢ value, which was listed as "Yosemite Falls" rather than the Golden Gate subject that was eventually issued. Here is the list of the approved subjects and denominations:

1¢ Franklin	2¢ Washington	3¢ Lincoln
4¢ Martha Washington	5¢ Roosevelt	6¢ Garfield
7¢ McKinley	8¢ Grant	9¢ Jefferson
10¢ Monroe	11¢ Hayes	12¢ Cleveland
14¢ American Indian	15¢ Statue of Liberty	20¢ Yosemite Falls
25¢ Niagara Falls	30¢ Buffalo	50¢ Arlington Amphitheatre
$1 Lincoln Memorial	$2 Capitol	$5 America

Planning the Series of 1922

The "America" listed for the $5 stamp was also engraved under the portrait of the issued stamp, but the image is the head of Crawford's Statue of Freedom from the Capitol. The name "America" was also used by mistake in listing the Bureau engraving from which the vignette was taken, and this is no doubt how the mistake came to be made.

Unfortunately we do not have any evidence of how the portrait subjects of the 12 lowest values were determined. There was no doubt some attempt to return to the traditional portraits used on past stamp series. Of the 14 portraits used on the Series of 1902, seven were used again in this new Series of 1922: those of Franklin, Washington, Grant, Lincoln, Garfield, Martha Washington and Jefferson.

Lincoln, Grant and Garfield had been Republican presidents. Three other Republican presidents were also added: Roosevelt, McKinley and Hayes. Only one Democratic president was included, Grover Cleveland, the most recently deceased. Cleveland died in 1908.

Once the choices for the subjects had been made, the choice of the specific portraits was relatively simple. For years the Bureau had adopted standard portraits of presidents and other noted individuals, and these were used uniformly on both stamps and currency.

For the higher values, some of the vignettes corresponded to subjects that the Bureau had been contemplating for a new series of currency in 1920: Niagara Falls, the American Indian and the U.S. Capitol. It is possible that the concept of national landmarks and sights had been suggested by the Bureau in conversations or meetings before Glover formally requested models for a new series of stamps. It seems to be more than a coincidence that the subjects used would be the same ones for which the Bureau had requested reference artwork in 1920.

Two of the scenes, however, were of recent historical significance. The Lincoln Memorial, which would be used as the subject for the $1 value, had been completed only recently and was dedicated on May 30, 1922, while the approval process for the designs was in progress.

Similarly, the Tomb of the Unknown Soldier, shown in the foreground of the 50¢ Arlington Amphitheatre stamp had been dedicated in an elaborate ceremony at which President Harding presided on November 11, 1921.

While the work of choosing designs was going on, Glover was also waging a small public-relations war in the press. As is noted in the previous chapter, Glover announced the coming series on July 12, in a release primarily concerning the new special delivery stamp. He was surprised, however, to hear the criticism that a new series of stamps would be a waste of money and was being issued primarily for the benefit of collectors.

In response, Glover put out a press release on July 28, stating that "thousands of letters suggesting a new issue of postage stamps have been received from employees of the postal service, who have pointed out the advisability of a more distinct variation in designs for postage stamps, as well as colors that do not possess striking similarity."[7]

Postal employees had indeed complained about the similarities in color and design of the Washington-Franklin stamps after they were issued in 1908 and 1909. But the colors had been changed to be more distinctive in 1912, and postal employees had been working with these stamps for more than a decade at this point.

In the correspondence between Glover and the Bureau in requesting the new series of stamps, there was virtually no reference to making the stamps more recognizable or to any problems that postal workers might be having.

But now, in the face of criticism that the new stamps would be a waste of the taxpayers' money, Glover argued that they would save money instead. The similarity of the current issue, he now said, "prevents postal employees from detecting short paid matter."

Glover could not make the same argument about the special delivery stamp he had just replaced — after all, clerks had no trouble distinguishing the old one — so he instead claimed that it was making money for the government. He had the cost of the labor involved in engraving the new die calculated at $438.91, while boasting that the sale of the new stamps to collectors, "for which no service was rendered," was $879.60 to date.

The choice of designs that Glover had made in August were released to the press on Friday, September 29, and embargoed for publication in morning newspapers on Monday, October 2, two days before the first of the new stamps, the 11¢ Hayes, was to be released at a ceremony in Fremont, Ohio.

Explaining how a series of 21 stamps with a mishmash of subjects — a variety of portraits, scenes, statues, buildings, and even a buffalo — somehow hung together was probably not an easy task, but here is the explanation as given in the Post Office Department's creative and imaginative press release:

"The subjects of the designs have not been selected without careful regard to their suitability, according to the Department's statement. The portraits include Washington and Jefferson as fathers of our institutions, Franklin as the First Postmaster General, Martha Washington to commemorate the pioneer womanhood of America, Lincoln, Garfield and McKinley as 'the martyr Presidents,' Monroe to mark the foreign policy associated with his name, with Grant, Hayes, Cleveland and Roosevelt carrying on the historical line to a recent day.

" 'The devices adopted for the higher denominations,' Mr. Glover says, stand in mind for a little story which aided him in selecting them. Together they stand for America as it might be viewed by a newly arriving immigrant. The

Planning the Series of 1922

stranger's first thought is of the primitive dwellers in the land, the aboriginal Indians, but on arrival the Statue of Liberty greets him, the symbol of a new civilization; the natural wonders opening to his view in this new world are represented by the Yosemite and Niagara, and its differing forms of animal life by the Buffalo; from these the alien's thoughts are supposed to turn to the deeds of men who lived and died to build and preserve the Nation, and this idea is marked by Arlington Amphitheatre and the Lincoln Memorial; then his mind turns to the Capitol itself as the center of national tradition and Government, and so to his vision of America, the final picture."[8]

The public, in reading this, had nothing to go on but a list of the denominations and subjects. No illustrations were released, as it was at this time against the law to illustrate stamps or currency, and would continue to be so for many more years. Nor was it possible for the public to get much of a picture of the entire series when the stamps were first issued, as they were released on nine different dates over a seven-month period that began on October 4, 1922, and ended on May 1, 1923. The following table shows the chronology of the release of the first 21 values of the Series of 1922.

Date	Den.	Subject	Occasion
10/04/22	11¢	Rutherford B. Hayes	Hayes' birthday
10/27/22	5¢	Theodore Roosevelt	Roosevelt's birthday
11/11/22	15¢	Statue of Liberty	Armistice Day
	25¢	Niagara Falls	"
	50¢	Arlington Amphitheatre	"
11/20/22	6¢	James Garfield	Garfield's birthday
1/15/23	2¢	George Washington	no stated occasion
	4¢	Martha Washington	"
	9¢	Thomas Jefferson	"
	10¢	James Monroe	"
1/17/23	1¢	Benjamin Franklin	Franklin's birthday
2/12/23	3¢	Abraham Lincoln	Lincoln's birthday
	$1	Lincoln Memorial	"
3/20/23	12¢	Grover Cleveland	Philatelic Show (Boston)
	30¢	Buffalo	"
	$2	U.S. Capitol	"
	$5	"America"	"
5/01/23	7¢	William McKinley	no stated occasion
	8¢	U.S. Grant	"
	14¢	American Indian	"
	20¢	Golden Gate	"

The release dates for several of the stamps were tied to some event or anniversary, and what we now know as the first-day ceremony was begun on

31

October 4, 1922, for the Hayes stamp in Fremont, Ohio. First-day cover collecting, which was only in its infancy, got a boost from this issue, although many of the stamps were released with only a few days advance notice of the date.

The new practice of issuing definitive stamps on a certain date and at a certain place was much appreciated by collectors, but it caused a number of difficulties for the Bureau, which had to produce the stamps against a set of tight deadlines set by the Post Office Department. It also would cause problems for the Department itself before too long, as postmasters and business groups and congressmen began to clamor to have their cities included as first-day sites.

Another Postmaster General

When the series had been ordered, Hubert Work was the postmaster general who approved each of the 21 designs. But he would not be in the post when the series was concluded, due to political problems in the Harding administration.

Albert Fall, the secretary of the interior whose financial troubles would ultimately result in the infamous Teapot Dome oil-lease scandal, had wanted out of the cabinet for some time, and was permitted to resign on March 3, 1923, as the second year of the Harding presidency came to an end. Postmaster General Work, who was from the west and had a good understanding of the issues facing the department, was named to replace Fall as secretary of the interior, having served exactly one year as head of the Post Office Department. He remained in the post long enough, however, to approve each of the models of the stamps of the new series.

Named to replace Work was Harry S. New, who would hold the post for the next six years. Work and New are shown together in Figure 15. New was a longtime friend and political advisor to President Harding. He had been

Figure 15. Postmaster General Hubert Work (right) was given another cabinet position, that of secretary of the interior, on March 4, 1923, after he had served only one year. Replacing him was Harry S. New, a former U.S. senator from Indiana and a political crony of President Harding.

Planning the Series of 1922

elected as a U.S. senator from Indiana in 1916, and had served in the Senate with Harding, who had represented the neighboring state of Ohio. New was an early supporter of Harding for the presidency, and had visited Harding to consult on the cabinet right after the election. During 1921 and 1922, he had continued serving in the Senate, but he was defeated for renomination in the 1922 elections. Harding took the occasion of New's political unemployment as an opportunity to put his friend in the cabinet, and New took office on March 4, 1923, the first day of the third year of the administration.

Still in production were several of the stamps of the Series of 1922. Although Glover was overseeing the production of the new stamps, New approved the die proofs of several values. Although he played no part in the selection of 20 of the 21 designs for the new series of regulars, he signed the final approval for the 20¢ Golden Gate stamp that replaced the Yosemite design. New, who was not without opinions, would have more to say about the commemorative issues that would follow.

The 20¢ Problem

We do not have much documentary evidence of the reason for the cancellation of the Yosemite stamp. The Bureau liked this stamp, and it had been approved by Postmaster General Work with the other models on July 26, 1922. The approval of the model was the authorization to proceed with the engraving of the die. It was fully engraved, and completed on November 1. But some time in November, probably after the die proof was sent to the Post Office Department for final approval, the Department decided that the design was not appropriate. A letter of November 27 shows that three new models for the 20¢ value, each showing the same Golden Gate view, were submitted in each of the frame formats: one in the oval portrait frame, one in the vertical "horseshoe" frame and one in the horizontal frame. These are shown in Figure 16. The engraving used for the vignette was the same sunset view, from a woodcut, that had been used on the 5¢ value of the Panama-Pacific stamps of 1913.

On December 4, another model for the 20¢ value was released, showing Mount Ranier, in Washington State. This was a handsome design that showed tall spruce trees in the foreground and the mountain peak in the background. It was submitted in the horseshoe frame, and is also shown in Figure 16.

On January 11, 1923, two more models were submitted. Although the subjects were not mentioned, these appear to have been Holy Cross Mountain in Colorado (the home state of Postmaster General Work), and another Yosemite view. This other Yosemite view is known in two frame designs, the horseshoe and the three-quarter portrait used for the original $5 "Goddess." Perhaps only one of these two new Yosemite models was submitted. These designs are also shown in Figure 16.

33

original Yosemite   *the three Golden Gate designs*

Mount Ranier   *Holy Cross Mountain*   *Yosemite designs*

Figure 16. ***Preliminary 20¢ Designs***
Why the original Yosemite Falls design (top left) was not approved is not known. Several new designs were submitted, but none of these was selected for the issued stamp.

None of these models seems to have pleased the Post Office Department, but perhaps it was difficult to get a decision from Postmaster General Work, who was about to change jobs and must have been preoccupied with more pressing matters.

On February 27, two final models were submitted for the 20¢ denomination. Both showed new views of San Francisco's Golden Gate, and are shown in Figure 17. One of these two designs, from a painting showing a sailing ship in the harbor, was finally chosen.

Figure 17. ***The Final Designs***
Two new designs, both based on paintings by W.A. Coulter, were submitted in February 1923. The model on the left, showing a ship and San Francisco's Golden Gate, was finally chosen.

But Bureau director Hill found nothing wrong with the original Yosemite design, and clearly wanted to use it. "I might say," he wrote, "that the 20¢ Yosemite Falls stamp already engraved is at your service in the event that you decide to make use of it under another denomination."[9]

By the time the new die was engraved for the 20¢ Golden Gate stamp, Harry S. New had taken office as postmaster general, and he approved the die proof on April 9, 1923. The planning and design phase of the Series of 1922, which had begun almost exactly a year earlier, was now complete, with 21 approved denominations instead of the original 20. The Yosemite stamp, despite the Bureau's prompting, never did get used.

Notes

1. W. Irving Glover to Louis A. Hill, April 24, 1922. Historical Resource Center, Bureau of Engraving and Printing.

2. Gary Griffith, "Preliminary Designs and Essays of the Fourth Bureau Issue," *The United States Specialist*, Vol. 65, No. 1 (April 1994), pp. 152-60.

3. Louis A. Hill to W. Irving Glover, June 2, 1922. Historical Resource Center, Bureau of Engraving and Printing.

4. W. Irving Glover to Louis A. Hill, July 13, 1922. Historical Resource Center, Bureau of Engraving and Printing.

5. Louis A. Hill to W. Irving Glover, July 19, 1922. Historical Resource Center, Bureau of Engraving and Printing.

6. W. Irving Glover to Louis A. Hill, July 26, 1922. Historical Resource Center, Bureau of Engraving and Printing.

7. Press release, Post Office Department, July 28, 1922.

8. Press release, Post Office Department, October 2, 1922.

9. Louis A. Hill to W. Irving Glover, February 26, 1923. Historical Resource Center, Bureau of Engraving and Printing.

United States Stamps 1922-26

Chapter 5

The Series of 1922

The original 21 values of these stamps, issued in 1922 and 1923, were planned together as a series. Although Scott catalogs the ½¢ and 1½¢ values, issued in 1925, with this series, they are more logically treated in their true chronology, particularly since the 1½¢ value followed the release of the Harding Memorial issue of 1923 and is based on its design.

The fractional values are treated in Chapters 20 and 21.

This series, employing three different frames, was designed by C. Aubrey Huston. The frames were engraved first, with Edward M. Hall engraving the basic frames and lettering and Joachim C. Benzing engraving the ribbons for the name of the subject and the acanthus leaves and other ornaments. Thus, for each of the stamps, Hall and Benzing get an engraving credit. The portraits, the denominations and the lettering of the name of the subjects were distributed among other engravers.[1] The engravers of this variable lettering are listed for each stamp as "variable lettering engravers."

Each of the stamps in this series was printed on the flat-plate press and perforated on the rotary perforator used for flat-plate work, with 11-gauge perforations. These stamps thus share these common characteristics:

Perforation: 11
Designer: Clair Aubrey Huston
Frame engravers: Edward M. Hall and Joachim C. Benzing
Press: flat plate

The other particulars of the stamps vary and are treated individually below. As noted in the previous chapter, these stamps were not issued all at once, but on a variety of dates, some of which had meaning for the individual value or its subject, such as a birth anniversary.

Booklet panes and coil stamps derived from these designs are treated in following chapters.

Because of the large number of plates used for these stamps, the plate numbers for all the values are not listed here. A complete list of the plate numbers for these stamps can be found in the current *Durland Standard Plate Number Catalog*, published by the Bureau Issues Association.

The practice of preparing printed cachets for first-day covers was not established at the time this series was issued, and printed cachets prepared in advance of the stamps' issue dates are not known for stamps of this series unless mentioned.

Plate layout and plate number blocks. The stamps from the 1¢ to the 50¢ denomination were printed with the standard flat-plate layout using 400 subjects. Plate number blocks were traditionally saved in blocks of six. Five positions are generally recognized: left, right, bottom, top left and top right. While the two bottom plate numbers are not easily distinguished from one another, the right-top plate number is usually preceded by a stamped letter "F" indicating the plate was approved and ready for hardening.

1¢ Benjamin Franklin

Scott Number:	552
First Day of Issue:	January 17, 1922
Scott Colors:	Deep green, green, pale green
Engravers:	Marcus Baldwin (vignette)
	Edward M. Hall and Joachim C. Benzing (variable lettering)
Plate Layout:	400 subjects cut into panes of 100
Quantity Issued:	4,015,109,977
Plates:	Total of 255: lowest, 14157; highest, 16571
Scott Varieties:	a. Booklet pane (see Chapter 10)
	Double transfer

The Subject and Design

Benjamin Franklin, who is credited with organizing the postal service, had been depicted on the lowest value of every new set of definitive stamps since 1847, and the tradition was kept alive with this series. The look of the previous Washington-Franklin series was also maintained by using the same portrait of Franklin for the new 1¢ value and the same portrait of Washington for the 2¢ value. In fact, no new engravings were made of the two portraits; they were transferred from the dies used for the Washington-Franklin series.

Although both the Post Office Department and the Bureau of Engraving and Printing described the Franklin portrait as "from Houdon's bust," recent scholarship has shown that the bust photographed for the model of this stamp (and all the Franklin designs of the Washington-Franklin series) was in fact of the type sculpted by Jean Jacques Caffieri, a contemporary of the better known sculptor Jean Antoine Houdon.[2] Caffieri sculpted Franklin's bust from life in 1777, a year before Houdon sculpted a similar bust. Although both busts were widely copied and reproduced, in sculpture and engravings, the Caffieri-type bust (shown in Figure 18) can be told easily from the Houdon type by the knotted jabot, or scarf, at the neck.

Philatelic Aspects and Varieties

First day of issue. This stamp had a first day of sale on January 17, 1923, at Washington, D.C., and at Philadelphia, Franklin's adopted city. The date was Franklin's birth anniversary. As the author of *Poor Richard's Almanac*, Franklin (who spent quite freely in his later years) was identified with thrift, and the release of the stamp was tied to National Thrift Week, which began the same day. A press release noted, "The Post Office Department is planning to participate in National Thrift Week ... by displaying pictures of Franklin, copied from a painting in the Postmaster General's office, on all postal trucks."[3]

Figure 18. The Caffieri bust of Franklin used for the vignette design of the Franklin stamps of the Washington-Franklin series, and the 1¢ value of the 1922 series. The photograph is a copy of the original in the files of the Bureau of Engraving and Printing.

On most first-day covers, a pair of stamps has been used to pay the 2¢ letter rate. There were fewer covers serviced from Philadelphia than from Washington, and these command a premium.

Shades. In the Post Office Department's description, this stamp was plain old green. When first listed in the 1924 edition of the Scott *Specialized Catalogue of U.S. Stamps*, deep green was listed as the major shade (as it still is) and green was added as a minor shade. Pale green was added in the 1927 edition. Johl listed several other shades, including bluish green and dark bluish green, which noted correctly that there is a shade of this stamp with a hint of blue in it.

Plate varieties. Although Scott began listing a double transfer for this issue in the 1926 edition of the *Specialized*, no specific position is given. Several double transfers are known. Johl listed positions 14159 UL 6 and 15990 UL 7 in 1935. A triple transfer was documented in the March 1938 *Bureau Specialist*. Cloudy French, in 1979, listed 26 different plate varieties, including a dramatic all-over double transfer, 15585 LL 27, first reported in 1930.

2¢ George Washington

Scott Number: 554
First Day of Issue: January 15, 1922, Washington, D.C.
Scott Colors: Carmine, light carmine
Engravers: Marcus Baldwin (vignette)
Edward M. Hall and Joachim C. Benzing (variable lettering)
Plate Layout: 400 subjects cut into panes of 100
Quantity Issued: 21,681,541,977
Plates: Total of 1,363: lowest, 14074; highest, 18828
Scott Varieties: Star plates (see Chapter 23)
    a. Horizontal pair, imperforate vertically
    b. Vertical pair, imperforate horizontally
    c. Booklet pane (see Chapter 10)
    d. Perforation 10 at top or bottom
Double transfer

The Subject and Design

George Washington had been one of the subjects on each series of definitive stamps since 1847, and was usually depicted on the value that represented the current first-class letter rate. This tradition was continued in this series. As with the 1¢ value, the 2¢ value carried over the portrait from the Washington-Franklin series.

The Washington portrait was based on the life mask and bust sculpted by Jean Antoine Houdon from life, at Washington's Mount Vernon home in 1785. However, the actual bust used for the model of this stamp was a reproduction of the Houdon bust made by Clark Mills in 1853 (shown in Figure 19).

No new engraving was made of the Washington portrait. The existing portrait was transferred from the die used to make the 2¢ Washington-Franklin stamp of 1908.

Philatelic Aspects and Varieties

Used to pay the domestic letter rate, this was the workhorse stamp of the series, and it was in nearly constant production from 1922 to 1927, when it

The Series of 1922

was finally supplanted entirely by the rotary-press version. With more than 21 billion flat-plate copies printed, we might expect a number of varieties, shades and errors. However, there are fewer varieties and shades of this stamp than we might imagine. While three major errors of this stamp do exist, two of the three are quite scarce.

First day of issue. This stamp had a first day of sale on January 15, 1923, only at Washington, D.C. The original plan was to issue this stamp on Washington's birthday, February 22. However, on January 5, 1923, the Post Office Department said in a press release that its plan had been "disrupted by the extraordinary heavy mailing during the past few months, especially during the holidays, which has so depleted the reserve stock of the old issues, that it was decided today to put out the new issues on January 15."[4]

Shades. To the Post Office Department, this stamp is just plain old ordinary red, and to the Bureau, it was regular red. When first listed in the 1924 edition of the Scott *Specialized,* carmine was given as the primary shade and light carmine as a secondary shade. These shades are the only ones given today. Johl listed in addition to these shades, pale carmine and deep carmine. In truth, there is not a great range of shades of this stamp, although in almost any accumulation, one will find that some appear somewhat lighter or darker than others.

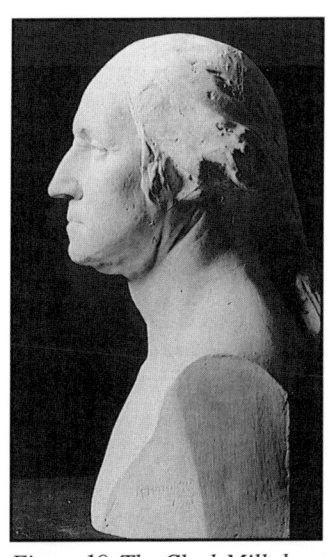

Figure 19. The Clark Mills bust used for the vignette design of the Washington stamps of the Washington-Franklin series, and the 2¢ value of the 1922 series. The Mills bust was sculpted after the bust by French sculptor Jean Antoine Houdon.

554a. This is listed by Scott in the form of a horizontal pair, imperforate vertically. The error occurred when the vertical perforations were skipped or not completed. The first discovery, made in a Michigan post office, was of a pane of 100, bearing the plate number 14689 at the right. It was reported in *Scott's Monthly Journal* in April 1924, which noted that "the stamps in several of the upper rows were perforated obliquely across the center."[5] Six good rows, or 30 error pairs, seemed to be saved from this find. This was the basis for the original listing. Subsequent finds added to the number of error pairs available. A pair with plate number 14545 is known. Johl also reported that a full pane was found imperforate vertically, but he does not give the plate number.

554b. This is listed by Scott as a vertical pair, imperforate horizontally, and is much more scarce than 554a. However, this error has been reported erroneously many times. The pane of

554a with plate number 14689 was described in several philatelic publications as being imperforate horizontally, rather than vertically, and Johl, for example, confused the horizontal and vertical perforations on this block in his 1935 book.

There may be only three to five genuine pairs of the imperforate horizontally error in existence, all from a pane bearing plate number 14213 at bottom. Most of this pane was perforated in both directions, but a small part of the lower-right corner did not receive the horizontal perforations. The Philatelic Foundation has given an opinion of genuine on only two pairs, both from this pane.

554d. This is a perforation error, with 10-gauge perforations at the top or bottom. This type of error exists on a number of stamps of this series, and was caused when a normal perforation 11 wheel was replaced, erroneously by an old-style perforation 10 wheel.

Several used singles and one unused single are known. More important, perhaps, are three documented covers, each bearing a readable postmark that helps to determine when this error was produced. The earliest postmark is November 23, 1923, at Albion, Michigan. The second is February 6, 1924, at Colorado Springs, Colorado. The third is July 11, 1924, at Syracuse, New York.

This type of "perforation 10 error" was first reported on the 11¢ value of the Washington-Franklin stamp (Scott 473) in 1931.[6] In 1934, Max Johl reported the find of a similar error on a block of the 25¢ value of this series (Scott 568).[7] In what is still the best explanation of how this error occurred, Hugh Southgate, later in 1934, wrote that all the errors of this type, both on this series and the Washington-Franklins, occurred during the period when both issues were at press — the last printings of the Washington-Franklins and the early printings of this series. "There is ... a known range of use of the perforator with the odd wheel," he concluded, "from probably the end of 1922 to at least the beginning or middle of May 1923."[8]

Plate varieties. Scott lists only a double transfer, but does not give a position. This listing was included with the first appearance of this stamp in the 1924 edition of the Scott *Specialized*, and it is no doubt based on the report by Philip Ward two months after the stamp appeared: "Mr. David H. Burr writes that the 25th stamp of the upper left pane of plate 14129 of the 2¢ stamp shows a decided double transfer."[9]

Over 10 years later, in 1934, George Sloane reported this same variety, but credited the noted philatelist Ezra Cole with its discovery, describing it further as "a marked double transfer with frameline doubled at bottom ... The block is from one of the upper panes (probably upper left), of plate 14129, the stamp is No. 26."[10] Note that Sloane makes this stamp 26 rather than 25 as reported by Ward. Johl illustrated this same variety the following year but gave the number of the stamp as 28, and this designation was used by French in his

Figure 20. The doubling of the bottom frameline is the easiest feature that distinguishes this well-documented double transfer from position 14129 UL 26.

book. However, an examination of an actual copy of this variety in a plate block of 16 confirms that Cole and Sloane were correct. The variety is 14129 UL 26 (Figure 20).

With 1,363 plates used to produce this stamp, many plate varieties should be expected. French reports a total of 33 on this stamp, including several other double transfers, but none is more dramatic (or better documented) than 14129 UL 26.

Carolyn Kuhn, who was a great student of plate varieties on this 2¢ design in all its forms, listed only two varieties of 554 in her 1956 summary of the best plate varieties on this design.[11] One of these was another double transfer, which shows a striking doubling in the word "postage." It is listed by French as the first of the plate varieties from unknown positions. Kuhn also listed a major recut in the hairlines, as recuts were relatively rare on flat-plate stamps. Using the transfer roll to re-enter or correct defects was the usual practice. The Kuhn recut is listed by French as the eighth plate variety from unknown positions. Note: For the booklet variety of this stamp, 554c, see Chapter 10. For the star plate varieties of this stamp, see Chapter 23.

3¢ Abraham Lincoln

Scott Number: 555
First Day of Issue: February 12, 1922
Scott Colors: Violet, deep violet, dark violet, red violet, bright violet
Engravers: George F.C. Smillie (vignette)
Edward M. Hall (variable lettering)
Plate Layout: 400 subjects cut into panes of 100
Quantity Issued: 372,593,077
Plates: Total of 44: lowest, 14296; highest, 18123
Scott Varieties: None

The Subject and Design

Abraham Lincoln, the 16th president of the United States, was then, as now, considered one of the greatest of the country's leaders. With the exception of the Washington-Franklin series, he had been included in each series of regular stamp issues since 1869, usually on one of the lowest and most frequently used values. As the first Republican president, Lincoln was also a natural choice for the Harding administration to include in the new series.

This portrait of Lincoln was taken by Mathew Brady, the leading commercial photographer of the day, on February 9, 1864, when Lincoln was only a few days short of his 55th birthday. This became the Bureau's official portrait of Lincoln. It was first used on currency in 1869, and was first used on a stamp in 1903, on the 5¢ value of the Series of 1902 (Scott 304). It can be distinguished from similar portraits of Lincoln by the curl or loop of hair on the forehead (Figure 21).

Figure 21. This Mathew Brady portrait of Lincoln was not only used on the 3¢ stamp, but on the $5 bill of 1928 that is still in circulation today.

No new engraving was made of this portrait for the stamp, as an existing one in the proper size, prepared for a bond coupon, had been made by George F.C. Smillie in 1898. It was transferred to the new stamp die using a transfer roll.

Philatelic Aspects and Varieties

First day of issue. This stamp had a first day of sale on February 12, 1923, in both Washington, D.C., and at Hodgenville, Kentucky, which was "three miles from the Rock Spring Farm where the martyred president was born."[12] The date was Lincoln's birth anniversary, and the $1 stamp of this series, depicting the Lincoln Memorial in Washington, D.C., was issued on the same day.

Only the 3¢ stamp was issued in Hodgenville, which was a very small town. The postmaster reported that only about 500 first-day covers were serviced there. These command a premium today.

The practice of issuing definitive or "ordinary" stamps on a given day was a new one for both the Post Office Department and the Bureau, and it often caught them both in a crunch, as it did with this stamp. Only a single plate, 14297, could be completed in time for the designated first day, and it went to press by itself. First-day covers cannot show stamps bearing any other plate number.

The Series of 1922

Shades. The Bureau called the color of this stamp regular purple, while the Post Office Department called it just purple. When it was first listed in the 1924 edition of the Scott *Specialized*, the major shade was given as violet, with deep violet listed as a secondary shade. Three additional shades, dark violet, red violet and bright violet, were added in the 1929 edition. These three shades were soon given small letter listings, which were subsequently removed. But the five shades continue to be listed.

Figure 22. A plate block of 10 signed in the top selvege on the first day of issue by Louis A. Hill, director of the Bureau of Engraving and Printing; Hubert Work, postmaster general; and W. Irving Glover, third assistant postmaster general. The blocks help to document the colors of the original printings.

Johl listed in addition to these, bright red violet, deep red violet and bluish violet. The bluish violet he attributed to the first printing from plate 14297. This shade can be documented from the first-day covers and the blocks autographed by Post Office and Bureau officials and sold on the first day of sale at the Philatelic Sales Agency. It exists only in a small quantity and should, if properly identified, command a premium. (See Figure 22.)

Plate varieties. Scott lists none. French lists only one: a shifted transfer in an unknown position.

4¢ Martha Washington

Scott Number: 556
First Day of Issue: January 15, 1922
Scott Colors: Yellow brown, brown
Engravers: Leo C. Kauffmann (vignette)
Edward M. Weeks (variable lettering)

Plate Layout:	400 subjects cut into panes of 100
Quantity Issued:	573,387,277
Plates:	Total of 36: lowest, 14094; highest, 16370
Scott Varieties:	Double transfer
	a. Vertical pair, imperforate horizontally
	b. Perforated 10 at top or bottom

The Subject and Design

Martha Washington, the wife of the first president, made her first appearance on a stamp in 1902, on the 8¢ value of the Series of 1902. Her reappearance in this series was probably a result of a desire by the new administration to be inclusive of women. Although not particularly noted for her own accomplishments, Martha Washington was at this time one of the few historical figures — and perhaps the only one — who was widely enough known to represent women in the series.

Women had been granted the right to vote in federal elections by the 19th Amendment to the Constitution, and had voted in a presidential election for the first time in 1920. They were heavily courted by the Republicans and helped to give Warren Harding his wide electoral majority. Harding shattered precedent by naming the first woman to the position of assistant attorney general, opened the diplomatic corps to women and was otherwise more receptive to appointing women to responsible positions. As one historian summarized, "All in all, the women's movement found promising advances under the administration."[13]

The portrait of Martha is one of the more troublesome — and interesting — ones in the series. The Post Office Department and the Bureau gave the source as "after a painting by Gilbert Stuart." This was true, for the face is indeed from the so-called Atheneum portrait of Martha Washington, painted by Stuart in 1792, when she was 61. But the Stuart portrait shows Mrs. Washing-

Figure 23. Not drawn from life, the portrait of Martha Washington, by French artist Charles Jalabert, combined the face of a well-known portrait by Gilbert Stuart with features from other portraits. The fichu, or lace scarf, is one distinguishing feature of the Jalabert portrait.

ton only in a cap, not in the fichu, or lace shawl, shown in the stamp.

This portrait of Martha in the fichu had been used on currency as early as 1886 and had become the official Bureau portrait. In a mirror image view, it was also used on the 1902 stamp.

The source portrait of Martha in the fichu seems to have been drawn in crayon by Charles Francois Jalabert, a French artist born in 1819, some 17 years after the death of Mrs. Washington. His crayon portrait was based on the face of Martha from the Stuart painting, but he softened it somewhat, giving her a slightly younger appearance. The fichu seems to be derived from a miniature by an unknown artist, painted from life.

The Jalabert portrait, which was widely engraved and shown in Figure 23, seems to be something of a composite of those two sources.[14]

A new engraving of the portrait was necessary for this stamp, and it was undertaken by Leo C. Kauffmann, who was then finishing his apprenticeship as a portrait engraver at the Bureau.

Philatelic Aspects and Varieties

First day of issue. This stamp had a first day of sale on January 15, 1923, only at Washington, D.C. Like the 2¢ value, this stamp was originally planned to be released on George Washington's birthday, February 22, 1923, but was moved up to January 15 because stamps (although not necessarily of this value) were needed.

Four stamps of the new series, the 2¢, 4¢, 9¢ and 10¢, were released on this same date. A relatively small number of combination covers are known, and these command a premium.

Shades. The Bureau called the color of this stamp brown, and so did the Post Office Department. When it was first listed in the Scott *Specialized*, the major shade was listed as yellow brown, and brown was given as a secondary shade. The listings remain today.

Johl, as usual, found several other shades, including light brown, light reddish brown, reddish brown, bright reddish brown and deep yellow brown. He is correct in noting that there is a shade of this stamp with a reddish-brown cast to it. Johl also notes that the stamp was first issued in the deep yellow-brown shade, which he says is "more desirable than any of the others." This shade can be documented by the first-day covers and the autographed sheets signed on the first day of issue and sold at the Philatelic Sales Agency.

556a. This is listed by Scott as a vertical pair, imperforate horizontally. Only a single undamaged pair is known, and this is therefore one of the rarest of the perforation errors. It was reported in 1924, as being from a block of "about a dozen," from the lower-right corner of a sheet, "much torn and wrinkled," with "a strip of brown paper stuck on the back."[15] This describes a common Bureau repair, where sheets of 400 or half sheets of 200 that were mangled in the perforating process were taped back together in order to salvage usable panes. Often, if one pane of 100 was damaged, the other three panes could be used. Sometimes these damaged and taped panes found their way into circulation, probably from being erroneously placed among the "good" or undamaged panes.

This block, reduced to a block of nine, became part of the Josiah K. Lilly collection and was photographed for the auction of that collection in 1968. The block shows tears in several places, and only shows one vertical pair, in the lower-right corner, as the undamaged pair.[16] The photograph also shows the plate finisher's initials "J.W.B." and "J.McF.," indicating that this can only be from the lower-right pane of plate 14095, one of the first to go to press.[17]

556b. This is the perforation 10 error, or perf 10 at top or bottom. (See the description of this type of error at 554d, above.) Only a few examples are known. One exists unused, perf 10 at bottom. One copy is known used, perf 10 at top. Two copies are known, perf 10 at bottom, precanceled: one at San Francisco, one at Cleveland.

Double transfer. This listing was added to the Scott *Specialized* in 1932. No plate number of position was given then, and none is listed now. The listing seems to be based on a find by J.C. Schenk reported in a *Shift Hunter Letter* of 1931 that described and illustrated a shift to the left that was "small but clear." This was also described as the best of several shifts on the 4¢ Washington.[18] French lists a total of 11 double transfers on this stamp.

5¢ Theodore Roosevelt

Scott Number:	557
First Day of Issue:	October 27, 1922
Scott Colors:	Dark blue, deep blue
Engravers:	John Eissler (vignette)
	Edward E. Myers and Edward M. Hall (variable lettering)
Plate Layout:	400 subjects cut into panes of 100
Quantity Issued:	780,624,677
Plates:	Total of 75: lowest, 14066; highest, 18060

The Series of 1922

Scott Varieties: a. Imperforate pair
b. Horizontal pair, imperforate vertically
c. Perforated 10 at top or bottom
Double transfer, 15571 UL 86

The Subject and Design

Theodore Roosevelt was the most recently deceased Republican president, having died in 1919. The administration of Woodrow Wilson, a Democrat, had not issued a stamp for Roosevelt, and this would be the new administration's opportunity.

As we have noted in the previous chapter, when this new series of stamps was requested, it was suggested that Roosevelt's portrait be used on the 5¢ value. This value, which paid the letter rate to most foreign countries under the Universal Postal Union, was one of the most frequently used stamps. The Post Office Department acknowledged in a press release that "this denomination is most widely used on letters to foreign countries, where the president's fame was believed to be more universal than that of any other."[19]

Only a few years deceased, Roosevelt was still something of a presence in Washington, and his family was quite active in Republican politics. His daughter Alice, who had become a celebrity during her father's presidency, had been married in a 1906 White House wedding to Congressman Nicholas Longworth, and Nick, as he was known, had now become one of the most influential members of Congress. In three more years, he would be elected Speaker of the House. In addition, Roosevelt's oldest son, Theodore Roosevelt Jr., had been appointed assistant secretary of the Navy in the new administration, a position Teddy had held in the first McKinley administration.

The Roosevelts and Longworths were frequent social guests in the Harding White House, and Nick and Ted were associate members of what was called Harding's "poker cabinet." There was a game twice a week.[20] Roosevelt's son, daughter and son-in-law had a role in choosing the portrait for the stamp and in approving the final engraving.

The portrait was taken in 1907 by the well-known Washington studio of Harris & Ewing. President Roosevelt was 49 years old at the time and in the seventh year of his presidency. The flamboyant Teddy was often photographed in gaudy neckties and suits with bold patterns, but this portrait captured him in a refined and forceful pose (see Figure 24).

A new engraving was made for the stamp by John Eissler, the leading portrait engraver at the Bureau. It was first engraved with a solid, or "dark," background, but this first engraving was not approved. According to philatelic writer Philip Ward, it "not only failed to please the proper officials, but did not please Colonel Roosevelt and Mrs. Longworth, children of the late President."[21]

49

United States Stamps 1922-26

They suggested a light, or plain, background, and the die was altered accordingly.

Philatelic Aspects and Varieties

First day of issue. This stamp had a first day of sale on October 27, 1922, at Washington, D.C.; at Oyster Bay, New York, where Roosevelt's well-known Long Island home, Sagamore Hill, was located; and at New York City, the place of his birth. The date was Roosevelt's birth anniversary. It was the second stamp in the series to be issued, after the 11¢ Hayes.

Figure 24. Taken by the Washington, D.C., firm of Harris & Ewing, this forceful photographic portrait of Theodore Roosevelt at the age of 49 was chosen for the stamp by his children.

There does not seem to have been a first-day ceremony as such, but a die proof of the stamp was sent to Roosevelt's widow, Edith, and five stamps from the first sheet printed were sent to daughter Alice and son Ted.

The first-day covers serviced at Oyster Bay are somewhat scarce, and command a substantial premium. In a contemporary report, Philip Ward wrote that "those who wrote to Oyster Bay for [first-day covers] were disappointed, for it seems that the supply was exceedingly small and the Postmaster retained those that he received for local use."[22]

Shades. To both the Bureau and the Post Office Department, this stamp was blue. When first listed in the 1924 edition of the Scott *Specialized,* the major shade was listed as dark blue, with deep blue given as a secondary shade. This seems a rather tough distinction. To these two shades Johl added simply blue.

557a. This is listed by Scott as an imperforate pair. A lower-left pane of 100 from plate 15568 was found in Stamford, Connecticut, in 1925. Again it was Ward who provides much of the information about this discovery. He wrote that it was found by George H. Quintard, and that the pane was "not even blue penciled," meaning that it was not marked for destruction at the Bureau. Ward added: "The sheet has full gum and is normal in every way with the exception of the vertical and horizontal perforations which are lacking."[23] The following month, it was reported that Ward had purchased this pane.[24] Ward later broke up the pane, the only one ever found, but wrote the position of each stamp on the gum in lead pencil. Stamps from this pane should show Ward's penciled numbers unless they have been regummed.

557b. This is listed by Scott as a horizontal pair, imperforate vertically. There is some question whether this item, if found today, would be listed the same way, as there may not be any complete pairs that are imperforate between. The contemporary description, again by Ward, may be a bit misleading. In the fall of 1926, Ward notified John Luff, editor of the Scott catalog that "he [Ward] has recently seen a sheet ... having plate number 16332," which was further described as follows: "The horizontal perforation is correctly placed but the vertical perforation is diagonal, running from the lower right to the upper left, and so misplaced as to leave at the right side of the sheet some pairs that have entirely escaped the vertical perforation."[25] Note here that Luff has apparently not seen the item, but is reporting Ward's description.

Johl notes that there were "some pairs, about ten, which were imperf vertically," but a few words later says "very few pairs remained where the diagonal perforations had entirely missed a pair of stamps."[26]

Although such pairs may exist, I have not seen one in actuality or in an illustration. Those that have been illustrated and purport to be this error, such as in the Caroline Prentice Cromwell collection[27] or the Wharton Sinkler collection,[28] show a diagonal perforation running through one stamp. The Philatelic Foundation, in rendering an opinion on one item clearly from this find, described it not as this Scott-listed error, but as having "misplaced perfs."[29]

557c. Perforation 10 at top or bottom. (See the description of this type of error at 554d above.) Several examples are known, including stamps with local precancels of Topeka, Kansas; South Bend, Indiana; and Minneapolis, Minnesota.

Double transfer. Scott lists the position as 15571 UL 86. This is a dandy overall double, and a relatively recent listing, having gone into the 1976 edition of the Scott *Specialized* after its discovery and verification in 1975. The authors of the discovery article, George Brett and James T. DeVoss, described it as a candidate for the title of "best double transfer known on a U.S. stamp" and had "no hesitancy in putting it in the top ten or maybe even the top five."[30] French lists a total of seven double transfers on this stamp, four in known positions, but this one, 15571 UL 86, is easily the most dramatic and outstanding.

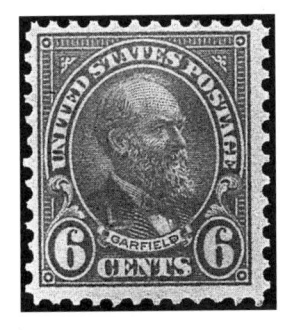

6¢ James A. Garfield

Scott Number:	558
First Day of Issue:	November 20, 1922
Scott Colors:	Red orange, pale red orange
Engravers:	John Eissler (vignette)
	Edward M. Hall (variable lettering)
Plate Layout:	400 subjects cut into panes of 100
Quantity Issued:	249,110,177
Plates:	Total of 22: lowest, 14169; highest, 16472
Scott Varieties:	Double transfer, 14169 LR 60, 70
	Same, recut

The Subject and Design

James A. Garfield was the 20th president of the United States, and the fourth Republican to hold the office. His place in history was cemented by his assassination rather than his accomplishments, as he was president for only four months before being shot by a disappointed office-seeker. He died two months later, in September 1881.

A stamp with Garfield's portrait (Scott 205) was prepared early the following year and went on general sale on April 10, 1882. His portrait remained on each new issue of ordinary or definitive stamps until the Washington-Franklin series appeared in 1908.

In part because Garfield died shortly into his presidential term, few portraits were taken of him in life. The portrait used on the 1882 stamp was derived from an artotype, a type of early photograph, taken of Garfield by New York photographer Edward Bierstadt. This photograph (see Figure 25) shows Garfield facing to his right, as does the 1922 stamp. It was reversed for the 1882 stamp, and for others that followed, including Scott 216 in 1888, Scott 224 in 1890, and Scott 256 in 1894. It was first used in its proper orientation on Scott 305 in 1903.

Figure 25. Because his presidential term was so short, few photographs exist of James Garfield. This one, used for the stamp, was taken in New York by Edward Bierstadt.

From 1890 to 1903, on three different definitive issues, Garfield was the portrait on the 6¢ stamp. He was returned to that value with the 1922 series.

The choice of Garfield, as one of the revered Republican presidents, was no doubt an easy one for the new Harding administration. Garfield was also, like Harding himself, an Ohioan.

The Series of 1922

A new engraving was made of the Bierstadt portrait by Bureau picture engraver John Eissler. He began his work on August 31, 1922, and was somewhat rushed to finish, as the Post Office Department announced that the stamp would be issued in honor of Garfield's birthday in November.

Philatelic Aspects and Varieties

First day of issue. This stamp had a first day of sale on November 20, 1922, only at Washington, D.C. There was little advance notice of this stamp, and some of the early reports created confusion. Philip Ward wrote that the stamp would be issued on November 19, the 91st anniversary of Garfield's birth, and that it would be placed on sale in Washington and "At Orange, Ohio, the birthplace of President Garfield."[31]

This was written, however, before the Post Office's official release on the stamp, which did not appear until November 17, three days before the stamp would be released. Garfield's birthday was indeed November 19, but since the date fell on Sunday, the stamp was to be released on Monday, November 20. With so little notice, relatively few first-day covers were serviced, and they command a premium over the other low values of this series.

The Bureau was also having some difficulty with the short deadline. The die was not finished until November 13. Although the usual four plates were assigned, only one, 14169, was completed in time to produce stamps in time for the first-day release. That plate was certified on Wednesday, November 15, and went to press the same day. All stamps sold on the first day were from that plate, and none of the other three plates went to press before February 7, 1923, as there was still a supply of 6¢ Washington-Franklin stamps in stock.

All stamps used on first-day covers must be from plate 14169.

Shades. Both the Bureau and the Post Office Department called this stamp orange, and most observers would be content to call this an orange stamp. Scott, however, uses the word orange to describe the 10¢ value, which is what anyone else would call yellow. When first listed in the 1924 edition of the Scott *Specialized,* this stamp was listed only as red orange. In the 1927 edition, pale red orange was listed as a secondary shade.

Johl, who noted that "there is little variation in the shades of this stamp," also added a bright red orange. Copies of this stamp can also be found in shades of brown, but these are color changlings whose ink has sulfuretted. They can be restored to their original shade with the application of hydrogen peroxide.

Plate varieties. Two days after the stamp was released, philatelic writer George Sloane discovered the marked double transfers that are listed by Scott as 14169 LR 60 and 14169 LR 70. Here is how Sloane told the story: "I made the original discovery of the double transfers one afternoon while tearing up a

Figure 26. The most significant double transfer on this stamp, 14169 LR 70, can be shown in the word "States."

number of sheets of the 6¢ stamps for postage. There were two double transfers, one above the other, sitting in a right side plate block which I soon identified as from the lower right pane of plate No. 14169."[32]

The orange ink of the stamp does not show this dramatic double transfer as readily as a darker colored ink would have, but there is a noticeable doubling of the word "States" and the top line of the arch (see Figure 26). Whether the rush to get this stamp into production helped to account for either the faulty transfers, or the fact that they were not noticed on the proof sheets, is a matter of speculation. We know, however, that the Bureau was working fast and probably faster than usual.

Sloane's involvement with the double transfers took another turn a few months after he discovered them. In January 1923, when Third Assistant PMG W. Irving Glover was a guest speaker at the Collectors' Club of New York, Sloane showed him the double transfers in a plate block that he had brought with him. Sloane picks up the story: "To my great surprise Mr. Glover took more than a casual interest in the things and in the end borrowed the block to take it back to Washington with him."[33]

Glover reported the faulty transfer to the Bureau, which repaired the two stamps. Sloane reports that it "recut the two positions by hand," although the normal method would be to hammer out the faulty transfers and re-enter the subjects. The repaired stamps, however, still show evidence of doubling, particularly in the upper corners, so Sloane's description is no doubt accurate. Scott has adopted it and lists in addition to the double transfers "Same, recut."

Both these items — the double transfers and the repaired stamps — are best collected in the form of a side plate block of six. Stamp 60 is adjacent to the side plate number and stamp 70 is the stamp below it.

Although these plate varieties were discovered by Sloane in 1922, they were not listed by Scott until 10 years later, first appearing in the 1932 edition of the Scott *Specialized*.

The Series of 1922

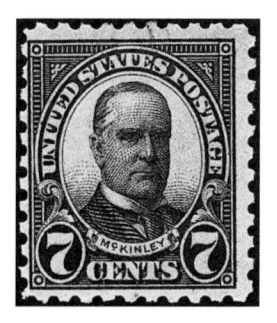

7¢ William McKinley

Scott Number: 559
First Day of Issue: May 1, 1923
Scott Colors: Black, gray black
Engravers: Louis Schofield (vignette)
Edward E. Myers (variable lettering)
Plate Layout: 400 subjects cut into panes of 100
Quantity Issued: 376,658,877
Plates: Total of 61: lowest, 14584; highest, 18166
Scott Varieties: Double transfer

The Subject and Design

William McKinley was the 25th president and the 6th Republican to hold the office. He was also the last Republican president before Theodore Roosevelt. McKinley was assassinated in the first year of his second term by an anarchist, and died a few days later, on September 14, 1901. His vice president, Theodore Roosevelt, then became president.

His portrait was put on a stamp for the first time in 1904 with the issue of the 5¢ value of the Louisiana Purchase issue. McKinley, of course, had nothing to do with the Louisiana Purchase and was not born when the purchase took place in 1804. Officially, the reason for including McKinley in this series was that he was the president who "approved the acts of Congress officially connecting the Government with the commemorative exposition."[34] This was a thin connection, but an opportunity for the Roosevelt postal administration to put McKinley on a stamp.

The Series of 1922 offered the new Republican administration the opportunity to give McKinley a stamp in his own right. Not only was he a past Republican president, but he was one of the three presidents — all Republicans — to be assassinated in office. Like Lincoln and Garfield, he was a "martyr President" and was a logical choice for inclusion in the series. If more ammunition was necessary, McKinley was also, like Harding, a native Ohioan.

Although contemporary Bureau records note that the source for the

McKinley portrait used on the stamp is from a photograph "origin unknown," it has recently been shown that the photograph (Figure 27) was taken by George Rockwood, who had a studio in New York City.[35]

The first engraving for the stamp was begun by George Wittenauer, a relatively new picture engraver at the Bureau, but his engraving was found to be unsatisfactory and was never completed. A new die was then undertaken on April 10, 1923, by Louis Schofield, a veteran picture engraver, and was completed two weeks later.

Philatelic Aspects and Varieties

First day of issue. This stamp had a first day of issue on May 1, 1923, in Washington, D.C., and in Niles, Ohio, the birthplace of McKinley. The date had no special significance. The 7¢, 8¢, 14¢ and 20¢ values were all issued on this date, in part to finish the series before the end of the Post Office Department fiscal year, which was to end on June 30.

First-day covers from Niles command a significant premium, as only 50 panes of stamps were sent to this site.

As with the 6¢ stamp, there was a race at the Bureau to complete this value in time for the Post Office Department's issue date. Problems with the first engraving of the die contributed to the delay, and the second engraving, by Louis Schofield, was not completed until Tuesday, April 24, 1923, one week before the first-day date.

Again, the usual four plates were assigned, but only one, 14584, was completed in time for the first-day date. It was certified on Thursday, April 26, and went to press the same day. Shipping stamps from Washington, D.C., to Niles, Ohio, for issue on Tuesday must have been a bit of a rush, and no doubt contributed to the short supply.

All stamps on first-day covers must be from plate 14584.

Shades. The Post Office Department originally termed the color of this stamp as bank note black, and it is clearly a black stamp. When first listed in the Scott *Specialized*, the primary shade was given as black, but gray black was included as a secondary shade. Johl added to these only intense black.

Plate varieties. Scott lists a double transfer on this stamp but gives no position. The listing went into the Scott *Specialized* for the first time in 1936,

Figure 27. The photographic portrait of McKinley from which the stamp design is derived has recently been identified as having been taken by George Rockwood in 1898.

and probably refers to the "upward shift" illustrated by Johl in 1935. This same variety was illustrated in the *Bureau Specialist* in December 1936, and referred to as "a shift to the north or 'back shift.' "[36] French illustrated the same variety, which he called a "backshift." It is also the only plate variety of this stamp that is illustrated by French. The position is still unknown.

8¢ Ulysses S. Grant

Scott Number:	560
First Day of Issue:	May 1, 1923
Scott Colors:	Olive green, pale olive green
Engravers:	Louis Schofield and John Eissler (vignette)
	Edward M. Hall and William B. Wells (variable lettering)
Plate Layout:	400 subjects cut into panes of 100
Quantity Issued:	367,196,477
Plates:	Total of 54: lowest, 14569; highest, 17920
Scott Varieties:	Double transfer

The Subject and Design

Ulysses S. Grant was the 18th president and the second Republican to hold the position. A Civil War general of renown, and Lincoln's final commander of all Union forces, Grant was elected to the presidency in 1868. He proved to be a mediocre president, but remained one of the nation's military heroes. His portrait was first placed on a stamp in the Series of 1890, under the Republican administration of Benjamin Harrison, and his portrait remained on a value of each new definitive series until the Washington-Franklin series of 1908.

With the 1922 series, Grant was restored. And again, like Garfield, McKinley and Hayes, he was not only a Republican president, but an Ohioan like President Harding.

A different portrait of Grant was used for the new stamp than had appeared on previous issues. The source of the new portrait was a photograph (Figure 28) taken by the popular Civil War photographer Mathew Brady and

Figure 28. The portrait of Grant used on the stamp is from a photograph by the renowned Civil War photographer Mathew Brady.

first used on currency in 1886. The photograph was apparently provided by the War Department, which also purchased many of the Brady negatives after the photographer's death in 1896.[37] Bureau designer C. Aubrey Huston also chose this portrait of Grant for a new series of currency in 1914, and it became the Bureau's official portrait of Grant.

As designed by Huston, this stamp was to have a dark background, and it was engraved that way by Louis Schofield, using an existing bond coupon die as the source. A die was fully engraved but found to be unsuitable. A new die was then made by transferring the Schofield engraving. This was reworked by John Eissler with a lighter background and approved on April 12, 1923.

Philatelic Aspects and Varieties

First day of issue. This stamp had a first day of issue on May 1, 1923, only at Washington, D.C. The date did not have any significance, and was the same date of issue as the 7¢, 14¢ and 20¢ values.

Each of the other three stamps issued on this date, however, had a first-day site in addition to Washington, D.C. It seems that there may not have been sufficient time to ship these stamps anywhere but Washington. The die was completed on April 12, giving ample time to lay out four plates of this stamp in time for the first-day date. However, the four plates did not go to press until Wednesday, April 25, less than a week before the issue date. This may well be the reason that there was no other first-day city.

Shades. To both the Bureau and the Post Office Department, this stamp was olive. When first listed in the 1924 edition of the Scott *Specialized*, the major shade was given as olive green, with pale olive green as a secondary shade.

Johl did not mention the pale shade, but added yellow olive green and deep olive green, the latter being described as being from the first printing, and that printing "being small, this shade is more desirable than the lighter ones which followed it."[38]

This shade can be distinguished by matching it to the stamps on first-day covers or from the blocks signed by Bureau and Post Office Department officials on the first day.

Plate varieties. Scott lists a double transfer, but gives no position. This, however, is undoubtedly the "distinct double transfer" described and illustrated in *Scott's Monthly Journal* in June 1927, which shows a marked eastward shift.[39] The listing went into the Scott *Specialized* with the 1928 edition.

This same double transfer is illustrated in French and is the one of only two plate varieties that he records on this stamp. The position remains unknown.

For the star-plate varieties of this stamp, see Chapter 23.

9¢ Thomas Jefferson

Scott Number: 561
First Day of Issue: January 15, 1923
Scott Colors: Rose, pale rose
Engravers: George F.C. Smillie (vignette)
Edward M. Hall (variable lettering)
Plate Layout: 400 subjects cut into panes of 100
Quantity Issued: 177,662,477
Plates: Total of 16: lowest, 14239; highest, 17524
Scott Varieties: Double transfer

The Subject and Design

Thomas Jefferson was the third president of the United States, and the third individual, after Washington and Franklin, to be depicted on a U.S. stamp. Jefferson made his first appearance on a stamp (Scott 12) in 1856 and with the exception of the 1869 Pictorials, he remained a subject on each definitive series until the Washington-Franklin series of 1908. Jefferson's portrait was also used on currency continually from 1869.

In addition to serving as president, Jefferson had framed or drafted the Constitution, he had been the first secretary of state and a governor of Virginia. Although any of his historical achievements would have justified his place on the new series of stamp, he also added some geographical balance, as he and Monroe were the only Southerners (other than the Washingtons) among the 12 portraits. None of the vignettes on the nine higher values depicts southern scenes.

The portrait of Jefferson that was used for the stamp derives from a portrait painted from life by Gilbert Stuart, one of America's great portraitists, in 1805. In the original portrait, Jefferson faces in the other direction (see Figure 29). The Bureau first engraved this portrait in the right-facing position in

1869, for use on currency, so Jefferson would look inward when the portrait was used on the left side of the bills.[40] It became the Bureau's official portrait of Jefferson and was used on Bureau-produced stamps for the 50¢ value of the 1902 series (Scott 310) and the 2¢ value of the Louisiana Purchase issue of 1904 (Scott 324).

No new engraving was made for the new stamp. The engraving by George F.C. Smillie for the 1904 Louisiana Purchase stamp was transferred to a new die using a transfer roll, and was restored by John Eissler and Leo Kauffmann.

Figure 29. The source of the Jefferson stamp was an oil portrait by Gilbert Stuart painted from life in 1805. In a reversed form, it became the official portrait of Jefferson used by the Bureau on both currency and stamps.

Philatelic Aspects and Varieties

First day of issue. This stamp was issued on January 15, 1923, only at Washington, D.C. According to a Post Office Department press release, the original plan was to issue this stamp on April 13, 1923, Thomas Jefferson's birthday.[41] But it was released on January 15, at the same time as the 2¢, 4¢ and 10¢ values. Although the press release speaks of the need for stamps, it was not really the 9¢ stamp that was needed, for it paid no special rate. It was probably issued with the other values because the dies and plates were ready and there was no real need to delay it.

A complete set of four plates for this stamp was certified on December 12, and they went to press together for the first time on December 16. Confirming the fact that there was no great shortage or demand for this value, the first press runs were rather small, and only 55,100 stamps were delivered to post offices during the 1923 fiscal year.

Shades. Both the Bureau and the Post Office Department described the color of this stamp as pink. When first listed in the 1924 edition of the Scott *Specialized*, only one shade, rose, was given. A pale rose shade was added in the 1927 edition.

Johl in 1935 added to these shades carmine rose and bright carmine rose. He gave the latter as the original shade, which he described as "the most desirable color variety." The Stanley Gibbons catalog of 1938 also noted, "The first shade of this stamp, bright carmine rose, is not at all common."[42] This early shade can be identified from first-day covers and from the panes signed on the first day of issue and sold at the Philatelic Stamp Agency.

Plate varieties. A double transfer listing went into the Scott *Specialized* in the 1933 edition. It is no doubt the shifted transfer reported by Edward T. Ferry in the *Bureau Specialist* in 1932, which was noted as the first report of "a shift of any kind on No. 561, the 9¢ 1922." The doubling was reported as showing "in the lower curve of the medallion, in 'Jefferson' and in the top of 'Cents.' "[43] The position was not established. This remains the only plate variety on this stamp listed by French.

10¢ James Monroe

Scott Number:	562
First Day of Issue:	January 15, 1923
Scott Color:	Orange
Engravers:	George F.C. Smillie (vignette)
	Edward M. Hall and Howard I. Earle (variable lettering)
Plate Layout:	400 subjects cut into panes of 100
Quantity Issued:	819,223,576
Plates:	Total of 103: lowest, 14229; highest, 18034
Scott Varieties:	a. Vertical pair, imperforate horizontally
	b. Imperforate pair
	c. Perforated 10 at top or bottom

The Subject and Design

James Monroe was the fifth president of the United States, and is probably best remembered in association with the Monroe Doctrine, a foreign-policy declaration against foreign colonization or intervention in the Americas.

Monroe had only appeared on a single previous stamp, the 3¢ value of the Louisiana Purchase issue of 1904 (Scott 325) and had only a brief appearance on currency. The use of his portrait on the 10¢ stamp, a popular value that paid both the registry and special delivery rates, is somewhat puzzling.

Here, perhaps, we have to raise the issue of the letter of Brother Cassian, an Ohio cleric, who reportedly wrote to the Post Office Department in early 1922 with suggestions for subject matter on a new series of stamps. We have never been able to locate the letter or the copy of the *Alverno Sentinel*, a house organ in which it was reportedly published in May 1922. But *Scott's Monthly Journal* reported in April 1923 that Brother Cassian had sent a letter "urging the selection of portraits including those of Lincoln, Washington, Grant, McKinley, Roosevelt, Monroe, Jefferson, Franklin, Martha Washington, and of scenes and symbols including the Statue of Liberty, Niagara Falls, the Capitol, an Indian and a Buffalo — all of which were later chosen."[44]

Brother Cassian's letter would have arrived at exactly the right time — when the Post Office Department was trying to pick subject matter. Perhaps the letter had a great deal of influence and was responsible for much of the subject matter of the series, including Monroe's portrait. We will probably never know.

In foreign policy the Harding administration stood against much of what the previous Wilson administration stood for. Harding campaigned for an end to the country's preoccupation with things and affairs European and a return to national interests. Mainly, this was a reaction against the idea of world government and the League of Nations that Wilson so much wanted the United States to join.

The Monroe Doctrine, enunciated in 1823, was not only having its centennial, but was having something of a revival of interest. Charles Evans Hughes, the new secretary of state, was convinced, according to Harding's biographers, "that the Monroe Doctrine was essential as a part of the foreign policy of the United States and was a cardinal rule of self-preservation."[45]

Figure 30. Although based on a portrait by John Vanderlyn in New York's City Hall, this engraving of Monroe by Asher Durand was in a book on the shelf of the engraving department of the Bureau of Engraving and Printing.

Nowhere, however, did the Post Office Department take much of an opportunity to sing the praises of Monroe or the Monroe Doctrine, except to say, as Glover did in the press release quoted earlier, that Monroe was included "to mark the foreign policy associated with his name."

The portrait of Monroe is based on a John Vanderlyn painting, but the painting was probably known to the Bureau in the form of an engraving by Asher Durand (Figure 30) that appeared in James B. Longacre's book, *The National Portrait Gallery*, which was published in 1833. This book was part of the library in the engraving division, and this portrait became the official one of Monroe.[46] It first appeared on currency on the $100 silver certificate of 1878.

The Series of 1922

No new engraving was made for the 1922 stamp. The portrait engraved for the 1904 Louisiana Purchase stamp by George F.C. Smillie was transferred to a new die and restored by Edward J. Hein.

Philatelic Aspects and Varieties

First day of issue. This stamp was issued on January 15, 1923, only in Washington, D.C. As with the 9¢ value, there was a plan, although short-lived, to release this stamp on a meaningful date — Monroe's birthday, April 28. But due to the need for stamps, and the fact that the die and plates were ready, it was released with the 2¢, 4¢ and 9¢ values on January 15, 1923, and only in Washington, D.C.

Some combination first-day covers are known, both with the 2¢ stamp and other values. These command a substantial premium over covers with only the 10¢ stamp.

Shades. Both the Bureau and the Post Office Department described this stamp as yellow, and few observers would probably argue with the designation. When first listed in the 1924 edition of the *Specialized Catalogue*, the shade was given as orange. A pale orange was added as a secondary shade in the 1927 edition.

Max Johl was among those who disliked these designations, arguing that "there is practically no red in the color that would give this orange cast, the color being more nearly a deep gold." He added that "there was little variation in the shade of this stamp, those listed being principally of the inking variety."[47] Johl called the shades light yellow orange, yellow orange and deep yellow orange.

562a. This is listed as a vertical pair, imperforate horizontally. Credited with the find of this variety, in early 1924, was Eugene Klein, the Philadelphia philatelist and dealer. One damaged pane was found, the upper right from plate 14816. Not all the stamps, however, were in undamaged condition.

Philip Ward, a fellow Philadelphian, was able to view the pane before it was divided into blocks and pairs, and gave us not only a good description of the pane, but a good theory of how the error stamps came about. He wrote:

"After the sheet of four hundred stamps had been printed, something happened to damage it at the right side, about at the arrow position, so that quite a portion of the sheet was torn. It was seen that the two right panes could be completed and made into a saleable stock so that this damaged portion was patched up with a dark kraft paper. The sheet was then perforated vertically and in this operation the sheet of four hundred stamps was cut into two panes of two hundred each. When the girl started to run the damaged pane through the perforating machine the other way, the paper adhering on the back caught and the horizontal perforations started in an upward diagonal course. These diagonal perforations only ran for a few inches when the sheet was removed and was heavily blue penciled across the lower right portion of the pane, which was a signal for the one counting the sheets to remove it and destroy it. Through error it was not noticed, and got into the regular stock."

To this no doubt accurate explanation, Ward added that because of the taping and blue pencil marks, "only twenty-three first class pairs are available."[48] The pane was soon broken up into pairs and blocks, and the plate block of six sent to John Luff of Scott for listing in the catalog.

Before the pane was broken up, however, the stamps were numbered by position on the reverse or gum side. These pencil numbers should still appear on copies that have not been regummed. This numbering of the stamps before rare panes were broken up was practiced by the two Philadelphia dealers, Klein and Ward, on several occasions. Klein, who bought the only known pane of the 1918 airmail invert (Scott C3a), numbered the stamps on the back before breaking it up, and Ward would also be known to number certain panes, including the panes of stamps we know now as 557a.

Johl writes that another pane of similar stamps, imperforate horizontally, was found in August 1923 from plate 14818 and had not been "blue penciled." This may not be true, as the writer has seen no plate number positions from such a pane. Nor did Scott seem to be aware of any such find until reported by Ward and Klein in 1924. Johl may have this pane confused with the imperforate pane found from plate 14818, which is described below.

562b. This is listed as an imperforate pair. Once again, it was Philip Ward who reported the find of this variety, noting that a lower-left pane from plate 14818 was found in Oklahoma in April 1925. "The pane," Ward wrote, "shows no traces whatsoever of perforations either horizontally or vertically."[49] This pane was marked for destruction with a blue crayon, and was ungummed. Ward noted that he was able to purchase it soon after its discovery.

562c. This is listed as "perf 10 at top or bottom" and was formed in the same way as the other perforation 10 errors. (See 554d above.) Several copies of this variety are known, all or nearly all, with local precancels of some type, including Brooklyn, New York; Osage, Iowa; Minneapolis, Minnesota; and Troy, Ohio.

Plate varieties. Scott has no listing for double transfers or other plate varieties on this stamp, and only two minor varieties are listed by French. While there were 103 plates of this stamp put to press, the yellow color has no doubt helped to mask from easy view the varieties that should be expected on a press run of more than 819,000,000 stamps.

The Series of 1922

11¢ Rutherford B. Hayes

Scott Number: 563
First Day of Issue: October 4, 1922
Scott Colors: Light blue, greenish blue, light bluish green, light yellow green
Engravers: John Eissler (vignette)
Edward M. Hall and Edward M. Weeks (variable lettering)
Plate Layout: 400 subjects cut into panes of 100
Quantity Issued: 298,510,877
Plates: Total of 28: lowest, 14058; highest, 19138
Scott Varieties: d. Imperforate pair

The Subject and Design

Rutherford B. Hayes was the 19th president of the United States and the third Republican to hold the office. Like Grant, Garfield and McKinley, he was also born in Ohio. Hayes was one of the two presidents (the other being Cleveland in his first term) to receive fewer popular votes than his opponent. He got 252,224 fewer votes than Democrat Samuel J. Tilden in the election of 1876, but received one more electoral vote and was declared president as a result.

Hayes' Republicanism and his Ohio birth should have been enough to qualify for inclusion on a stamp in the Harding administration, but his son, Scott R. Hayes, waged a campaign to have his father honored on a stamp for the 100th anniversary of his birth.

Philip Ward was one of the writers who criticized the selection of Hayes almost immediately after the news broke that he would be among the subjects. "Hayes never did anything that history will remember," he wrote, "and I imagine our only reason for having him was because he happened to be born just a hundred years ago."[50]

While one Bureau record attributes the portrait of Hayes on the stamp to Charles Parker of Washington, D.C., this record appears to be in error. A Mathew Brady portrait of Hayes, nearly identical to the stamp, is known in the Library of Congress and is shown in Figure 31. This portrait was probably

Figure 31. The portrait of Hayes used for the stamp was from the Brady studio, and was probably taken by Mathew Brady himself or one of his associates.

taken by Brady himself or one of his assistants. In addition, a souvenir portrait of Hayes, based on the Brady photograph, was engraved in 1877.

Hayes had not previously appeared on a stamp. A new engraving was made for the stamp by John Eissler.

Philatelic Aspects and Varieties

First day of issue. This was the first value of the new series to be issued, on October 4, 1922, in Washington, D.C., and in Fremont, Ohio, which was Hayes' hometown. The date was the 100th anniversary of Hayes' birth, and a ceremony of that anniversary was scheduled for Fremont. To meet the date, the Bureau had to rush the stamps into production.

The die was begun on August 10, but not completed until Thursday, September 28. A set of four plates were assigned the following day, but only one was certified before the first day of issue. Plate 14058 was certified on Saturday, September 30, and went to press by itself on the same day.

This first printing was small, just 600 sheets of 400, or 240,000 stamps. Once the plates went to press, the stamps had to be dried — usually at least an overnight process — then gummed and perforated. The process was not completed until the morning of Tuesday, October 3. Press releases from the Post Office Department noted that the first 32 panes of stamps were autographed by W. Irving Glover, Louis A. Hill and Michael Eidsness. Eidsness was also personally dispatched to Fremont, with 50,000 stamps, or 500 panes.

The ceremony at Fremont has been noted by several writers as the first first-day ceremony for a stamp.[51] Scott R. Hayes, the son of the president, was presented with a die proof of the stamp and was sold a sheet that was described as "the first sheet."[52]

A handful of first-day covers serviced at Fremont exist today and command a substantial premium over those postmarked in Washington, D.C. One of these, addressed to Herman Boers, a well-known collector, is shown in Figure 32.

Shades. This stamp has more shades — and a more interesting history of shades — than any other 20th-century stamp. The Post Office Department described the original color as peacock blue, and it is a shame that Scott never adopted this description, as specialist collectors still use it to describe this unique and beautiful shade of the first printing. It can be documented from the first-

The Series of 1922

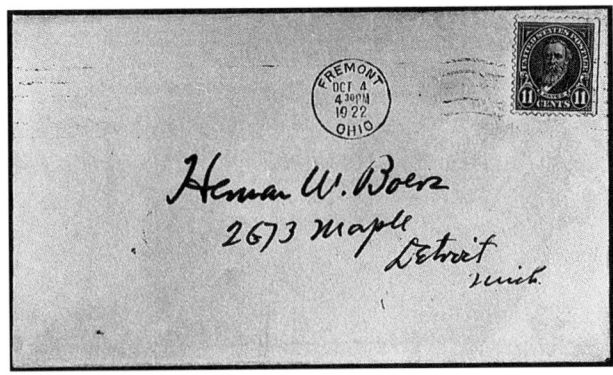

Figure 32. The 11¢ value was the first of the series to be issued and had something of a ceremony in Fremont, Ohio. Fremont first-day covers command a high premium over those serviced in Washington D.C.

day covers and the signed blocks from plate 14058.

John Luff, who was assigning the Scott colors, evidently didn't like this shade or its description, but admitted somewhat begrudgingly that he hadn't seen it before. "The color is delicate and lady-like, not what we would associate with a man," he wrote. "It is officially termed 'peacock blue.' If we had a peacock of that color we would feel that it needed a 'pink pill' or something to improve its physical condition."[53] Luff termed the shade a pedestrian light blue when he listed it for the first time in the 1924 edition of the *Specialized Catalogue*, and that has remained the primary shade in Scott catalogs to this day, although Scott has listed a few other shades over the years, and even gave one shade its own catalog number for a while.

While the first shade of this stamp was established with the first printing from plate 14058, the second shade probably occurred on October 9, 1922, when the rest of the plates from what was meant to be the first set of plates went to press. The shade produced was a bit deeper or darker than the printing from plate 14058 alone. Over the next three years, the stamp was produced in a wide variety of shades.

So wide, in fact, was the variety that in February 1925, according to philatelic writer Ross Frampton, the Post Office Department "felt that the color spread was too great, and requested the Bureau to submit specimens."[54] As a result, "a lighter blue" shade than the original peacock blue was selected.

By 1928, the stamp was being produced in a decidedly greenish shade. In the 1929 Scott *Specialized,* the greenish blue shade was added. This was the first shade Scott recognized in addition to its original light blue. But a discussion soon got under way.

Luff, in July 1929, reported that "a gradual change has been observed in the color of the current 11¢ stamp." In Luff's opinion, "The color changed from blue to greenish blue and finally to a light green." Backing up his opinion was a letter from a Charles Rubel, enclosing two blocks of the new shade and the information that "the Director of the Bureau admitted to me that the 50,000 issued in this color went through by mistake and that additional issues would come out in a light blue run."[55]

As a result of this letter and the blocks of stamps submitted by Rubel, Scott assigned a totally new number, 652, to the light green shade of what otherwise would be 563. This new catalog number went into the Scott *Specialized* in the 1930 edition and was removed in the 1937 edition. There is now no such Scott number, but the discussion over the shades of this stamp went on for some time.

One of the first collectors to specialize in this stamp, L.E. Eastman, described shades of this stamp in December 1929 as follows: "I have it ... ranging from blue, turquoise blue, several shades of blue-green, chalky blue, green, yellow-green and about six shades of yellowish-green."[56]

Ross Frampton wrote in 1931 that after the discovery of the green shade, which was termed an "error" due to the Bureau's description of this being printed "by mistake," another sheet was pulled to standardize the color on April 20, 1929. This was described as "the milky shade now in service."[57]

By the time Johl tackled this stamp in 1935, he listed and named 26 shades. He argued that what Scott called 652 "was neither intentional nor official and therefore should not be listed as a separate major variety." He also interpreted the "50,000" of the light green to be 50,000 panes, not 50,000 stamps, for a total of 5,000,000 copies. Thus, he also disputed the scarcity of this shade over the early peacock blue shades. Scott was putting a premium price on the greens. "These earlier colors," Johl predicted, "are likely to prove more desirable than the later greens and milky blues."[58]

This view has prevailed in the main. In 1937, when the 652 variety was removed from the Scott *Specialized*, it listed, as it always had, light blue as the primary shade, greenish blue as 563a, light bluish green as 563b, and light yellow green as 563c. (The light yellow green had replaced the light green of 652 in 1933.)

The small-letter designations and the premiums for the other shades have now been removed, but Scott continues to list only these four shades for this stamp. Although Scott does not recognize the early peacock blue shade or give it a premium, specialized collectors know it when they see it and are willing to pay more for it.

563d. This is listed as an imperforate pair. Only two examples are known, and both have local precancels "San Francisco, California." The first report of this variety was a pair reported in *Scott's Monthly Journal* in September 1925. The brief notice said, "We are indebted to Mr. Adolph , Jr., for show-

The Series of 1922

ing us a pair of this novelty."[59] This pair was evidently purchased by Scott, as Ward reported several months later that he had "acquired [it] from Scott Stamp & Coin." He noted further, "I understand it was used in sending out catalogs by a firm in that city." Ward also quoted Hugh Clark, manager of the Scott firm, as writing:

"In regard to the pair of 11¢ imperforate stamps, I first learned of this variety when in California last summer. I heard several rumors of further supplies in San Francisco and in consequence I made a special trip to San Francisco to run down these rumors. I was unable to find any basis whatever in fact."[60]

In 1938, another writer, W.L. Babcock, told this second-hand story of this unusual pair:

"In 1923 or 1924 a boy about 17 yrs. of age named Christensen, employed by the Pacific Mutual Life Ins. Co. law department, salvaged an imperf. horizontal pair from a package containing a shipment of law books from a San Francisco firm. The pair was precanceled. The young man finally traded it for a few cheap stamps and a small amount of cash. I was told the party acquiring the pair later sold it to the Scott Stamp and Coin Co., N.Y."[61]

This pair was further described in 1968, when it was sold as part of the Josiah Lilly collection, as being "almost severed by scissors," and "the only known pair."[62]

In 1982, however, a vertical strip of three, also with a San Francisco precancel, appeared in an auction sale by the firm of Jacques C. Schiff Jr. Inc. It was photographed and described[63] and is almost certainly from the same pane as the horizontal pair.

The fact that these items were precanceled means that not only did the error first escape the Bureau inspectors, but it also escaped detection by the San Francisco postmaster who had the precanceling done. And finally it escaped notice by whoever affixed the precanceled stamps to the packages!

Plate markings. Scott lists no plate varieties or marginal-marking varieties for this stamp. However, there are some well-known and well-documented varieties of the marginal markings. Plate 14058, the first plate to go to press, had the "F" marking at the lower-right side on the first printing, instead of before the top upper-right plate number as was customary. This "F" was moved to its proper position on later printings of this plate, so there are four distinct varieties of marginal markings on this pane. Top upper-right plate blocks exist with and without the "F." Lower-right plate blocks also exist with and without the "F." On this same plate, 14058, which we know to have been hurriedly put to press, stamps 7, 17, 27 and 37 are misaligned on the upper-left pane.

On plate 14060, the "F" marking was originally placed before the plate number on the side of the upper-left pane, then moved to its normal position

69

before the top upper-right plate number. Thus there are also four distinct varieties of marginal marking on this pane. Left side upper plate numbers of 14060 exist with and without the "F." Top right plate numbers also exist with or without the "F."[64]

12¢ Grover Cleveland

Scott Number:	564
First Day of Issue:	March 20, 1923
Scott Colors:	Brown violet, deep brown violet
Engravers:	John Eissler (vignette)
	Edward M. Week and Frank Lamasure (variable lettering)
Plate Layout:	400 subjects cut into panes of 100
Quantity Issued:	447,511,777
Plates:	Total of 35: lowest, 14404; highest, 19442
Scott Varieties:	Double transfer, 14404 UL 73, 74
	a. Horizontal pair, imperforate vertically

The Subject and Design

Grover Cleveland holds the distinction of being the only person to be elected to the U.S. presidency for two nonconsecutive terms. He was the 22nd person to be president, and served as both the 22nd and 24th president. Cleveland, who died in 1908, was the most recently deceased Democratic president, and he is the only Democrat among the 12 persons whose portraits appear in the series. It is perhaps not too difficult to believe that he was included in the series to provide some balance and some representation for his party.

The source of the portrait used on the stamp is given in Bureau records as "unknown." It was first engraved in 1886, during Cleveland's first term, when Cleveland was less obese than he became in later life. A lithograph of this same portrait on deposit at the Library of Congress is credited to Courier Litho Co. of Buffalo, New York, and has the name "A. J. Maerz" in the lower-right corner.[65] (See Figure 33.)

This portrait was first used on currency on the $20 Federal Reserve note of 1914. It had never before been used on a stamp, and was engraved for the series by John Eissler.

Philatelic Aspects and Varieties

First day of issue. This stamp was issued on March 20, 1923, in Washington, D.C.; in Caldwell, New Jersey, which was Cleveland's birthplace; and in Boston, Massachusetts, where a philatelic exhibition was taking place.

The 30¢, $2 and $5 denominations were issued on the same day. Although several writers have noted that "the date of this issue had no significance relating to the subject,"[66] the Post Office Department's press release notes, "It is issued in honor of Cleveland's birthday, which falls on Sunday, March 18."[67]

Instead of the Sunday date (on which post offices would be closed), the Post Office Department chose the following Tuesday, to coincide with the exhibition at the Boston Public Library sponsored by the Boston Philatelic Society. Ten thousand stamps were sent to Boston. A smaller quantity, reported as 3,000, was sent to Caldwell, New Jersey, which was Cleveland's birthplace.

Johl noted that the Washington postmark on this stamp is most common — which is true — but he also remarked that "the advance notice did not mention the Department's intention to issue the new 12¢ stamps in Boston on March 20th."[68] This is incorrect. The press release not only mentions the sale and the date, but says "Because of the desire of collectors to obtain these stamps together with a special Boston postmark being used in honor of the philatelic convention, it is expected the sale of Cleveland stamps in the Hub city will be enormous."[69] This release no doubt escaped Johl's notice.

To meet the March 20 deadline was another challenge for the Bureau. The die was not approved until March 3. The normal set of four plate numbers were assigned the same date, but only plate 14404 went to press before the first-day date. All first-day items must therefore be from this plate and from a small initial printing.

Shades. The Bureau and the Post Office Department gave the color of this stamp as purplish brown. When first listed in the 1924 edition of the *Specialized Catalogue*, the major shade was given as brown violet, with deep brown violet listed as a secondary shade. The two shades are still listed today.

Johl added to these only light brown vio-

Figure 33. The portrait used on the Cleveland stamp shows the president as he appeared in 1886, during his first term, before he became heavier.

let, noting, "This stamp has shown a slighter variation in color than any of the lower values except the seven cent."

Fred J. Melville, the British writer, described this color as plum, which is perhaps as descriptive as any.[70]

564a. This is listed as a horizontal pair, imperforate vertically. It was first listed in the second edition of the 1936 Scott *Specialized* and was based on a find reported by Spencer Anderson in April of that year. According to Anderson's report, one pane was discovered "some 10 years ago" on which the "top three rows show no vertical perforations" and on which "the lower seven rows show slightly diagonal extra perforations."[71] This would make only 15 pairs that were imperforate vertically.

564b. There is no such variety. This listing appeared in the Scott *Specialized* in the 1982 edition, as an imperforate pair, but was later questioned by assistant editor William Hatton, who had the note inserted into the 1993 edition, "The status of No. 564b has been questioned." We know from examples that the pane that contained 564a, listed above, was a lower-right pane. Thus, the top row was straight edge. This made five pairs that were imperforate on all sides but the bottom. The erroneous listing was no doubt based on a pair of stamps that had the perforations at bottom cut off. Such a pair was sold in a Schiff auction in 1981, and illustrated, but was properly identified as having the bottom "perfs trimmed off."[72] The listing was removed in the 1996 edition of the *Specialized*.

Plate varieties. A double transfer listing went into the Scott *Specialized* in the 1926 edition. In 1932, George Sloane reported that "an extremely distinct double transfer," which he had noticed a few years earlier, could now be identified as 14404 UR 2, coming from the first plate to press.[73] This is indeed a distinct double transfer, visible in many places in the lower third of the stamp. It is in fact a more pronounced example of a double transfer than the two positions Scott currently lists.

In the 1943 edition of the *Specialized*, the listing was changed to specify positions 14404 UL 73 and 74. These were described by Johl in *Stamps* in 1934. Both, it should be noted, are from plate 14404, the first, hurried plate to go to press. Johl calls 14404 UL 73 "a two-way double or triple transfer which can be easily seen." He describes 14404 UL 74 as a stamp that "had three entries before it was finally correct." It is more distinct than its partner. Johl ended his article with the opinion that "these items are of major importance and their discovery is a worthwhile contribution to our knowledge of this stamp."[74] These stamps were loaned to Johl by the Alvonis Company, a stamp firm that took an ad on the same page as Johl's column. Perhaps this affected Johl's opinion. For the star-plate varieties of this stamp, see Chapter 23.

The Series of 1922

14¢ American Indian

Scott Number: 565
First Day of Issue: May 1, 1923
Scott Colors: Blue, deep blue
Engravers: Louis Schofield (vignette)
Frank Lamasure and Edward M. Hall (variable lettering)
Plate Layout: 400 subjects cut into panes of 100
Quantity Issued: 151,114,177
Plates: Total of 20: lowest, 14512; highest, 19441
Scott Varieties: Double transfer

The Subject and Design

The American Indian at this point had become a popular symbol of the country. Only a few decades earlier the Indian was viewed as an obstacle to western expansion and a threat to the safety of settlers. But now, like the eagle, the Indian represented strength and a natural nobility.

The so-called Buffalo nickel that was in current circulation had an Indian head on the obverse, and while the Indian-head penny had been replaced with the Lincoln-head cent in 1909, they were still quite common in any handful of change.

The Bureau had used an Indian in a full warbonnet on the $5 silver certificate of 1899 and had in mind using another Indian on the currency it was redesigning in 1920. Carter Glass, the second secretary of the treasury in the Woodrow Wilson administration, had instructed the director of the Bureau in January 1920 "to consider the whole matter of currency designs and to submit for the Department's consideration any suggestions in the form of definite models which you may have to offer. ..."[75]

As part of this project of submitting new currency designs, the superintendent of the Bureau's engraving department, George F.C. Smillie, visited the Smithsonian Museum to view photographs taken by De Lancey Gill, the staff photographer at the Smithsonian's Bureau of American Ethnology. On April 15, the Bureau made a formal request for about 20 "prints from the negatives of Indians ... in the collections shown by Mr. De Lancey Gill to Mr. Smillie."[76]

The plan to change the currency was nixed by the incoming secretary of the treasury, Andrew Mellon. But one of the Indian portraits, that of Hollow Horn Bear, a Brule Sioux, obviously caught the attention of the engravers as a representative Indian portrait. (See Figure 34.) The print was kept in the files, and on March 30, 1922, less than a month before the new issue of stamps was requested, engraver Louis Schofield began working on a large engraving of an "Indian Head," using the Hollow Horn Bear photograph. This engraving was listed as originating from a "Miscellaneous Die," and does not appear to have been used in the larger form. It was, however, engraved in smaller size by Schofield for the stamp.

De Lancey Gill was a careful photographer, who recorded the names of each subject, as well as tribe, place of birth and approximate date of birth. The name of the Indian was not only known at the Bureau, but the name "Hollow Horn Bear" was included in the ribbon under the portrait on the model for the stamp.

Figure 34. Taken at the Smithsonian Institution by De Lancey Gill, the photograph of Brule Sioux tribal leader Hollow Horn Bear struck Bureau personnel as an excellent representation of the American Indian.

As there was no intent to honor Hollow Horn Bear himself, the caption in the ribbon was changed to "American Indian." There was some temporary concern that the individual might still be living, and Glover telephoned the Bureau's director, Louis A. Hill, before he approved the model of the stamp. Hill replied in writing: "This man died March 13, 1913. We never use the face of a living person on any security issued by the Government."[77]

After the stamp appeared, there was more discussion of who the Indian was. Much of what we know comes from the *Handbook of American Indians North of Mexico*, a reference work published by the Smithsonian in 1912. According to the biographical entry, Hollow Horn Bear was born in what is now Sheridan County, Nebraska, in March 1850, and eventually became a captain of the police on the Rosebud reservation.

A closer look at Hollow Horn Bear shows that he was a relatively minor figure in Sioux history. He is often noted as being an orator, but we have few examples of his oratory or its effect, other than one instance where he spoke on behalf of opening the reservation lands to white settlement. A subchief of the Brule group of Sioux, he traveled in delegations to Washington on several occasions.

The photograph used for the stamp was taken in March 1905, when Hollow Horn Bear and three other members of his tribe came to Washington for the inauguration of Theodore Roosevelt. A group of Indians, including the 76-year-old Geronimo, once the proud leader of the Chiricahua Apache, marched in the inaugural parade as examples of "conquered" tribes.

Hollow Horn Bear was photographed in several poses at Gill's studio at the 1905 sitting. From a group photograph, we know that he arrived in single-breasted suit, not totally unlike one that any Washington office worker might have worn. The headdress and breastplate were apparently part of his parade regalia. The feather-trimmed blanket or robe he is wearing was put on over his suit coat. Around his neck is a kerchief, fastened with a horseshoe-shaped pin, and lower on the kerchief is attached a campaign or inauguration button for Theodore Roosevelt. A good portion of this Roosevelt button remains in the engraving on the stamp.[78]

Hollow Horn Bear spent some time in Washington as a representative of the Brule Sioux. He marched again in the inaugural parade for Woodrow Wilson in 1913, and died a few days later of pneumonia. Like many Rosebud Reservation Indians, he had been instructed in the Roman Catholic faith, and his funeral services were held at St. Paul's Roman Catholic Church in Washington. His body was returned to South Dakota for burial at the Rosebud.

Among the more interesting philatelic articles published not long after the stamp appeared was one by J.E. Paddock, who said he knew Hollow Horn Bear for about 20 years prior to his death. "Hollow Horn Bear was an excellent type of Sioux manhood," he wrote, "though his word could not be depended on, as many found out who let him have credit."[79]

Philatelic Aspects and Varieties

First day of issue. This stamp was first placed on sale on May 1, 1923, at Washington, D.C., and Muskogee, Oklahoma.

That the portrait was to represent the American Indian, and not any particular person or tribe was reinforced by the decision to have a first day of sale at Muskogee, which, a Post Office Department press release said, "was selected as the representative Indian town of America, being as it is, the headquarters of the Five Civilized Tribes. ..."[80]

This may have seemed good politics of the day, but was probably not very well researched. The Five Civilized Tribes were the Cherokee, Chickasaw, Choctaw, Creek and Seminole, who had been largely forced into agreements with the government to give up their eastern lands to settlement and be "relocated" in Indian Territory, traveling along routes collectively known today as "the trail of tears." After the Civil War, the Five Civilized Tribes were declared to have been allies of the Confederacy and were forced to sell their western lands at prices of 15¢ to 30¢ an acre. What had been Indian Territory and Oklahoma Territory became the state of Oklahoma in 1907, but not before representatives of the Five Civilized Tribes met at Muskogee in July 1905 and adopted a constitution establishing the state of Sequoia. Congress refused to recognize it.

The notice from the Post Office Department that this stamp would be issued in Muskogee is dated April 24, not April 27 as Johl states. Nevertheless, there was still not much notice to collectors, and first-day covers from Muskogee are relatively scarce and command a substantial premium over those from Washington, D.C.

The May 1 date of issue had nothing to do with the subject matter of any of the four stamps issued on this date: the 7¢, 8¢, 14¢ and 25¢. The May 1 date was a reflection of the Post Office Department's desire to have the entire series issued during the 1922 fiscal year, which was to end on June 30.

This was the first 14¢ stamp ever issued in the United States, and was not in great demand. It replaced the 13¢ value of the Washington-Franklin series, which made more sense between November 1917 and July 1919, when the domestic letter rate was 3¢ an ounce.

Shades. The Post Office Department's original plan was to issue this stamp in what it called regular yellow-green, the same shade as the 13¢ Washington-Franklin stamp that it was to replace. A cigarette-blue color — which was used on revenue stamps — was going to be used on a 20¢ Yosemite design, which was never issued.

Several different trial color proofs were struck before the Post Office Department finally settled on the Bureau's cigarette blue, which was called indigo blue in a Department press release, and just indigo in later descriptions.

Scott, when it first listed this stamp in the 1924 *Specialized Catalogue*, called the primary shade dark blue and the secondary shade deep blue, which were exactly the same shades it listed for the 5¢ Roosevelt of the same series. Today, Scott calls the major shade of the 14¢ stamp just blue, while the major shade of the 5¢ stamp is still dark blue. But both stamps still have minor shades of deep blue, which is the name of the major (and only) shade of the $2 stamp. This is of course confusing.

Johl listed in addition bright deep blue and picked up the Post Office Department's description of indigo.

This stamp does come in a very deep shade of blue that is not found on either the 5¢ or $2 stamp. It is unique to this stamp and is probably better described as indigo than any other shade.

Relief breaks. Although not listed or mentioned by Scott, the most significant plate varieties on this stamp are the relief breaks, which show up in the top line of the ribbon that contains the label "American Indian." The majority of the copies of this issue will show one or more breaks in this line.

The Series of 1922

A relief is the raised part of the design on the transfer roll, which is used to enter the stamp design into the steel plate. When a bit of steel breaks off the relief, it creates a constant variety, and that is what happened here.

Three reliefs existed on the transfer roll used for this stamp, but only two were used on this stamp. The first, relief A, started to break after it had been used on three plates, and was used in its broken form on 14 of the 20 plates used to produce this stamp. As it was used, other small breaks occurred. This is what is termed a progressive relief break. Well more than half of the stamps of this issue will show one, two or three breaks in the top line of the ribbon. See Figure 35.

Relief B was used to transfer three of the 20 plates. These will show a strong top ribbon line.[81]

Plate varieties. A double transfer listing went into the *Scott Specialized* in the 1937 edition, but no plate or position was listed. Johl, in his 1935 book, listed three double transfers, one at 15795 LL 91 and two at unknown positions. These are no doubt the basis of the Scott listing.

Figure 35. Although not listed by Scott, relief breaks are the most common plate variety on this stamp. Breaks can be found in the top line of the ribbon, over the "ER," the "I" and the "C" of "AMERICAN."

This stamp, with its fine engraving and dark ink color, shows plate varieties well. French lists no fewer than 15 double transfers on this stamp.

Wide spacing. A note was added in the 1941 Scott *Specialized* regarding a wide spacing variety on the upper-right pane of plate 14515. It was a confused and erroneous listing that has been changed and amended in later editions. In the current catalog it is rather lengthy, but still incomplete and reads: "Horizontal pairs of No. 565 are known with spacings up to 3¾mm instead of 2mm between. These are from the 5th and 6th vertical rows of the upper right pane of Plate 14515 and also between stamps Nos. 3 and 4 of the same pane. A plate block of Pl. 14512 is known with 3 mm spacing."

Spacing varieties, whether intentional, as in the star-plate varieties (see Chapter 23), or unintentional, as is the case here, are somewhat inconsequential, and not that uncommon. If all of them were listed, we would have a lengthy catalog indeed. This is the only spacing variety of this series that is noted in the catalog, but there are many others. Measurements of these spaces can also be highly inaccurate, as Scott seems to be in its current listing.

The spacing variety on plate 14515 was first reported in the *Bureau Specialist* in 1935 by Hugh Southgate, who gave the wide spacing as "0.115 of an inch" against 0.095 for the adjacent row.[82] Southgate used hundredths of an inch, as this was the unit of measurement used by Bureau siderographers. Southgate apparently had seen only an upper-right pane, but lower-right panes, of course, show the same spacing, as the margin was laid out on a sheet of 400 subjects, not on a single pane.

Johl, in his 1935 book, made this correction, referring to "right panes" but gave the measurements in millimeters, 2mm and 3mm.

Scott, in 1941, used Johl's millimeter measurement, but reverted back to Southgate's upper-right pane. How the current note got to 3¾mm for the wide measurement is not clear, but it is wrong. My own measurement of wide margin on the certified plate proofs at the National Postal Museum is identical to Southgate's: .115 inch. This is mathematically close to Johl's 3mm (.118 inch). Scott's 3¾ mm (.148 inch) just isn't accurate. This Scott note should be corrected — or better yet — dropped entirely.

15¢ Statue of Liberty

Scott Number: 566
First Day of Issue: November 11, 1922, Washington, D.C.
Scott Colors: Gray, light gray
Engravers: Louis Schofield (vignette)
Edward M. Hall (variable lettering)
Plate Layout: 400 subjects cut into panes of 100
Quantity Issued: 661,479,477
Plates: Total of 41: lowest, 14070; highest, 19463
Scott Varieties: Star plate (see Chapter 23)

The Subject and Design

In the Post Office Department's letter to the Bureau requesting this series of stamps, it was suggested that one of the subjects be "the Goddess of Liberty." This was interpreted both as the Statue of Liberty that is familiar to us today and as the full-faced allegorical figure that was eventually used for the vignette of the $5 value. Designs of both figures were submitted with the original set of models.

The Series of 1922

For what became the 15¢ value, designer Huston chose as the subject the gigantic statue by Frederic August Bartholdi that sits in New York Harbor. A gift of the people of France to the United States in 1886, its correct title is *Liberty Enlightening the World*. Although it has now become a symbol or icon of America, this was the first time it was used on a U.S. postage stamp.

As a vignette, Huston chose an 1888 engraving by Charles Skinner of the American Bank Note Company. This engraving, according to the records of that firm, was "taken from a drawing and a photograph."[83] No doubt one was of the statue and the other was of the harbor scene.

Figure 36. A stamplike label used by National Wholesale Liquor Dealers Association is similar in design to the 15¢ stamp.

Although we do not know the original purpose of Skinner's engraving, it was used both for a certificate of some sort and later for a "protective stamp" used by an association of liquor dealers during the temperance movement. The liquor "stamp" — actually a label in philatelic terms — appears to have been used by members of the liquor industry to authenticate their correspondence. Figure 36 shows one of these labels. The earliest use of these labels appears to have been in 1915.

We do not know if designer Huston ever saw one of these labels, but he had a larger copy of the Skinner engraving and used it to make the model for the stamp. Figure 37 shows this engraving, which has the same background as

Figure 37. The American Bank Note engraving by Skinner from the Bureau files has the same background as the stamp and was no doubt used for the model.

79

the issued stamp.[84]

This value has a different frame from all the other issued stamps. This so-called horseshoe-shaped frame was designed to accommodate vertically oriented scenes, like the Statue of Liberty. It was originally intended to be used on both the 15¢ and 20¢ values, but a change in the subject matter of the 20¢ stamp left only the 15¢ with this frame.

Like the other two frames used for this series, the horseshoe-shaped frame was engraved primarily by Edward M. Hall, with Joachim C. Benzing adding the scrolls and the ribbon. The vignette was engraved by Louis S. Schofield.

Philatelic Aspects and Varieties

First day of issue. This stamp was issued on November 11, 1922, only at Washington, D.C. It was one of three stamps issued on Armistice Day. The others were the 25¢ Niagara and the 50¢ Arlington Amphitheatre, which was directly related to World War I.

There was no first-day ceremony. For publicity purposes, stamps and die proofs of each value were presented to President Harding at the White House by Frances Glover, the six-year-old daughter of the third assistant postmaster general. A press release was issued, and photographs of "Little Miss Glover" were provided to the Washington newspapers.

First-day covers of this stamp are relatively scarce due to several factors. One was the early date. Only two other issues of the Series of 1922 had been issued at this time, and first-day cover servicing had not become as large a business as it soon would. The price of this stamp, and the others issued that day — a total of 90¢ — no doubt kept the numbers of covers low. And as with many of the early issues, there was not much notice to collectors.

Shades. The Post Office Department described the color as dark gray in one press release, and mouse-gray in another. Scott, in its initial listing of this stamp in the 1924 edition of the *Specialized Catalogue*, gave gray as the primary shade and light gray as a secondary shade. These shades remain in the catalog today.

Johl added to these pale gray, deep gray and light gray, noting, "there has been little variation in the shade, those that are listed are mainly differences in the value or quantity of the ink used on the plates, although at the end of 1930 a very pale gray shade was on sale at numerous post offices."

For the star-plate varieties of this stamp, see Chapter 23.

20¢ Golden Gate

Scott Number:	567
First Day of Issue:	May 1, 1923
Scott Colors:	Carmine rose, deep carmine rose
Engravers:	Louis Schofield (vignette)
	Edward E. Myers (variable lettering)
Plate Layout:	400 subjects cut into panes of 100
Quantity Issued:	1,077,488,777
Plates:	Total of 76: lowest, 14559; highest 20274
Scott Varieties	Star plates (see Chapter 23)
	Double transfer, 18925
	a. Horizontal pair, imperforate vertically

The Subject and Design

This value was originally to have depicted a view of the Vernal Falls in Yosemite, and was announced as such in the press release of October 11, 1922. The production of the 20¢ Yosemite went almost to completion. A die was fully engraved, and finished on November 1. The Bureau liked the engraving, but someone at the Post Office Department did not. By November 27, new models were completed, showing the same view of California's Golden Gate as had been used on the 5¢ value of the Panama-Pacific issue of 1913 (Scott 399).

In December, another model was prepared, showing a view of Mt. Ranier with cedar trees in the foreground. In January 1923, two other models were prepared, one showing Holy Cross Mountain in Colorado, the home state of Postmaster General Work, and another with a different view of Yosemite. None of these seemed to be satisfactory.

The Golden Gate stamp was being promoted by the San Francisco Chamber of Commerce, which engaged one of California's U.S. senators, Hiram Johnson, to join in the lobbying effort. Through Johnson, new artwork of the Golden Gate was supplied, including a photograph of a painting by William A. Coulter.

It was this Coulter painting that was the basis for the vignette of the issued stamp. Coulter was an Irish-born artist who settled in California about

Figure 38. The large painting by W.A. Coulter that was the source of the 20¢ stamp design hung in the office of J.B. Levison, chairman of the Fireman's Fund Insurance Company in San Francisco.

1869. He exhibited at the San Francisco Art Academy between 1874 and 1890, and was commissioned to paint several views of Golden Gate Harbor. The painting used for the stamp apparently does not have a title, but was commissioned by Jacob B. Levison of the Home Fire and Marine Insurance Company. Levison, who later became chairman of the board of his company's parent firm, the Fireman's Fund Insurance Company, had the painting done for his home, and took it to his office in 1907. The full-rigged ship is reported to be the "W.F. Babcock," and the flag flying on the shore at the left of the stamp is raised over Fort Mason.[85] A photograph of the painting is shown in Figure 38.

The design was selected at a time of administrative change at the top of the Post Office Department. Hubert Work, the postmaster general who had approved the designs for the other values, was being moved to the head of the Interior Department, to replace Secretary Albert Fall, who was involved in what would later become known as the Teapot Dome scandal. Replacing Work as postmaster general was Harry S. New, a former U.S. senator from Indiana who was a friend and political ally of President Harding.

The Golden Gate stamp was the last that Work would approve, signing the model on February 23, 1923, during his last week in office. Harry New, who took over on March 4, would approve the die proof a few weeks later, on April 11.

The Post Office Department offered little explanation for the change in designs from the previously announced Yosemite. A press release stated: "The difficulty of making a good engraving of Yosemite, which would bring out details and do justice to the picture, made it necessary to abandon the Falls as the subject for the 20¢ stamp."[86]

The Bureau, although silent, must have felt otherwise. Not only had the die been fully engraved, but during the process, director Hill mentioned in a letter, "I might say that the 20¢ Yosemite Falls stamp already engraved is at your service in the event that you decide to make use of it under another denomination."[87] This clearly indicates that the Bureau did not share the Post Office Department's opinion that there was a problem with the engraving.

The 20¢ Golden Gate was the lowest of the seven values to use the horizontal frame. Unlike the two other frame designs, the horizontal frame did not have a name ribbon engraved as an integral part of the frame. Louis S. Schofield engraved both the vignette and the ribbon.

Philatelic Aspects and Varieties

First day of issue. This stamp was issued on May 1, 1923, at Washington, D.C., and San Francisco, California. Other stamps issued on the same date were the 7¢ McKinley, the 14¢ Indian and the 8¢ Grant.

The date of issue had no relationship to any of the stamps. There was only a week's notice that the stamps would be issued, and this left little time for collectors or dealers to arrange to have covers serviced from San Francisco. The high face value of the stamp also kept down the number of covers serviced. Covers from San Francisco are scarce.

Shades. Both the Bureau and the Post Office Department referred to the color of the new stamp as crimson. Scott listed the color in the 1924 *Specialized Catalogue* as carmine rose, and added deep carmine rose in the 1937 edition.

Johl reported that "there was but little variation in shade although several sheets were found in a deep carmine lake." Johl also listed a bright carmine rose. Scott has never recognized the carmine lake and this is probably just as well, as these shades are difficult if not impossible to identify without a reference copy.

The Stanley Gibbons catalog, in 1938, also remarked about the lack of shades: "In spite of the immense quantity used of this stamp, we find only very slight variation in shade, the color having remained remarkably constant." Gibbons noted only a dull red in addition to Scott's carmine rose, and no carmine lake.

567a. Horizontal pair, imperforate vertically. A complete pane of 100 was found in South Pasadena, California, in August 1929 and divided between two collectors into a top half of 50, showing the plate numbers, and a lower of half of 50. Its find was reported the same month in *Scott's Monthly Journal*.[88] This would seem to make 50 known pairs.

The plate number on this upper-left pane was 19646. The top part of this pane, at least, has been broken up into pairs and blocks.

Plate varieties. The Scott *Specialized* currently lists a double transfer, which is designated only as "Pl. 18925." This listing went into the catalog in 1937, based on the Johl book, and remains undefined by position to this day. Double transfers do exist on this stamp, but perhaps not on this plate number.

A double-transfer listing first appeared in the *Specialized Catalogue* in the 1932 edition, and was no doubt based on *Shift Hunter Letter 19*, which reported a double transfer as follows: "This is an outstanding shift but only one copy has been reported. It is easily seen with the naked eye. Plate number is not known."[89] An accompanying illustration showed a curved line in the "tage" of "postage," as if the doubling were in the bottom line of the arch containing the words "United States Postage."

In the following number of the *Shift Hunter Letters* was a note that said: "Please check your post office at once for upper left plate number 18925 on the 20¢ stamp. Get blocks of six ... you will have one good and one minor shift."[90] But it was noted that "this shift will be illustrated later." This variety was not illustrated later, as it appeared that no one could find it. It does not exist on the certified plate proofs, and was no doubt not a constant variety.

Johl, however, seemed to marry these two *Shift Hunter* reports in his 1935 book, illustrating the variety from *Shift Hunter Letter 19* but using the plate number designated for a different — and phantom variety — in *Shift Hunter Letter 20*.

French slightly improved on this muddled situation by illustrating the variety shown in *Shift Hunter Letter 19* and Johl but giving it no plate-number designation. For the star-plate varieties of this stamp, see Chapter 23.

25¢ Niagara

Scott Number: 568
First Day of Issue: November 11, 1922
Scott Colors: Yellow green, green, deep green
Engravers: Charles Chalmers (vignette)
Edward E. Myers (variable lettering)
Plate Layout: 400 subjects cut into panes of 100
Quantity Issued: 107,616,077
Plates: Total of 12: lowest, 14062; highest, 17445
Scott Varieties: Double transfer
b. Vertical pair, imperforate horizontally
c. Perf 10 at left or right

The Subject and Design

This, more than any other design, helped to define the higher values of the series as depicting the country's natural wonders. The Bureau had for sev-

The Series of 1922

Figure 39. A stereoscope view of the American Falls from Goat Island by the firm of Underwood & Underwood. While no source photograph is cited in the records, this view is nearly identical to the view on the stamp.

eral years been contemplating using a view of Niagara Falls on currency, and had requested a photograph of the painting *Niagara* by Frederic Church from the Corcoran Gallery of Art in Washington, D.C. But the painting was not used as the artwork for the stamp.

The source for the stamp, in Bureau and Post Office Department records, is given only as "a photograph of Niagara Falls taken from Goat Island." Goat Island, sometimes called Luna Island, splits the cataract into the American Falls on the east or American side, and the Horseshoe Falls on the west or Canadian side.

This view of the falls was a common one. Several similar photographs exist in the files of the Library of Congress, and all seem to have been taken from the same convenient spot, where there was a paved overlook. Many of these were made into stereoscope slides. Figure 39 shows a stereoscope view, by Underwood & Underwood, a large photographic studio and publisher, that shows a view of the falls that is nearly identical to the view on the stamp.

In part because the source of the photograph was never given, some philatelic writers supposed that the Church painting in the Corcoran was the source, and one even went so far as to criticize the design as "not being a true delineation of an actual scene."[91]

The vignette of the stamp was engraved by Charles Chalmers, who is also credited with engraving the ribbon below the scene. Edward E. Myers is given credit for the lettering "Niagara."

The Philately

First day of issue. This stamp was issued on November 11, 1922, only at Washington, D.C. This was the same date as the 15¢ and 50¢ values. The date, Armistice Day, was appropriate for the 50¢ value, which depicted the tomb of the unknown soldier.

As noted above for the 15¢ value, first-day covers were scarce for several reasons. The high denomination of the 25¢ stamp undoubtedly kept the number of covers serviced low.

Shades. The Post Office Department originally described this stamp as note green, referring to the color of currency. The first printing of this stamp was in a deep green color, not unlike the color on the reverse of the Federal Reserve notes of today.

When Scott first listed this stamp in the 1924 *Specialized Catalogue*, it gave the primary shade as deep green, and green and a minor shade. The yellow-green shade went into the 1929 catalog as a minor shade, and was listed as 568a in the 1932 catalog.

Yellow green became the primary shade in the 1937 edition. This reflected a philosophy of making the most common shade in which the stamp was found the major shade, regardless of chronology. Deep green was then given the small-letter listing, which was later dropped.

Johl lists, in addition, deep yellow green, dark yellow green, deep bluish green, and dark bluish green. He is correct in noting that there is also a shade of this stamp with a blue-green cast to it.

568b. This is listed as a vertical pair, imperforate horizontally. It was discovered in Georgia in 1927, and reported by Ward as being in the light green shade. The pane, he said, was "normal with this small corner receiving the vertical perforations only ..."[92] indicating that less than a full pane was found. We know from existing examples that this was from a right side pane of plate 14063.

568c. Perforated 10 at left or right. For a discussion of these perforation 10 errors and how they occurred, see the description under 554d earlier in this chapter. This error on the 25¢ stamp was discovered in an unused block of eight by C.B. Durland, the Boston stamp dealer, and first reported by Johl in the *Bureau Specialist* in 1934.[93] This block, the largest multiple of any denomination showing the perforation 10 error, found its way into a number of important collections, included those formed by Josiah K. Lilly and Louis Grunin.

Double transfer. Although French lists several double transfers on this stamp, the catalog listing, which first appeared in the first edition of the 1936 Scott *Specialized*, is based on one reported in *Scott's Monthly Journal* in 1934 and described as "a clear double transfer to the right," which showed "particularly outside the right frame line."[94] The plate and position are still not recorded.

Bridge Over Falls. Although not listed by Scott, this is one of the most dramatic and best publicized plate varieties of this series (see Figure 40). Appearing at 17445 LL 26, it consists of four parallel scratches at the bottom

The Series of 1922

of the vignette. It was discovered by Henry C. DeWitt in 1931, but named and reported by Ward, who said, "it almost appears as if the engraver placed a bridge across the Falls." Ward commented further, "As a rule we think little of scratched plate varieties, for they are quite prevalent, but this shows such a sharp and distinct scratch that it is worthy of attention."[95]

Figure 40. The Bridge Over the Falls plate variety, at 17445 LL 26. Although not listed by Scott, this is one of the more dramatic plate varieties of the series.

Ward's report of this variety was apparently not known to George Sloane, who wrote up, and illustrated this variety two years later, describing it as "sort of a bridge, or a tight wire rope, suspended over the Falls."[96]

Plate scratches often occur during production, when the plates are transferred from storage and placed on and off the press. These scratches, however, appear on the certified plate proofs, and were not noticed by the plate finisher.

30¢ Buffalo

Scott Number:	569
First Day of Issue:	March 20, 1923
Scott Color:	Olive brown
Engravers:	Louis Schofield (vignette)
	Edward M. Hall (variable lettering)
Plate Layout:	400 subjects cut into panes of 100
Quantity Issued:	282,608,477
Plates:	Total of 24: lowest, 14436; highest 20194
Scott Varieties:	Double transfer, 16065 UR 52

The Subject and Design

Like the American Indian on the 14¢ value, the buffalo had also become a symbol of American strength and freedom. It had been used on coinage since 1913, and gave the name to the "buffalo nickel" that was in current circulation when the stamp issue was being designed.

87

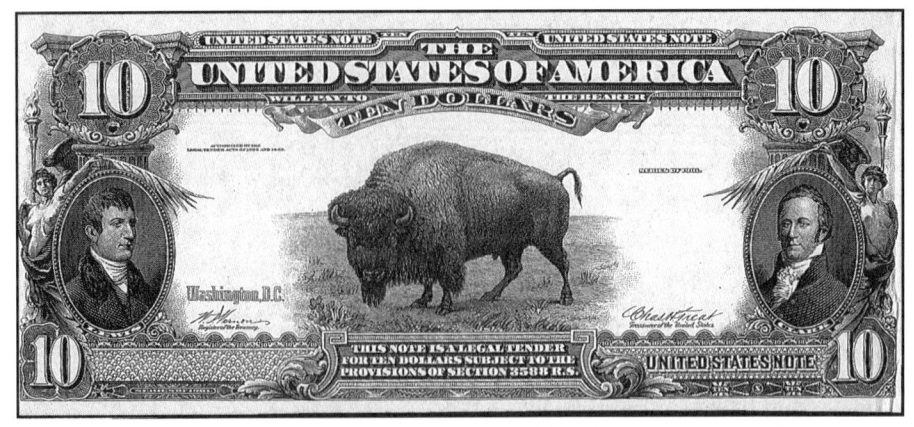

Figure 41. The so-called "Buffalo Bill" was issued for the Pan American Exposition in Buffalo, New York, in 1901. The explorers Lewis and Clark are shown on either side.

This value is a good example of the recycling of designs that went on at the Bureau of Engraving and Printing. The drawing of the buffalo that would be used on the stamp had already been employed, over 20 years earlier, on currency. The same buffalo was the central figure on the so-called "buffalo bill," a $10 U.S. note created in 1901 for the Pan American Exposition held in Buffalo, New York. A proof copy of the bill is shown in Figure 41.

The drawing of the buffalo is now well-documented as having been done by Charles R. Knight, a New York artist who achieved fame as a painter of wildlife. His original drawing is shown in Figure 42. For over 15 years, however, the source was given as a photograph of a group of stuffed bison at the Smithsonian Museum. Johl illustrated the museum photo in his 1935 book, but in 1939, Catherine Manning, the philatelist at the Smithsonian Institution, traced back the true source after it had been questioned by philatelic writer F.L. Ellis.[97]

Figure 42. Charles Knight's 1901 drawing of a bison was created for currency, but it was used again for the new series of stamps.

Contacted about the drawing, Knight wrote to the Smithsonian that in 1901 he had come across Marcus Baldwin, a Bureau engraver, trying to make a drawing of a buffalo from the mounted group at the Smithsonian. "I offered to do this," Knight wrote, adding that Baldwin then got him a commission to do the drawing. Knight stated that he completed the drawing by observ-

The Series of 1922

ing a live specimen at the Zoological Park in Washington.[98]

The 30¢ stamp is the only one in this series that does not include a ribbon under the vignette. Whether this was intentional or not is not known, but it seems no less redundant for the ribbon under the buffalo stamp to read "Buffalo" than it would for the Lincoln stamp to read "Lincoln."

A new engraving was made for the stamp by picture engraver Louis Schofield.

Philatelic Aspects and Varieties

First day of issue. This stamp was issued on March 20, 1923, only at Washington, D.C. This stamp became another rush job at the Bureau, in order to meet the announced first day of March 20, 1923. The first plate, 14436, was not assigned until March 12, and it went to press alone on March 16. All first-day covers must bear stamps from this plate. There was no significance of the 30¢ stamp to its first-day date. It was released at the same time as the 12¢, $2 and $5 values. Because of the high denomination, few first-day covers were serviced.

Shades. While the Post Office Department listed this stamp's color as sepia, Scott called it olive brown when it was first listed in the 1924 *Specialized Catalogue*. No other shade has been added. This is a stamp that does not vary much in shade. Johl added only bright olive brown and deep olive brown.

Double transfer. This is listed as 16065 UR 52, and it is a stunner, one of the most dramatic double transfers in U.S. philately. It shows a heavy downward shift on the right side of the stamp, and is particularly visible in the right numeral. It seems to have been reported for the first time in *Shift Hunter Letter Number 9* on January 22, 1930, some four years after plate 16065 went to press. The Scott *Specialized* listed another double transfer at the time, showing doubling at the left in the word "United," but C.W. Bedford argued that it "deserves listing, since it is larger in misplacement than the left side shift and easily seen with the naked eye."[99] (See Figure 43.) The plate number was not determined at this time, but Bedford reported that it was position 52 in an upper-right pane.

Figure 43. The double transfer on the 30¢ Buffalo is one of the most dramatic plate varieties found on a U.S. stamp. The position is 16065 UR 52.

Others who have described this stamp have also described it in usual terms. George Sloane commented in 1933, "This is one of the most remarkable double transfer varieties I have ever seen, and no magnifying glass will be necessary to locate the duplicated area."[100]

Johl, too, was impressed, comment-

89

ing, "This needs no glass and it is hard to understand how such a defect could pass the careful plate inspection at the Bureau."[101]

Scott made the transition slowly from its original double-transfer listing, changing it simply to "double transfer" in the 1932 edition of the *Specialized Catalogue*, and finally listing 16065 UR 52 first in the 1936 edition, although it ran the listing erroneously under the 50¢ stamp until the 1938 edition.

50¢ Arlington Amphitheatre

Scott Number: 570
First Day of Issue: November 11, 1922
Scott Colors: Lilac, dull lilac
Engravers: Louis Schofield (vignette)
Edward E. Myers (variable lettering)
Plate Layout: 400 subjects cut into panes of 100
Quantity Issued: 220,810,977
Plates: Total of 16: lowest, 14042; highest, 19146
Scott Varieties: None

The Subject and Design

Arlington Memorial Amphitheatre, which is located in Arlington National Cemetery, was completed in 1920, just two years before this stamp was issued, and had been the location of an enormously intricate ceremony on November 11, 1921, when the Unknown Soldier was entombed. England had buried an unknown from the World War in Westminster Abbey; France had buried an unknown under the Arch de Triomphe in Paris, but America had not yet involved itself in this symbolic recognition of the unknown dead of the war.

The Harding administration prepared the American ceremony for Armistice Day, 1921, and President Harding himself officiated, accompanied by regiments of infantrymen, battalions of sailors and marines, and squadrons of cavalry with muffled hooves. Harding's speech was carried by telephone wire not only to crowds in Washington, but to audiences in auditoriums in New York and San Francisco.

The request for an Arlington Amphitheatre stamp came late in the pro-

The Series of 1922

cess. On July 26, 1922, after most of the other designs for the series had been submitted, Glover wrote to the Bureau requesting a 40¢ value, "the subject to contain a reproduction of the Arlington Amphitheatre, showing the Unknown Soldier's tomb."[102]

Shortly, however, the denomination was changed from 40¢ to 25¢, and a model similar to the 50¢ stamp we know today was submitted. The source was a photograph taken of the east facade of the amphitheatre, showing the tomb of the unknown soldier in the foreground.

Johl noted that the tomb of the unknown was not accurately depicted on the stamp, writing that "had the view of the tomb, as large as shown on the stamp been pictured in its true position, nothing but pillars would appear on the stamp" and commenting that "this change greatly increased the beauty of the design."[103]

But he was mistaken. Figure 44 shows the actual photograph from which the stamp was designed. The original white marble tomb, or cenotaph, placed in 1921 was a very simple one, and is shown more or less in scale at the foreground of the stamp. A larger and more elaborate sarcophagus, with carved pilasters and sculptured wreaths, was placed over it in 1931. This tall sarcophagus is what Johl is referring to. It is what he would have seen had he visited the site after 1931 or viewed a newer photograph.

A new engraving was made for the stamp by Louis Schofield. The lettering "Arlington Amphitheatre" is attributed to Edward E. Myers.

Scott's John Luff didn't think much of the design, saying that it "suggests a bank or small commercial building." He also felt that the tomb of the unknown got lost in the design, and that it "appears to be a light slab in the pavement."[104]

Figure 44. The photograph from which the stamp design was made shows the original plain white marble cenotaph in which the unknown soldier was entombed. It was later replaced with a more elaborate sarcophagus.

Philatelic Aspects and Varieties

First day of issue. This stamp had a first day of issue on November 11, 1922, only in Washington, D.C. The date was Armistice Day, and was exactly two years after the ceremony for the burial of the unknown soldier. Also issued on the same day were the 15¢ and 25¢ values. First-day covers are not plentiful for any of these values, due to the high denominations, the early date and perhaps the fact that the issue date was on a holiday.

Shades. The Bureau and the Post Office Department gave the color of this stamp as lavender. When first listed in the 1924 edition of the *Specialized Catalogue*, the shade was given as lilac. In the 1927 edition, dull lilac was added as a secondary shade. To this Johl added only a deep dull lilac.

Plate varieties. Scott currently lists none. Johl listed one double transfer and one shifted transfer, both from unknown positions. French had little to add. Only 16 plates went to press for this stamp, and the light color of the ink does not show plate varieties well.

$1 Lincoln Memorial

Scott Number:	571
First Day of Issue:	February 12, 1923
Scott Colors:	Violet black, violet brown
Engravers:	Louis Schofield (vignette)
	William B. Wells (variable lettering)
Plate Layout:	200 subjects cut into panes of 100
Quantity Issued:	47,217,960
Plates:	14268, 18642, 18680, 18681, 18682
Scott Varieties:	Double transfer, 18642 L 30 and 18682

The Subject and Design

Like the 50¢ value, this showed a recently completed monument in Washington. The Lincoln Memorial was very much in the news as this stamp was being designed. The corner stone had been laid in 1915 on Lincoln's birthday, February 12. After many delays, it was scheduled to be dedicated in 1922, on Memorial Day, May 30. The new series of stamps had been requested in

Figure 45. The Signal Corps photograph of the Lincoln Memorial as it was being completed, but before its dedication in 1922. The stamp design was derived from this photograph.

April 1922.

The source of the design is a photograph taken by the Signal Corps of the U.S. Army before the structure was dedicated. It is shown in Figure 45. Bureau director Hill requested a set of photographs from the Corps in June, "for official use in this Bureau."[105]

The stamp shows the east facade of the Memorial, which was designed by architect Henry Bacon and constructed of white Colorado marble.

A new engraving was made for the stamp by Louis S. Schofield.

Philatelic Aspects and Varieties

First day of issue. This stamp was issued on February 12, 1923, at Washington, D.C., and at Springfield, Illinois, which was Lincoln's home for many years and the place of his burial. The date of the issue coincided with Lincoln's birth anniversary. The 3¢ value of this series was released on the same day.

Although notice of the first-day sites was not given until February 8, several individuals were able to obtain first-day covers from both the Washington and Springfield locations. However, due to the high denomination, the number of covers serviced was small.

A survey of the known first-day covers in 1992 showed 23 covers canceled at Washington, D.C., and 17 canceled at Springfield. Of these 40 covers, 13 were serviced by Edward Worden, the first-day cover enthusiast from Milburn, New Jersey. Few other individuals serviced more than a single cover.[106]

Only one plate, 14268, went to press before the first day of issue, and all stamps on first-day covers must be from this plate.

Plate layout and plate number blocks. This stamp and the $2 denomination were produced from plates of 200 subjects, rather than the 400 subjects of the lower denominations. For issue, the sheets of 200 were cut into two panes, an upper and a lower, of 100 subjects each. Thus these stamps were not issued with straight edges on the left or right. Straight edges do appear at the top and bottom.

Four plate numbers appeared on each sheet of 200, two at the bottom and two at the top. There are no side plate numbers. Plate blocks are collected in blocks of six. Three positions can be found: bottom, top left and top right. The top-right number is preceded by the letter "F" indicating that the plate was approved and ready for hardening.

Pairs and blocks showing stamps on either side of the vertical guideline are also found on the two panes of 100, with the top and bottom arrow blocks being the most desirable.

Shades. The Post Office Department called the color brown, which is the same designation it gave to the 4¢ value, which is quite different in color. Scott called the shade violet brown in the 1924 *Specialized Catalogue*. To this Johl added light violet brown and deep violet brown. In the 1939 *Specialized Catalogue*, Scott changed the major shade to violet black, and listed the violet brown shade as 571a, at a premium. Scott now maintains violet black as the major shade, with violet brown as a minor shade at no premium.

Double transfer. The first double-transfer listing went into the 1936 *Specialized Catalogue*, specifying "pl. 18682." This was based on publication of Johl's book, which described a compound transfer at 18682 U 5 and a double transfer at 18682 U 15.

In the 1941 catalog, another listing was added for 18642 L 30, based on a report of this variety in the *American Stamp Journal* for January 1938.

$2 U.S. Capitol

Scott Number: 572
First Day of Issue: March 20, 1923
Scott Color: Deep blue
Engravers: Louis Schofield (vignette)
Edward M. Hall (variable lettering)

The Series of 1922

Plate Layout: 200 subjects cut into panes of 100
Quantity Issued: 3,189,578
Plate: 14306
Scott Varieties: None

The Subject and Design

The U.S. Capitol had been one of the first suggestions as a stamp subject when the series was requested. Three designs showing the Capitol were submitted, and this was the one chosen. It is based on a photograph, by an unknown photographer, which still exists in the Bureau records. It is shown in Figure 46. This same photograph became the basis for the standard engraving of the Capitol, and it is likely the engraving, rather than the actual photograph, that was reduced in size to make the models for this stamp.

It is the House of Representatives side of the Capitol that appears in the foreground of the stamp. The building, as shown, was the result of several additions and remodelings, which were completed in 1863. Its classical architecture is similar in style to that of the Arlington Amphitheatre used on the 50¢ stamp and that of the Lincoln Memorial used on the $1 stamp. The unity of building style gives the three stamps a unified appearance as well.

A new engraving for the stamp was made by Louis A. Schofield. Edward M. Hall is credited with the lettering, "U.S. Capitol" and "Dollars."

Philatelic Aspects and Varieties

First day of issue. This stamp was issued on March 20, 1923, only at Washington, D.C. The date had no significance to the subject of this stamp. The 12¢, 30¢ and $5 values were issued on the same day.

Figure 46. Taken by an unknown photographer, this photograph of the U.S. Capitol was the source for the design of the $2 stamp.

A 1993 survey reported only 12 known first-day covers. Of these, four were addressed to Edward C. Worden. The addressees on three of the covers could not be read. The others were John R. Rood, Herman E. Boers, George D. Frost, Orville Ballard and Clara Helff. [107] These individuals, we can imagine, were among the most serious of first-day cover collectors during this early period of 1923.

Plate layout and plate number blocks. Like the $1 denomination this stamp was printed from a plate with a 200-subject layout. Only one plate of this denomination went to press, plate 14306. For issue, the sheets of 200 were cut into two panes, an upper and a lower of 100 subjects each. Thus these stamps were not issued with straight edges on the left or right. Straight edges do appear at the top and bottom.

Four plate numbers appeared on the sheet of 200, two at the bottom and two at the top. There are no side plate numbers. Plate blocks are collected in blocks of six. Three positions can be found: bottom, top left and top right. The top-right number is preceded by the letter "F" indicating that the plate was approved and ready for hardening.

Pairs and blocks showing stamps on either side of the vertical guideline are also found on the two panes of 100, with the top and bottom arrow blocks being the most desirable.

Shades. The Post Office Department listed the color of this stamp as regular blue, the same color as the 5¢ value. When first listed in the 1924 *Specialized Catalogue* the color was given as deep blue, and no other shades have been added. Johl found light blue, bright blue and deep bright blue.

Plate varieties. Scott lists none, and no double transfers are known. Johl listed a plate flaw at 14306 U 40, showing a series of dots in the margin. To this, French added only a few minor scratches.

$5 America

Scott Number: 573
First Day of Issue: March 20, 1923
Scott Colors: Carmine & blue, carmine lake & dark blue
Engravers: John Eissler (vignette)

The Series of 1922

	Howard I. Earle (variable lettering)
Plate Layout:	100 subjects
Quantity Issued:	1,652,167
Plates:	Vignette: 14326; frame: 14327
Scott Varieties:	None

The Subject and Design

When this series was ordered, one of the subjects suggested was the "Goddess of Liberty." This caused Bureau designer C. Aubrey Huston to submit models using images of Bartholdi's Statue of Liberty, which was used on the 15¢ value, and of Thomas Crawford's Statue of Freedom, which was called the "Goddess of Liberty" in some Bureau records pertaining to the newspaper stamps of 1875.

It was the head of Crawford's *Armed Freedom*, the sculpture atop the dome of the U.S. Capitol, that was eventually used on this stamp. An engraving of the head existed in the Bureau's engraving files, and this was the image Huston used on his stamp model (see Figure 47). The engraving was labeled "America" in the Bureau's file books of engravings, however, and it was this name that appears on the ribbon on the issued stamp.

Crawford's bronze statue was erected on the tholus of the Capitol dome on December 2, 1863. An engraving of the statue was used on the newspaper stamps produced for the Post Office Department by the Continental Bank Note Company in 1875. Newspaper stamps of similar design were produced by the Bureau in 1895.

Figure 47. This engraving of the head and helmet of the Statue of Freedom was incorrectly labeled "America." It was used for the model of the $5 stamp.

Although models for most of the other values of this series were approved on July 26, 1922, the $5 value was not. "The $5 denomination has not been approved," Third Assistant PMG W. Irving Glover wrote, "because it is desired to have this stamp in rectangular shape instead of oblong."[108] The initial model had been prepared in a vertical format like the lower-denomination stamps. A new model was prepared showing the same design in the horizontal format that is familiar to us today. The laurel leaves surrounding Freedom's head were a late addition, and were added directly to the stamp-sized model.

Bureau records list the source of the stamp design as a plaster model of the Statue of Freedom (Figure 48) that was on display at the National Museum of the Smithsonian Institution, but new scholarship has shown that the existing engraving in the Bureau's records was the true source of the face used on the stamp model.[109]

A new engraving of the vignette was made by John Eissler.

Philatelic Aspects and Varieties

First day of issue. This value was issued on March 20, 1923, only at Washington, D.C. The 12¢, 30¢ and $2 values were issued on the same day.

Of the eight documented first-day covers, two are addressed to Edward C. Worden, the collector and chemist from Milburn, New Jersey, and one is addressed to his assistant, Leo Rutstein. The only other covers with readable addresses were to Herman W. Boers and William O. Siebold.[110]

Figure 48. The plaster model of Crawford's Statue of Freedom was once on display at the Smithsonian's National Museum. But this is not the face on the stamp.

Plate layout and plate number blocks. This was the only stamp of the series to be printed in two colors, and the only one laid out on 100-subject plates. Two plates were used. The frame plate, 14327, went to press first to print the red frames. The vignette plate, 14326, then printed the blue vignettes. Both plates had only one number at the top of the plate. Although the frame plate was divided into quarters with guidelines, the sheets of 100 stamps were not divided into panes for sale in post offices. These guidelines meet at the center of the sheet. Centerline and arrow blocks are collectible positions.

The plate block is usually a block of eight, which includes both the red and blue plate numbers and the top arrow.

Shades. The Post Office Department described the colors of this stamp as regular red for the frame and regular blue for the vignette. When first listed in the 1924 edition of the *Specialized Catalogue*, the color was given as carmine and dark blue.

This stamp went to press several times. One early printing, but apparently not the first, was in a deeper shade of carmine, which was eventually recognized by the 1947 edition of the *Specialized Catalogue* when the major shade combination was changed to carmine and blue, and carmine lake and dark blue was added as 573a. The small letter was eventually dropped, but both shades are listed today, with the carmine lake and dark blue carrying a slight premium in value.

The late printings of this stamp show both a lighter carmine and a lighter blue than the early ones.

Plate varieties. Scott lists none and French lists none. With only one vignette plate and one frame plate, we should not expect a great number of varieties.

Missing plate number. Although not listed by Scott, at least two blocks of this stamp are known without a blue plate number at the top. This variety probably occurred because the vignette plate was not inked in that area.

Notes

1. For a discussion of the engraving and engraving credits of this series, see Gary Griffith, "Engraving the Fourth Bureau Issue," *United States Specialist*, Vol. 65, No. 9 (September 1994), pp. 390-98.

2. See Gary Griffith, "The Source of the Benjamin Franklin Design of 1908-1938," *United States Specialist*, Vol. 63, No. 7 (July 1992), pp. 364-69.

3. Press release, Post Office Department, January 5, 1923.

4. *Ibid.*

5. John N. Luff, "Notes of the Month," *Scott's Monthly Journal*, Vol. 5, No. 2 (April 1924), p. 25.

6. See Philip H. Ward Jr., *Mekeel's Weekly Stamp News*, October 12, 1931.

7. Max Johl, "A New and Unusual Compound Perforation," *Bureau Specialist*, Vol. 5, No. 8 (August 1934), pp. 73-74.

8. Hugh Southgate, "11 and 10 by 11 Compound Perforation," *Bureau Specialist*, Vol. 5, No. 12 (December 1934), pp. 110-11.

9. Philip H. Ward Jr., "Chronicle of New Issues and Varieties," *Mekeel's Weekly Stamp News*, Vol. 37, No. 11 (March 17, 1923), p. 152.

10. George B. Sloane, *Sloane's Column*, (Bureau Issues Association, 1961), p. 313.

11. Carolyn Kuhn, "The Twelve Best Plate Varieties on the 2¢ Washington," *Bureau Specialist*, Vol. 27, No. 3 (March 1956), p. 63.

12. Press release, Post Office Department, February 8, 1923.

13. Eugene P. Trani and David L. Wilson, *The Presidency of Warren Harding* (University Press of Kansas, 1977), p. 106.

14. For illustrations of the Stuart and Jalabert portraits, see Gary Griffith, "Design Sources of the Fourth Bureau Issue," *United States Specialist*, Vol. 63, No. 10 (October 1992), p. 524.

15. John Luff, "News of the Day," *Scott's Monthly Journal*, Vol. 5, No. 9 (November 1924), p. 205.

16. Robert A. Siegel Auctions, *The Josiah K. Lilly Collection: Part VII* [auction catalog], 327th Sale (February 7-8, 1968), Lot 555.

17. See the listing of plate numbers and marginal markings in John S. Meek, "The 4¢ Martha Washington: Scott 556," *United States Specialist*, Vol. 54, No. 2 (February 1983), p. 68.

18. C.W. Bedford, *Shift Hunter Letter No. 36* (August 1931).

19. Press release, Post Office Department, October 2, 1922.

20. See Francis Russell, *The Shadow of Blooming Grove: Warren G. Harding and His Times* (New York: McGraw-Hill Book Company, 1968), p. 447.

21. Philip H. Ward Jr., "Chronicle of New Issues and Varieties," *Mekeel's Weekly Stamp News*, Vol. 36, No. 49 (December 9, 1922), p. 602.

22. Philip H. Ward Jr., "Chronicle of New Issues and Varieties," *Mekeel's Weekly Stamp News*, Vol. 36, No. 46 (November 18, 1922), p. 564.

23. Philip H. Ward Jr., "Washington Philatelic News," *Mekeel's Weekly Stamp News*, Vol. 39, No. 33 (August 17, 1925), p. 389.

24. Kent M. Stiles, "Notes of the Month," *Scott's Monthly Journal*, Vol. 6, No. 7 (September 1925), p. 145.

25. John M. Luff, "Notes of the Month," *Scott's Monthly Journal*, Vol. 7, No. 7 (September 1926), p. 145.

26. Johl, Vol. III, p. 82.

27. Irwin Heiman, Inc., *The Caroline Prentice Cromwell Collection of United States Stamps, Proofs, Essays* [auction catalog], 179th Sale (November 7-8, 1957), Lot 383.

28. Eugene Klein, 116th Auction Sale [auction catalog] (March 8, 1940), Lot 459.

29. This item bears Philatelic Foundation certificate 215240.

30. George W. Brett and James T. DeVoss, "A Super, Unreported U.S. Double Transfer: 5¢ Ordinary, 1922 Series, Perf 11," *United States Specialist*, Vol. 46, No. 10 (October 1975), pp. 461-65.

31. Philip H. Ward Jr., "Chronicle of New Issues and Varieties," *Mekeel's Weekly Stamp News*, Vol. 36, No. 47 (November 25, 1922), p. 516.

32. George B. Sloane, "1922, 6¢ Garfield, Double Transfers," *Stamps* (April 7, 1956), reprinted in *Sloane's Column* (Bureau Issues Association, 1961), p. 313.

33. *Ibid.*

34. Post Office Department, *A Description of United States Postage Stamps* (U.S. Government Printing Office, 1937), p. 36.

35. See Gary Griffith, "Design Sources," *op. cit.*, p. 526.

36. See F. E. Stanton Jr., "Plate Varieties Committee," *Bureau Specialist*, Vol. 7, No. 12 (December 1936), pp. 162, 168.

37. See Gary Griffith, "Design Sources of the Fourth Bureau Issue; Part II," *United States Specialist*, Vol. 63, No. 12 (December 1992), p. 614.

38. Johl, Vol. III, p. 96.

39. Herman Toaspern, "Additions and Corrections Affecting the Specialized Catalogue of United States Stamps," *Scott's Monthly Journal*, Vol. 8, No. 4 (June 1927), p. 118.

40. See Griffith, "Design Sources ... Part II," *op. cit.*, p. 615-16.

41. Press release, Post Office Department, January 5, 1923.

42. Stanley Gibbons Inc., *The Postage Stamps of the United States*, Vol. IV, 16th Edition (New York: 1938), p. 73.

43. C.W. Bedford, "Plate Varieties Committee, *Bureau Specialist*, Vol. 3, No. 2 (February 1932), p. 18.

44. "The U.S. Designs," *Scott's Monthly Journal*, Vol. 4, No. 2 (April 1923), pp. 42-43.

45. Trani and Wilson, *op. cit.*, p. 134.

46. See Griffith, "Design Sources ... Part II," *op. cit.*, p. 616.

47. Johl, III, pp. 102-3.

48. Philip H. Ward Jr., "Chronicle of New Issues and Varieties," *Mekeel's Weekly Stamp News*, Vol. 38, No. 5 (February 4, 1924), p. 70.

49. Philip H. Ward, Jr., "Washington Philatelic News," *Mekeel's Weekly Stamp News*, Vol. 39, No. 22 (June 1, 1925), p. 281.

50. Philip H. Ward Jr., "Chronicle of New Issues and Varieties," *Mekeel's Weekly*

Stamp News, Vol. 36, No. 41 (October 14, 1922).

51. See for example Allison W. Cusick, "Modern First Days Began with Hayes Issue," *Linn's Stamp News,* April 27, 1987, p. 8.

52. Press release, Post Office Department, October 5, 1922.

53. John N. Luff, "The Month," *Scott's Monthly Journal,* Vol. 3, No. 9 (November 1922), p. 185.

54. Ross Frampton, "The Hayes Eleven Cent Stamp," *American Philatelist,* Vol. 44, No. 5 (February 1931), p. 238.

55. John N. Luff, "Notes of the Month," *Scott's Monthly Journal,* Vol. 10, No. 5 (July 1929), p. 130.

56. L.E. Eastman, "The Current Type 11¢," *Mekeel's Weekly Stamp News* (December 23, 1929), p. 788.

57. Frampton, *op. cit.,* p. 240.

58. Johl, Vol. III, p. 108.

59. Kent B. Stiles, "Notes of the Month," *Scott's Monthly Journal,* Vol. 6, No. 7 (September 1925), p. 145.

60. Philip H. Ward Jr., "Chronicle of New Issues and Varieties," *Mekeel's Weekly Stamp News,* Vol. 40, No.14 (April 15, 1926), p. 192.

61. W.L. Babcock, M.D., "United States Stamps," *Mekeel's Weekly Stamp News,* Vol. 52, No. 8 (February 21, 1938), p. 90.

62. *The Josiah K. Lilly Collection, op. cit.,* Lot 560.

63. Jacques C. Schiff Jr. Inc., *Elite Auction X: United States Major Errors* (December 2, 1982), Lot 62E.

64. For a detailed description of these varieties, see Jerry A. Katz, "Plates 14058 and 14060 of the Eleven-Cent Hayes of 1922," *United States Specialist,* Vol. 64, No. 3 (March 1993), pp. 113-18.

65. See Griffith, "Design Sources ... Part II," *op. cit.,* p. 617-18.

66. Jack V. Harvey, *First Day Covers of the Regular Postage Issue of 1922-1935,* Second Edition (American First Day Cover Society, 1985), p. 16.

67. Press release, Post Office Department, March 15, 1923.

68. Johl, III, p. 111.

69. Post Office Department, press release, March 15, 1923.

70. Fred J. Melville, *United States Postage Stamps, 1922-1925* (London: Philatelic Institute, 1925), p. 56.

71. Spencer Anderson, "A New Major Error in 20th Century U.S.," *Stamps*, Vol. 15, No. 3 (April 18, 1936), p. 90.

72. Jacques C. Schiff Jr. Inc., *Elite Auction IX: United States Major Errors* [auction catalog], December 10, 1981, Lot 32.

73. *Sloane's Column, op. cit.*, p. 313.

74. Max G. Johl, "Max G. Johl Replies on 20th Century U.S.," *Stamps*, Vol. 8, No. 11 (September 15, 1934), p. 374.

75. Carter Glass to James L. Wilmeth, January 14, 1920, National Archives.

76. James L. Wilmeth to Secretary, Smithsonian Institution, April 15, 1920, National Archives.

77. Louis A. Hill to W. Irving Glover, July 19, 1922, National Archives.

78. For photographs of Hollow Horn Bear on several of his Washington visits, see Gary Griffith, "Hollow Horn Bear," *United States Specialist*, Vol. 64, No. 4 (April 1993), pp. 152-63.

79. J. E. Paddock, "Hollow-Horn-Bear," *Mekeel's Weekly Stamp News*, June 2, 1923, p. 290.

80. Press release, Post Office Department, April 24, 1922.

81. For a more detailed explanation of these breaks, and a plate-by-plate breakdown, see Gary Griffith, "The Relief Breaks on the 14-Cent Indian," *United States Specialist*, Vol. 67, No. 10 (October 1996), pp. 405-11.

82. Hugh M. Southgate, "14 Cent 1922, No. 565," *Bureau Specialist*, Vol. VI, No. 3 (March 1935), p. 20.

83. Letter from Aurelia Chen of American Bank Note Company to Anthony M. Callendrello, May 10, 1991, Copy in possession of the author.

84. See Gary Griffith, "Design Sources of the Fourth Bureau Issue, Part IV," *United States Specialist*, Vol. 64, No. 5 (May 1993), p. 207.

85. See Max Johl, "The Twenty-Cent 1922 Design," *Stamps*, August 23, 1941; "Twentieth-Century Golden Gate Stamp," *Stamps*, February 25, 1950.

86. Press release, Post Office Department, April 11, 1923.

87. Louis A. Hill to W. Irving Glover, February 26, 1923, Bureau of Engraving and Printing.

88. See John N. Luff, "Notes of the Month," *Scott's Monthly Journal*, Vol. 10, No. 6 (August 1929), p. 163.

89. C.W. Bedford, *Shift Hunter Letter Number 19* (Akron, Ohio, undated).

90. C.W. Bedford, *Shift Hunter Letter Number 20* (Akron, Ohio, undated).

91. "Americus" [pseud.], "Philatelic Gossip," *Weekly Philatelic Gossip*, Vol. 7, No. 19 (January 1, 1923), p. 411.

92. Philip H. Ward Jr., "Chronicle of New Issues and Varieties," *Mekeel's Weekly Stamp News*, Vol. 41, No. 36 (September 5, 1927), p. 494.

93. Max G. Johl, "A New and Unusual Compound Perforation," *Bureau Specialist*, Vol. 5, No. 8 (August 1934), p. 73.

94. Eugene N. Costales, "Notes on General Issues," *Scott's Monthly Journal*, Vol. 15, No. 10 (December 1934), p. 266.

95. Philip H. Ward Jr., "Washington News," *Mekeel's Weekly Stamp News*, Vol. 45, No. 35 (August 31, 1931), p. 535.

96. *Sloane's Column, op. cit.*, p. 314.

97. See F. Ellis, "Buffalo Design on the 30-Cent United States Stamp," *Stamps*, Vol 36, No. 4 (July 26, 1941), pp. 125-27.

98. Charles R. Knight, letter to J.C. Bryant of the Smithsonian Institution, November 3, 1939, Historical Resource Center, Bureau of Engraving and Printing.

99. C.W. Bedford, *Shift Hunter Letter Number 19*, January 22, 1930, p. 8.

100. *Sloane's Column, op. cit.*, p. 315.

101. Johl, Vol III, p. 133.

102. W. Irving Glover to Louis A. Hill, July 26, 1922, Historical Resource Center, Bureau of Engraving and Printing.

103. Johl, Vol. III, p. 136.

104. John N. Luff, "The Month," *Scott's Monthly Journal*, Vol. 3, No. 10 (December 1922), p. 210.

105. Louis A. Hill to Col. C.A. Secane, Executive Officer, Signal Corps, U.S. Army, June 16, 1922, National Archives.

106. Robert P. Colby and Robert F. Drummond, "A Listing of the Dollar Value FDCs, Sc. 571-3, Part I: Sc. 571, Washington, D.C.," *First Days*, Vol. 37, No. 7 (October 15, 1992), pp. 547-50, and "Part II: Sc. 571, Spring-

field, IL," Vol. 38, No. 2 (March 1, 1993), pp. 121-23.

107. Robert P. Colby and Robert F. Drummond, "A Listing of the Dollar Value FDCs, Sc. 571-3, Part III: Sc. 572, Washington, D.C.," *First Days*, Vol. 38, No. 4 (June 1, 1993), pp. 292-94.

108. W. Irving Glover to Louis A. Hill, July 26, 1922. Historical Resource Center, Bureau of Engraving and Printing.

109. Gary Griffith, "The Statue of Freedom," *United States Specialist*, Vol. 64, No. 8 (August 1993), pp. 344-53.

110. Robert P. Colby and Robert F. Drummond, "A Listing of the Dollar Value FDCs, Sc. 571-3, Part IV: Sc. 573, Washington, D.C.," *First Days*, Vol. 38, No. 6 (September 1, 1993), pp. 470-71.

United States Stamps 1922-26

Chapter 6

The Rotary Press

While the bulk of the new series of stamps would initially be printed on the Bureau's flat-plate presses, there was a great interest at both the Post Office Department and the Bureau in using the faster rotary press to print a greater share of stamps.

Designed by Benjamin Stickney, the Bureau's "mechanical expert" in 1910, the rotary intaglio press at the Bureau became known as the Stickney press, and was used to print coil stamps beginning in 1914. The press worked well for coils, as it printed from a long or "continuous" web of paper, and eliminated the tedious process of pasting half-sheets of flat-plate stamps together to be cut into coil stamps, which were becoming more and more popular. On the Stickney press (see Figure 47), the stamps were also gummed in the same process, eliminating the need for a separate gumming operation. Perforating, however, still required a separate step, as the process of perforating, even with newly devised two-way perforating machines, was much slower than the process of printing.

To make sidewise coils, a 170-subject plate was laid out on flat steel, then bent in a semicircle. Two such plates were locked around the cylinder of the press, which rotated to make the stamp impressions on the moving web of paper.

Figure 47. The small Stickney rotary press used to print coil stamps used two plates curved to fit around a cylinder. The stamps were gummed on the same machine, but were perforated in a separate process.

Because the plates were bent in a sidewise direction, rotary-press coil stamps were slightly wider than sheet stamps printed on the flat-plate press.

The first coil stamps printed on the Stickney press and issued to the public were 2¢ Washington-Franklin stamps, coiled sidewise. One-cent sidewise coils, and endwise coils in the 1¢ and 2¢ denominations, were released within a few months.

For endwise coils, 150-subject plates were used and bent in the length-

107

wise direction. Thus endwise coils are slightly taller than sheet stamps printed on the flat-plate press.

For coil work, the Stickney press was found to have few problems, or perhaps more correctly, the problems it had were fixed by Benjamin Stickney. It was soon used to produce all coil stamps. By the end of the Wilson administration, this included endwise coils in 1¢, 2¢ and 3¢ denominations, and sidewise coils in 1¢, 2¢, 3¢, 4¢ and 5¢ denominations.

The 10¢ Washington-Franklin coil that we know as Scott 497 was actually produced during the Harding administration, having been issued on January 28, 1922, a little less than a year before the 10¢ value of the new series appeared. It stayed in production for the next three years, until the 10¢ Monroe coil was issued in December 1924 (see Chapter 7).

Rotary Sheet Stamps Problems

Encouraged by the success of the Stickney press in printing coils, the Bureau experimented with a larger version of the press, with a cylinder large enough to print 400-subject sheet stamps. The first of these presses was installed in early 1920 and was used to produce the 1¢ Washington-Franklin stamp we know as Scott 542. Because the 400-subject plates were curved, the stamps (like endwise coils) were taller than sheet stamps printed on the flat-plate press.

This first printing was regarded as experimental, and the stamps were perforated 10 horizontally by 11 vertically. This compound perforation was soon found to be unacceptable, however, as the stamps tended to curl and split along the vertical perforations.

To combat this problem, the perforation gauge was changed to 10 in both directions. Stamps with the perf 10 gauge were issued in May 1921, giving us the 1¢ stamp we know as 543. Although this variety was issued during the Harding administration, the Post Office Department seems to have had little to do with its development, as it was regarded as simply a perforation variety of an existing design. There was no announcement of this perforation change to collectors.

The change in perforation gauge did not entirely solve the problem with these rotary-press sheet stamps. Because they had been printed from rolls of paper, they tended to revert back to their curled state. This made them difficult to handle in post office drawers, and more specifically, made them difficult to precancel at local post offices. There were numerous complaints, which soon became the problem of the new administration. Just a few weeks after taking the job, Glover and his staff began hearing both good things and bad things about the rotary presses.

On the positive side, the presses were expected to save money, and they did. Treasury Secretary Andrew Mellon, under whose jurisdiction the Bureau of Engraving and Printing fell, was also new on the job and was happy to report in July 1921 that the price of postage stamps would be going down. The Treasury Department sold stamps to the Post Office Department, and it was its only supplier.

Where the price for "ordinary" or definitive stamps had been 9½¢ per thousand under the Wilson administration, Mellon was quoting a cost of only 8¢ for the first fiscal year that he would head the Treasury. This was due, he wrote, to "a decrease in the cost of materials and of improved efficiency of the employees."[1] Mellon would be doing what the Republicans promised during the campaign: running the government more efficiently and saving the taxpayers' money.

At the Bureau, meanwhile, Stickney was completing his plan for what he described as "the gradual elimination of the old process of producing stamps." Four small rotary presses were in place and were running at capacity to make coil stamps. Two large rotary presses were also in operation, making sheet stamps — but only in one denomination: the 1¢ Washington-Franklin. Two more large presses were on order.

Now, in the beginning of 1921, Stickney was requesting permission to purchase two additional large presses, which would bring the number of large presses up to six. By the following year, he wanted to purchase four more, to bring the total up to 10 by the beginning of the 1923 fiscal year, which began July 1, 1922. Ten large presses, he believed, would be sufficient to "produce the entire requirements for postage stamps."[2]

But even as Stickney was requesting more presses, postmasters were complaining about the 1¢ sheet stamps produced on the rotary press. Even after the perforations were changed from perf 10 x 11 to perf 10 all around, local post offices still had problems with curling. The hot gumming and gum-drying operations also contributed to the problem, as the gum shrunk more than the paper, causing the sheets of stamps to curl toward the back, or gummed side.

"The chief difficulty," Glover wrote to Bureau director Wilmeth the following September, "is on account of the backward curling of stamp sheets." When the decks or packages of stamps were opened, he wrote, "unless the sheets are weighted down, they curl to such an extent that they easily break in the perforations."[3]

This letter was forwarded to Stickney, who replied, "Regarding the curling, I have to say that this is materially improving, and I am providing mechanical means for treating the product while being perforated so that this trouble of curling may be prevented."[4]

This mechanical means became what we now know as gum breakers, or lines impressed into the gum side of the stamp to make it noncontiguous. Although the problem was not immediately solved, the Bureau was confident that Stickney, its resident mechanical expert, could solve this problem the way he had solved so many other technical difficulties with the presses that he had designed.

At the start of the new year of 1922, Bureau director Wilmeth told Glover that the Bureau would be able to save the Post Office Department a good deal of money in the coming fiscal year, due to the use of the large rotary presses.

"It is estimated," he wrote, "that the cost of stamps printed from these presses will be 5½¢ per 1,000 stamps," while stamps "printed on the other presses is 8¢ per 1,000." With two more large rotary presses on order and expected to be in use by July 1, Wilmeth estimated that "the four machines ... would reduce the stamp cost next year $108,000, or a conservative estimate of $90,000."[5]

But these optimistic plans ran into a number of serious problems within weeks. On March 31, Wilmeth and Stickney were dismissed from the Bureau with 23 others in the so-called Liberty Bond scandal that later proved baseless (see Chapter 2). Wilmeth and some of the other supervisors who were dismissed were really managers. But others, like Stickney, were craftsmen who held superintendent positions so they could be paid a competitive salary. The mass dismissals had a devastating effect on the Bureau.

At approximately the same time, complaints about the quality of rotary sheet stamps reached a critical stage.

The most serious complaint was that the stamps could not be precanceled efficiently if at all. Although smaller post offices applied the local precancels themselves, the larger offices contracted this work out to local printers, who ran the stamps through sheet-fed letterpress presses. The narrow margins on the rotary stamps, and their tendency to curl and break apart, made them difficult if not impossible to precancel.

The postmaster of Detroit was one of several who wanted to return the stamps for their flat-plate printed equivalent. "This office," he wrote, "has received five million one-cent rotary process stamps on which the mucilage is so thick and heavy that as soon as a package is opened the stamps curl up to such an extent that it is almost impossible to do anything with them, and at the slightest handling they break apart along the lines of the vertical perforations ... the printer cannot run them through the press on account of their condition."[6]

The postmaster of Jersey City, New Jersey, had a similar complaint about three million stamps he had received. "The patrons of this office who buy large quantities," he wrote, "have been objecting to accept them when offered to them, and station clerks have returned those sent to them." The stamps, he complained, "have become unsalable."[7]

Glover had liked the prospect of lower stamp costs, but he concluded that the quality of the rotary sheet stamps was simply unacceptable. He was aware that the Bureau had ordered two additional presses, but the prospect of the return of millions of stamps from dozens of the largest post offices was too much. On July 19, 1922, he pulled the plug on rotary sheet stamp production.

"Complaints are of such concern to this Department," he informed the Treasury Department, "as to warrant the recommendation that sheet work manufactured by the rotary press be discontinued."[8]

This was big trouble at the Bureau, for a number of reasons. Stickney had been let go in the Liberty Bond fiasco and was not around to fix the production problems. More importantly perhaps, the Treasury quotation for the price of the stamps had been predicated on the use of the rotary presses. Without using the large presses, production of sheet stamps would not only fall behind, but it would also be more expensive. And if all that weren't enough, the company that was making the new presses wanted to be paid for them. The new Bureau director, Louis A. Hill, who had been named to replace James Wilmeth as director, had problems.

On top of all this, Hill soon was told that the Bureau was seriously behind in its deliveries of coil stamps, and could not produce the number of coils the Post Office Department had ordered unless they were printed on overtime hours. That, in turn, would drive his stamp-production costs even higher.

Hill chewed over his options and spelled out the financial implications in some detail to his superior, Treasury Secretary Mellon. "As the situation now stands," Hill wrote, "it appears that unless the Government can cancel the order for the two large 'Web Rotary Presses,' which amounts to $21,204.00, the presses would be delivered to the Bureau and it would have no immediate use therefor, in view of the complaints made by the Post Office Department relative to the sheet stamps being produced from these particular presses."

His recommendation was to see if the supplier, the Universal Machine Co., would substitute two small rotary presses (for producing coils) for the two large ones on order and to have the matter "submitted to the proper legal officer of the Department."[9]

The lawyers and accountants worked on the details for a few days. Universal Machine Co. replied that the Bureau would be responsible for $6,804.63 in parts and labor if the contract was canceled. The Bureau would also be responsible to another company, Griscom-Russell, for the costs to date for the additional two-way perforating machines it had ordered to service the new presses.

To get coil production up to demand, it was determined that "at least one" small press would be necessary, at a cost of approximately $10,000, and this would require another $4,000 for the related heating units and perforator. But here was the hitch from the lawyers:

"This equipment would necessarily be purchased out of the appropriation for 1923, which could not legally be done unless the price received from the Post Office Department for postage stamps furnished during the current fiscal year were such as to justify this additional expenditure, as the machinery would be used entirely in the production of postage stamps for the Post Office Department."[10]

But of course the price of stamps to be produced on these machines had been cut to 5½¢ per thousand, not raised to buy new equipment.

To get the Bureau out of its bind, the Treasury Department came up with a plan. Everything might work out "if the Bureau could make arrangements with said Department whereby a straight price of 8 cents per thousand stamps would be paid to the Bureau, with the understanding that 15 per cent of this number of stamps would be printed from the 'Web Rotary Presses.' "

While this proposal might be good for the Bureau, it was not such a good deal for the Post Office Department. The Department would pay more for its total stamp order, and it would get some rotary-press sheet stamps after all.

The Bureau argued that, under this plan, the Post Office Department would get its coils on time. And as for the hated rotary sheet stamps, they might be sent to small cities that had no need to have precancels applied. In addition, the Bureau said it was confident that these sheet stamps could be improved.

In August the Post Office Department approved the deal, and established a joint committee with the Bureau "for the purpose of examining the methods and details of the manufacture of postage stamps by uses of the rotary presses in the Bureau of Engraving and Printing."[11]

Figure 48. Benjamin Stickney at the two-way perforator he also developed. After returning to the Bureau following his groundless firing, he continued to improve the manufacture of stamps using rotary intaglio presses.

The Rotary Press

Rotary sheet stamp production, which might have been killed for years, not only got a reprieve, but received a mandate to go forward. The Bureau's modernization plan also continued. Benjamin Stickney, like his colleagues, was eventually cleared of all charges, and he rejoined the Bureau on February 25, 1924. Precanceling of stamps at the Bureau, as we shall see in Chapter 11, would eliminate the problems postmasters had with precanceling rotary-press stamps. Stickney, shown in Figure 48 at the two-way perforating machine he also developed, would continued to improve and refine the rotary-press stamp operation. Before the Series of 1922 was retired, all but the three highest values were produced exclusively on the rotary presses Stickney had designed.

Notes

1. Andrew W. Mellon, secretary of the treasury, to Will H. Hays, July 20, 1921, National Archives.
2. Benjamin Stickney to James L. Wilmeth, October 13, 1921, National Archives.
3. W. Irving Glover to James L. Wilmeth, September 21, 1921, National Archives.
4. Benjamin Stickney to James L. Wilmeth, September 26, 1921, National Archives.
5. James L. Wilmeth to W. Irving Glover, January 12, 1922, National Archives.
6. John W. Smith, postmaster, Detroit, Michigan, to W. Irving Glover, July 12, 1922, National Archives.
7. Matt Ely, postmaster, Jersey City, New Jersey, to W. Irving Glover, July 14, 1922, National Archives.
8. W. Irving Glover to Eliot Wadsworth, assistant secretary of the treasury, July 19, 1922, National Archives.
9. Louis A. Hill to Andrew Mellon, July 20, 1922, National Archives.
10. A.E. Thomas, chief of Division of Assignments and Reviews, Treasury Department, to Louis A. Hill, July 24, 1922, National Archives.
11. W. Irving Glover to Louis A. Hill, August 16, 1922, Smithsonian Institution, Post Office Department Manuscript Collection.

United States Stamps 1922-26

Chapter 7

The Sidewise Coils

The rotary-press coil stamps that had been introduced in 1914 turned out to be a good product that was soon in high demand. Businesses found them more efficient to use, and a number of hand-stamping affixing machines were developed to make letter-stamping a more automated chore at the office. Vending machines also used coils and were becoming more prevalent, particularly in drug and stationery stores, which had traditionally kept stamps as a no-profit convenience item.

"The demand for coil stamps is increasing rapidly from year to year," Glover wrote in July 1922, as the new series of stamps was being designed, "the records of this office showing an increase from 1,234,196,500 stamps in this form in fiscal year 1917 to 2,322,525,410 in the fiscal year 1922. ..."[1]

In the early years of coil-stamp production, endwise coils had been the preferred type, but affixing manufacturers favored the sidewise coil, and it was in most demand by large post offices. The Multipost Company claimed 80 percent of the hand-stamping market by 1923, and its model that used sidewise coils was its most popular.

Although there was a stock of 1¢ coils available, 2¢ coils could not be produced fast enough to meet requisitions. As Glover complained to the Treasury Department, "This condition has frequently resulted in serious delays and materially inconvenienced the public."[2]

The coil version of the new 2¢ Washington design was originally intended to be released with the sheet stamp on Washington's birthday, February 22, 1923. But the demand for coil stamps moved up the issue for both varieties of the 2¢ stamp to Monday, January 15.

Sidewise coils were produced from the same dies as sheet stamps. No new engraving was made, so the design and engraving credits are the same as for the flat-plate sheet stamps. Because the plates were bent in a sidewise direction (in terms of the design), the designs will be wider than flat-plate stamps. Scott gives these dimensions in millimeters, but the stamps were laid out precisely in hundredths of an inch. The flat-plate stamps of this series should measure .75 x .87 inch. While there can be slight variations due to paper shrinkage, it is usually negligible, and sidewise coils are always wider. Sidewise coils usually measure .78 x .87 inch.

Because two 170-subject plates were fitted around a cylinder, a slight gap existed between the two plates. During printing, this gap would fill with ink

Figure 49. A one-way coil perforator, about 1923, set up for sidewise coils. Rolls or webs of printed stamps were taken from the press to machines like this, where the perforations were applied. The perforated web was removed from the other end and taken to another machine that slit the web into strips and rolled the stamps into coils.

and produce a line. When the gap was particularly wide, two parallel lines might be printed. These gap or joint lines appear after every 17 stamps. They are usually collected in pairs and command a premium.

What was produced on the small rotary press was a roll of printed and gummed stamps. This roll was removed from the press and moved to other equipment for perforating, counting and slitting into coils.

Coil stamps were perforated on what the Bureau called a "one-way perforator" that was quite different from the flat-plate perforator. Rather than wheels of pins, the coil perforator used bars of pins, set around a cylinder, that placed the vertical perforation across all 10 rows of the printed stamps at one time. An early version of this perforator is shown in Figure 49. Later a strobe light was affixed to help the operator keep the perforations centered. The one-way perforator also trimmed the margins on either side of the web, but did not slit the web into coils.

After perforation, the web was handled by another worker, who measured it into 500- or 1,000-stamp units by unrolling the web across a table. At the forward end of the web, this worker attached a strip of brown paper that would form the core. Then after each 500 or 1,000 stamps (depending on which coils were being measured) the web was cut and another length of brown paper

The Sidewise Coils

was attached. The other end of this paper was attached to the rest of the web and the counting began again, until another length of brown paper was added. When cut later on, this brown paper would form the core at one end and the outer wrapper at the other.

When the web had been measured and processed with the lengths of core and wrapper paper, it was moved to another station, where another worker would slit the web into 10 coils using a coiling machine. This device used rotary cutting wheels to slit the web between the horizontal rows of stamps and wind them into coils. Once the slitting had begun, the brown-paper core at the end was placed into a slot in one of the 10 spindles of the coiling machine. As the stamps were slit, the operator wound the coils on these spindles until the next length of brown paper appeared. This was then cut, with one portion used as the outside wrapper of the coils, and the remaining portion used as the core for the next coil.[3]

Splices. Several types of perforated splices are known on the gum side of coils of this period. Brown-paper splices, when found, usually occur at the joint lines. These were used by the workers who counted and measured coils, and used them to join two webs of stamps. White-paper splices are also found, with at least two different types of gum. These were used by the workers who wound the coils, to join the coils when they broke during this process. Both the white- and brown-paper splices are perforated 11, as they were prepared on the perforators used for flat-plate sheet stamps.

Rolls. When first issued, these stamps were available in coils of 500 or 1,000. On December 1, 1927, a roll of 3,000 became available, coiled gum side out, to be used in motorized affixing machines. These coils eliminated the need for the privately perforated flat-plate stamps that had previously been used in these affixing machines (see Chapter 9).

Bureau precancels. Coil stamps were not precanceled until the Bureau had met with some success in precanceling sheet stamps (see Chapter 11). The method of precanceling coil stamps was nearly identical to that for sheet stamps. An attachment to the rotary press applied the precancels on the same press, but with a different set of plates. The precanceling attachment was positioned on the press in front of the gumming unit, and used the letterpress process to apply the precancels with curved plates of raised metal type. For coil stamps, four plates were used, each five subjects wide by six subjects deep. The plates were bent so that two fit around a cylinder. Two cylinders were placed side-by-side. The plates applied the black precanceling ink to a section of the web that had already been printed by the intaglio plates.

The first Bureau precanceled coil stamps, 11,405,000 of the 1¢ denomination, were shipped on January 17, 1924, to New York City. Other cities were added rapidly.

1¢ Side Coil

Scott Number:	597
First Day of Issue:	July 18, 1923
Perforation:	10 vertical
Scott Colors:	Green, yellow green
Press:	Small rotary press
Plate Layout:	170 subjects, cut into coils
Quantity Issued:	2,147,680,500
Plate Numbers:	Total of 104: lowest, 14563; highest 20103
Scott Varieties:	Joint line pair; Gripper cracks; Double transfer

Philatelic Aspects and Varieties

First day of issue. This stamp was issued on July 18, 1923, only in Washington, D.C. This was more than six months later than the 2¢ coil. While the first-day date had no historical significance, it tells us that no 1¢ coil stamps of the new design were put on sale during the 1923 fiscal year, which ended on June 30. There was no announcement of the issue date, but some collectors were able to prepare first-day covers. These are not common, however, and command a high premium. Most first-day covers show pairs to make up the 2¢ letter rate.

Shades. This stamp remained in production for more than 14 years. It shows a wide range of shades, with the darker greens and bluish greens generally produced earlier than the yellow greens. When first listed in the 1924 edition of the Scott *Specialized*, the color was given only as deep green. In the 1927 edition, this shade was changed to just green. In the 1932 edition, yellow green was added as a secondary shade.

To these Johl added "bright yellowish green, dull greyish green, deep greyish green, deep bright green, deep bluish green, blue green, deep blue green."

Plate numbers. The 170-subject plates used for these coils were numbered in sequence with flat plates of the period. In normal coil production, however, the plate numbers were trimmed off. Only when the stamps were miscut do we find portions of plate numbers appearing at the top or bottom of the stamps. Stamps showing 100 percent of the plate number are difficult to find.

On most of these coil plates, the plate number appears only once, at the upper left to the right of a small, five-point star. Beginning with plate 19756, certified in July 1929, a second number was added at the lower right of the plate, but no star was added to this position.

Double transfer. This listing first appeared in the 1934 Scott *Specialized* and was based on a report in *Scott's Monthly Journal* in March 1933 of "one of the most interesting double transfers we have seen in some time."[4] It was later called a twisted double transfer, and is quite distinctive, as it shows some additional lines in Franklin's forehead in the vignette, as well as doubling in other areas.

Gripper cracks. This listing first appeared as a "cracked plate" in the 1929 Scott *Specialized*. In the 1939 edition, this listing was changed to "gripper cracks" to reflect the growing understanding that cracks occurring on coil stamps at the edges of the plates were caused by a weakness in the steel due to the slots cut into the rotary plate in order to attach the plates to the cylinder. Norman Kempf, an early coil specialist, referred to a crack on this stamp as "a prominent gripper slot crack" in January 1937.[5] He later explained, "These sections of the plate are under severe mechanical strain and at times the surface over the slot cracks open."[6]

Precancels. This stamp is known with 296 different Bureau precancels.

2¢ Side Coil

Scott Number:	599
First Day of Issue:	January 15, 1923
Perforation:	10 vertical
Scott Colors:	Carmine, deep carmine
Press:	Small rotary press
Plate Layout:	170 subjects, cut into coils
Quantity Issued:	24,946,522,000
Plate Numbers:	Total of 685: lowest, 14098; highest, 20799
Scott Varieties:	Joint line pair; Gripper cracks; Double transfer

Figure 50. One of the 37 first-day covers prepared by Philip Ward. Two of the 37 are known with strips of six, which is the largest multiple of this stamp on first-day covers.

Philatelic Aspects and Varieties

First day of issue. This stamp was issued on the same day as the sheet version, January 15, 1923, only at Washington, D.C. Most of the first-day cover enthusiasts of the era missed this issue entirely. Although there was advance notice of the sheet stamps that would be issued on January 15, there was no advance notice that the coil version would be released on the same day, and copies were not available at the Philatelic Stamp Agency until January 17.

Coils were sent to post offices as early as January 6, but were not to be released to the public until the issue date.[7] Some post offices released them early, and a few early release dates have been noted. The earliest recorded is January 10.

Philip Ward, the stamp columnist and dealer, seems to have been the only person to service first-day covers of this stamp on January 15. He explained in an advertisement that he did not find the stamps at the agency, but that "the wholesale clerk ... kindly hunted around and found a coil for me. ..."[8] In the same advertisement Ward said that he had mailed out "exactly 37 covers." Two of these are known with strips of six stamps, paying the special delivery rate (see Figure 50).

Shades. When first listed in the 1924 edition of the Scott *Specialized*, the color was given as carmine. In the 1926 edition, deep carmine was added as a secondary shade. Although only these two shades are listed today, this stamp

The Sidewise Coils

was in production for more than 16 years and appears in a variety of shades.

Johl lists in addition only bright carmine. This stamp went to press many times, and there is certainly a light carmine shade.

Plate numbers. On most of the plates used for these coils, the plate number was placed only at the upper-left corner, to the right of a small five-point star. Beginning with plate 19752, certified in April 1929, a second number was added at the lower-left corner.

Double transfer. The double transfer listing went into the Scott *Specialized* in the 1935 edition, and was apparently based on the one double transfer listed and illustrated in Johl. Since coil stamps do not usually appear with plate numbers, and since we do not see the plates themselves except in the proof stage, specific positions for plate varieties can seldom be given. A number of other double transfers are known on this stamp. French lists 14.

Gripper cracks. This listing began as a "cracked plate" in the 1936 edition of the Scott *Specialized*, and was based on a report in *Scott's Monthly Journal* in April 1935 of a variety that showed a "well defined crack extending from the mouth of Washington upwards through the 'S' of States and terminating directly above that letter in the upper left triangle."[9] The stamp was described as "the right hand one of a guide line pair," which made it one of the stamps on the far left side of the plate. In the 1939 edition, this listing was changed to "gripper cracks."

Other plate varieties. In addition to shifted transfers and gripper cracks, rotary press stamps often show another type of variety, the recut. When flat plates were damaged or scratched, the plate could be repaired by hammering and burnishing out the damage and making a new entry with the transfer roll. But this type of repair was not possible on rotary press stamps, as the plates had been bent or curved. Thus, plate damage was often repaired by hand recutting. A few recuts are known on this stamp, but none is outstanding.

In 1952, Carolyn Kuhn, one of the great students of this issue, reported a single coil stamp with a number of corrosion stains appearing near the left side of the design. She later included this variety among her "Twelve Best Plate Varieties on the 2¢ Washington." Usually, she wrote, "great care is taken to preserve stamp plates from rust and corrosion. ..." But on this stamp, which she called "a beautiful example of its kind," the corrosion is shown clearly on the stamp.[10] This same stamp was also listed and illustrated by French in his article, "Important Plate Varieties on the Bureau Issues" published in the British journal *Stamp Lover* in 1972.[11]

Bureau precancels. This stamp is known with 113 different Bureau precancels.

The Type II of this coil, cataloged as Scott 599A, was issued in 1928, and is not treated here.

3¢ Side Coil

Scott Number:	600
First Day of Issue:	May 10, 1924
Perforation:	10 vertical
Scott Colors:	Violet, deep violet
Press:	Small rotary press
Plate Layout:	170 subjects, cut into coils
Quantity Issued:	499,091,500
Plate Numbers:	Total of 20: lowest, 14720; highest, 20377
Scott Varieties:	Joint line pair; Cracked plate

Philatelic Aspects and Varieties

First day of issue. This stamp was issued on May 10, 1924, only at Washington, D.C. There was little need for a 3¢ coil, and this stamp was not issued until well over a year after the 2¢ coil. Although there was no announcement of this stamp, the servicing of first-day covers had become a small but popular business by this time, and several stamp dealers prepared covers. The difference in the values and scarcity between first-day covers of the 2¢ coil and this 3¢ coil are an indication of how popular first-day cover servicing had become in the 16 months between the issue dates.

Shades. When first listed in the 1926 edition of the Scott *Specialized*, the color was violet. In the 1937 edition deep violet was added as a secondary shade. To this Johl added pale violet and bright violet.

Plate numbers. All but two of the 20 plates of this stamp have only one plate number, at top left. Plates 20376 and 20377 also have plate numbers at the lower right. Each of these plates has a small, five-point star at the upper left.

Cracked plate. This listing went into the Scott *Specialized* in the 1937 edition and is apparently based on a report in *Stamps* magazine in January 1936. As this crack was described as appearing at the left end of a plate,[12] it is no doubt a gripper crack, and should be listed as such. Unlike the early "cracked plate" listings for the 1¢ and 2¢ design, this listing was never changed.

Bureau precancels. This stamp is known with 62 different Bureau precancels.

The Sidewise Coils

4¢ Side Coil

Scott Number:	601
First Day of Issue:	August 5, 1923
Perforation:	10 vertical
Scott Colors:	Yellow brown, brown
Press:	Small rotary press
Plate Layout:	170 subjects, cut into coils
Quantity Issued:	228,288,000
Plate Numbers:	14189, 14190, 14294, 14321, 17937, 17938, 17939, 17940
Scott Varieties:	Joint line pair

Philatelic Aspects and Varieties

First Day of Issue. Although the records seem to indicate that this stamp was issued on August 5, 1923, only at Washington, D.C., no first-day covers are known. Since this stamp paid the double-weight letter rate, it was in some demand and was issued earlier than all of the coils except the 1¢ and 2¢ side coils. Its release, however, seems to have escaped the notice of all the first-day enthusiasts of the day. Jack Harvey, the noted specialist of first-day covers of this series, wrote: "Why did Ward, Hammelman and the other early servicers miss the 4¢ coil? The author must confess that he does not know and cannot construct any reasonable explanation."[13]

Shades. When first listed in the 1924 edition of the Scott *Specialized*, the color was yellow brown. In the 1932 edition brown was listed as a secondary shade. Johl added pale brown, reddish brown and deep reddish brown. While the quantities produced of this stamp were not large, it remained in production for 10 years and appeared in a number of shades.

Plate numbers. Only eight plates went to press for this issue, as it began to be replaced in 1930 by a new design depicting William Howard Taft. All of the plates have only one plate number, at the upper left following the small, five-point star.

Gripper cracks. While Scott lists no plate varieties of this stamp, a gripper crack variety was reported in 1932, and is illustrated in French.

Bureau precancels. This stamp is known with 34 Bureau precancels.

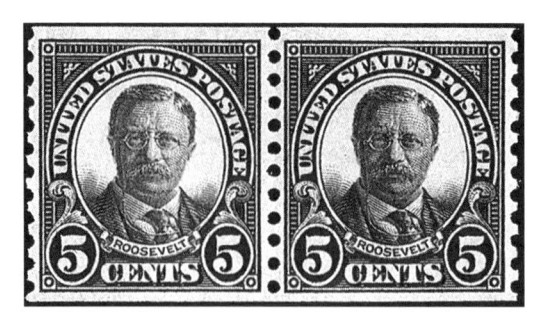

5¢ Side Coil

Scott Number:	602
First Day of Issue:	March 5, 1924
Perforation:	10 vertical
Scott Color:	Dark blue
Press:	Small rotary press
Plate Layout:	170 subjects, cut into coils
Quantity Issued:	Unknown
Plate Numbers:	Total of 10: lowest, 15279; highest, 17948
Scott Varieties:	Joint line pair

Philatelic Aspects and Varieties

First Day of Issue. This stamp was issued on March 5, 1924, only at Washington, D.C. Like the 3¢ and 10¢ coils, this stamp was not issued until 1924 and more than a year later than the 2¢ coils. As with most of the other coils, no release date was publicized, but some of the earlier first-day enthusiasts, including Edward Worden and C.E. Nickles, were able to prepare first-day covers.

Shades. Scott lists only one shade, dark blue, and Johl seems to have agreed that there was only a single shade, although he listed it as plain blue.

Plate numbers. Only 10 plates were used to print this stamp, and all have the plate numbers only at the upper left, following the star.

Plate varieties. Scott lists none, and French lists only a few minor varieties.

Bureau precancels. This stamp is known with 36 different Bureau precancels.

The Sidewise Coils

10¢ Side Coil

Scott Number: 603
First Day of Issue: December 1, 1924
Perforation: 10 vertical
Scott Color: Orange
Press: Small rotary press
Plate Layout: 170 subjects, cut into coils
Quantity Issued: Unknown
Plate Numbers: 16339, 16340, 16341, 16342, 17610, 17961, 17962, 17963, 17964
Scott Varieties: Joint line pair

Philatelic Aspects and Varieties

First day of issue. This stamp was issued on December 1, 1924, only in Washington, D.C. It replaced the sidewise coil of the Washington-Franklin design, which had not been issued until 1922 and was still available in rather large quantities when the new designs were issued. As with most of the other new coils, there was no first-day publicity, but some enthusiasts were able to service covers.

Shades. Since it was first listed in the 1926 edition of the Scott *Specialized*, the only color ever given by Scott for this stamp is orange. While this is clearly a yellow stamp, Scott followed the same convention it used with the 10¢ flat-plate stamp, which it also called orange. Johl added yellow orange and deep yellow orange.

Plate numbers. Only nine plates were used for this stamp, and all have plate numbers only at the upper left, following the star.

Plate varieties. Neither Scott nor French lists any plate varieties for this stamp.

Bureau precancels. This stamp is known with 32 different Bureau precancels.

Notes

1. W. Irving Glover to Eliot Wadsworth, Assistant Secretary of the Treasury, July 19, 1922, National Archives.

2. *Ibid.*

3. The coil production process of this period is described in Harold F. Whittaker, "Through the Bureau of Engraving and Printing," *Scott's Monthly Journal*, Vol. 4, No. 2 (April 1923), pp. 45-48.

4. Beverly S. King, "Notes on General Issues," *Scott's Monthly Journal*, Vol. 14, No. 1 (March 1933), p. 7.

5. Norman Kempf, "Current Coils," *Bureau Specialist*, Vol. 8, No. 1 (January 1937), p. 4.

6. Norman W. Kempf, "Plate Varieties Committee: Plate Cracks," *Bureau Specialist*, Vol. 22, No. 7 (July 1951), p. 130.

7. Johl gives this date as January 8 (Vol. III, p. 55), but a Bureau memorandum in the correspondence files at the National Archives gives the date of January 6, 1923, noting: "First delivery of 2¢ ordinary stamps, Series 1922, put up in coil form, 170 subjects, has this day been made to the Post Office Department."

8. Philip H. Ward, Jr., "Did You Get the New 2-Cent Coil Used the First Day of Issue" [advertisement], *Mekeel's Weekly Stamp News*, Vol. 37, No. 5 (February 3, 1923), p. 72.

9. Hugh M. Clark, "Notes on General Issues," *Scott's Monthly Journal*, Vol. 16, No. 2 (April 1935), p. 69.

10. Carolyn P. Kuhn, "The Twelve Best Plate Varieties on the 2¢ Washington," *Bureau Specialist*, Vol. 27, No. 3 (March 1956), p. 65.

11. Loran C. French, "Important Plate Varieties on the Bureau Issues," *Stamp Lover*, Vol. 64, No. 3 (May-June 1972), pp. 84-88.

12. See George B. Sloane, "3¢ Lincoln Coil, Cracked Plate," *Stamps*, January 18, 1936, reprinted in *Sloane's Column, op. cit.*, p. 317.

13. Jack V. Harvey, *First Day Covers of the Regular Postage Issue of 1922-35*, Second Edition (American First Day Cover Society, 1985), p. 50.

Chapter 8

Coil Waste

Coil-waste stamps are among the most difficult and interesting stamps of this series, and among the most difficult to find on cover legitimately used during the period.

The practice of salvaging waste from coil production began in 1919, during the Washington-Franklin period, when the Bureau had accumulated 85,000 sheets of 170 subjects of 1¢, 2¢ and 3¢ stamps that had been "laid aside as mutilated because they cannot be made into coils on account of some defect, but are otherwise commercially perfect."[1] Bureau director James Wilmeth proposed to the Post Office Department that these stamps be perforated and shipped to post offices for use.

Wilmeth's plan was approved, as was his packing scheme, in which 12 decks of 100 sheets of 170 subjects would be made up into packages. That would make packages of 204,000 coil-waste stamps, instead of the usual 200,000 sheet stamps.

The stamps that Wilmeth's workers were salvaging had come from webs of stamps printed on the small rotary press and designed for sidewise coils. Most of it consisted of short ends, and all of it had already been run through the one-way perforator.

Cutting the webs of paper on the joint lines yielded sheets of 170 subjects. Cutting the webs into panes of 100 might have made them easier to pack and count. But this would have been against the normal Bureau procedure of keeping records by plate number. Cutting the sheets on the guidelines maintained the integrity of the plate system. Flaws or damage detected in the printing could also be isolated to a particular printing plate. Some examples are known where the sheets were not cut on the guidelines, but these are the exception, not the rule.

Since these sheets had already received 10-gauge vertical perforations on the one-way perforator, they needed only to be run through another perforator in the horizontal direction to complete their transformation to sheet stamps. The perforators used for the horizontal perforations were the same ones used to perforate sheet stamps, and these had 11-gauge pins. This created the 11 x 10 coil waste Washington-Franklin stamps that we now know as Scott 538, 539, 540 and 541. We know that these stamps were used as early as June 1919.

At some post offices, however, these sheets of 170 did not fit easily into the normal drawers, and were often cut into panes of 100 and panes of 70.

127

At some later time, and probably not until the spring of 1921, webs of 1¢ and 2¢ coil waste that had not yet gone through the one-way perforator were also salvaged. These sheets had to be run through the sheet-stamp perforator twice, and resulted in 11-gauge perforations on all four sides. These became the Washington-Franklin stamps we know as 545 and 546. These may well be the first Scott-numbered stamps printed during the Harding administration, although they were not considered new varieties by the Bureau or the Post Office Department.

All of these coil-waste stamps will be wider than sheet stamps and exactly as wide as sidewise coil stamps, as that is the way they began.

Coil Waste of the New Series

When the new coil stamps of the Series of 1922 began to be produced, the same policy of salvage was in place. But it ended within 19 months. Johl credits stamp collectors for helping to put an end to the coil-waste policy. "This change of policy," he writes, "was entirely due to the efforts of certain outstanding collectors who realized the hardship to the average collector, as the distribution was limited and the output small." In Johl's version of the story, Bureau director Hall, "having been shown the attitude of collectors, gave instructions that all further coil waste be treated as such and be destroyed."[2]

Unfortunately, we have no documentation for this account, nor any date for the cessation of the policy. If the story is true, it must have been essentially a one-way conversation, as these collectors failed to answer many of the questions that other collectors still have, and they failed to learn of the existence of valuable waste varieties that were not discovered until years later.

With or without the intervention of collectors, the discontinuation of the coil-waste salvage policy should not have been a hard one to make. Salvaging coil waste was a labor-intensive operation that involved a great deal of handwork at a time when the Bureau was trying to automate and update its production methods. It was also an idea originated by Bureau director Wilmeth, who was now gone.

Waste salvage also made less economic sense after January 1, 1923, when the Treasury Department consented to the Post Office Department's request to again charge a lower rate for rotary press stamps. Treasury Secretary Mellon agreed to a rate of 6¢ per thousand for stamps printed by the rotary presses and a rate of 8¢ per thousand for stamps printed by the flat-plate presses.[3]

Where the 85,000 sheets of coil waste were worth 9½¢ per thousand, or $1372.75 in 1919, the same number of coil-waste stamps were worth only $867.00 at 6¢ per thousand in 1923. The labor of cutting so many sheets by hand and running them through flat-plate perforators probably just wasn't worth it.

2¢ Coil Waste, Perforated 11 x 10

Scott Number:	579
Earliest Documented Use:	February 20, 1923
Scott Colors:	Carmine, deep carmine
Press:	Small rotary press
Plate Layout:	170 subjects, cut into sheets of 170
Quantity Issued:	Fewer than 17,918,000
Plate Numbers:	Total of 181 reported: lowest, 14098; highest, 15921
Scott Varieties:	Recut in eye, plate 14731

Philatelic Aspects and Varieties

Earliest use. As was discussed above, this variety was more of a Bureau economy measure than anything else, and it was not considered a new issue. Thus, there was no notice to collectors. Bureau records show that the first delivery of these stamps was made on February 17, 1923. Within a month, there was a report in the philatelic press that copies were in the hands of Scott Stamp & Coin in New York.[4] Collectors and dealers found supplies of these stamps at New York post offices. By the end of March, there were reports of several plate numbers. Thus we can surmise that many of the unused plate blocks that exist today were saved by New York dealers and collectors.

No first-day covers were prepared, however, and we have very few examples of these stamps used on cover during the period. The earliest documented cover is dated from New York on February 20, 1923. This is three days after the delivery date to post offices, and it seems likely that this date will hold up for some time.[5]

Only after this stamp was discovered by collectors did it go on sale at the Philatelic Agency in Washington. Although the sheets of 170 were usually broken into sheets of 100 and 70 for sale in post offices, several full sheets of 170 are known.

Quantity issued. The last delivery of this variety was made on September 29, 1924. A total of 17,918,000 stamps were delivered in sheet form

United States Stamps 1922-26

from plates of 170 subjects. The Bureau kept careful records of stamp formats, but did not differentiate between perforation varieties. Thus, we do not know how many of these stamps were perforated 11 x 10 and how many were perforated 11.

Each quantity delivered by the Bureau is divisible by 17,000, indicating that these stamps were delivered in decks of 100 sheets of 170 subjects. The total quantity is also divisible by 17,000 and yields 1,054 decks or 105,400 sheets of 170.

Plate numbers. The large number of plate numbers known derives from the fact that these were the waste ends of sheets. While 181 different plate numbers have been recorded, others may be reported in the future.

Imperforate at bottom. Most but not all sheets of these stamps were imperforate at bottom. This bottom margin is wider than the straight edge found on flat-plate stamps. Collectors sometimes call this variety a "fantail."

Recut in eye. This listing specifies "plate 14731," which should be made more specific, as we know that this is stamp 14731-3, that is the third stamp on that plate of 170. Collectors who have actually seen the stamp sometimes call it the "black-eyed Washington," as the recut appears to give George a shiner.

The listing went into the Scott *Specialized* in the 1936 edition and was based on a report by George Sloane, who speculated correctly: "I am convinced it is actually a retouch and an attempt by an engraver working over the subject by hand, after the plate was made, to conceal a flaw in the metal or to improve an unsatisfactory transfer."[6]

Figure 51. Although they are not often found, joint lines exist on coil-waste stamps, just as they do on coils. The four stamps to the left of the joint line in this block of six were printed from a plate other than plate 14148.

Joint line pair. While this variety is not listed in Scott, it exists, and is the equivalent of a coil line pair. It was formed exactly the same way as a coil line, that is by the crack between the two rotary-press printing plates filling with ink. Nearly all coil-waste sheets were cut on these joint lines, which usually show up on either the right or left side of the sheet of 170, but a few examples are known with the joint line running between two stamps. These are also known in blocks and plate number blocks. See Figure 51.

2¢ Coil Waste, Perforated 11 x 11

Scott Number:	595
Earliest Documented Use:	June 25, 1923
Scott Colors:	Carmine, deep carmine
Press:	Small rotary press
Plate Layout:	170 subjects, cut into sheets of 170
Quantity Issued:	Unknown
Plate Numbers:	Total of 95 reported; lowest, 14098; highest, 14926
Scott Varieties:	Recut in eye, plate 14731

Philatelic Aspects and Varieties

Earliest Use. As we have noted above, this variety was produced from webs of printed paper that were originally intended for coil stamps. Unlike the waste that became Scott 579, these stamps had not gone through the one-way perforator. Webs of imperforate printed stamps were cut on the joint lines into sheets of 170 subjects, and were then run twice through the 11-gauge perforator: once for the vertical perforations and once for the horizontal perforations. Some of this imperforate waste no doubt occurred when the one-way perforator used for sidewise coils was "threaded."

There was not as much of this imperforate waste as there was of waste with 10-gauge perforations, and it did not accumulate as rapidly. It was not reported until a month later that Scott 579 existed, when Philip Ward wrote that Arthur Owen of New York had discovered examples showing five different plate numbers.[7]

Very few of these stamps have been found on cover. The earliest documented cover is canceled June 29, 1923, and was used from New York City.

As with Scott 579, full sheets of 170 subjects of Scott 595 are known.

Plate numbers. Fewer plate numbers are reported on this stamp than on Scott 579. Many of these plate numbers, however, appear on stamps with both perforation varieties. Thus, a plate number alone does not tell us whether the stamp should be Scott 579 or 595. With Scott 595 however, the vertical perforations cross the top margin. They do not cross the top margin on Scott 579.

Recut in eye. As with Scott 579, this variety is given as being from plate 14731, and should be identical to the variety described above. As both perforations appear on stamps with this plate number, this variety should appear on both Scott 579 and 595, as well as on the coil stamp itself, Scott 599.

1¢ Coil Waste, Perforated 11 x 10

Scott Number:	578
Earliest Documented Use:	November 1923
Scott Color:	Green
Press:	Small rotary press
Plate Layout:	170 subjects, cut into sheets of 170
Quantity Issued:	Fewer than 3,077,000
Plate Numbers:	Total of 25 reported: lowest, 14563; highest, 15810
Scott Varieties:	None

Philatelic Aspects and Varieties

Earliest use. The first delivery of these stamps was made on October 17, 1923, exactly eight months after the first delivery of Scott 579. It was reported in the philatelic press a month later, and again it was Arthur Owen who discovered it in New York.[8] As with the 2¢ coil-waste varieties, we have very few stamps reported on cover, the earliest being postmarked sometime in November 1923, as the datestamp on this cover is indistinct.

Coil Waste

It was eventually placed on sale at the Philatelic Stamp Agency and is known in full sheets of 170 subjects.

Quantity issued. Like the 2¢ coil waste, the last delivery of 1¢ sheet stamps printed from 170-subject plates was made on September 29, 1924. The total was 3,077,000 stamps, but we do not know how many of these were perforated 11 x 10 and how many were perforated 11.

The delivery numbers divide equally by 17,000, and the total makes 181 decks of 100 sheets of 170-subject stamps.

Plate Numbers. As with the 2¢ variety, there are a large number of plate numbers for this stamp due to fact that this stamp was created from waste ends. Additional plate numbers may be reported.

Imperforate at Bottom. Most but not all sheets of these stamps were imperforate at bottom. This bottom margin is wider than the straight edge found on flat-plate stamps. Collectors sometimes call this variety a fantail. Figure 52 shows a fantail copy.

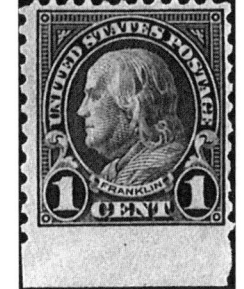

Figure 52. On most coil-waste sheets of 170, there were no perforations at the bottom. This created stamps with an imperforate bottom margin, often called a fantail.

Fakes. These stamps are more frequently faked than the 2¢ variety, but both can be made from coil stamps, by adding counterfeit perforations to the top and bottom.

1¢ Coil Waste, Perforated 11 x 11

Scott Number:	594
Earliest Documented Use:	March 24, 1924
Scott Color:	Green
Press:	Small rotary press
Plate Layout:	170 subjects, cut into sheets of 170
Quantity Issued:	Unknown
Plate Numbers:	Unknown
Scott Varieties:	None

Figure 53. A pair of Scott 594, canceled at Grand Central Station in New York. Most known copies were mailed from three New York post offices.

Philatelic Aspects and Varieties

Scarcity. This has become one of the most highly priced U.S. stamps of the 20th century, and for a time was the most valuable. It has been the subject of a great deal of reporting and speculation.

The first report that this stamp existed was made in April 1925, more than four months after the last delivery of the stamps had been made. C.L. Gabel was the name of the collector who sent Philip Ward the first copy of this stamp, with the information that it had been in his possession for "nearly a year." Ward then reported that "inquiry at Washington produces the information that some of the imperforated coil waste of the 1¢ denomination was perf 11 and went out with the general stock."[9]

As with the 2¢ stamps, the Bureau kept no separate record of perforation differences, only the total number of sheet stamps issued from 170-subject plates, which was 3,077,000.

None of the 1¢ perf-11 variety was sent to the Philatelic Stamp Agency, and none was found in unused form at New York post offices. To this day, we have no plate numbers reported on this stamp, nor do we have any blocks, the largest known multiple being a pair.

Early in 1934, 18 copies of this stamp were found by Ernest E. Fairbanks, a New York writer who had mailed out postcards bearing these stamps and had several returned to him. These nine returned cards each bore two stamps and were dated October 4, 1924, and postmarked at the Madison Square Station in New York.[10]

In the same year as the find of the Fairbanks copies, the first unused example was found by Max Wulson of the Uptown Stamp Company in a collection of stamps that it had purchased. This stamp, without gum, was auctioned on November 15, 1934, and brought the startling price of $1,975 — quite a sum during the Depression. Prescott Thorp noted "with silent amazement" that this stamp had brought such an "astounding price."[11] The news of this stamp sale reached not only the philatelic press, but the popular press as well, and became known as one of the great rarities. Not only did it bring a high price, but it looked like the hundreds of millions of ordinary 1¢ stamps that were in current use.

It was soon reported that these stamps were known with cancellations from three New York post offices: Grand Central, Madison Square and Station Y.[12] If each of these post offices received a deck of 17,000 stamps, this would be a minimum of 51,000 stamps. We do not know whether these stamps were packed with Scott 578, but it would make sense that these imperforate waste sheets were stockpiled until there was a large enough quantity to run them through the flat-plate perforators twice.

A pair canceled at Grand Central Station is shown in Figure 53.

Earliest use. Although Scott does not list an earliest-use date, the earliest documented use is March 24, 1924.[13] Max Johl also reported a cover dated March 31, 1924, mailed from New York City.[14]

Fakes. There are many fakes of this stamp, as might be expected. In 1968, the Philatelic Foundation reported that eight unused singles had been found genuine, out of 25 submitted, and that 37 used copies had been found genuine, out of 106 submitted.[15] In 1983, the Foundation reported that there were 13 unused copies and 74 used copies.[16]

In the Foundation's report, two copies were reported known with "the same indistinguishable perforated cancel." This appears to be what we know as perforated initials. The perfin on these two stamps is a "W" encircled by a "C" and was used by P.F. Colliers & Sons, a New York publishing firm, and was used by *Collier's Weekly*, a magazine, on prepaid return postcards.[17]

Notes

1. James L. Wilmeth to Third Assistant PMG, March 25, 1919, Bureau of Engraving and Printing.
2. Johl, Vol. III, p. 59.
3. Andrew W. Mellon to Hubert S. Work, January 12, 1923. Smithsonian In-

stitution, Post Office Department Manuscript Collection.

4. Philip H. Ward Jr., "Chronicle of New Issues and Varieties," *Mekeel's Weekly Stamp News*, Vol. 37, No. 10 (March 10, 1923), p. 140.

5. See Gary Griffith, "2¢ Coil Waste Issues of 1923: Earliest Known Uses of Sc. 579 and Sc. 595," *First Days*, Vol. 36, No. 3 (April 15, 1991), pp. 276-77.

6. George B. Sloane, in *Stamps*, July 15, 1933, reprinted in *Sloane's Column*, *op. cit.*, p. 316.

7. Philip H. Ward Jr., "Chronicle of New Issues and Varieties," *Mekeel's Weekly Stamp News*, April 21, 1923, p. 216.

8. Philip H. Ward Jr., "Chronicle of New Issues and Varieties," *Mekeel's Weekly Stamp News*, November 12, 1923, p. 580.

9. Philip H. Ward Jr., "Chronicle of New Issues and Varieties," *Mekeel's Weekly Stamp News*, Vol. 39, No. 15 (April 13, 1925), pp. 197-98.

10. Max G. Johl, "A Find of the Rarest U.S. Twentieth Century Non Error Stamp," *Stamps*, Vol. 7 (April 7, 1934), p. 15.

11. Prescott H. Thorp, "Notes of the Month," *Scott's Monthly Journal*, Vol. 15, No. 10 (December 1934), p. 251.

12. R.A. Barry, "Number 594," *American Philatelist*, Vol. 48, No. 3 (December 1934), p. 181.

13. Edward J. Siskin, *Checklist of First Days and Earliest Documented Covers: 1847-1931* (American First Day Cover Foundation, 1990), p. 35.

14. Max G. Johl, "Max G. Johl Reports on 20th Century United States," *Stamps*, Vol. 32, No. 9 (August 31, 1940), p. 304.

15. "Philatelic Foundation Expert Committee," *Stamps*, Vol. 42, No. 3 (January 20, 1968), p. 131.

16. Brian La Vane, "Less than a Millimeter, Thousand of Dollars, Opinions (The Philatelic Foundation, 1983), p. 72.

17. George B. Sloane, "1922-26m 1c Perf. 11, No. 594," *Stamps*, June 29, 1946, reprinted in *Sloane's Column, op. cit.*, p. 317.

Chapter 9

The Imperforates

In 1923, as the new designs were issued, they were produced in imperforate form for only one reason: to fill requisitions for flat-plate printed sheets of 400 from the Mail-o-Meter Company, the last supplier of privately perforated coils for affixing machines.

The Mail-o-Meter Company pasted together the sheets of 400, perforated them with two rectangular holes and cut them into coils of 3,000 subjects. These coils were then sold, at a slight premium over face, to users of its electric-powered envelope-sealing and stamp-affixing machines.

The two rectangular holes in the stamps, which we now know as Schermack Type III perforations, permitted the stamps to be advanced in the machine by two steel fingers. Mail-o-Meter was a successor company to the Schermack firm. Its machines could only affix a single stamp at a time. No pairs or strips or blocks of these stamps were affixed by its machines. Figure 54 shows a typical use of the 2¢ stamp.

Mail-o-Meter had been known to sell imperforate sheets, perforated-to-order blocks and unused perforated coils to stamp dealers, and that is the source of most if not all of the pairs, strips and blocks of these privately perforated stamps that exist in collections today.

The imperforate sheets of the new designs were also sent to the Phila-

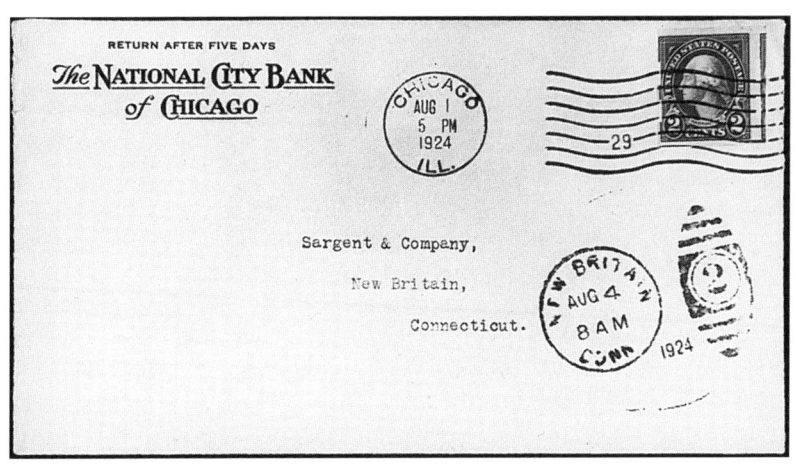

Figure 54. Large mailers, like the National City Bank of Chicago, used privately perforated coils affixed by machines.

137

telic Stamp Agency for the benefit of collectors.

Imperforate sheets were manufactured exactly like other flat-plate stamps, except that they did not go through the cutting and perforating process. Because they were not cut into panes, pairs and blocks showing the guidelines between the stamps could be cut from the sheets, as could the so-called centerline block, where the vertical and horizontal guidelines crossed. Line blocks from the top, bottom, and side margins are known as arrow blocks, whether they actually show an arrow-line marking or not.

It was common for dealers and collectors to purchase sheets of 400, cut out the centerline block, plate blocks, corner blocks, and/or arrow blocks, and then use the remainder of the stamps for postage. Thus there was some use of these stamps on cover, but it is generally considered a "philatelic" use.

The more desirable "commercial" uses of these imperforate stamps are on covers showing the privately perforated stamps.

1¢ Imperforate

Scott Number:	575
Earliest Documented Use:	March 16, 1923
Scott Colors:	Green, deep green
Press:	Flat-plate press
Plate Layout:	400 subjects, uncut
Quantity Issued:	16,072,400
Plate Numbers:	Total of 47 reported: lowest, 14157; highest, 16569

Philatelic Aspects and Varieties

First day of issue. Although Scott lists March 20, 1923, as the issue date of this stamp, some first-day covers were prepared by Harold F. Whittaker on March 16 from Washington, D.C. The Post Office Department did not consider this a new issue, only a perforation variety, and there was no official announcement. Philip Ward reported that both the 1¢ and 2¢ imperforates went on sale at the Philatelic Stamp Agency on March 20 in sheets of 400.[1]

The Imperforates

Scarcity. In April 1925, the third-class circular rate was raised to 1.5¢, eliminating much of the need for this stamp, as it was at that time mainly used in Chicago in privately perforated and precanceled form for mass-mailing circulars.

After this stamp went "off agency" or was depleted at the Philatelic Stamp Agency in 1930, there was some attempt by dealers to manipulate its price. As Johl has described it, "a few dealers and speculators realized the possibility of the relative 'scarcity' of this stamp, laid aside large quantities ... and as a consequence the prices asked were much higher than the facts warranted."[2]

Schermack Type III perforations. When the stamp was first issued, imperforate stamps were needed in both New York and Chicago, but the use of the stamps in New York was short-lived. According to George Howard, the best scholar of these issues, the Postage Meter Company bought out the Mail-o-Meter company in 1924, "and from then on the private perforation was used only in the Chicago district."[3] The earliest use of this stamp on cover from New York is May 5, 1924; the earliest use from Chicago is February 7, 1924.[4]

Unused pairs are somewhat scarce. These can occur with guidelines and as paste-up pairs, where the sheets joined together. Unused singles are somewhat easier to find, as one Chicago firm used these stamps to prepay return postcards, and these stamps could be soaked off those cards.

Most of the other 1¢ stamps were precanceled "Chicago, Illinois." These are somewhat common off cover, but difficult to find on cover. Figure 55 shows a use of the Chicago precancel.

Figure 55. The Chicago precancel is the only one known on this stamp, which was often used on third-class mailings like this.

2¢ Imperforate

Scott Number:	577
Earliest Documented Use:	April 12, 1923
Scott Colors:	Carmine, light carmine
Press:	Flat-plate press
Plate Layout:	400 subjects, uncut
Quantity Issued:	36,085,600
Plate Numbers:	Total of 117 reported: lowest, 14091; highest, 18228

Philatelic Aspects and Varieties

First day of issue. Scott lists no date of issue for this stamp; Johl uses March 20, 1923, the same date that Ward reported as the date the stamps were placed on sale at the Philatelic Stamp Agency. However, the earliest-reported use is April 12, 1923.

Schermack Type III perforations. Unlike the 1¢ variety, no examples of this stamp are known to have been used from New York. The earliest-known postmark is from Milwaukee on May 31, 1923; the earliest known from Chicago is October 12, 1923.[5] The bulk of the firms that owned Mail-o-Meter affixing machines were located in Chicago, and it is probable that nearby Milwaukee was supplied with coils from Chicago.

A large number of mass-mailing firms used these stamps in Chicago, including the city's water department, which used the affixing machines to mail water bills. Used copies are not uncommon. Copies on cover are not common, but are much more plentiful than the 1¢ variety.

As with the 1¢ stamp, guideline and paste-up pairs can be found. Precancels are not known. An unused strip of five is shown in Figure 56.

After 1925, when the spacing of the vertical margins between the stamp was widened, two spacing varieties could be found. These will be covered under the Star Plates in Chapter 23.

Figure 56. A strip of five stamps with Schermack Type III perforations. The affixing machines used these holes to advance the stamps. A knife in the machine separated the stamps.

Notes

1. Philip H. Ward Jr., "Chronicle of New Issues and Varieties," *Mekeel's Weekly Stamp News*, April 7, 1923, p. 192.

2. Johl, Vol. III, p. 29.

3. George P. Howard, *The Stamp Machines and Coiled Stamps* (New York: H.L. Lindquist Publications, 1943), p. 25.

4. See James G. Baird, "Schermack Perforation Types: History and Postal History," *Collectors Club Philatelist*, Vol. 71, No. 1 (January-February 1992), p. 50.

5. *Ibid.*, p. 51.

United States Stamps 1922-26

Chapter 10

Flat-Plate Booklets

Stamps in booklets were first produced by the Bureau of Engraving and Printing in 1900, and the format did not change much by the time the Series of 1922 was introduced. In the new series, only the 1¢ and 2¢ stamps were issued in booklet format from the flat-plate press. Booklets consisted of panes of six stamps bound with staples between cardboard covers. Depending on denomination, booklets could contain two, four, eight or 16 panes, and always sold for 1¢ above face value. Glassine or waxed paper interleaves were placed between the panes to keep them from sticking to one another.

Booklet covers, and the wording on the back and the inside of the covers, varied from time to time. These are described more fully in *The BIA Check List of the Postage Stamp Booklet Covers of the United States*, published by the Bureau Issues Association in 1955, and updated in 1975.

Combination Booklets

Booklet 57

In addition to booklets containing all 1¢ and all 2¢ stamps, combination booklets of four 1¢ panes and four 2¢ panes were produced. These sold for 73¢. The 2¢ stamp of the new design was issued in booklet form about six months before the 1¢ because there were existing stocks of the 1¢ Washington-Franklin stamp in booklet form. The first combination booklets contained four panes of the 1¢ stamp of the Washington-Franklin series (Scott 498e) and four panes of the 2¢ stamp of the new series (554c). Scott calls this BK57.

After the stock of 1¢ Washington-Franklin panes was exhausted, these booklets were issued with 1¢ stamps of the new design (552a) and 2¢ stamps of the new design (554c). Scott calls this BK68.

A tabular listing of these booklets follows.

Scott Booklet	Scott Stamp #	Panes	Value	Cover Design	Cover Stock	Cover Ink	Price
BK57	498e	4	24¢	PO building	white	red	73¢
	554c	4	48¢				
BK68	552a	4	24¢	PO building	white	red	73¢
	554c	4	48¢				

1¢ Booklets

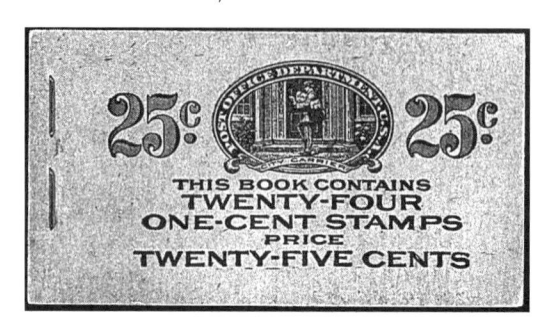

Booklet 66

Booklets containing only 1¢ stamps were not in great demand. They were issued later than the booklets containing only 2¢ stamps. Only two sizes were issued, and the 97¢ booklet is somewhat scarce.

Scott Booklet	Scott Stamp #	Panes	Face Value	Cover Design	Cover Stock	Cover Ink	Price
BK66	552a	4	24¢	Carrier	green	green	25¢
BK67	552a	16	96¢	PO building	lavender	green	97¢

2¢ Booklets

Booklet 71

Booklets containing only 2¢ stamps were issued in three sizes. Although these booklets were issued in large numbers, they were in use for a relatively short period.

Flat-Plate Booklets

Scott Booklet	Scott Stamp #	Panes	Face Value	Cover Design	Cover Stock	Cover Ink	Price
BK69	554c	2	24¢	Post Rider	buff	red	25¢
BK70	554c	4	48¢	Post Rider	pink	red	49¢
BK71	554c	8	96¢	Steamship	blue	red	97¢

Booklet pane positions. Flat-plate booklet stamps of this series were printed only from plates of 360 subjects, cut into booklet panes of six stamps. The plates had guidelines similar to 400-subject plates, but had only two plate numbers: one at the top and one at the bottom. The plate number at the bottom was trimmed off and does not ordinarily appear on booklet panes.

When the panes were cut from these sheets, 12 different positions could be determined by the plate number and guidelines (or lack thereof) that showed on the pane. These can best be understood by looking at Figure 57, but can be described as follows:

Position	Description	Occurrences in 60 Pane Plate
A	No guidelines or plate number.	31
B	Partial arrow at top and guideline at right.	1
C	Partial arrow at top and guideline at left.	1
D	Plate number in top selvage.	1
H	Guideline	3
I	Guideline	3
J	Guideline at bottom.	8
K	Guideline at bottom and right.	1
L	Guideline at bottom and left.	1
M	Guideline at top.	8
N	Guideline at top and right.	1
O	Guideline at top and left.	1

Position A is the most common pane, making up more than half of all panes produced. While it seems that positions N and O should be found as frequently as the plate number pane, position D, they are not. Guidelines were often trimmed off and were often not noticed by collectors at the top, where the booklets were bound together. Positions N and O are in fact found less frequently than any other positions. Plate number panes were saved more frequently, and are thus not as uncommon as some of the other positions.

Booklet construction. There was quite a bit of hand work involved in booklet construction. The proper number of sheets of 360, covers and interleaving paper were stacked like sandwiches, then stapled, then cut. Thus, each booklet ordinarily showed panes from the same position. A booklet of eight panes that showed a plate number on any one pane would ordinarily show plate numbers on the other seven panes as well. Some booklets are known contain-

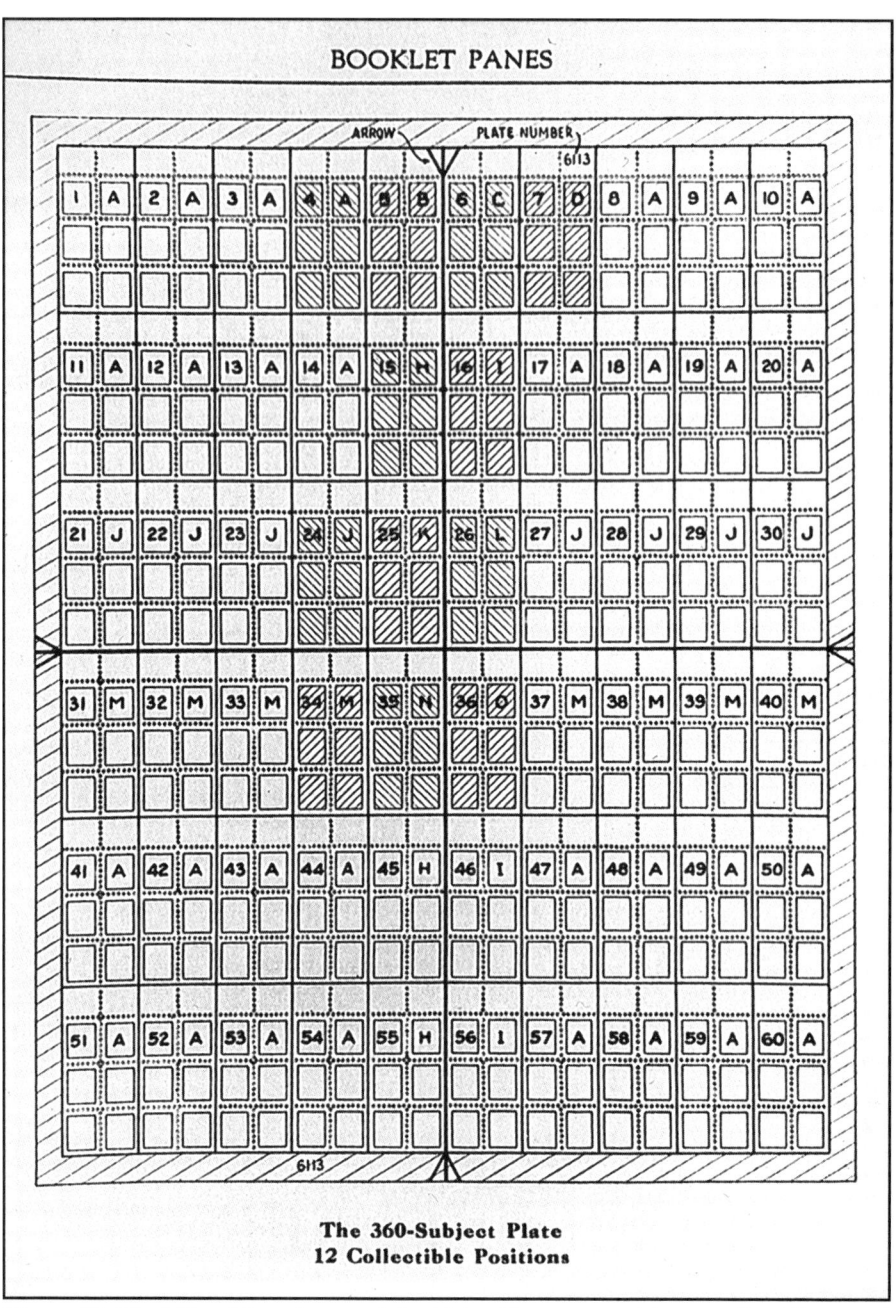

Figure 57. The 360-subject sheet and the 12 booklet pane positions, as first illustrated in the 1937 Scott Specialized. *Courtesy Amos Press.*

ing the wrong number of panes, but these are quite uncommon. Over the life of these booklets, some differences can be found in the interleaving paper used.

Panes. These panes of six stamps have selvage only at the top, with straight edges at the bottom and at the outside edges at the left and right. The stamp positions on the pane can be described as stamps 1 through 6, with stamp 1 at the upper left and stamp 6 at the lower right.

Paper grain. Flat-plate booklet stamps were ordinarily printed on paper with the grain running horizontally. This differs from the direction of the grain of the paper used for sheet stamps, which ordinarily ran vertically. Booklet-pane stamps can thus be told from flat-plate stamps with straight edges as the booklet stamps are wider, due to the shrinkage in the horizontal direction of the paper used for sheet stamps. Booklet stamps are also slightly shorter than sheet stamps for a similar reason.

1¢ Booklet Pane

Scott number:	552a
Earliest Documented Use:	January 10, 1924
Perforation:	11
Scott Color:	Deep green
Press:	Flat-plate press
Plate Layout:	Plates of 360, cut into panes of 6
Quantity Issued:	327,708,000
Plate Numbers:	Total of 20: lowest, 14221; highest, 15968
Scott Varieties:	None

Philatelic Aspects and Varieties

First day of issue. There was no announcement of the issue of this stamp, and no first-day covers appear to have been serviced. Johl gives an issue date of August 11, 1923, which Scott has also adopted, but this cannot be true. The first plate did not go to press until August 13, and the first delivery to the Post Office Department was not until October 27, after the second set of plates went to press. The earliest documented use is January 10, 1924.[1]

Shades. Scott lists only deep green, and to this Johl added only green. There is not a wide range of shades in this stamp.

Plate varieties. Scott lists none. There is one well-described double transfer, which occurs on a position 1 stamp. This shows doubling in several areas, including the bottom frameline.[2]

2¢ Booklet Pane

Scott number:	554c
Earliest Documented Usage	April 6, 1923
Perforation:	11
Scott Color:	Carmine
Press:	Flat-plate press
Plate Layout:	Plates of 360, cut into panes of 6
Quantity Issued:	2,672,028,000
Plate Numbers:	Total of 194: lowest, 14181; highest, 18521
Scott Varieties:	None

Philatelic Aspects and Varieties

First day of issue. This pane was issued about six months earlier than the 1¢ pane, but it, too, was released with no official announcement. Johl gives an issue date of February 10, 1923, which is plausible, as the delivery date to the Post Office Department was January 30. No first-day covers are known. A purported cover dated February 10 was used as a first day in establishing the issue date, but this cover has been found to be a fake.[3] Philip Ward reported in the February 24 edition of *Mekeel's* that "new booklets of the 2¢ Washington are being placed on sale," but he gave no issue date. Ward also noted in this column that "the first combination booklets will have the old 1¢ Franklin and the new 2¢ Washington."[4]

William J. Hart, a specialist in early use covers, gives April 6, 1923, as the earliest-known use of this booklet-pane stamp.[5]

Shades. Scott lists only carmine for this stamp. To this Johl adds only deep carmine. With well over two billion copies of this stamp printed, we might expect a wider variety of shade, but these booklet stamps do seem to be rather constant in terms of shade.

Plate varieties. Scott lists none and Johl lists none. However, French reported and illustrated a "recently discovered and not previously described" twisted double transfer in 1975.[6] This is the most important of the 11 plate varieties he includes in his encyclopedia.

Notes

1. Richard A. Larkin, "Earliest Known Use," *United States Specialist*, Vol. 58, No. 2 (February 1987), p. 61.

2. Fred A. Neill, "Booklet Plate Varieties," *Bureau Specialist*, Vol. 12, No. 8 (August 1941), p. 100.

3. See Jack V. Harvey, *First Day Covers of the Regular Postage Issue of 1922-1935*, Second Edition (American First Day Cover Society, 1985), p. xii.

4. Philip H. Ward Jr., "Chronicle of New Issues and Varieties," *Mekeel's Weekly Stamp News*, Vol. 37, No. 8 (February 24, 1923).

5. William J. Hart, letter to the author, April 17, 1989.

6. Cloudy French, "Plate Varieties," *United States Specialist*, Vol. 46, No. 9 (September 1975), p. 445.

United States Stamps 1922-26

Chapter 11

A New Sheet Rotary

Understanding the chronology of the first sheet rotary of the new design, the stamp we know as Scott 581, is important for a thorough understanding of this new series, for it marks the beginning of Bureau precanceled stamps and was issued relatively early in the life of the series. Despite its high catalog number, this stamp went to press before several of the flat-plate designs.

The Bureau began printing sheet stamps by the rotary process in 1920, with the 1¢ Washington-Franklin stamp we know as 542 (see Chapter 6). The perforations were changed to perf 10 in 1921 and made the Washington-Franklin stamp we know as 543. That stamp remained on the press all through 1922 and well into 1923. In fact, it remained at press even after plates of the new design were issued. The last two plates used to print the Washington-Franklin stamp 543 were not removed from the presses until September 17, 1923.

The first rotary-press plates of the new Series of 1922 design were certified in December 1922 but did not go to press until April 2, 1923.

The Bureau's plate records clearly show that both Washington-Franklin 1¢ stamps and 1922 1¢ stamps were on the presses at the same time during a six-month period of 1923.

Bureau Precancels

As discussed in Chapter 6, local postmasters found the rotary-printed 1¢ Washington-Franklin stamps to be objectionable, mainly because they curled after printing and were thus difficult to precancel at local printing companies.

The Bureau and Post Office Department had considered several times the possibility of precanceling stamps at the Bureau. In 1916 flat-plate stamps were overprinted for three cities at the Bureau, but the process was found to be too costly. Another experiment was conducted in which a bold precancel was engraved into the orginal die, but this scheme, too, proved impractical.

By early 1923, however, the development of the rotary press for sheet stamp use offered an opportunity to produce precancels in an efficient manner. The Bureau's idea to precancel stamps on the new large rotary presses was a clever solution to two problems: (1) that rotary sheet stamps were hard to precancel locally and (2) that postmasters were clamoring for stamps with precancels already applied.

The Bureau experimented with an attachment to the large rotary press that would precancel rotary stamps as they were printed. The final arrangement used two sets of small raised-type plates of 50 subjects (10 x 5), which applied a fast-drying black ink to the intaglio-printed stamps. The Stickney press thus became a two-color and two-process press. The green ink was applied using engraved plates, while the black ink was applied using letterpress plates.

Johl gives the date of issue for the first precancels on Scott 581 as April 21, 1923. Gilbert Noble gives the date as May 2.[1] Bureau records indicate the first delivery was made to New York on May 3.

But something is wrong here. This author has located the letter authorizing the Bureau to make plates "for precanceling postage stamps on the rotary presses" for four cities, New York, Chicago, Cleveland and Kansas City. It is dated May 31.[2] None of the other cities had deliveries before June 6. A letter specifying the delivery dates gives the New York delivery as "May 3rd-June 8th."[3] My guess is that this was a bad transcription of the actual record, which was probably June 3 to June 8.

At any rate, Bureau precancels, as we know them now, quickly became a success. Not only did they eliminate the need for local precanceling, but the costs were lower. By August, St. Louis, Philadelphia and Cincinnati were added to the list of cities authorized to receive Bureau precancels, and orders were pending for 11 more cities. By June 1927, when this stamp was replaced by Scott 632, some 64 cities had been provided with 1¢ stamps precanceled at the Bureau of Engraving and Printing.

1¢ Sheet Rotary

Scott number:	581
Earliest Reported Use:	May 18, 1923
Perforation:	10
Scott Colors:	Green, yellow green, pale green
Press:	Large rotary press
Plate Layout:	Sheets of 400, cut into four panes
Quantity Issued:	Unknown
Plate Numbers:	Total of 56: lowest, 14205; highest, 18732
Scott Varieties:	None

A New Sheet Rotary

Philatelic Aspects and Varieties

Earliest usage. This is another stamp that has some mystery and intrigue related to its date of issue and earliest-known covers. Since precanceled stamps did not go through the normal canceling process, they would not ordinarily have received any datestamping.

If we accept the fact that the precanceling plates were not ordered until May 31, and that the first plates went to press on April 2, we must assume that the stamps printed between these dates did not have precancels. This assumption is born out by the recent discovery by George Wagner of Chicago of a copy of 581 canceled on May 18 in Wilmington, California.

Some rotary-press sheets must have been sent to post offices in unprecanceled condition.

Johl wrote that the stamps were first placed on sale at the Philatelic Stamp Agency on October 17, 1923. There was no official announcement of this date. Philip Ward reported the same October 17 date in his *Mekeel's* column of November 5, 1923, noting that he had appealed to Glover to issue the stamp in unprecanceled form.[4] A first-day cover showing this October 17 date was illustrated by Jack Harvey but has been found to be a fake. Harvey reports in a later edition that a genuine October 17 use is known.[5] Such a cover surfaced in the auction of the Lawrence S. Fisher collection in May 1996. It was not a serviced cover, but a personal postcard mailed from Washington, D.C.

Plate layout. Like flat-plate plates, the rotary-press plates were laid out with 400 subjects. But gutters measuring 5/16 of an inch separated the four panes, and the plate numbers were placed only at the four corners of the plates. This arrangement changed the collecting of plate blocks from blocks of six stamps to blocks of four (see Figure 58). The

Figure 58. With the rotary press, only four numbers were placed on each plate, in the corners. This changed the format of the plate number block to four stamps instead of six on the normal flat-plate press plate block.

early plates had a series of horizontal dashes in the center gutter to aid in perforation registration. These are referred to as Type A marginal markings. On the later plates these horizontal dashes were replaced by a short center cross and short vertical and horizontal markings like the "arrows" of the flat plates. These are referred to as Type B marginal markings.

153

Perforation and division. Like rotary-press coils, these stamps were printed on a continuous web of paper. At the end of the printing and gumming process, the web was wound in a roll and removed. These rolls were then taken to so-called "two-way perforators," which applied the vertical and horizontal perforations in a single operation. The vertical perforations were applied by perforating wheels similar to the rotary perforators used for flat-plate stamps, while the horizontal perforations were applied by bars of pins that also rotated.

This two-way perforator also cut the web into sheets of 400 using a wavy-edged cutting knife. The sheets of 400 were stacked in units of 100 sheets, with a piece of cardboard at the top or bottom and stapled once on each of the four sides. Then they were cut with a guillotine-style paper cutter into quarters. The cuts fell in the gutters of the printed sheets and created four decks of 100 panes of 100 stamps.

Shades. When first listed in the 1924 edition of the Scott *Specialized*, this stamp was listed as deep green, as was the flat-plate stamp. But the first printings of the stamp were not as deep a green as the flat-plate stamp. In the 1925 edition, this difference was noted, and the stamp was listed as just green. Scott added the pale green shade in 1927. In the 1938 edition, yellow green became 581a, and Scott maintained that listing until 1978.

Johl found a much wider range of shades, and added grayish green, dark grayish green, dull bluish green, bluish green, bright yellowish green and deep yellowish green.

Double paper. Where two webs of paper were spliced together, a double layer of paper resulted. Although most of the stamps printed on this double paper were "supposed to be caught and destroyed" at the Bureau, according to Ward, some examples were found and reported in early 1927.[6] Scott added a double-paper listing in the 1928 edition of the Scott *Specialized*. In 1932, the double-paper listing became 581a and was changed to 581b in 1938, when the yellow-green shade (see above) was listed as 581a. In the 1945 edition, Scott dropped all rotary-press double-paper listings with the explanation that "double paper varieties were first listed because of their novelty and scarcity," but were being discontinued "as all Rotary Press stamps may exist on double paper." The explanation also noted that "interest has lessened due to increasing finds."

Notes

1. Gilbert W. Noble, editor, *The Noble Official Catalog of Bureau Precancels*, 58th Edition (Privately published, 1976), p. 16.

2. W. Irving Glover to Andrew Mellon, May 31, 1923. Historical Resource Center, Bureau of Engraving and Printing.

3. W. Irving Glover to John H. Bartlett, August 20, 1923. Historical Resource

Center, Bureau of Engraving and Printing.

4. Philip H. Ward Jr., "Chronicle of New Issues and Varieties," *Mekeel's Weekly Stamp News*, Vol. 37, No. 44 (November 5, 1923), p. 566.

5. Jack V. Harvey, *First Day Covers of the Regular Postage Issue of 1922-1935*, Second Edition (American First Day Cover Society, 1985), p. viii.

6. John N. Luff, "Notes of the Month," *Scott's Monthly Journal*, Vol. 7, No. 11 (January 1927), p. 305.

United States Stamps 1922-26

Chapter 12

The Death of Harding and Accession of Coolidge

The Harding Administration came to an abrupt halt on August 2, 1923, when the president died unexpectedly in San Francisco, after falling ill during a trip across the country.

Harding had left Washington, D.C., six weeks earlier by train, spoke in St. Louis in favor of joining the World Court, toured Yellowstone Park, boarded a steamship on July 4 at Tacoma, Washington, for a sightseeing side trip to the Territory of Alaska, where no previous American president had set foot. He fell ill in Seattle during his return. The initial explanation, by White House physician Charles Sawyer, a family friend of the Hardings, was that he had eaten some bad crabmeat.

With Harding on the trip was a large entourage that included Hubert Work, the former postmaster general who was now secretary of the interior. Work, a physician by profession, consulted with the other doctor on the trip, Harding's medical and naval aide Lieutenant Commander Joel T. Boone. Work and Boone agreed that Harding was suffering from something more than tainted seafood and arranged to have two heart specialists meet the president's train in San Francisco.

Five days later, Warren Harding died in bed in the Palace Hotel.

Calvin Coolidge, his vice president, was vacationing at his father's home in Plymouth, Vermont, and was sworn in as president by lamplight in the middle of the night. Coolidge pledged that he would carry out Harding's policies, and asked his Cabinet to stay on (see Figure 59).

Figure 59. With the sudden death of Warren Harding, Vice President Calvin Coolidge assumed the presidency. Coolidge is shown here wearing a mourning band on his left arm shortly after Harding's death. He made few changes in the Cabinet, and none in the Post Office Department.

Coolidge was a native New Englander who both looked and acted the part. A graduate of Amherst College, Coolidge entered law practice in Massachusetts, became the mayor of Northampton and worked his way up through a succession of offices, reaching the governorship in the 1918 election. In 1919, he gained national prominence for breaking the Boston police strike by calling up the state militia. New England Republicans were talking him up as a presidential candidate in 1920, but without much support elsewhere. Yet when his name was placed in nomination at the Chicago convention, "it struck off an unexpected spark ... and in a sudden blaze of enthusiasm,"[1] Coolidge became Harding's running mate.

After Harding's death, many of the shady dealings of Attorney General Daugherty, former Secretary of the Interior Fall and other officials came to light, but Coolidge managed to control the political damage by appointing untainted special prosecutors from both parties. Coolidge, the reserved and efficient Yankee, believed in saying little and working long and hard. The economy was fortunately on an upswing, and the American people did not believe they needed a change. Coolidge ran for election in his own right in 1924, and outpolled his Democratic rival, John W. Davis, nearly two-to-one in the popular vote. As one historian put it, "Coolidge, through his stern austere conception of the presidency, rehabilitated the Republican Party in an amazingly short time."[2]

For the Post Office Department, the change in presidents brought about little change in personnel or policy. Harry S. New remained as postmaster general, and W. Irving Glover remained as third assistant. Coolidge did not tamper with the Department or its politics. In terms of personnel and direction, the Harding postal administration simply remained in operation during the Coolidge presidency.

Notes

1. Francis Russell, *The Shadow of Blooming Grove* (New York: McGraw-Hill Book Company, 1968), p. 396.

2. Eugene P. Trani and David L. Wilson, *The Presidency of Warren G. Harding* (University of Kansas Press, 1977), p. 186.

Chapter 13

Night Flying and the Transcontinental Airmails

One of the priorities of the Harding postal administration had been the revival of airmail and the establishment of a transcontinental route that would enable planes to carry mail efficiently and safely from one part of the country to another. From the beginning of the administration, airmail was a priority, but planning was interrupted by the untimely death of Second Assistant Postmaster General Edward H. Shaughnessy in early 1922 (see Chapter 1).

Succeeding Shaughnessy was Paul Henderson, who like Shaughnessy, was a former Army officer. But Henderson was essentially a businessman, and a well-connected one at that, having married the daughter of powerful Chicago Congressman Martin Madden. Henderson took over the crucial position at a critical time and built a lighted airway that allowed pilots to fly safely at night.

Night-flying experiments had been conducted under the Wilson administration, most notably at its very end, in a February 1920 cross-country test when pilot Jack Knight risked his life to fly several legs of a dark route.[1] Under Henderson, however, a practical night airway was constructed in a professional and businesslike fashion.

Lighting the way was an enormous logistical and technical feat, particularly in an era when much of rural America had not yet been wired for electricity. All of the major or "terminal" airfields on the Transcontinental Route from New York to San Francisco were already constructed by this time, but mail was only flown between them during daylight hours. It was then transferred to the Railway Mail Service, which advanced it during the night by train.

Lighting the entire cross-country route was not practical. The mountainous sections of the west, and even the Alleghenies of the east, were considered unsafe for night flying, and dangerous enough during the day, particularly when an emergency landing was necessary. But the flat midwest, roughly a third of the route, was considered suitable. Not only were there no significant mountains to contend with, but its location in the center of the country meant that mail could depart from San Francisco or New York in the morning, travel through the middle of the country at night, and then continue toward either coast during daylight again. Figure 60 shows the route.

The 885-mile section between Chicago and Cheyenne, Wyoming, was chosen to be the lighted section. The major airfields in between were North Platte and Omaha, Nebraska, and Iowa City, Iowa. With Chicago and Chey-

159

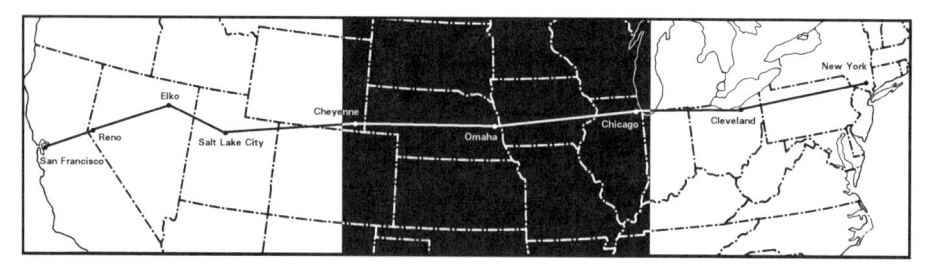

Figure 60. Roughly a third of the Transcontinental Route, from Cheyenne to Chicago, was relatively flat, and it was this section that was initially lighted for night flying. This is the dark area on the map. Planes traveled by day over the Rockies in the west and the Alleghenies in the east.

enne, each of these five "terminal" fields were equipped with a 53-foot high tower topped with a revolving, 450-million-candlepower beacon that could be seen, under ideal conditions, from a hundred miles away. Searchlights illuminated the landing fields, and spotlights were fixed on hangars and other buildings and obstacles. Figure 61 shows a hangar with its lighting devices.

Figure 61. Hangars and other buildings on the illuminated airway were also lit so they could be seen by pilots. A De Havilland DH-4, the standard plane of the Air Mail Service, is in the foreground.

Along the route, at intervals of approximately 25 miles, were 34 additional emergency landing fields. These had smaller beacons and spotlights. Between the emergency fields the way was marked with another 250 beacons, spaced approximately three miles apart, on six-foot pylons. Where electricity was not available, acetylene gas or battery-powered lights were used.

Henderson had hired an outside engineer, Joseph V. Magee of Cincinnati, to work with the Air Mail Service on the details, and Magee in turn contracted with General Electric, Sperry Gyroscope and the American Gas Accumulator Company for the beacons and lighting.[2]

By February 1923, a test field was established in North Platte, and after successful trials there, Henderson ordered the entire 855-mile stretch to be illuminated. Postmaster General Harry S. New, who had taken over in March, was also an advocate of the night-flying plan and predicted it would involve "scarcely more hazard than day flying."[3]

Money, however, was a problem. While many in Congress believed airmail was only something of a novelty, one of its chief foes was a member of the president's own administration, budget director Herbert Lord, who submitted the Harding budget to Congress. He cut the airmail service funds before Congress had the chance. Where Henderson had wanted $2,500,000 in the fiscal year that began on July 1, 1923, Lord cut the amount to $1,500,000. Even as the Post Office Department began constructing its lighted airway, it seemed apparent that the money would not be there to actually fly the route that year, at least not for the entire 12 months. When New wrote his annual report at the end of July, he noted that the work of constructing the transcontinental route was practically finished and that "a service over this route ... will be the first attempt made in the world to operate aircraft at night on a regular schedule."[4]

When that schedule was to begin was anyone's guess, but New ordered stamps for the new route that July, with the hope that the service might begin as early as September. A series of cross-country tests were to be conducted in August, and the stamps would at least serve as something of a publicity device.

The De Havilland DH-4

Just as the airfields had to be modified for night flying, so did the aircraft. The De Havilland DH-4 had become the standard mail plane of the Air Mail Service during the Harding administration, and would become, somewhat by default, the plane to fly the new lighted route. Shaughnessy, who began to reorganize the Air Mail Service in 1921, eliminated all other planes. As Karl Weber has pointed out, "This did not mean that the DH-4 was the most suitable plane available, but ... it was considered good business to standardize on it because the Army had a large surplus which was transferred to the Air Mail Service as needed without any expense to the Post Office Department."[5]

Designed in England in 1916 as a bomber, thousands of DH-4s had been mass-produced in the United States under license for the Army Air Corps. Since 1919, when the first DH-4s had first been used by the Air Mail Service, the design of the plane was modified several times by the Post Office Department to make it sturdier, safer and more suitable to the purpose. Originally dubbed a "flying coffin," by early 1923 the DH-4 had compiled a good safety and service record, and had become popular with pilots. The Air Mail Service had 79 of the planes and a large stock of spare engines, but the plane was not up-to-date when Henderson began lighting airways, and he put out bids for a replacement aircraft.

Chief among his specifications was that a new plane land more slowly than the 60-mile-an-hour speed the DH-4 required. Three manufacturers were awarded contracts for experimental aircraft, but it became apparent that none would be available in time for the August trials. Therefore, 10 DH-4s were altered with a new wing design that reduced the landing speed, and these planes were also rigged with an array of special night-flying equipment. This included powerful, automobile-type headlights mounted on both wings, emergency flares that could be dropped on parachutes, navigational lights like those on ships at sea and an illuminated instrument panel.

The Rates and Stamps

The rate structure for the new night-and-day airmail was to be similar to that of the parcel post system established in 1913; that is, the rate would be determined in part by the distance traveled.

Under the legislation passed in 1918 for the first airmail service between Washington and New York, the postmaster general was authorized "in his discretion, to require the payment of postage on mail carried by airplane at not exceeding 24 cents per ounce or fraction thereof."[6]

Thus, 24¢ became the maximum rate the Post Office Department could charge without going to Congress for new legislation that would no doubt be troublesome, as the route would fly through 12 different states and a large number of congressional districts.

The same three divisions the Post Office Department used for day-and-night flying would become the zones for the rates. San Francisco to Cheyenne was one zone. Cheyenne to Chicago was another. And Chicago to New York was the third. The rate for each zone would be 8¢.

In July a set of three stamps was ordered in denominations of 8¢, 16¢ and 24¢. Test flights were scheduled for August, and there was hope that a limited schedule might be flown as early as September. The first stamp, the 8¢ value, was scheduled for release at the convention of the American Philatelic Society in Washington, D.C., on August 15.

The stamp designs were not approved until July 23, and the Bureau found itself in a race to meet the deadline, just as it had with several values of the regular series that had just been completed.

President Harding's death on August 2, and the news relating to the transportation of his body across the country from San Francisco — a four-day trip — suppressed much of the news relating to the new stamps and to all other national news for that matter. Harding's body was placed in state in the rotunda of the Capitol on August 8, and he was buried in Marion, Ohio, on August 10.

That the Post Office Department had new airmail stamps in the works was a well-kept secret and was first reported by Philip Ward in *Mekeel's* issue of August 11. "A piece of news that will come as a great surprise," he wrote, "is the fact that the Post Office Department is about to issue a new series of airplane stamps consisting of three denominations, each in a different design."[7]

Only the 8¢ stamp was ready for the convention, and was placed on sale at the convention and at the Philatelic Stamp Agency on August 15. Figure 62 shows a first-day cover with the corner card of the Shoreham Hotel, where

Night Flying and the Transcontinental Airmails

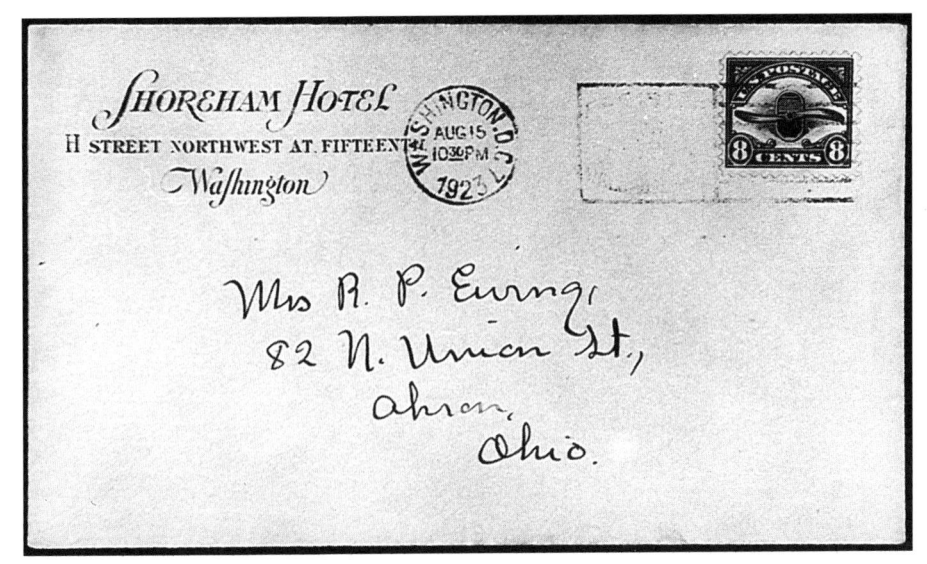

Figure 62. Although few first-day covers of Scott C4 were serviced, some have the corner card of the Shoreham Hotel in Washington, D.C., where the American Philatelic Society was meeting. The stamp was first put on sale at the hotel.

the American Philatelic Society held its convention. The 16¢ stamp was placed on sale at the agency on August 17, and the 24¢ stamp was placed on sale at the agency on August 21, the same day that the first of the three sets of demonstration flights was to take place. The stamps were also distributed to 16 post offices along the route on August 24, but word quickly went out to the postmasters not to place the stamps on sale until further notification.

Although some airmail collectors prepared covers for the test flights, ordinary mail made up most of the cargo. There was no separate airmail rate in effect. The 1918 rates had been suspended on July 18, 1919, and although much mail had been flown from point to point, there was no guarantee of air service. All first-class mail traveled at the standard rates. For letters, this remained at 2¢ per ounce or fraction thereof.

Test Flights and a New Route

Four days of air trials began on August 21, with flights leaving both New York and San Francisco. Henderson went to Omaha to view the night part of the operations in action. The westbound flight left New York at 11:01 a.m., the rather late time being set to avoid early morning fog. After scheduled stops in Bellefonte, Pennsylvania, and Cleveland, the mail reached Chicago at 4:14 p.m. The Chicago-to-Omaha leg was also on time, landing at 11:02 p.m. Jack Knight, the hero of the 1921 flight, flew the next leg from Omaha, stopping at North Platte and arriving at Cheyenne at 2:50 a.m. on August 22. Bad weather delayed the leg from Cheyenne to Rock Springs, Wyoming, but the mail reached San Francisco at 6:24 p.m., having been carried by air the entire way.

The eastbound flight was hampered by fog near Rock Springs, and the schedule was broken. Eastbound mail leaving Cheyenne, however, made it to New York entirely by air. The second and third series of flights on August 22 and 23 were all completed on schedule, and all under 30 hours. The fastest was 26 hours and 14 minutes, a new transcontinental record. The Railway Mail Service took 90 hours to complete the same trip.

Postmaster General New termed the test flights "100 per cent perfect" and the aviation world hailed the accomplishment with such terms as "an epoch-making performance." But the year's budget was already established, and there were not sufficient funds for actually flying the route. It remained a battle with the budget office and Congress to get the necessary money, but Henderson, with the help of Postmaster General New, a former senator, finally got Congress to appropriate $2,750,000 for the fiscal year beginning July 1, 1924.

Philip Ward reported that the night-flying airmail service would "formally begin early in September,"[7] but this was not the case. There was no money, and it was not until the following May that the Post Office Department announced that "a daily, regular, and permanent" schedule would be flown between New York and San Francisco. Postmasters were instructed not to put the airmail stamps on sale until June 16.

By the time the new service began on July 1, 1924, the first day of the new fiscal year, the lighted airway had been extended in both directions. Now it ran almost 1,600 miles, from Cleveland in the east to Rock Springs in the west. This gave an extra measure of safety to delayed flights. By all apparent statistics, the new service was a success, and New, in his next annual report, cited a flurry of them. In its first year of operation, the new night-flying Air Mail Service had carried nine million letters. It had flown a total of 2,501,555 miles, 696,126 of them at night. Only two pilots had been killed in crashes, and the average miles flown per crash was 208,463, a new record for safety.

Behind the scenes, however, New and Henderson were disappointed. Volume was only about half of what they expected it to be. Costs, too, remained high. While airmail rates were at least four times that of surface mail, the costs were more than 10 times as great. One of the problems, Henderson said, was simply getting businesses and individuals to change their habits. Another was the cost, which he felt could be brought down by better equipment, specifically a plane that was faster and carried more weight than — ironically — the plane currently depicted on the postage stamps.

8¢ Propeller and Radiator

Scott:	C4
First Day of Issue:	August 15, 1923
Perforation:	11
Scott Colors:	Dark green, deep green
Designer:	Clair Aubrey Huston
Engravers:	H.P. Dawson (vignette)
	E.M. Weeks (frame and lettering)
Plate Layout:	Flat plate; plates of 400 cut into panes of 100
Quantity Issued:	6,414,576
Plate Numbers:	14824, 14825, 14826, 14827
Scott Varieties:	Double transfer

The Subject and Design

In the official description, this stamp shows "a mail airplane radiator with propeller attached," but it is clearly the front of the De Havilland DH-4, or more correctly the radiator of the Liberty engine and the DH-4 propeller. The Liberty, developed by the Aircraft Production Board during the war, had 12 cylinders and delivered 400 horsepower. It replaced the sluggish 275-horsepower Rolls-Royce engines in the original British-built De Havillands.

Bureau records indicate that the model was prepared from a "photograph of propeller of airplane submitted by the Post Office." For Bureau designer Clair Huston, this must have been an appealing photo, for he adopted symmetrical designs in all of his stamp frames, and this was a symmetrical vignette.

Each of the three stamps in this series has a slightly different frame design, but in Huston's neoclassical style, the three are integrally related. The words "air mail" do not appear on this stamp, and although intended for use in the night-flying airmail service, they were valid on any type of mail.

Philatelic Aspects and Varieties

First day of issue. Only one plate, 14824, went to press before the August 15, 1923, first day of sale, and all first-day covers must be from this plate. Even though these stamps were put on sale at the convention of the American Philatelic Society in Washington, D.C., a relatively small number of first-day covers exist. First-flight covers, postmarked July 1, 1924, are somewhat common.

Stamps not distinctive. Not long after the stamp had been issued, a number of complaints were received that mail franked with this stamp was not receiving airmail service and was being confused with regular mail, due to the green color, which was the same as the 1¢ stamp. This led to a campaign by the Post Office Department to have airmail envelopes clearly marked "Air Mail." To aid in this marking, rubber stamps with the Air Mail Service insignia, similar to the design of the 16¢ stamp, were delivered to postmasters along the route.

By August 18, Third Assistant Postmaster General Glover was defensively writing that "this procedure has already been inaugurated at some of the larger offices with splendid results." However, he admitted that "even at this moment I am turning over in my mind the thought that a special sticker, which could be adopted by the Department for use on the face of such envelopes, might be used to great advantage in this respect."

In effect, Glover was admitting that the new stamps were failing their purpose. This would be the last issue of airmail stamps under his administration that were the same size and shape as regular postage stamps.

Shades. To the Post Office Department, this stamp was just plain green. Scott originally cataloged this stamp as dark green in the 1924 edition of the *Specialized Catalogue*, and added deep green in the 1926 edition.

Double transfer. This listing went into the *Specialized Catalogue* in the 1936 edition, but the basis for it is vague. French lists only a single plate variety, a plate scratch below the bottom frameline of 14824 UR 1.

16¢ Air Service Emblem

Scott: C5
First Day of Issue: August 17, 1923
Perforation: 11
Scott Color: Dark blue
Designer: Clair Aubrey Huston

Engravers:	H.P. Dawson (vignette)
	E.M. Hall (frame and lettering)
Plate Layout:	Flat plate; plates of 400 cut into panes of 100
Quantity Issued:	5,309,276
Plate Numbers:	14828, 14829, 14830, 14831
Scott Varieties:	Double transfer

The Subject and Design

The vignette of this stamp, in the Post Office Department's description, is "the official insignia of the air-mail service." This insignia is based on the "wings" pin awarded to pilots of the Air Mail Service, which had the lettering "Pilot" at the top and "Aerial Mail" at the bottom. This pin also served as the basis for a similar handstamp distributed to postmasters at airmail fields, which had the words "Via" at the top and "Air Mail" at the bottom.

In the Bureau records, the source of the design is listed as a "sketch of official insignia of Air Mail Service by C.A. Huston." Huston evidently altered the insignia by enlarging the lettering, with the word "Air" at the top and "Mail" at the bottom. This is the only one of the three stamps in this series to use the words "Air Mail," and it appears in the design, rather than in the frame lettering.

Like the propeller on the 8¢ value, this is a completely symmetrical vignette, which fit in well with Huston's symmetrical frame design. This design is particularly well-balanced horizontally as well as vertically. It marks Huston's mature style as a designer.

Philatelic Aspects and Varieties

First day of issue. Like the 8¢ version, this stamp was produced in something of a hurry, but it was not completed in time for the convention of the American Philatelic Society, and was placed on sale at the Philatelic Stamp Agency in Washington, D.C., on August 17, 1923. Few covers were serviced, and the relatively high denomination helped to keep the number low.

Shades. Scott listed this stamp in the 1924 *Specialized Catalogue* as dark blue, and the listing has remained constant. Johl added to this deep blue, but this seems to be nit-picking, as all plates of this stamp went to press only once, during an eight-day period. The shade should not and does not vary much. It was at first reported by Ward that this stamp would be issued in black.

Double transfer. The dark color of this stamp helps to make plate varieties more noticeable, and a number have been reported. The listing went into the Scott *Specialized* in the 1936 edition. Johl listed six double and shifted transfers in his 1935 book, and French also lists a number of them. The most outstanding seems to be 14828 UL 16.

24¢ De Havilland Biplane

Scott:	C6
First Day of Issue:	August 21, 1923
Perforation:	11
Scott Color:	Carmine
Designer:	Clair Aubrey Huston
Engravers:	John Eissler (vignette)
	E.M. Hall (frame and lettering)
Plate Layout:	Flat plate; plates of 400 cut into panes of 100
Quantity Issued:	5,285,776
Plate Numbers:	14840, 14841, 14842, 14843
Scott Varieties:	Double transfer, plate 14841

The Subject and Design

The official description of this design is "a mail airplane in flight." The airplane is clearly a DH-4 and is based on a photograph provided by the Post Office Department. The original photograph (see Figure 63) is still in the Bureau files and shows a photograph of a DH-4 in flight, apparently taken from another airplane. Huston incorporated this plane in a drawing that added a hill and trees in the background. On the stamp it appears somewhat crowded.

Several distinguishing characteristics of the DH-4 are apparent even in the small engraving of the final stamp. The pilot sits far back in the plane, in what was originally the rear cockpit of the twin-cockpit bomber. The front cockpit was eliminated to make the cargo area for mail sacks. As engraved, the six cylinder heads on the left side of the 12-cylinder Liberty engine can also be counted. The DH-4 on the stamp was not one of the planes equipped for night-flying, however. If it were, it would show a lamp on the bottom wing.

Philatelic Aspects and Varieties

First day of issue. The die proof for this stamp was not approved until August 14, and it, too, went into production quite quickly. It was placed on sale at the Philatelic Sales Agency in Washington, D.C., on August 21, 1923. Only plate 14840 had gone to press by that time, and all first-day covers must be

Figure 63. The design of the 24¢ airmail is based on this photograph of a DH-4 in flight, taken from another airplane. It does not show the landscape scene, which was added to the finished stamp.

from that plate. As with the 16¢ denomination, few covers were serviced, in part because of the high denomination.

Shades. When first listed in the 1924 edition of the *Specialized Catalogue*, the shade was given as carmine rose. This was changed to carmine in the 1926 edition, and it has remained constant since. Johl lists deep carmine as well, but as with the 16¢ value, each plate of this stamp went to press only once, and during a period of less than two weeks. There should not be a great variation in shades. It was at first reported by Ward that this stamp would be issued in brown.

Double transfer. This listing first appeared in the 1935 edition of the *Specialized Catalogue* and was based on a 1933 report by Beverly King in *Stamps*, which included an illustration, but not a position.[10] In the second edition of the 1936 *Specialized* the notation of plate 14841 was added, but no pane or position was given, and this notation continues in the current edition. This is no doubt the double transfer illustrated by Johl in his 1935 book and is well-established as 14841 UL 6.

Notes

1. For a short but accurate account of Knight's heroic flight see Donald B. Holmes, *Air Mail: An Illustrated History, 1793-1981* (New York: Clarkson N. Potter Inc., 1981), pp. 118-22.

2. Further details of the illumination scheme can be found in William M.

Leary, *Aerial Pioneers: The U.S. Air Mail Service, 1918-1927* (Smithsonian Institution Press), 1985, pp. 171-85.

3. Quoted in Donald Dale Jackson, *Flying the Mail* (Alexandria, Virginia: Time-Life Books, 1982), p. 84.

4. Harry S. New, *Annual Report of the Postmaster General, 1923* [fiscal year ending June 30, 1923] (Washington: Government Printing Office, 1923), p. 32.

5. Karl B. Weber, in Weber and Thomas J. O'Sullivan, *History of the United States Pioneer and Government-Operated Air Mail Service, 1910-1928* (American Air Mail Society, 1973), p. 143.

6. Post Office Department, *United States Domestic Postage Rates: 1789-1956* (Washington: Government Printing Office, 1956), p. 74.

7. Philip H. Ward Jr., "Chronicle of New Issues and Varieties," *Mekeel's Weekly Stamp News*, August 11, 1923, p. 408.

8. Philip H. Ward Jr., "Chronicle of New Issues and Varieties," *Mekeel's Weekly Stamp News*, September 3, 1923, p. 444.

9. Quoted in Philip H. Ward Jr., "Chronicle of New Issues and Varieties," *Mekeel's Weekly Stamp News*, August 18, 1924, p. 440.

10. Beverly S. King, "Notes on U.S. Stamps," *Stamps,* Vol. 4, No. 5 (July 29, 1933), p. 156.

Chapter 14

The Black Hardings

The death of President Harding was a shock to the American public. He was not known to be ill, and he was the first president in more than 20 years to die in office, the last being McKinley in 1901. He had been elected by a large majority, and the scandals that would later mar his place in history were not yet known. As the historian Mark Sullivan said in 1935, "The event provided one of the rare occasions America has for national emotion."[1]

His body was placed at window level in the *Superb*, the presidential train that had carried him across the country, and now it carried him back across the full length of the country. All along the tracks people lined up, waiting for hours for the train to pass, on its slow, solemn journey back to Washington, D.C. In Stockton, California, the crowd was reported at 15,000. In Omaha, it was 40,000. In Chicago, the Illinois National Guard fired a 21-gun salute as more than 100,000 gathered.

In Washington, Harding's body was placed in state in the Rotunda of the Capitol as thousands filed by, four abreast. The *Superb* then took the casket to Harding's hometown of Marion, Ohio. Again the tracks were lined with people. Thousands more filed past the home of Harding's father, where the body lay in state for one more day before the burial service. "Harding," a more modern historian has summed up, "had died in the love he desired."[2]

Two days after Harding's death, as the president's body was still on its way across the country, the first suggestion for a Harding stamp was received at the Post Office Department from Herman Boers, a stamp and first-day cover collector from Detroit, Michigan. "No doubt many suggestions will come up now," it began, "but let me suggest ... a mourning stamp of Harding, say a one or two cent issue ... to be used for say 30 or 60 days."[3]

Although addressed to Howard Mount, the agent of the Philatelic Sales Agency, it was answered by W. Irving Glover, the third assistant postmaster general. "This is a splendid suggestion on your part," Glover

The body of President Harding leaving the White House, with a military escort, to be placed in state in the rotunda of the United States Capitol. Suggestions for a stamp had already been received.

wrote back, "and I personally would like to see some tribute of this sort adopted." But then Glover's reply reverted to the standard form letter that was used to answer most stamp suggestions: "However due to lack of appropriations for the manufacture of postage stamps it cannot be given consideration at this time."[4]

Glover had been personally close to President Harding, and it seems difficult to imagine that he actually put the idea of a stamp out of consideration. This seems only to have been a bureaucratic first reaction. Glover would backtrack later and claim that the suggestion for a Harding stamp had first come from Postmaster General New himself.

Several other suggestions for a stamp were received, including one from Brother Cassian of Cincinnati, who had suggested many of the designs that were used for the regular series that had just been issued (see Chapter 5). Brother Cassian's suggestion, received on August 11, was for a 13¢ Harding denomination to be added to the regular series. This he said would set a precedent for the series, "depicting the very President who nominated the very officials of the existing post office government."[5]

Harding's portrait would be added to this series of stamps eventually, but it was essentially Boer's suggestion that the Post Office Department followed now. On August 15, word went out that a stamp would be issued, and models for "a new Harding Memorial stamp" were ordered from the Bureau on August 16. The Post Office Department issued a press release on August 17 saying that a stamp would be issued on September 1, having been "suggested by the Postmaster General as a tribute to his Chief and friend."

Boer's suggestion that the stamp be issued for 30 or 60 days was also acted upon, only the period was extended to 90 days. "For three months," the Post Office Department release continued, "the engraving of George Washington, the first president, which has been traditionally memorialized on the two cent stamp will give way to the late President Harding."[6]

Replacing the 2¢ Washington stamp for a period of 90 days was not only an ambitious goal, but also an impossible one. The initial order for the stamp was 300 million copies. "It is probable that more will be ordered," the release said. But the number of ordinary 2¢ stamps the Post Office Department was ordering each year was more than 9 billion at this point. That would average 750 million stamps a month, or 2.25 billion for 90 days. In addition, the heavy Christmas mailing period was coming up, requiring an even greater number of stamps.

Producing enough new Harding stamps just to fill postmasters' 2¢ stamp requisitions beginning September 1 was an impossible task for the Bureau of Engraving and Printing. But emotion, not logic, was ruling the day, and the Bureau would deliver 1.56 billion copies of the stamp, in three formats, during the next four months.

The Black Hardings

The black color of the stamp, the traditional one for mourning, created two problems, neither of which concerned the Post Office Department. First, the Universal Postal Union treaty specified that letter-rate stamps were to be printed in red. The UPU was simply advised that the United States would be varying from this specification for a 90-day period. Secondly, there was some irony in issuing a black Harding stamp, for there had been a persistent rumor that Harding had Negro blood. During the 1920 campaign, William Estabrook Chancellor, a professor of economics at Wooster College, had circulated pamphlets purporting to show that Harding's father was a mulatto who had passed for white, and that "Warren Gamaliel Harding is not a white man. ..."[7] Will Hays, who managed the campaign, had been forced to distribute thousands of Harding genealogies, and the *New York Herald* editorialized shortly before the election against what it called "an assiduous assertion that Warren G. Harding ... is of Negro blood."[8]

2¢ Black Harding

Scott Number:	610
First Day of Issue:	September 1, 1923
Perforation:	11
Scott Colors:	Black, intense black, grayish black
Designer:	Clair Aubrey Huston
Engravers:	Frederick Pauling (vignette)
	E.M. Hall (lettering)
	J.C. Benzing (scrolls and ribbon)
Plate Layout:	Flat plate; sheets of 400 cut into panes of 100
Quantity Issued:	1,459,487,085
Plate Numbers:	Total of 166: lowest, 14852; highest, 15195
Scott Varieties:	Double transfer

The Subject and Design

This was a rush order for Bureau designer Huston. From Bureau and Post Office Department records we find that the model ordered on August 16 was completed and approved on the same day.

Huston had faced and solved a similar design problem in the past. In 1909, when a Lincoln Memorial issue was requested for the centennial of Lincoln's birth, he simply used a portrait of Lincoln in the Washington-Franklin frame and altered the ribbon a bit. In this new case, Huston simply modified the frame design used on the regular stamps of the Series of 1922 by blacking in the "ladders" at the top and sides, and using the years of Harding's birth and death instead of corner triangles. Not only did this allow him to produce the model so quickly, but it also meant that the existing frame die could be used, eliminating much of the time-consuming frame engraving that would otherwise have been necessary.

Because the stamp was to be produced in black, the traditional color for mourning, a profile view of Harding was used. Had a full-face view of Harding been used, the stamp might have been easily confused with the existing black 7¢ McKinley stamp.

Frederick Pauling, a picture engraver, had recently completed a large-size etching of Harding based upon a photograph showing a left profile. The completed etching (Figure 64) was readily on hand in the Bureau's engraving department, and it was reduced photographically by Huston for the model.

Figure 64. The Frederick Pauling etching, used for the model of the Harding stamp, was on hand at the Bureau. A profile view was needed to avoid confusion with the black 7¢ McKinley stamp.

Figure 65. The source photograph of Harding from which the Pauling etching was derived. It can now be identified as from the Moffett Studio of Chicago and taken in 1920.

174

The Black Hardings

Bureau records note that the "origin of photograph used for making the etching is unknown," but this author has identified it, from a copyright deposit photograph in the Library of Congress (Figure 65). It was taken by the Moffett Studio of Chicago in 1920, before Harding was sworn in as president. Harding attended the Republican convention in Chicago in the summer of 1920, and the photograph may well have been taken at that time.

In light of later statements that this was not a suitable portrait of Harding, it is interesting to note that the Post Office Department called the Pauling etching Harding's "favorite engraving," and described the first proof as "one of the finest stamp engravings ever produced."[9]

Philatelic Aspects and Varieties

First day of issue. This stamp was placed on sale at Marion, Ohio, Harding's hometown, and at Washington, D.C., on September 1, 1923. Few if any previously issued stamps received more publicity than this one. Collectors, in particular, acted on the notice that the stamp would be issued, and ordered first-day covers in large numbers. Stamp magazine publisher George Linn of Columbus, Ohio, prepared envelopes for his covers with a preprinted message, and serviced them himself at the Marion post office. These have come to be considered the first commercially cacheted first-day covers (see Figure 66).[10] Linn also promoted the sale of these covers in his publication, and helped to popularize this aspect of the hobby.

September 1 was a Saturday, and dozens of people were in line to buy stamps when the post office opened. F.W. Hitchings, a doctor who had driven

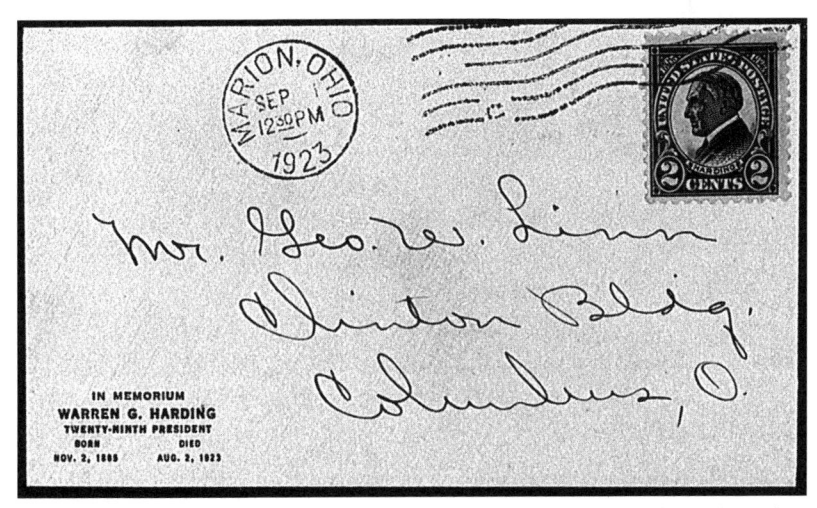

Figure 66. George Linn, founder of Linn's Stamp News, *prepared this first-day cover for the 2¢ Black Harding Memorial stamp.*

175

overnight from Cleveland to be the first in line, purchased the first pane. The president's father, George Harding, had been presented a pane of the stamps and mailed a letter for the benefit of the newsreel cameras. Also on hand was Michael Eidsness Jr., the superintendent of the Post Office Department's Division of Stamps, who had personally carried from Washington the 200,000 stamps to be placed on sale. The following morning, French Crow, the postmaster, wired Postmaster General New that the stamps had sold out, "as fitting testimonial of love and esteem in which people held late president."[11]

Shades. This seems to be a black stamp, but with such a large press run, we might expect some variation in shade. Ward reported that the stamps sold on the first day at the Philatelic Stamp Agency in Washington were in "two very distinct shades, a deep black and a light gray, due to the heaviness and lightness of the inking."[12] This description seems to have stuck. When the first listing appeared in the 1924 edition of the *Specialized Catalogue*, black was given as the major shade, and intense black and gray black were listed as additional shades. Gray black was changed to grayish black in the 1927 edition.

610a. Horizontal pair, imperforate vertically. In April 1924, Samuel Konwiser, a New Jersey collector, was reported to have purchased from the stamp clerk of the Newark post office a block of 40, imperforate horizontally. Ward recorded this as being the last four horizontal rows from an upper-left pane. Konwiser stated that this block was "the entire lot, and that he knows of no others."[13] However, the balance of this pane surfaced a little more than a year later and was reported to be from plate 15056. This was reported as being somewhat mangled, torn and "held together by a Manila paper patch on the back," but yielded "seven good blocks of four."[14] This would add up to a total of 34 pairs: 20 from the original block of 40 and 14 from the mangled block of 60.

The listing first appeared in the 1926 edition of the *Specialized Catalogue* and was given the small-letter listing of 610a in the 1932 edition.

Double transfer. With a large number of plates produced in a hurry, and the dark color of this stamp, we might expect a number of plate varieties, and many have in fact been reported. The double-transfer listing first appeared in the 1926 edition of the *Specialized Catalogue*. French lists more than 50 plate varieties on this stamp.

Imperforate error. Although the date of the discovery is not recorded, Arthur Owen, the plate number specialist, was reported to have acquired an upper-left pane of 100 stamps from plate 14870. This, according to Johl, "was found in a usual post office package of 100 sheets of regularly perforated stamps, and had been blue penciled at the Bureau, but somehow had gotten out by mistake."[15]

The value and uniqueness of this pane was nullified by the issue of the stamp in imperforate form in November 1923 (see below). The pane was broken up in 1950. The top plate block of 15 was purchased by C.B. Durland, who wrote, "I believe that no one will argue that it can properly be classified under [the imperforate listing, 611] which was not printed at the time the error got out. ..."[16]

2¢ Rotary Black Harding

Scott Number:	612
First Day of Issue:	September 12, 1923
Perforation:	10
Scott Colors:	Black, gray black
Plate Layout:	Rotary press; sheets of 400 cut into panes of 100
Quantity Issued:	99,950,300
Plate Numbers:	14866, 14867, 14900, 14901, 14938, 14939, 14995, 14996
Scott Varieties:	Pair with full vertical gutter between

The Political Background

The Post Office Department's plan to replace the 2¢ Washington stamp with the Harding Memorial stamp during a 90-day period taxed the production facilities of the Bureau, and led to the use of the rotary press for this stamp in an attempt to meet the Post Office Department's request for 300 million. Where the flat-plate presses could turn out a maximum of 1.6 million stamps — or 4,000 sheets of 400 — a day, the rotary press could turn out 6 million stamps — or 15,000 sheets of 400.

Only two other sheet stamps had been produced on the rotary press: the 1¢ Washington Franklin (Scott 542 and 543) and the 1¢ Franklin of the new design (581).

Philatelic Aspects and Varieties

First day of issue. The first rotary plates for the 2¢ Harding went to press on September 6, five days after the first day of issue of the flat-plate stamp, and the stamps went on sale at the Philatelic Stamp Agency on September 12, with only two days notice. Relatively few first-day covers were serviced, and within a month these were advertised at four times the price of the flat-plate first-day covers.

Complaints. By September 29, the Post Office Department found that its 300 million order would not meet the requisitions for 2¢ stamps, and ordered an additional 300 million. Five days later, on October 4, it ordered one billion more.

However, complaints were coming in from the public and from postmasters about the quality of the rotary-press stamps The postmaster of Indianapolis wrote on October 4, for example, "to advise that patrons generally are complaining relative to the Harding Memorial Stamps ... printed on a rotary press."[17] The stamps were usually lighter in color than those from the flat-plate press, and to some, this was something of an improvement. As Ward himself remarked, "the rotary variety ... shows the lines of the engraving more clearly and softer so that it has a more pleasing appearance."[18]

Although there had been complaints about the quality of rotary-press sheet stamps for some time, the quality of the Harding stamps probably had more to do with the production demand than anything else. Stamps from worn plates, and those that were badly perforated, were not rejected by Bureau inspectors in order to meet the production schedule. Glover himself acknowledged that for both the flat-plate and rotary stamps a lower quality was tolerated, with the explanation that "this condition was necessary to meet demands."[19]

Nevertheless, by late October or early November, the Post Office Department directed the Bureau to stop producing the Harding stamp by the rotary press. Ward, who had previously praised the rotary stamp, reported that the stamp was being discontinued with this explanation: "It seems that the black ink does not produce a satisfactory product for they vary from a deep black to a grey black that borders almost on a white."[20] Johl, in describing the rotary stamps, noted among their distinguishing marks "the weak color" and "lack of final detail."[21]

Plate markings. All plates of this stamp were laid out like the 400-subject rotary plates used for the 1¢ stamp (581), with gutters rather than guidelines, and plate numbers in the corners. Each of the eight plates that went to press had the Type A marginal markings, with 19 horizontal dashes in the center gutter to aid in perforating.

Double paper. A listing for this variety went into the 1928 edition of the *Specialized Catalogue*, based on a find of what Johl described as a pane in which four rows, or 40 stamps, were printed on double paper. This variety was given a small "a" variety listing in the 1932 edition, and was eliminated, with other double-paper listings, in the 1945 edition.

Pair with full vertical gutter between. This listing first appeared in the 1948 edition of the *Specialized Catalogue*. Such varieties could be produced on these rotary sheet stamps by error when the paper knife or guillotine was used to cut the sheets of 400 into panes of 100. When a foldover or other abnormality occurred in the stacking of sheets, some panes might contain stamps on either side of the gutter. Stamps showing a full gutter and some part of the next stamp are known as "gutter snipes." The listed error requires a pair of stamps with the full gutter between. Some of these full-gutter-between varieties were favor items, not errors. An unused block of 18 of this stamp is known, with three pairs showing the full vertical gutter between.

2¢ Imperforate Black Harding

Scott Number: 611
First Day of Issue: November 15, 1923
Perforation: None
Scott Color: Black
Plate Layout: Flat plate; full sheets of 400
Quantity Issued: 770,000
Plate Numbers: 15019, 15025, 15027, 15028, 15054, 15059

The Political Background

The Post Office Department announced on October 31, 1923, that the Harding stamp would be issued in imperforate form on November 15 at the Philatelic Stamp Agency. The reason, as stated in the press release, was to meet "the great demand from collectors, members of Congress, and others" who wanted imperforate sheets "so that they might be framed as a memorial to the late president."[22]

If there was in fact a great demand for imperforate sheets, it must have been verbal, for there is little supporting evidence for that assertion in the official records that are available today. What was in demand, however, were die proofs, particularly from members of Congress, other officials and relatives of the late president. Postmaster General New had primed the pump for these requests by announcing that the first die proof of the stamp, "bound in black morocco" would be presented to Mrs. Harding, and that the second and third die proofs would be presented to Mrs. New, his wife, and to Emily B. McLean, the two-year-old daughter of Edward McLean, a friend of the president who was also the publisher of the *Washington Post*.

This set off a flurry of demand. On September 25, 10 more "specially mounted die-proofs" were requested for other administration officials and VIPs, including the late president's father. Many others wanted a philatelic memento of President Harding, and it seems that the imperforate sheets helped to satisfy the demand.

First day of issue. This stamp was issued on November 15, 1923, only at Washington, D.C. There was adequate notification to allow collectors to buy the sheets and prepare first-day covers.

Position pieces. As with other imperforate sheets sold at the agency, collectors tended to save the plate blocks, centerline blocks and other position pieces, and use the remainder for postage. Only the flat-plate sheets were issued in imperforate form. Imperforate sheets were taken from the ordinary flat-plate production before the stamps went through the perforating process. While four of the six known plates of this issue are rather common, two — 15054 and 15059 — are quite scarce.

Private perforations. This stamp is known with genuine Type III Schermack perforations, but it seems that these were mostly perforated as favor items for collectors and dealers, rather than perforated for use by business mailers. At least one commercial usage is known, however, from Evanston, Illinois, in 1924.[23]

Note: Scott 613, the Black Harding printed from the rotary press with 11-gauge perforations is treated in the following chapter.

Notes

1. Mark Sullivan, *Our Times: The United States 1900-1925*, Volume VI (New York: Charles Scribner's Sons, 1935), p. 252.

2. Geoffrey Perrett, *America in the Twenties* (New York: Simon & Schuster, 1982), p. 143.

3. Herman Boers to Howard M. Mount, August 4, 1923, Smithsonian Institution Libraries, Post Office Department Manuscripts.

4. W. Irving Glover to Herman Boers, August 7, 1923, Smithsonian Institution Libraries, Post Office Department Manuscripts.

5. Cassian Brenner to Glover, August 9, 1923, Smithsonian Institution Libraries, Post Office Department Manuscripts.

6. Post Office Department, press release, [untitled], August 17, 1923.

7. Quoted in Francis Russell, *The Shadow of Blooming Grove: Warren Harding and His Times* (New York: McGraw-Hill Book Company, 1968), p. 414.
8. *Ibid*, p. 415.
9. Press release of August 17, 1923, *op. cit.*
10. This judgment is expressed, among other places, in Monte Eiserman, *The Handbook for First Day Cover Collectors* (American First Day Cover Foundation Inc., 1979), p. 77.
11. Western Union Telegram; French Crow, Postmaster, Marion, Ohio, to Harry S. New, September 2, 1923, National Postal Museum.
12. Philip H. Ward Jr., "Chronicle of New Issues and Varieties," *Mekeel's Weekly Stamp News*, September 17, 1923, p. 468.
13. Philip H. Ward Jr., "Chronicle of New Issues and Varieties," *Mekeel's Weekly Stamp News*, May 19, 1924, p. 278.
14. H.M.K. [Harry M. Konwiser], "Discovering Some More Harding Stamps, Part Imperf.," *American Philatelist*, Vol. 38, No. 10 (July 1925), pp. 673-74.
15. Max G. Johl, *The United States Commemorative Stamps of the Twentieth Century*, Volume 1 (New York: H.L. Lindquist, 1947), p. 84.
16. C.B. Durland, "2¢ Harding Memorial, Plate 14870, Rare Imperforate Variety," *Stamps*, Vol. 71, No. 4 (April 22, 1950), p. 206.
17. Robert H. Bryson, Postmaster, Indianapolis, Indiana, to W. Irving Glover, October 5, 1923, Smithsonian Institution Libraries, Post Office Department Manuscripts.
18. Philip H. Ward Jr., "Chronicle of New Issues and Varieties," *Mekeel's Weekly Stamp News*, October 8, 1923, p. 504.
19. Glover to Robert H. Bryson, Postmaster, Indianapolis, Indiana, October 10, 1923, Smithsonian Institution Libraries, Post Office Department Manuscripts.
20. Philip H. Ward Jr., "Chronicle of New Issues and Varieties," *Mekeel's Weekly Stamp News*, November 5, 1923, p. 566.
21. Johl, *Commemorative Stamps, op. cit.*, p. 86.
22. Post Office Department press relase, November 1, 1923.
23. See James Baird, "The Proprietary Coils: A Summary," *Collectors Club Philatelist*, Vol. 73, No. 1 (January-February 1994), p. 34.

United States Stamps 1922-26

Chapter 15

The Sheet Rotary Rarities

The first three sheet stamps printed on the large Stickney rotary press were the 1¢ Washington-Franklin, the 1¢ Series of 1922 and the 2¢ Black Harding. A small number of each of these three stamps is known with 11-gauge perforations, and these stamps, known as Scott 544, 596 and 613, respectively, have become 20th-century rarities.

Although 544 is a Washington-Franklin series design, it was produced at roughly the same period as the two others, and will be treated here in an attempt to give the reader a better understanding of these often-confused stamps.

There was no announcement of the production of these stamps, and the first of them was not discovered until some 13 years after they were originally produced. Max Johl, writing in the *Bureau Specialist* in 1936, described the stamps we know as 544 and 596 in the same article.[1]

Johl called these "two new major varieties," and he was correct. A Chicago collector, E.F. Hartwell, had sent Johl three copies of the Washington-Franklin rotary stamp with 11-gauge perforations. One of these was a single (shown in Figure 67), and one was a pair with a sheet margin at bottom. "A checkup of size," Johl wrote, "quickly showed that the stamps were from the sheet rotaries and were perforated 11 instead of 10 x 11 or 10 x 10." By "a checkup of size" Johl meant that the stamps were taller than flat-plate stamps. This was caused by bending the plates to fit around the rotary-press cylinder. Rotary sheet stamps and endwise coils were bent vertically, and thus produced "tall" stamps, while sidewise coils were bent horizontally and produced "wide" stamps.

Figure 67. One of the three discovery copies of Scott 544, from the collection of Max Johl.

The sheet margin at the bottom of the pair, however, indicated that the pair had to have been produced from a 400-subject rotary plate, as this sheet margin was in fact the central gutter. "There seems to be no question that these are ... a new variety, perf 11 x 11 from sheet rotaries," Johl concluded.

He had also been sent a similar stamp in the new design. It was also a "tall" rotary, with 11 x 11 perforations. Although this stamp had its full gum, it carried a "Kansas City, Mo." Bureau precancel. The precancel on this stamp helped Johl identify it as "a sheet rotary intended for a perf 10 stamp." Had this stamp received the usual 10-gauge perforations, it would have been Scott 581. Figure 68 shows a similar copy with a Kansas City precancel.

Both these varieties were reported accurately by Johl, who also had the assistance of other specialists, including Arthur Owen and Hugh Southgate, in making his identifications. Later, however, both of these stamps were erroneously reported as originating from endwise coil waste. As Johl noted, the bottom sheet margin on the pair of 544 eliminated that possibility on the Washington-Franklin stamps. As for 596, the Kansas City precancel eliminated the possibility as well, as endwise coils were never precanceled at the Bureau.

Figure 68. One of the seven known copies of Scott 596 with a Kansas City, Missouri, Bureau precancel.

About two years after Johl discovered these two varieties, a similar stamp in the Black Harding design was discovered by Leslie Lewis, of the Stanley Gibbons stamp firm in New York. While sorting a quantity of 50,000 Black Harding stamps for stock in August 1938, Lewis found a top-margin pair (Figure 69) with 11-gauge perforations.[2] This stamp, first reported in January 1939, is the stamp we know now as 613. As there were no coil versions of the Black Harding, this stamp, too, cannot have been produced from anything other than 400-subject rotary plates.

Figure 69. The discovery pair of Scott 613, found by Leslie Lewis of the Stanley Gibbons firm.

All three of these stamps, 544, 596 and 613, were produced during a short period of time, and probably in the same way.

Waste Salvage or Experiment?

How and why were these stamps produced? As was discussed in Chapter 8, the Bureau began salvaging rotary coil waste in 1919. Sheet stamps were not issued from the rotary presses until May 1920. One theory, and perhaps the most plausible, is that the Bureau also decided to salvage sheet-stamp waste and set up a perforator for that purpose. It is possible that the rotary sheets were quartered first and sent through a perforator set up for flat-plate stamps. We know for certain that the coil waste was not processed until a sufficient amount of it had accumulated. Then it was perforated on the same type of perforators used for flat-plate stamps, and with the same 11-gauge perforations.

The Sheet Rotary Rarities

Coil waste was somewhat easily recognized, as the sheet size was 170 subjects. Sheet waste would be more difficult to identify, as it would result in the same pane size as the finished stamps; that is panes of 100. The only thing that would be different would be the gauge of the perforations.

The earliest use, documented by an expertizing certificate, of any of the sheet-rotary rarities is a 544 postmarked December 21, 1922.[3] Only the Washington-Franklin sheet rotary was in production at this time. As stocks of waste accumulated over the next year, they were perforated on a flat-plate perforator.

The first plates that could have produced 596 did not go to press until April 1923, and the first plates that could have produced 613 did not go to press until August 1923.

Waste salvaging was ended sometime in late 1923 or early 1924. In terms of quantities, we have the most of 544, which seems logical, as waste from the Washington Franklin sheet rotary could have accumulated over a period of a year or more. Next in quantity, we have 613, which makes sense because of the large numbers of stamps produced on the rotary press during a short time — nearly 100 million stamps in a four-month period. Last in quantity is 596.

It is also interesting to note that all three of these stamps were in production at roughly the same time. Records were kept on a fiscal year basis. From July 1, 1923, to June 30, 1924, here are the number of sheet stamps produced on the large rotary presses:

1¢ Washington-Franklin rotary:	618,498,170
1¢ Series of 1922 rotary precancel:	722,770,000
1¢ Series of 1922 rotary:	152,200,000
2¢ Black Harding rotary:	99,950,300

During this period, rotary-press sheet stamps were printed from rolls of paper that measured 24 inches in diameter and yielded 6,000 sheets of 400 stamps, or 2,400,000 stamps per roll. The large Stickney press printed and gummed the stamps, then wound the roll again at the other end of the press. In normal production, this roll of printed and gummed paper was then removed and taken to the two-way perforator. (A two-way perforator is shown in Figure 48 in Chapter 6.)

The two-way perforator not only applied the vertical and horizontal perforations, but also cut the web of paper into sheets of 400. These sheets of 400 were then stacked in piles of 100 sheets between thin cardboard covers and cut into quarters on a guillotinelike paper cutter. The resulting decks of 100 panes of 100 stamps were stapled and sent to postmasters.

If waste sheets were perforated on flat-bed perforators, how were the resulting panes of 100 stamps issued? Were they made up into decks of 100?

185

Or were individual panes added to decks to replace panes that did not pass inspection?

If waste ends of the various press runs were saved until there were sufficient quantities to run through the perforators — as was the case with coil waste — why do we have only Kansas City precancels on 596, and not New York, Chicago, Cleveland and Boston, which were also in production during the period?

Some students of these varieties have suggested that these stamps were produced as the result of experiments. Richard Kiusalis, for example, attributed the existence of these rarities to experimentation, rather than salvage, writing that "experiments in different perforation gauges had been going on for a number of years in an effort to find the ideal perforation for sheet and coil stamps; these experiments were not quite finished when experimenting with precancel printing was begun."[4] There is not, however, much in the way of evidence for this experimentation in the Bureau records, and Kiusalis offered none.

We do know that the Bureau was experimenting with changes in paper and gum, in order to make rotary sheet stamps curl less, and these experiments were noted by Ward in December 1923, when he also wrote that "it is thought that they will soon be in a position to perforate these stamps 11 instead of 10 as heretofore."[5]

The experiments to which Ward was referring were conducted under the request of a committee appointed by the postmaster general to study whether rotary-press sheet stamp production should be continued and/or expanded. Chaired by Michael Eidsness, the superintendent of the Post Office Department's Division of Stamps, the committee also included two Bureau supervisors. Its final report, issued in February 1924, noted that "one of the most serious complaints received recently relative to rotary postage stamps is that they do not tear readily at the perforations." The recommendation was made "that consideration be given to adopting the 11 perforation with a view of eliminating the criticisms regarding tear."[6]

There is no indication in the lengthy report that experiments were actually conducted with the 11-gauge perforation, only that consideration be given to using the 11-gauge. A few months later, when the 2¢ stamp was about to be released in rotary sheet format, Ward reported that "these will possibly come with a perforation 11 later on, but the cost for making the change in the perforating wheels is greater than the department at present cares to pay, so that the change will most likely come when the old wheels begin to wear out."[7] This, as we know, happened in part. A new gauge of 11 x 10½ was chosen for rotary sheet stamps in late 1926.

There should be no doubt that experiments with perforation gauges were conducted, but these could have been conducted on unprinted stock. The Post Office Department was also quite sensitive at this time about intentionally creating philatelic varieties, and we have no record, for example, of any premature release of the 11 x 10½ perforations.

In the 60 years since the perf 11 sheet rotaries were first reported researchers and scholars of these issues have learned little. Despite the Post Office Department's philatelic sensitivity, the Bureau did not view perforation varieties as an accountable matter. To the Bureau, these rarities were simply sheet stamps printed from 400-subject plates and were no doubt accounted for in those totals. There appear to be no records or correspondence that tells us how or why these 11-gauge sheet rotaries were produced. Today we have little more than the stamps themselves as evidence.

1¢ Sheet Rotary, Perforated 11

Scott Number:	596
Perforation:	11
Scott Color:	Green
Press:	Large rotary press
Plate Layout:	Sheets of 400, cut into four panes
Quantity Issued:	Unknown
Plate Numbers:	Unknown

Philatelic Aspects and Varieties

After Max Johl wrote up this stamp's discovery in 1936, a few other reports trickled in. Johl reported the find of a second copy in 1938, which, he said, "checks with the discovery copy and is undoubtedly another example."[8]

Several other people, however, also claimed to have discovered this stamp and, in the process, confused its true origin. Lester Brookman, the distinguished student of 19th-century stamps, reported a copy of this stamp without a Kansas City precancel, writing in 1944 that "the writer has just discovered a new U.S. stamp. ..." Brookman's stamp had been sent to him as an example of 594, but in measuring it, he found it to be tall rather than wide. "Careful checking," Brookman wrote, "has revealed that it is absolutely identical in size and appearance as the endwise coil and there is no doubt in my mind that this new variety is from endwise coil waste."[9]

Brookman apparently never considered that this stamp could be waste from the sheet stamp, and his article did a great deal to confuse the understanding of this stamp. For many years to come, this stamp would be regarded erroneously as endwise coil waste.

W.B. Hoover, the precancel dealer and specialist, also claimed responsibility in 1951 for discovering the precanceled version of this stamp, which he called "an unlisted variety of Scott No. 604" and "a brand new U.S. variety."[10] This was, however, simply another copy of the stamp with a Kansas City precancel, the same stamp that Johl had reported in 1936. Hoover had the stamp sent to the Philatelic Foundation, which examined the stamp, and agreed — erroneously — that "it is a variety of No. 604."

Scott, too, adopted the idea that this stamp was endwise coil waste, and listed 596 for the first time in the 1963 edition of the *Specialized Catalogue*, with the note, "Made from coil waste of No. 604."

This listing did not sit well with several specialists, however, including Richard Kiusalas, whose 1967 article (see above) and letters to Eugene Costales, the editor of the Scott catalog, eventually convinced Scott to change the listing. In the 1970 edition of the catalog, Scott removed from the listing the notation that it was from coil waste. However, Scott did not give any other information about its origin, and the coil-waste label stuck. Many writers and publications continued to describe this stamp as being from endwise coil waste.

In 1978, Joe Moberly, another specialist, again took on the issue of the origin of this stamp. By this time seven copies were known, five with a Kansas City precancel and two without. In an article in the *United States Specialist*, Moberly wrote that "the precancelation alone makes nonsense out of any claims that the five precanceled copies are vertical coil waste." The Bureau, he explained, never precanceled anything other than sheet stamps and horizontal coils. "Bureau precanceled vertical coils and hence Bureau precanceled vertical coil waste do not exist."[11]

Nevertheless, the idea that this stamp was endwise coil waste was hard to shake. This writer took up the issue again in the January 1994 edition of the *United States Specialist*, arguing that the concept of endwise coil waste should be rethought, as no collector has ever produced a stamp that can be proven to be endwise coil waste, and that the Bureau surely would have kept records of sheet stamps produced from 150-subject plates if it had issued any. This would have been an accountable format. It was probably simply not a Bureau practice to salvage waste from endwise coil production.[12]

In addition, 1¢ endwise coils of the new series, as we shall see in the

The Sheet Rotary Rarities

next chapter, were not produced until July 1924. They were not in production at the same time as the Black Harding, and they were produced in relatively small quantities. There is simply no evidence of any rotary-press endwise coil waste ever being produced.

In the 1996 edition of the *Specialized Catalogue*, the listing for this stamp was changed to indicate that it was produced as "rotary press sheet waste."

Size and identification. To identify this stamp, it must first be determined that this is a "tall" stamp printed by the rotary press. Scott confuses the issue of the size of this stamp (and all other U.S. stamps) by giving the size in metric measurements. Scott says the design of this stamp measures "approximately 19¼ by 22½ mm." U.S. stamps, however, were laid out using inch measurements, which are relatively simple.

Flat-plate stamps of this issue are generally $^{75}/_{100}$ inch wide and $^{87}/_{100}$ inch long, or .75 x .87. This is ¾ inch by ⅞ inch and can be measured on a schoolboy's ruler. Scott 596 will be about a frameline taller than ⅞ inch and will be the same height as 581, which is roughly .75 x .89 in inches, or by my measurement in millimeters about 19.00 by 22.50.

Each person, however, seems to measure these stamps differently, and when we are dealing with such small increments, paper shrinkage and whether one measures from the outsides or centers of the framelines can make a difference. The best way to measure these stamps is by using another stamp as a guide. Many collectors cut a common 1¢ stamp in half and use it for comparison.

Scott 596 will be taller than 552 (the flat-plate stamp) and the same size as 581, the rotary sheet stamp of this period. Scott 596 will also have genuine 11-gauge perforations. Confirmation of this stamp's identity from an expertizing service should be considered essential.

Rarity. To date only 12 copies of this stamp have been documented, seven with Kansas City precancels, and five without. It is the rarest non-error U.S. stamp of the 20th century, and has been selling at increasingly high prices. In the 1996 edition of the *Specialized Catalogue* it was first priced in two different ways: with a Bureau precancel, and with a machine cancellation. Copies without a precancel carry the higher catalog price.

Only used singles have been found. No unused copies are known, nor are any blocks or pairs. No stamps on cover or on piece have been reported, and no stamp shows a dated postmark. Thus, no date of earliest use has been determined.

2¢ Rotary Black Harding, Perforated 11

Scott Number: 613
Perforation: 11
Scott Color: Black
Press: Large rotary press
Plate Layout: Sheets of 400, cut into four panes
Quantity Issued: Unknown
Plate Numbers: Unknown

Philatelic Aspects and Varieties

There has never been as much misunderstanding about this stamp as there has been with 596, as this stamp was produced only in two formats: 400-subject flat-plate sheet stamps and 400-subject rotary-press sheet stamps.

In the first report of the discovery of this stamp by the Stanley Gibbons firm, its origin was correctly surmised. "The theory of its existence," the *New York Journal and American* reported, "... is that the pair came from the torn end of a rotary press printing which was perforated on a flat press."[13] The hurry to produce the Harding stamps was also cited as a factor.

"Careful examination leaves no doubt that this pair is an entirely new major variety," *Mekeel's* editorialized a few days later.[14] Catalog listing came rather quickly (compared to 596) and the stamp was first listed in the 1943 edition of the Scott *Specialized Catalogue* as 613B.

Johl included this stamp in his book on commemorative stamps, writing in 1947: "No information is available as to how or why these were made. The Bureau of Engraving and Printing has no record of setting up a special perforating machine for sheet rotaries using 11 gauge pins and wheels." Johl then assumed that "these must, therefore, have been some short lengths or odd sheets which were salvaged by being perforated along with some coil waste of the regular issue on machines set for the utilization of coil waste."[15] Johl seems wrong here.

The perforating machines set up for coil waste had to accommodate sheets that were 17 stamps wide and 10 deep. Sheets of rotary-press Black

Hardings (and the 1¢ stamps that became 596) were 20 stamps wide by 20 stamps deep, with gutters between the panes, rather than the guidelines used on the flat-plate sheets of 400. Whether the Bureau had a record of setting up a special perforator — and Johl would be checking 24 years after the fact — it seems that it would have been necessary to set up a perforating machine that would accommodate the gutters in order to perforate full sheets of 400 of rotary-press sheet waste.

If, however, the sheets were first reduced to quarter sheets of 100 by cutting through the gutters, they might well have been run through the existing perforators set up for flat-plate stamps. This scenario for 613, 596 and 544 would make sense if this waste was used only for the purpose of replacing damaged panes in decks of 100 — perhaps those removed by inspectors — rather than as an attempt to utilize large amounts of waste. This might also explain why such small quantities of these stamps are known.

Size and identification. This stamp will be taller than the flat-plate version of this stamp, and the same size as the perforated-10 version of the rotary stamp 612. As with 596, confirmation of identity by an expertizing service should be considered a necessity.

Rarity. By 1984, some 30 copies of this stamp had been examined by the Philatelic Foundation and found to be genuine. Interestingly, two copies are noted as having straight edges.[16] Rotary-press sheet stamps do not have straight edges in normal production, which may add credence to the theory that these stamps were produced by first cutting down the sheets of 400 and running them through the flat-plate perforators.

No unused copies have been reported. Two pairs are known, one of them being the discovery pair. No copies are known on cover, and no copies are known with dated cancels. Thus no date of earliest use is known.

Notes

1. Max G. Johl, "Two New Major Varieties," *Bureau Specialist*, Vol. 7, No. 11 (November 1936), pp. 149-50.

2. "Rare Variety Found in 2¢ Harding Stamp," *Stamps*, Vol. 26, No. 1 (January 14, 1939), p. 46.

3. A postcard with a copy of Scott 544 canceled on this date has been examined by the Philatelic Foundation and found to be genuine in its opinion. The card was illustrated in the auction catalog, *The Connoisseur Collection*, produced by Superior Galleries of Beverly Hills, California, October 26, 1992, p. 86.

4. Richard A. Kiusalas, "The Era of Experimentation," *United States Spe-*

cialist, Vol. 38, No. 10 (October 1967), p. 374.

5. Philip H. Ward Jr., "Chronicle of New Issues and Varieties," *Mekeel's Weekly Stamp News*, Vol. 37, No. 48 (December 3, 1923), p. 627.

6. Michael L. Eidsness Jr., et al., to Harry S. New, February 28, 1924. National Postal Museum.

7. Philip H. Ward Jr., "Chronicle of New Issues and Varieties," *Mekeel's Weekly Stamp News*, Vol. 38, No. 17 (April 28, 1924) p. 236.

8. Max G. Johl, "Max G. Johl Reports on 20th Century United States," *Stamps*, Vol. 23, No. 5 (April 30, 1938), p. 160.

9. L.G. Brookman, "New United States Stamp Discovered," *American Philatelist*, Vol. 57, No. 10 (July 1944), p. 733.

10. W.B. Hoover, "Kansas City, Mo. No. 51a," *Precancel Forum*, Vol. 12, No. 9 (September 1951), p. 289.

11. Joe Moberly, "Is the 1¢ Franklin, Scott 596, Vertical Coil Waste?" *United States Specialist*, Vol. 49, No. 4 (April 1978), pp. 164-65.

12. See Gary Griffith, "Once Again, Scott 596 Is Not Coil Waste," *United States Specialist*, Vol. 65, No. 1 (January 1994), pp. 8-17.

13. Justin L. Bacharach, *New York Journal and American*, December 30, 1938, reprinted as "2¢ Harding Error Discovered," in *Weekly Philatelic Gossip*, Vol. 27, No. 17 (January 7, 1939), p. 469.

14. "A Most Remarkable Find," *Mekeel's Weekly Stamp News*, Vol. 53, No. 4 (January 23, 1939), p. 40.

15. Max G. Johl, *The United States Commemorative Stamps of the Twentieth Century*, Volume 1 (New York: H.L. Lindquist, 1947), p. 87.

16. See Brian LaVane, "Rare or Common? The Harding Memorial Issue" in *Opinions II* (Philatelic Foundation, 1984), p. 129.

Chapter 16

The Endwise Coils

Endwise coils were not in heavy demand during this period and were issued in relatively small quantities. The first endwise coil of this series was the 2¢ value, which was not issued until December 31, 1923, more than 11 months later than the sidewise coil. The 1¢ value was not issued until even later, on July 19, 1924.

The plates used to print endwise coils on the rotary press had 150 subjects and were laid out with 10 subjects horizontally and 15 subjects vertically. As with the sidewise coils, the plates were laid out like flat plates, then bent into a half circle. Two plates fit around the cylinder of the Stickney rotary press. Where the two plates joined, a crevice filled with ink. This printed a joint line where the two plates met. When the stamps were coiled, this joint line would appear after every 15 stamps.

Endwise coil stamp plates were curved vertically, and went through the press "head first." This made the stamps slightly taller than flat-plate stamps, due to the curvature of the plate. The production process was otherwise similar to that used for the sidewise coils (see Chapter 7). The stamps were printed and gummed on the Stickney press but perforated in a separate process, on a one-way perforator.

As with the sidewise coils, brown paper was used at both ends of the coil. A short length was used as the core and a longer length was used for the leader, which was wrapped around the finished coil of stamps. Coils were issued in quantities of 500 and 1,000. The same types of paper splices as occur on the sidewise coils occur on the endwise coils.

While short ends of the sidewise coils were salvaged as coil-waste sheet stamps (see Chapter 8), it seems that it was never a Bureau practice to salvage the waste from endwise coils. As we have noted in the previous chapter, it simply may be that the practice of salvaging waste ended in late 1923, before either of the endwise coil stamps was produced. In addition, there would have been relatively little waste from endwise coils, as the quantity produced was less than one-tenth of the quantity of sidewise coils.

1¢ End Coil

Scott Number: 604
First Day of Issue: July 19, 1924
Perforation: 10 horizontal
Scott Colors: Yellow green, green
Plate Layout: 150 subjects, cut into coils
Quantity Issued: 174,848,250
Plate Numbers: 15179, 15180, 15239, 15240, 20355, 20356, 20357, 20358
Scott Varieties: Joint line pair

Philatelic Aspects and Varieties

First day of issue. This stamp was issued on July 19, 1924, only at Washington, D.C. The first plates were certified on January 7, but there was a large stock of Washington-Franklin endwise coils on hand, and the demand for this stamp was, as Johl has put it, "practically nil."[1] The first plates did not go to press until June, and the stamps were placed on sale at the Philatelic Stamp Agency before they were issued to postmasters. Although there appears to have been no advance notice of its sale in the philatelic press, collectors were watching for it, as the plate numbers had been reported as being certified some time earlier. Several individuals were able to prepare first-day covers. Most of these are pairs paying the 2¢ letter rate.

Used vs. unused. This stamp is rather common in unused condition. Dealers could buy a coil of 500 for $5 and have a ready stock of singles, pairs and joint-line pairs. In used condition, however, this is not as common a stamp. The quantity issued is rather small by comparison to sidewise coils; about 12 sidewise coils issued for every endwise coil. Most of these stamps were used in hand-affixing machines by mailers of commercial advertising flyers and postcards. Stamps on cover during the period of use are relatively difficult to find.

Shades. Although issued in a relatively small quantity, this stamp remained in use for nearly 15 years and appears in a number of shades. The earliest printings are a dark green, and this stamp was listed simply as green when it first appeared in the 1926 edition of the Scott *Specialized*. In the 1938 edition, yellow green became the primary shade, with green listed as 604a. The small-letter listing was dropped in the 1978 edition. To these two shades Johl added bright yellow green, bright green, dull grayish green, deep grayish green and deep green.

Plate numbers. Only eight plates were used to produce this stamp. On the first four plates, the plate number appeared only once, preceded by a small

The Endwise Coils

five-point star, at the lower-left corner of the plate. On the four later plates, the plate number also appeared at the upper right of the plate. These plate numbers did not appear on the finished coils, however. Only when the coils were cut off-center do we find plate numbers, or more usually, partial plate numbers on these coil stamps. Figure 70 shows a partial plate number on a used line pair on cover.

Figure 70. Detail of used endwise coil line pair on cover shows a partial plate number at the left of the bottom stamp. The number comes from the upper right of a 150-subject rotary plate. As on endwise coils, the line was formed by the gap where the two plates met. The top stamps of the pair thus come from one plate and the bottom stamp from another

Plate varieties. Scott lists none. However, there is a rather dramatic plate crack that appears on the first stamp below the joint line on an unknown plate. This was first reported and illustrated in a 1934 *Shift Hunter Letter*, which noted "this type of crack seems quite common."[2] Johl described this as a "curving crack," which "shows in the gutter adjacent to the joint line." This crack is also illustrated in French. A similar crack also is well documented on the 2¢ variety (see below).

2¢ End Coil

Scott Number:	606
First Day of Issue:	December 31, 1923
Perforation:	10 Horizontal
Scott Color:	Carmine
Plate Layout:	150 subjects, cut into coils
Quantity Issued:	301,134,500
Plate Numbers:	Total of 18; lowest, 14155; highest 17573
Scott Varieties:	Joint line pair Cracked plate

Philatelic Aspects and Varieties

First day of issue. This stamp was issued on December 31, 1923, only at Washington, D.C. The first plate was certified on January 20, but as there was little demand for endwise coils, it did not go to press until November 22, 10 months later. As with the 1¢ variety, some collectors were watching for this issue. It was put on sale at the Philatelic Stamp Agency and a number of individuals were able to prepare first-day covers. Figure 71 shows a

195

Figure 71. A first-day cover with a strip of five paying the special delivery fee on a stamped envelope. The sender, W.O. Siebold, and the addressee, Karl Kaslowski, were among the early collectors of first-day covers.

strip of five on a first-day cover paying the special delivery rate. Issued on the last day of the year, this was obviously the final stamp of 1923.

Used vs. unused. As with the 1¢ value, unused copies of this stamp are quite common, but used copies, and those used on cover during the period of issue, are difficult to find. Carolyn Kuhn, a student of the 2¢ Washington stamp in all its forms, was one of the first to take note of the difficulty of finding used copies of this stamp, writing in 1954: "So few copies of No. 606, the vertical coil, are seen that a dated copy (off cover) might be said to be nearly a rarity."[3]

Plate numbers. On 12 plates, the plate number appeared only once, preceded by a small five-point star, at the lower-left corner of the plate. On six other plates the number appears only on the right side of the plate, at the top, preceded by a small five-point star. These plates are listed in the *Durland* catalog.

Shades. Scott lists only carmine as the shade of this stamp, but like the 1¢ value, it was in service for some 15 years and appears in a range of shades. Johl added rose carmine and bright carmine. The later printings are somewhat lighter than the early ones.

Plate varieties. The very visible and dramatic plate crack on this stamp was first reported in the *Shift Hunter Letters* in 1932, but with the mistake that it appeared on plate 18757 — an error that has been continually repeated. Although a line pair that shows this variety shows a portion of plate 18757 at the top, the crack appears on the stamp below, which is from the companion plate 18758. This crack is shown in Figure 72. This crack not only appears on the stamp below the joint line, but extends to the stamp next to it, or stamps 18758-1 and 18758-2. The *Shift Hunter Letters* referred to this as "a Type III crack" or

The Endwise Coils

one that "developed during the bending of late plates to fit the rotary press."[4] George Sloane also reported and illustrated this crack in *Stamps* in 1934,[5] which led to the listing in the Scott *Specialized* in the 1936 edition. But Sloane apparently followed the *Shift Hunter* report and repeated the plate number error. French, depending on these prior reports, also reported the crack on the wrong plate.

A series of gripper cracks, quite different from the crack described above, is also known on this stamp. It was noted by Johl in the addenda to his 1935 book as "a series of horizontal cracks in the left margin which run into the design opposite the 'U' of 'United.' "[6] This crack was identified as position 19287-141 and illustrated in the *Bureau Specialist* in 1939.[7]

Another rather common plate variety, which can be found on some joint-line pairs, is one that shows unerased layout lines at one or both sides of the top stamp's top frameline. These are thin lines used by the siderographer to lay out the plate. These lines should have been erased or burnished out by the plate finisher.

Figure 72. Detail of the major plate crack on the first stamp of plate 18758. The top stamp of the pair was printed from companion plate 18757.

Notes

1. Max G. Johl, *The United States Postage Stamps of the Twentieth Century*, Volume III (New York: H.L. Lindquist, 1935), p. 36.

2. C.W. Bedford, *Shift Hunter Letter No. 56* (February 1932).

3. Carolyn P. Kuhn, "2¢ Washington 1922," *United States Specialist*, Vol. 25, No. 2 (February 1954), p. 39.

4. C.W. Bedford, *Shift Hunter Letter No. 47* (January 1932) and *Shift Hunter Letter No. 42* (August 1931).

5. George B. Sloane, "1922-23, 2¢ Carmine, Rotary Coil, Plate Cracks," *Stamps*, February 8, 1934, collected in *Sloane's Column* (Bureau Issues Association, 1961), p. 318.

6. Johl, Volume III, *op. cit.*, p. 266.

7. Norman Kempf, "Plate Varieties," *Bureau Specialist*, Vol. 10, No. 11 (November 1939), p. 154.

United States Stamps 1922-26

Chapter 17

Huguenot–Walloon Issue

The Political Background

This was the first commemorative series of the new administration. Although some collectors treat the Black Harding issue as a commemorative, it was more properly termed a memorial issue. The three stamps of the Huguenot-Walloon issue follow the pattern set by the Pilgrim Tercentenary issue of 1920. Had the original plan been carried through, this set would have been even more like the Pilgrims, but as finally issued, the Walloons — as the stamps are often known — like the Pilgrims, show a ship on the 1¢ value and a landing scene on the 2¢ value.

The lobbying for this issue, which commemorates the role of European Protestants in colonizing America, began more than two years before the stamps were issued. The National Huguenot-Walloon New Netherland Commission, the sponsoring organization, planned an elaborate religious observation for April 27, 1924 — what it called "a memorial Sunday" to commemorate the 300th anniversary of the landing of the Huguenots and Walloons and the founding of the Presbyterian or Reformed Church in America.

Overshadowed in the history books by the Mayflower Pilgrims of 1620, the religious descendants of these sects — mostly Presbyterian churchmen — lined up the broadest possible alliance of religious and historical groups, and was successful in getting hundreds of prominent Americans and Europeans to take honorary or actual positions on its board. President Harding accepted the honorary chairmanship in December 1922 in a letter stating that "it is good for us to be reminded of so great a debt to those who laid the foundations of our Nation, and we cannot do too much honor them on occasions of this sort."[1] After Harding's death, President Coolidge became the honorary chairman, accepting the position on September 27, 1923.

Also convinced to become honorary co-chairmen were Queen Wilhelmina of the Netherlands, King Albert of Belgium and President Alexandre Millerand of France. Several senators and congressmen served on the commission, which also had the support of dozens of historical and church organizations, including the Daughters of the American Revolution and the Federal Council of the Churches of Christ in America.

This was one of the very few commemorative issues of Postmaster General Harry New's term that New and his administration did not oppose. As we shall see in forthcoming chapters, New quickly learned that commemorative issues were troublesome and expensive. But there is no record of his opposition to this issue, perhaps because it was the first of his administration, but more likely because so many groups and individuals, including President Coolidge, were supporters. The Huguenots and Walloons were, after all, followers of religious reformer John Calvin, the man after whom the new president, John Calvin Coolidge, was named.

With so many individuals and groups on the commission's board, the selection of subject matter got a bit complicated, and the subject matter itself was never very simple. Rather than commemorating a single event, the commission was attempting to commemorate a religious immigration about which most Americans had no knowledge at all. The stamps may have helped to popularize the terms Huguenots and Walloons among stamp collectors, but the history was somewhat arcane and the message a bit muddled. The 2¢ stamp, for example, shows the landing of a group in New York, while the 5¢ stamp shows a monument in Florida.

The Commemorative Subjects

The Huguenots were French Protestants, followers of Protestant reformer John Calvin. They founded the Presbyterian church in France in 1559 and soon became one of the nation's most industrious political and religious groups. The Edict of Nantes, in 1598, gave them certain liberties, including the right to worship in public and to hold office. However, under Louis XIV and Cardinal Richelieu, the Huguenots were systematically stripped of their political power. In 1685 the Edict of Nantes was revoked, and in 1715, Louis XIV announced that he had ended all exercise of the Protestant religion in France. The Huguenots fled the country, primarily to England, Prussia, Holland, and eventually, to America.

Walloons was a term given to an ethnic group in northern France and southern Belgium who spoke a French dialect. Like many of the Huguenots, many Calvinist Walloons emigrated first to Holland and then to the new world.

What the commission wanted to commemorate was essentially the emigration of a religious group, not ethnic groups, and this religious group included French, Belgian and Dutch Protestants. As its literature said: "Besides the Walloons and Dutch who kept coming to the Middle colonies, there were Christian people likewise holding the Reformed faith driven out of France who came to America. These, whether Belgic or French, were called Huguenots."[2]

While the 1¢ and 2¢ values depict events of 1624, the 5¢ value makes reference to a much earlier landing of the French Huguenots on what is now U.S. soil. Under the leadership of Jean Ribaut, a navigator sailing under the authority of Gaspard de Coligny, admiral of France, a Huguenot colony was established near what is now Port Royal, South Carolina, in 1562. This was not a successful venture, to say the least.

While Ribaut returned to France for supplies, the colonists abused the local Indians whom Ribaut had previously befriended and upon whom the colony relied for support. This small group of about 26 Huguenots eventually murdered the man left in charge, the dictatorial captain Albert de la Pierria. Unable to fend for themselves, the remaining colonists returned to France in a makeshift boat, surviving only by cannibalism. Historian Samuel Eliot Morison summed up this first group of Huguenot colonists as "ill led" and "unenterprising."[3]

Ribaut returned in 1564 to resupply another French Huguenot settlement that had been established in northern Florida by Rene Goulaine de Laudonniere. This settlement, however, was located "so near the homeward route of treasure fleets that Spain could not ignore it,"[4] and it was wiped out within the year by the brutal Menendez de Aviles, who hung Ribaut and massacred the colonists who had surrendered. It is a monument to Ribaut and this group in Florida that is shown on the 5¢ value.

The Protestant Walloon colonists, who sailed for the new world some 60 years later, were more successful, and it is their voyage and landing in 1624 that is depicted on the 1¢ and 2¢ values.

Like the Mayflower Pilgrims of 1620, they had first emigrated to Holland to practice their religion. In March 1624 a group of them petitioned the Dutch West India Company to form a colony in what was then New Netherland. Sailing on the Dutch ship *Nieu Nederland* and probably one or two other vessels, they landed in Hudson River country in May or June. The majority of the colonists settled at Fort Orange, which eventually became the city we know as Albany. As the commission that sponsored the stamps wrote, these colonists "conducted services daily," and "this may be regarded as the beginning of the Reformed Church in America."[5]

1¢ Ship Nieu Nederland

Scott Number: 614
First Day of Issue: May 1, 1924

Perforation:	11
Scott Colors:	Dark green, green
Designer:	Clair Aubrey Huston
Engravers:	L.S. Schofield (vignette)
	E.M. Hall (frame)
	H.P. Dawson (scrolls and ribbons).
Printing:	Flat plate; plates of 200 cut into panes of 50
Quantity Issued:	51,378,023
Plate Numbers:	15756, 15757, 15758, 15759, 15778, 15779, 15780, 15781, 15782, 15783, 15784, 15785
Scott Varieties:	Double transfer

The Subject and Design

All of the reference artwork for this series was provided to the Post Office Department by the Reverend John Baer Stoudt, a minister of the Reformed Church in the United States, who was the director of the National Huguenot-Walloon New Netherland Commission.

Although the name of the flagship on which the Walloons sailed in 1624 was known, there is no existing painting or drawing of the ship *Nieu Nederland*. The commission provided a drawing, which Johl says was prepared for the memorial half dollar that was issued and "which was based in turn on a marine painting by the Belgian artist, A. Musin."[6] This drawing (shown in Figure 73) had been collected by Johl's partner, Beverly King, and was listed by Brazer as an essay for this value. This pencil drawing shows the starboard side of the ship, as if it were sailing east, and Brazer notes that it also contains "pencilled criticism," probably on the back that reads "Reverse — sailing to

Figure 73. The drawing of the ship, Nieu Nederland, *provided by the stamp's sponsors, was turned in the other direction and redrawn for the issued stamp.*

Figure 74. One set of models for the stamps showed the subjects in a more squared-off frame than the issued designs. The 5¢ value shows a De Bry print of the column Ribault erected in Florida in 1564.

America, not away from America — J.B. Stoudt."[7]

The letter requesting models for this stamp on March 6, 1924, indicates that the designs "were discussed ... several days ago." It requests that the models be submitted "as soon as possible," since "these stamps are desired for issue ... on April 24th."[8]

Two days later the Bureau submitted two sets of models, one in the familiar frame that was eventually issued, one in a slightly different frame. The set of rejected models is shown in Figure 74. The other set was approved on March 11.

Bureau artist C. Aubrey Huston evidently took Stoudt's note to heart and shows the port side of the ship, as if sailing west. Huston's adopted frame, used on all three values of this series, employs elements that had become staples of his design: acanthus leaves at both sides, ribbons, arches and the banknote Roman typeface.

The size of this stamp is the same as the parcel post stamps of 1912 and is somewhat unusual, being slightly larger in both directions than what would later become the standard size for commemoratives — that of the special delivery stamps. The Bureau gave the measurement of the Huguenot-Walloon stamps as 1.375 inches x .875 inch.

A design change on the 5¢ value delayed the issue somewhat, and the series was released on May 1, 1924, instead of the April 24 date that had been planned.

The beauty of these stamps, as with most others, was in the eye of the beholder. Philip Ward didn't care much for them, writing that "they look like large colored labels."[9] Ralph Kimble, however, found them "of unusually handsome appearance."[10]

Philatelic Aspects and Varieties

First day of issue. This stamp was issued on May 1, 1924, in Washington, D.C., and 10 different cities: Albany, New York; Allentown, Pennsylvania; Charleston, South Carolina; Jacksonville, Florida; Lancaster, Pennsylvania; Mayport, Florida; New Rochelle, New York; New York, New York; Philadelphia, Pennsylvania; and Reading, Pennsylvania.

With so many church groups, congressmen and organizations involved in the sponsoring committee, it was perhaps inevitable that there would be a clamor for inclusion as first-day cities. This was by far the most that had ever been designated as first-day sites. There was adequate notice for dealers and collectors to prepare covers. First-day cover collecting was becoming increasingly popular, and the fact that this was a commemorative issue added to the large number of covers prepared. Covers affixed with all three stamps in the series generally command a substantial premium. Otherwise, Scott prices all 11 cities equally. Figure 75 shows a combination first-day cover serviced by Philip Ward from Jacksonville, Florida.

Shades. Scott listed dark green as the major shade, and green as a minor shade when this stamp first appeared in the 1926 edition of the Scott *Specialized,* and continues to list the stamp this way. Johl had no additions.

Double transfer. This variety has never been well-defined. It was included with the first listing of this stamp in the 1926 Scott *Specialized*. Johl, in the 1947 edition of his *Commemoratives* noted only that a double transfer was

Figure 75. A combination first-day cover, serviced at Jacksonville, Florida, by the stamp columnist and dealer Philip Ward.

"listed — no data." French lists only one double transfer, based on a 1938 report of a single copy, which "shows almost the entire right outside frame line shifted to the right."[11] Johl included this variety, but called it a "shifted transfer."

2¢ Walloons Landing at Fort Orange

Scott Number:	615
First Day of Issue:	May 1, 1924
Perforation:	11
Scott Colors:	Carmine rose, dark carmine rose
Designer:	Clair Aubrey Huston
Engravers:	H.P. Dawson (vignette, scrolls and ribbons)
	E.M. Hall (frame and lettering)
Plate Layout:	Flat plate; plates of 200 cut into panes of 50
Quantity Issued:	77,753,423
Plate Numbers:	15744-47, 15760-63, 15766-69, 15786-89
Scott Varieties:	Double transfer

The Subject and Design

The reference artwork for the design of this value, like the others, was provided by the stamp's sponsor, the National Huguenot-Walloon New Netherland Commission. It was a print titled *Landing of the Walloons at Albany*, which was taken from the book *A History of New York* by Martha J. Lamb, published in 1877.

Designer Huston used the print itself for the large working model and actually extended the scene a bit on the sides to make it fit the aspect ratio of the stamp. Huston's altered print is shown in Figure 76. This large working model was reduced to stamp size for approval. It was then copied rather carefully by picture engraver Harry Dawson. The scene shows a group of Walloons landing on the banks of the Hudson River. Some, including a woman with an infant, are seated, while others are unloading supplies. Their sailing ship is moored in the background. This was a rather complex scene to engrave in stamp

Figure 76. The print Landing of the Walloons at Albany *was extended at the sides so that it would fit the stamp design. This is the artwork used by the Bureau of Engraving and Printing for the working model of the stamp.*

size, but Dawson carried it off rather well.

The Post Office Department, described this scene as Lamb's book did, as "the landing of the Walloons at Albany, N.Y.," but this was a bit of an anachronism, and the scene is of course imaginative and idealized. The Walloons probably landed at Fort Nassau, a temporary post on the west bank of the Hudson that had been established by the Dutch in 1614. They built Fort Orange on the same site, which became the first permanent settlement there. It became the Dutch town of Beverwyck in 1652. It was not called Albany until the British took control in 1664 and renamed it after the Duke of York and Albany, who later became King James II.

Philatelic Aspects and Varieties

All three values of this stamp were released on May 1, 1924, at 11 cities (see the listing at the 1¢ stamp above). The 2¢ value was printed in the largest quantity, as it paid the first-class letter rate of the time. It is a somewhat better-studied stamp than either of the other two values, although as we discuss below, the 5¢ value has the most dramatic of the plate varieties.

Shades. The Bureau and the Post Office Department described the color of this stamp as just plain old red. When first listed in the 1926 edition of the Scott *Specialized*, the major shade was given as carmine rose, with deep carmine rose as a minor shade. Scott continues to list the stamp this way. Johl added only dark carmine rose.

Double transfer. The variety was listed with the first appearance of this stamp in the 1926 edition of the Scott *Specialized*. There are several well-documented double transfers of this stamp in known positions. Three of them are adjacent stamps: 15745 UL 16, 17 and 18.

The double at 15745 UL 16 has been discussed and illustrated at some length. In 1934 Johl called it "easily seen and a major plate variety."[12] This stamp is included in the side plate block and was often saved. The doubling shows in both numerals and in the lower frameline. The stamp next to it, 15745 UL 17, is also included in the side plate block. It also shows doubling in both numerals, and in the bottom and left framelines. The stamp at 15745 UL 18 is not included in the plate block. It also shows doubling at the bottom and left framelines.

Damaged transfer. A constant variety is also known on several stamps of plate 15746, which shows as a spot in the letter "A" of postage. George Sloane described this as "a pear shaped spot" caused by a bit of foreign material adhering to the relief. This shows on stamps 5, 6 and 7 of the lower-right pane, and on stamps 6, 7, 8, 9 and 10 of the lower-left pane. Sloane described this mark as "gradually fading in distinctness until it disappears."[13]

5¢ Jean Ribault Monument

Scott Number:	616
First Day of Issue:	May 1, 1924
Perforation:	11
Scott Colors:	Dark blue, deep blue
Designer:	Clair Aubrey Huston
Engravers:	F. Pauling and E.M. Hall
Plate Layout:	Flat plate; plates of 200 cut into panes of 50
Quantity Issued:	5,659,023
Plate Numbers:	15752-55
Scott Varieties:	"Broken circle": 15754, UR 2, 3, 4, 5

The Subject and Design

This value of the series represents the Huguenot part of the emigration and shows a stone pillar, known as the Jean Ribaut Monument, at Mayport, Florida, which is now part of Jacksonville. This was the site of Fort Caroline, the French Huguenot settlement established by Rene Laudonniere in 1564. Jean Ribaut, who formed the first disastrous colony in South Carolina in 1562, was killed here in 1565 by the Spanish when he tried to relieve the colonists.

The Ribaut monument is a replica of a stone marker, reportedly carved with a French coat of arms, that was erected at Fort Caroline in 1564. The Daughters of the American Revolution of Florida erected this replica in 1924 and dedicated it on May 1, the same date as the stamps were released.

The reference for the original monument was a print, apparently by the Dutch engraver Theodor De Bry, showing this monument, Florida Indians, Ribaut and gifts that were given to the Indians by the French. This artwork was used on the rejected models with the squared-off frames shown in Figure 74, and it was also used in the arched frame models of the issued stamps, which were approved on March 11.

However, a week later the approval of the 5¢ design was rescinded. The Bureau was supplied with new artwork provided by the Huguenot-Walloon Commission, and the Post Office Department stated that "it is desired to have an additional model prepared for the five-cent denomination along the lines of the accompanying exhibit."[14] In the meantime, work on the series was suspended.

The new artwork showing the monument, a palm tree and the sun rising over the St. John River was provided by the Reverend John Baer Stoudt, who seems to have taken credit for creating it. Johl and King quote him as saying: "In drawing the sketch I found that by point of compass the sun rose over an island directly in line with the monument. This gave me the idea of incorporating the symbolism and I sketched in a rising sun."[15]

However, several years later F.P. Mills, a Florida architect, wrote to the Post Office Department stating that he drew the sketch while he was working for the Jacksonville architectural firm of Greely & Benjamin, which was commissioned by the Florida chapter of the Daughters of the American Revolution to provide a sketch.

"I was sent to Mayport on the St. John's River," Mills wrote, "to make a sketch of the site and on returning to the office I made a finished drawing of the site and for the monument for this five cent stamp and it was given to the above society." Mills further wrote that

Figure 77. Bureau designer C. Aubrey Huston's original artwork for the vignette of the 5¢ value. The matting and inscription have been added.

"it seems a pretty small thing for Dr. Stoudt to assume credit for the work of a $50-per-week draftsman."[16]

Bureau designer Huston modified this drawing for the stamp. Mills' original drawing is not preserved, but the Huston drawing used for the working model was collected by Beverly King and is now listed as an essay for this stamp. It is shown in Figure 77, with a mat and inscription that has been added.

Figure 78. The replica of the Ribault monument, unvieled by the Daughters of the American Revolution in 1924, at its present location.

Huston's new model was approved on March 20, and work went forward on the series.

The official Post Office Department notice for this stamp said that the 5¢ denomination "represents a marker located at Mayport, Fla., showing the landing place of one colony of Walloons." This is in error, of course, as it relates not to the Walloons but to a specific colonization effort of the French Huguenots under the auspices of the admiral of France. Like most Americans, Post Office Department officials had trouble completely understanding what this series was about.

The replica of the Ribault column is no longer in the same place where it was unveiled on May 1, 1924, in conjunction with the issue of the stamp, and it has been moved around a bit in the ensuing years. As World War II was breaking out in 1941, a U.S. Naval Station was established at Mayport, Florida, and the area on the south bank of the river became inaccessible to the public. The replica column was moved in early 1942 to a new location on the naval base, but this too, was unsuitable, and it was then moved just outside the base.

The Daughters of the American Revolution, at its annual meeting in 1957, voted to move the monument again, and on July 8, 1958, it was moved to donated property on St. John's Bluff that was to become part of the Fort Caroline National Memorial, which is maintained by the National Park Service. Figure 78 shows the replica monument in its present location.

Philatelic Aspects and Varieties

Like the 2¢ value, this stamp had both its admirers and detractors. King and Johl, in describing the design, called it "this rather uninteresting picture" while Ralph Kimble called it "by far the most lovely stamp of all, and one of the finest in our history."[17]

The most interesting aspect of this stamp, however, is the relief break that is known on one plate, which is discussed below.

First day of issue. While this stamp was issued with the others on May 1, 1924, and at the same cities (see the list at the 1¢ stamp above), the date was tied to the unveiling of the replica of the Ribault column in Mayport, Florida, by the Daughters of the American Revolution. There was a ceremony for the monument's unveiling, but there seems to have been no ceremony for the issuing of the stamp.

Shades. When this stamp was first listed in the 1926 edition of the Scott *Specialized*, the major shade was given as dark blue with deep blue as a minor shade. The stamp continues to be listed the same way. Johl had no additions. There is not, however, much variety in shade in this stamp. Only four plates were used, and they all went to press together for one printing.

Broken circle. This is an outstanding example of a relief break, and no doubt the best example of a progressive relief break in 20th-century U.S. philately. Although the Scott listing has changed a bit over the years, it was included in the first listing of the stamp in the 1926 edition of the Scott *Specialized*.

The break occurs in the inner circle of the right numeral on stamp 15745 UR 2. The next stamp shows a further break, as the thin piece of steel on the relief drops lower on 15745 UR 3 (see Figure 79). Stamps 15745 UR 4 and 5 show the relief breaking further. By stamp 15745 UR 7 the steel has completely broken off the relief, but a piece of it can be seen lodged in the white space just above the lower frameline.

The current Scott listing mentions four stamps, 15745 UR 2, 3, 4, 5, as making up this variety, but George Sloane probably had the matter right when he wrote that "the ideal form in which to obtain the variety is in a block of ten stamps comprising the two top rows of the sheet."[18] Sloane found three varieties, which he called "the normal circle, the broken circle, and the defective circle." The normal circle shows on all copies of plates 15752, 15753 and 15742, and the left panes of 15745. It will also show on the 15745 UR 1. The broken circle, or perhaps more correctly, the breaking circle, shows progressively on stamps 15745 UR 2, 3, 4 and 5. The de-

Figure 79. The circle at left is from stamp 15745 UR 3 and shows the broken relief. The circle at right, from an adjacent stamp, shows the normal configuration of the circle.

fective circle, which is the circle after the break has occurred and after the steel has broken off the relief, shows on all copies below 15745 UR 6 and on all copies of the lower-right pane of plate 15745.

Notes

1. *The National Huguenot-Walloon New Netherland Commission* [brochure], New York, 1923, p. 15.

2. *Ibid.*, p 10.

3. Samuel Eliot Morison, *The European Discovery of America: The Northern Voyages* (New York: Oxford University Press, 1971), p. 470.

4. *Ibid.*

5. *Commission* brochure, *op. cit.*, p. 6.

6. Johl, *Commemoratives*, Vol. 1, p. 89.

7. Clarence W. Brazer, *Essays for U.S. Adhesive Postage Stamps* (Quarterman Publications, reprint, 1976), p. 195.

8. W. Irving Glover to W.W. Kirby, director, Bureau of Engraving and Printing, March 6, 1924. Bureau of Engraving and Printing.

9. Philip H. Ward Jr., "Chronicle of New Issues and Varieties," *Mekeel's Weekly Stamp News*, Vol. 38, No. 20 (May 19, 1924), p. 278.

10. Ralph A. Kimble, *Commemorative Postage Stamps of the United States* (New York: Grosset & Dunlap), 1933, p. 103.

11. James H. Obrig, "Plate Varieties," *Bureau Specialist*, Vol. 9, No. 6 (June 1938), p. 72.

12. Max G. Johl, "Max G. Johl Replies on 20th Century U.S.," *Stamps*, Vol. 9, No. 10 (October 8, 1934), p. 346. As printed here, this variety is mentioned as from plate 15744, but Johl corrected this error in a later column, to be plate 15745. See Johl's same column in *Stamps*, Vol. 12, No. 9 (August 31, 1935), p. 302.

13. George B. Sloane, "1924 2¢ Huguenot-Walloon" in *Stamps*, January 28, 1933, reprinted in *Sloane's Column* (BIA, 1961), p. 322.

14. Harvey Lovejoy, acting third assistant postmaster general, to W.W. Kirby, March 19, 1924. Bureau of Engraving and Printing.

15. Beverly S. King and Max G. Johl, *The United States Postage Stamps of the Twentieth Century*, Volume II: Commemoratives 1923-1933 (New York:

H.L. Lindquist, 1934), p. 11.

16. F.P.L. Mills to Post Office Department, August 28, 1956. Smithsonian Institution Libraries, Post Office Department Manuscripts.

17. Kimble, *op. cit.*, p. 104.

18. George B. Sloane, "Huguenot-Walloon, 5¢ Blue Broken Circle," *Sloane's Column*, *op. cit.*, p. 322.

Chapter 18

Another Rotary Experiment: The 2¢ Perf 10

While it makes for neat album placement to group all the perf-10 rotary sheet stamps together, the stamps we know as Scott 581-591 were issued over a long stretch of time. As was discussed in Chapter 11, the 1¢ value was an experimental one and was the first to be issued, as early as April 1923, in precanceled form. Until it was determined to be a success, no other values were produced.

The 2¢ stamp was the next to be issued in rotary sheet format perforated 10. This too, as we shall see, was an experimental stamp, and it was issued by itself, sometime in the spring of 1924, at least six months before the next value to be issued — the 5¢ — and about two years before the last stamps of the series — the 7¢, 8¢ and 9¢ values — which were not issued until May 1926.

This entire series will be discussed in Chapter 24. But to understand the development of these stamps, and of the large rotary press, the events of early 1924 are crucial. There was a flurry of developments in the first two months of the year that assured not only continued experiments with the large rotary press, but its eventual domination of postage-stamp printing at the Bureau.

The Large Rotary Press and Sheet Stamp Production

On January 12, a committee established by the Post Office Department for studying the use of the rotary press for sheet stamps recommended that it be expanded by producing 2¢ sheet stamps with precancels "in order that further experimentation can be made of the precanceling of postage stamps other than the 1¢ denomination."[1] But before this "experimentation" could be conducted and evaluated, other developments would step up the pace of the use of the large rotary press (shown in Figure 80) for stamp production.

On January 17, the first delivery of Bureau-precanceled coil stamps was made to Chicago and Boston in 1¢ and 2¢ denominations, and to Washington, D.C., in only the 1¢ denomination. As with the previous coil stamps, there were virtually no complaints about these sidewise coils, and their precanceling at the Bureau was a money-saving convenience.

On February 15, the Bureau of Engraving and Printing went through a major change, coming under new management, with the resignation of Louis

213

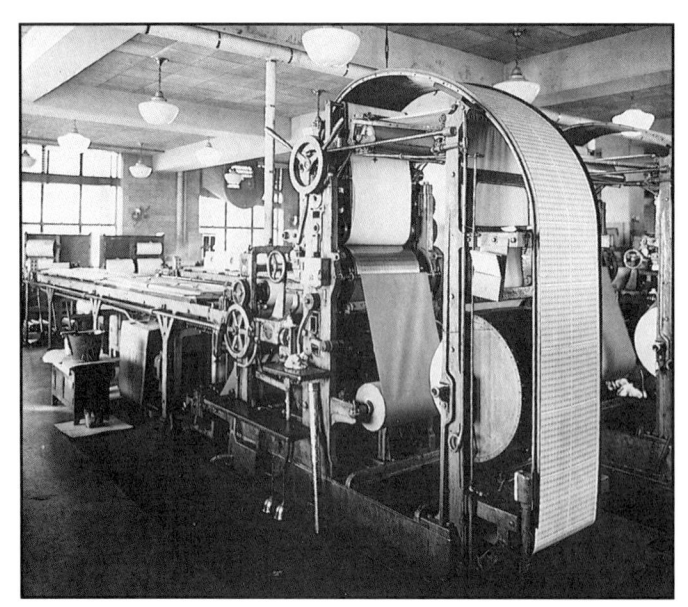

Figure 80. The large rotary press was designed to print sheet stamps from two 400-subject plates. The diameter of the printing cylinder was larger than that of the original press, which was used only for coils. The large press printed on rolls of paper that were 18½ inches wide, while the coil press printed on rolls 10⁵⁄₁₆ inches wide.

A. Hill as director and the temporary appointment of Wallace W. Kirby, an officer of the Army Corps of Engineers, as director. Kirby had been a Bureau supervisor in the offset plate-making division until 1920. The investigation into the so-called Liberty Loan scandal (see Chapter 6) that had resulted in the dismissal of the Bureau's top managers in March 1922 had finally proved that the charges were unfounded, and Kirby set out to rebuild the demoralized staff. "It was found that one of the first things to be done," he wrote, "was to devise ways and means to gain the confidence of the employees and build up the morale."[2]

All of the dismissed employees who wished to return were reinstated, and 17 of the 25 came back to their previous positions. One of these was Benjamin Stickney, the mechanical expert who had invented the rotary press, and who had been developing a plan to eventually convert all Bureau stamp production to these presses. Stickney returned to the Bureau on February 25, at a critical point.

Three days after Stickney returned, the committee studying the rotary press issued a lengthy report to Postmaster General New. It found that "rotary stamps are not in keeping with the superior quality that the Post Office Department desires." It also made a series of recommendations, the first of which was "that the rotary presses be used exclusively for the manufacture of coils and precanceled stamps, except in cases of unusual emergencies, when, upon authorization of the postmaster general, they may be used for printing ordinary stamps."[3]

Another Rotary Experiment: The 2¢ Perf 10

Michael Eidsness, the superintendent of the Division of Stamps, was the chairman of this committee. He, his assistant and two Bureau superintendents signed this report. One other member of the committee, B.L. Andrus, the chief Post Office Department inspector, wrote something of a minority report, in which he recommended that the rotary presses also be used for nonprecanceled sheet stamps "as may be necessary to keep the machines used in the rotary process fully occupied at all times."[4]

Andrus, who had evidently become a supporter of the rotary press for several reasons, explained them in an additional memorandum to the postmaster general. He argued that the complaints about the rotary stamps were somewhat overstated. Although some postmasters had been quite vocal about their dislike of these stamps, Andrus argued that a questionnaire to 566 postmasters showed that "only twelve reported that any complaint had been received. ..."

Andrus went on to argue that "the work produced by the rotary presses is excellent and from the standpoint of the needs of the Post Office Department, fully meets the requirements." Moreover, he said, whatever some might think about the differences between flat-plate and rotary sheet stamps, the difference was "of such minor importance that it has no comparison to the financial advantage of the rotary process."[5]

This was a well-reasoned argument, but it could not be accepted for political reasons. To do so would overturn the majority report. W. Irving Glover, and Harry S. New in turn, thus approved the committee's report on March 1, stating that Andrus' minority position was "not material by reason of the fact that the authority to permit the production of stamps for regular purposes in addition to the precanceled and coiled stamps, is lodged in this Department, and if the product consisting of precanceled and coiled stamps is improved within a short time ... the Department can authorize the issue of stamps for regular purposes, which will no doubt meet the views of Mr. Andrus."[6]

Andrus' minority report that rotary-press stamps were acceptable, and in fact preferable because of their cost, was buttressed by Stickney's return and his work with gum-breaking experiments, which would help to reduce the major criticism — the curl of rotary-press sheet stamps. Referring to Stickney's work on this problem, Paul Twyman, acting director of the Bureau, wrote to the Post Office Department on April 10 that a "mechanical improvement" had been made on the presses.

Eidsness, the chairman of the committee, was also being given more and more responsibility for stamp production as Glover, his immediate supervisor, became more involved and interested in airmail. Eidsness immediately visited the Bureau to see Stickney's work, and on April 14, Glover reported that Eidsness had "noted the improvement in the quality of the stamps furnished."

On this same date, Glover in effect reversed the recommendation that the committee had made less than a month earlier, and authorized "the manufacture of 300,000,000 1¢ and 300,000,000 2¢ by the rotary process." He stated that "it is believed that one of the most objectionable features of the rotary process stamps will be largely, if not entirely, overcome by the new attachment to the web perforating machines" and ordered this somewhat experimental press run so that these stamps "may be given a thorough trial."[7]

Thus, at least on an experimental basis, the rotary press was OK'd for sheet-stamp production. The crucial bridge had been crossed. In a period of less than four months, the rotary press moved from being unacceptable for normal sheet-stamp production to acceptable.

The long process of converting stamp production from the flat-plate presses to the rotary-press production got under way again. Stickney was back to see things through, and he no doubt made sure that the crucial, experimental 2¢ rotary sheet stamp was a success.

2¢ Washington Rotary

Scott Number:	583
Earliest Reported Use:	May 15, 1924, unprecanceled
Perforation:	10
Scott Colors:	Carmine, deep carmine
Press:	Large rotary press
Plate Layout:	Plates of 400 cut into panes of 100
Quantity Issued:	Unknown
Plate Numbers:	Total of 284: lowest, 15412; highest, 18952
Scott Varieties:	None

Philatelic Aspects and Varieties

This has been a somewhat mysterious stamp, as there was no advance notice of its issue, and no first-day covers are known. The precanceled variety was authorized first, but because precancels are not normally canceled, we do not seem to have a very substantial basis for determining when these stamps were first issued. As usual, it was Philip Ward who reported the appearance of this variety, in his hometown of Philadelphia, stating in his column of May 5, 1924, that "we saw the first of the 2¢ during the week of April 14th."

Since April 14 was a Monday, this could mean that the stamps appeared sometime between that date and Saturday, April 19. We have Ward's usually good recollection to go on, but no dated cover, as precancels were not usually given additional cancellations that would provide a date. Ward and others could not legally produce covers from these stamps, as precancels required a permit.

Ward gave the shade as "deep carmine" and noted that "as yet the variety is not available in unused condition, although it no doubt will be at an early date, as the Department has been requested to make these available to collectors through the Philatelic Agency."[8]

Although Ward and other collectors were looking for this stamp to appear unused at the Philatelic Stamp Agency in Washington, D.C., it was first reported from Chicago. Ward noted in his June 9 column that "through the kindness of Mr. George Soulman we are able to report that this stamp in an unused condition is now on sale at the Chicago office."[9] No first day was established, and no first-day covers were prepared.

Jack Harvey has speculated that there may have been an attempt by the Post Office Department to make no notification of this new issue and to keep its release a secret. "Since there had been so many complaints from post offices," Harvey wrote, "... the Department may have decided to circulate the 2¢ value rotary ... without telling the post offices that it was a rotary press printing on the theory that this was the only fair test of the process."[10]

To date, the earliest-documented cover of an unprecanceled example of 583 is May 15, 1924, on a nonphilatelic picture postcard from Washington, D.C. This was found rather recently by early use specialist Bill Hart.[11]

Shades. As we have mentioned above, Ward reported this stamp as deep carmine, and Scott, in first listing this stamp in the 1926 edition of the *Specialized Catalogue*, gave carmine as the primary shade and deep carmine as a minor shade. Scott continues to list the stamp this way. To these, Johl added rose carmine, bright carmine, dark carmine and lake.

Plate layout. As with the 1¢ value (581) and the rotary Black Harding (612), some plates, mainly the earlier ones, have what we know as Type A marginal markings with horizontal dashes in the center vertical gutter.

On the later plates, which comprise the great majority of the total, these horizontal dashes were replaced by a short cross in the center of the sheet where the vertical and horizontal gutters met, and short vertical and horizontal marks, like the so-called arrows of the flat plates, at the ends of the horizontal and vertical gutters. These are referred to as Type B marginal markings.

Figure 81. The two types of marginal markings are shown on blocks of Scott 583. Type A (left) has short horizontal lines at the left of the stamps. These are from the center vertical gutter of the sheets of 400 that were cut into panes of 100. Type B (right) shows a portion of the central cross where the vertical and horizontal gutters met on the sheets of 400.

Figure 81 shows these two types of marginal markings.

Plate varieties. With so many plates — 284 — we should expect a number of plate varieties. However, Scott lists none. This issue has been a bit troublesome since the rotary process often produces "ink drags" on the stamps, which are blots or strands of ink that have been deposited on the stamps due to the fast rotary process, which sometimes spins off, or flips off, ink. A number of smears and other pseudo-varieties are also known. Thus, while determining true plate varieties on these stamps, it is necessary to have at the very least two clear copies of the exact same variety.

This being said, a few good plate varieties have been reported. A double transfer from an unknown position was illustrated in Johl, and French lists some 26 varieties. Carolyn Kuhn, a student of the 2¢ Washington stamp in all its varieties, noted that "the perf 10 stamp is represented by the fewest number of plate varieties," but included a combination scratch and gouge over Washington's ear in her "Twelve Best Plate Varieties on the 2¢ Washington,"[12] which contains a good illustration. Another easily seen and constant plate variety on this stamp is a deep gouge through the right numeral, which was first reported and illustrated by Kuhn in 1951.[13]

Double paper. Before 1946, Scott listed double-paper varieties on a number of rotary-press stamps, including this one. This double paper occurs where two webs of paper were spliced together, and can appear on all rotary-press stamps. The double-paper listing first appeared for this stamp in the 1927 edition of the Scott *Specialized*. Beginning in the 1932 edition, it was listed as 583a. This listing was dropped in the 1946 edition.

Note: The booklet version of this stamp, 583a, which appeared in 1926, is covered in Chapter 38.

Notes

1. W. Irving Glover to W.W. Kirby, January 12, 1924. Bureau of Engraving and Printing.

2. Wallace W. Kirby, *Annual Report of the Director of the Bureau of Engraving and Printing*, 1924 (Washington: Government Printing Office), p. 1.

3. Michael Eidsness Jr., et al, to Harry S. New, February 28, 1924, p. 19. Smithsonian Institution Libraries, Post Office Department Manuscripts.

4. *Ibid.*, p. 20.

5. B.L. Andrus to Harry S. New, February 29, 1924. Smithsonian Institution Libraries, Post Office Department Manuscripts.

6. W. Irving Glover to Harry S. New, March 1, 1924. Smithsonian Institution Libraries, Post Office Department Manuscripts.

7. W. Irving Glover to Paul Twyman, acting director, Bureau of Engraving and Printing, April 14, 1924. Bureau of Engraving and Printing.

8. Philip H. Ward Jr., "Chronicle of New Issues and Varieties," *Mekeel's Weekly Stamp News*, Vol. 38, No. 19 (May 12, 1924).

9. Philip H. Ward Jr., "Chronicle of New Issues and Varieties," *Mekeel's Weekly Stamp News*, Vol. 38, No. 23 (June 9, 1924), p. 320.

10. Jack V. Harvey, *First Day Covers of the Regular Postage Issue of 1922-1935*, Second Edition (American First Day Cover Society, 1985), p. 30.

11. See William J. Hart, "The Elusive First Day of Use: Sc. 583, the 2¢ Perf 10 of 1924," *First Days*, December 1, 1991, p. 890-91.

12. Carolyn P. Kuhn, "The Twelve Best Plate Varieties on the 2¢ Washington," *Bureau Specialist*, Vol. 27, No. 3 (March 1956), p. 64.

13. Carolyn P. Kuhn, "2¢ Washington 1922," *Bureau Specialist*, Vol. 22, No. 9 (September 1951), p. 165.

United States Stamps 1922-26

Chapter 19

The Election of 1924 and New Postal Rates of 1925

During the year and a half that Calvin Coolidge filled out the presidential term of Warren Harding, he made no changes in the Cabinet and was determined to carry on the policies of his predecessor. While he soon found that he had to ask for the resignation of Attorney General Daugherty and to accept the resignation of Navy Secretary Denby, both of whom were caught up in scandals during the Harding administration, Coolidge for the most part let his Cabinet secretaries manage their portfolios. Historian Geoffrey Perrett writes that Coolidge "allowed them the widest freedom in running their departments."[1]

Although he was anything but a charismatic personality, Silent Cal, as he became known, had no opposition in his own party for the 1924 Republican nomination. The Democrats had one of the most raucous conventions in history, taking 103 ballots to finally come up with a compromise candidate, John W. Davis. In the fall campaign they continued to be disorganized, and failed to make a cutting issue of the Teapot Dome oil affair or the other scandals of the Harding administration that had come to light. Robert LaFollette, a populist senator from Wisconsin, ran as the Progressive Party's candidate and took almost five million votes. Davis won just over eight million. Coolidge took nearly 16 million, in what was a rather unexciting campaign. Coolidge was portrayed as honest and thrifty, and the economy was robust. One of the campaign slogans that stuck was "Coolidge or Chaos." The majority of American voters, and particularly those who were doing well, did not want a change.

"They did not want a man of action in the Presidency," Frederick Lewis Allen has written of the mood. "They wanted as little government as possible, at as low cost as possible, and this dour New Englander who drove the prosperity bandwagon with so slack a rein embodied their idea of supreme statesmanship."[2]

After the election, Coolidge made a few key changes in his Cabinet, but kept on the most able administrators brought in by his predecessor, including Herbert Hoover as secretary of commerce, Hubert Work as secretary of the interior, and Andrew Mellon as secretary of treasury. Postmaster General Harry S. New was not quite of the same caliber, but he, too, stayed on.

New Rates

After the election, the "Coolidge prosperity" that the nation was experiencing also meant more money for members of Congress. Then, as now, Congress liked to put as much distance between election days and their own pay raises as possible. Then, however, members had the luxury of a long, four-month lame-duck session between the November elections and the March 4 inauguration. This was viewed as a perfect time for passing unpopular legislation and casting anonymous votes. On February 17, 1925, the Senate approved a House-passed pay raise.

All of their salaries would be increased by a whopping 25 percent, to $10,000 a year from $7,500. Cabinet members also received the same increase, from $12,000 to $15,000. The measure passed on voice votes in both houses, so that no one was recorded as voting yes or no.

In the same spirit, Congress voted more money for many government employees, including postal workers. On February 28, in one of the final moments of the 68th Congress, its members passed a comprehensive bill that gave most Post Office Department workers some kind of a raise. Postal clerks and city letter carriers received an additional $300 a year, taking their salaries to a maximum of $2,400. Temporary clerks and carriers received a raise of 5¢ an hour, making their hourly wage 70¢. The pay increases were to take place on January 1, 1925, and it was estimated that the bill would cost the Post Office Department $68,000,000 for the first year.

To pay for the pay raises, the same piece of legislation raised a number of postal rates. The Post Office Department was not expected to break even. Somewhat like the military, it was viewed as a necessary service of government. Postal rates helped to offset its costs, but the Department ran a multimillion-dollar deficit every year. Postal rates were somewhat arbitrary and were always set in round amounts. First-class letters were 2¢. Postcards were a penny. Special delivery and registry services were 10¢ in addition. Many of these rates had been in effect for years, simply because the Post Office Department and Congress had not felt it necessary or politically expedient to change them.

Under the Republican administration that had come in with Harding, there was an increased effort to look at all government costs, and Secretary Mellon, in particular, wanted to reduce or eliminate the federal deficit. As early as 1921, the Post Office Department and a special committee of Congress set out to look at postal rates and the costs of carrying and handling all classes of mail. But the work was frustrated several times, once by a railroad strike and then by the failure of Congress to further fund the study. However, during the 1923 fiscal year, Congress appropriated $500,000 for a rate study, the results of which were finally transmitted to Congress on December 2, 1924.

This report, according to PMG New, was "voluminous and contained a vast array of important information," not the least of which was that the postal service "showed a loss in the performance of service for every class of mail

The Election of 1924 and New Postal Rates of 1925

Figure 82. The 1¢ rate for what we would call "junk mail" today was a bargain in the early 1920s, and the amount of it being sent in the mail during the "Coolidge prosperity" was increasing. The rate would be raised to 1½¢ under a new law that provided a pay raise for postal workers.

matter and special service, excepting first-class mail and postal savings. ..."[3]

The new law attempted to correct this situation, raising a number of new rates to make them more self-supporting.

By far the most important new rate in terms of stamps and stamp production was the increase in third-class matter from 1¢ to 1½¢ for the first two ounces. This related mostly to what we call "junk mail" today: circulars and miscellaneous printed matter (see Figure 82). The amount of this material that was being carried in the mails had increased with the economy and the advertising boom of the 1920s, but the rate had not changed since 1879.

This new rate meant that there would have to be fractional postage stamps for the first time. A 1½¢ stamp was called for, as was a ½¢ stamp and a ½¢ postage due stamp. The rate was to go into effect on April 15, which left the Post Office Department and the Bureau little time to prepare these stamps, which would be needed in rather large quantities.

A new service called "special handling" was also created for fourth-class mail. By paying a 25¢ fee in addition to the normal postage, parcels would receive "the same expeditious handling, transportation, and delivery" as first-class mail. A new stamp was required for this service.

Special delivery rates were also increased for heavier mail, which had previously been delivered by special messenger, regardless of weight, for a 10¢ fee in addition to the postage. Under the new law, mail for special delivery weighing over two pounds was charged 15¢ in addition to postage, and mail weighing over 10 pounds was charged 20¢ in addition for special delivery. These rates, too, required new stamps.

Many other rates that did not require new stamps were also changed, and new charges for some previously free services were instituted. No longer, for example, was a return receipt delivered at no charge when requested for registered mail; a fee of 3¢ would be charged. "Private mailing cards," which were postcards not produced by the government, went up to 2¢ from 1¢. Rates also were increased for parcel post, insured mail, collect-on-delivery service, money orders, and several other classifications and services.

In some ways the Post Office Department was a microcosm of the country. Business was good. Employment was growing. And everyone seemed to be making more money.

Notes

1. Geoffrey Perrett, *America in the Twenties* (New York: Simon & Schuster, 1982), p. 180.
2. Frederick Lewis Allen, *Only Yesterday: An Informal History of the Nineteen-Twenties* (New York: Harper & Brothers, 1931), p. 185.
3. Harry S. New, *Annual Report of the Postmaster General* (Washington: Government Printing Office, 1925), p. 5.

Chapter 20

The 1½¢ Harding

This was not only the first 1½¢ stamp to be issued by the United States, but also the first fractional denomination postage stamp. It represents well the businesslike precision of the Coolidge administration: charging as much as necessary — but no more — for government service.

There are six formats of the 1½¢ Harding stamp of 1925. Although these have Scott numbers ranging from 553 to 633, four of the six were issued within 60 days of one another in 1925. For album-page layout purposes Scott has included them with the Series of 1922, and has numbered them in series with the regular issues, coils and imperforates. This has somewhat obscured their real place in the chronology and philatelic history.

The Political Background

After Congress passed the pay-raise and postal-increase bill discussed in the preceding chapter, the Post Office Department found itself in a potentially embarrassing position. Postmaster General Harry S. New had been pushing for passage of the new law, but once it went into effect — which was rather quickly — his Department might not have any stamps to pay the new rates. Congress passed it on February 28, 1925, and the rates were to go into effect on April 15. This was only a six-week period, and the Post Office Department was also committed to producing a series of stamps for the 150th anniversary of the battles of Lexington and Concord, which had to be issued before April 18.

On February 27, the day after the Senate acted on the pay-raise and postal-rate bill, Michael Eidsness, superintendent of the Division of Stamps, wrote a detailed memo to Third Assistant Postmaster General W. Irving Glover, spelling out the challenges his division faced, and offering some suggestions.

"The Act," he wrote, "so far as I have been able to interpret, requires the issuance of a 1½¢ stamp for third class matter, a 15¢ special delivery stamp for first class matter ... and a 20¢ special delivery stamp for parcel post matter above ten pounds." He also noted that a new stamp would be required for the special handling rate, but advised that it be delayed.

In order "to expedite the printing" of the new stamps, Eidsness continued, "I suggest that the present Harding Memorial stamp be changed to read '1½¢' as well as a corresponding change in color." This would eliminate nearly all of the design work, it would require only minimal new engraving, and it would also speed up the approval process, as the subject already existed.

"I believe that a large quantity of these stamps could be made available for sale at post offices on April 15th," Eidsness continued, "and thereby saving a great deal of embarrassment to the service."[1]

This was a suggestion that no doubt went down easy with the top executives at the Post Office Department. Not only would it be expedient, but it would put the revered former president, who had personally appointed all of them, on an ordinary or regularly issued stamp. The Harding Memorial stamp was long out of production by this time, and there had been suggestions to some day include his portrait as part of the regular series.

Glover and New approved the suggestion quickly, if not immediately, as work on the die began at the Bureau on the following day with no formal approval of a model. The model was sent to the Post Office Department on March 2, was returned for an unspecified change and was approved on March 5. The approval model is shown in Figure 83. A die proof was approved on March 7.

Figure 83. The stamp-size approval model for the 1½¢ Harding was made by simply changing the denomination of the Harding Memorial issue and replacing the dates in the upper corners with triangular ornaments.

In addition to changing the denomination, corner ornaments were added to replace the years of birth and death on the Harding Memorial stamp. Perhaps this was the change suggested when the model was returned unapproved. Transfer roll 1335, which had been made from the 2¢ Black Harding die 721, was used to make a new die for the 1½¢ design. This new die was numbered 734, and reworked to make the changes required in the denomination and ornaments. Because of the lighter ink used — brown instead of black — some lines of the engraving were deepened.

A Joint Issue

In order to get as many stamps as possible to post offices, it was decided to use both the flat-plate and rotary presses to produce this stamp. With the 2¢ Black Harding, the rotary printings were added after the flat-plate printings had begun. In this case, they were coterminous, and were the first flat-plate and rotary-press stamps to be jointly issued. A sidewise coil version was also produced and issued at the same time.

Issuing this stamp in a rotary version made sense as well because there would be a large demand for it in precanceled form. It would replace most of the 1¢ precancels that were used for third-class mailings.

The first numbered plates, 16825 and 16826, were 400-subject rotary plates. The next numbered plate used for this design was 16828, a 170-subject rotary coil plate. Next were 400-subject flat plates 16829, 16830, 16831 and

The 1½¢ Harding

16832. All of these plates were assigned on the same day, March 7.

The flat-plate stamp (Scott 553), rotary stamp perforated 10 (582) and sidewise coil stamp (598) were all issued on March 19. It is important to note that Scott's numbering system is not chronological, and that all of these stamps were issued more than year and a half after the higher numbered Black Hardings (610-13). A stamped envelope (U481) was also prepared for release on the same day.

The flat-plate imperforate version of the 1½¢ Harding was issued only a few days later, on April 4, and the endwise coil was issued on May 9. So within a period of less than 60 days, five varieties or formats of this stamp were issued, not including the stamped envelope. There was no booklet version, as this stamp was used mainly by business mailers.

While these stamps are correctly included in what we know as the Series of 1922, or the Fourth Bureau issue, they have a different frame design, which derived from the Black Harding. They are the fourth frame design of the series, following the vertical frame used for the values from 1¢ to 14¢, the so-called horseshoe frames used for the 15¢ Liberty, and the horizontal frame used for values from 20¢ to $5.

1½¢ Harding Flat Plate

Scott Number:	553
First Day of Issue:	March 19, 1925
Perforation:	11
Scott Colors:	Yellow brown, pale yellow brown, brown
Designer:	Clair Aubrey Huston
Engravers:	Frederic Pauling (vignette)
	E.M. Hall (frame and lettering of "Harding")
	J.C. Benzing (scrolls and ribbon), and E.M. Weeks (numerals)
Press:	Flat plate
Plate Layout:	400 subjects, cut into panes of 100
Quantity Issued:	1,208,187,883
Plate Numbers:	Total of 66: lowest, 16829; highest, 16984
Scott Varieties:	Double transfer

Philatelic Aspects and Varieties

First day of issue. This stamp was issued on March 19, 1925, only at Washington, D.C. There was rather subdued departmental publicity about the release of this stamp for several reasons, not the least of which was the uncertainty of production schedules. There was no first-day event, and the stamp was issued only in Washington, D.C. News that there would be a 1½¢ stamp was officially announced on March 9, stating that stamps and stamped envelopes would be shipped to postmasters "as soon as sufficient stocks are available."[2] No mention was made of a portrait subject or color, but this announcement gave first-day-cover enthusiasts ample notice.

It was not until March 13 that the Post Office Department announced that former President Warren Harding would be the subject, but again, no date of release was given, only the information that "the first issue of the 1½-cent stamp will be off the press Tuesday, March 17."[3] This obviously helped inform the first-day crowd, but the short notice seemed to prevent anyone from preparing printed cachets or other embellishments. Most first-day covers of this stamp are plain. Figure 84 shows a combination cover with the stamped envelope.

A rumor surfaced that there were two dies made for this stamp, but it was probably based on the fact that the stamp was issued from both the flat-plate and rotary presses at the same time, resulting in two different size stamps. Philip Ward, in researching the basis of the rumor, reported that "there has been no second die" but attributed to Bureau director Alvin W. Hall the information

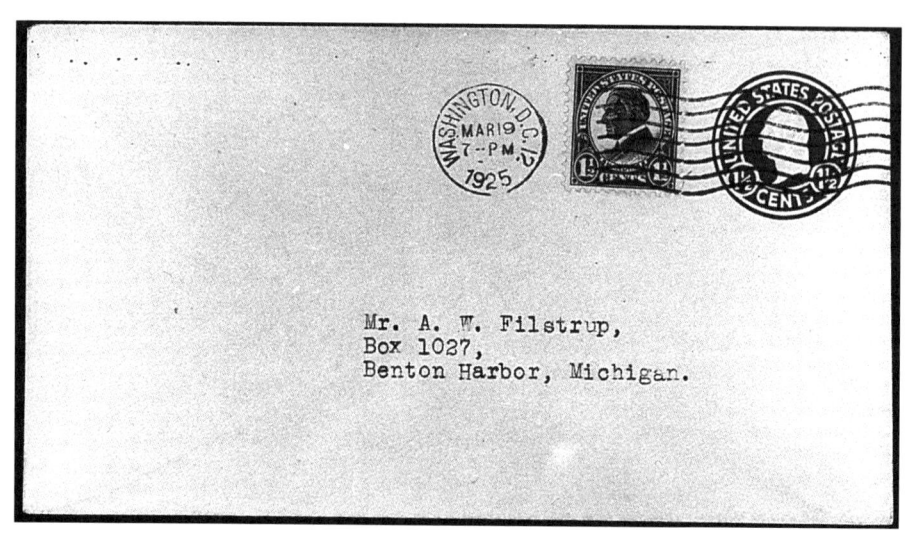

Figure 84. Most first-day covers of the 1½¢ Harding stamps are plain, as the short notice prevented servicers from preparing any type of printed cachet or other embellishment. This is a combination of the flat-plate stamp and the stamped envelope (Scott U481), which were issued on the same day.

The 1½¢ Harding

that "it was necessary to work over the entire stamp, especially the portrait, in order to give it depth for the new color in which it is printed."[4]

Shades. The Post Office Department release of March 13 gave the color as "sepia brown, the same color as that used on the present 4-cent Martha Washington stamp" but in other places the color was given as "light brown."[5] Ward, in reporting on this stamp within a month of its issuance, noted that it "has appeared in two very distinct shades, one a deep brown, and the other a yellow brown."[6]

Scott, when it first listed this stamp in the 1926 edition of the *Specialized Catalogue,* gave the major shade as yellow brown, and gave brown and pale yellow brown as minor shades. The listings remain the same today.

Johl found a much wider range, as usual, and listed in addition light yellow brown, yellowish brown, deep yellow brown, reddish brown and deep brown.

Double transfer. Some "191 shifted transfers" were reported on plate 16872 alone in a 1934 article.[7] Johl noted that the best of these are positions 46-56 in the upper-left pane. The double-transfer listing went into the *Specialized Catalogue* in the 1936 edition and was no doubt based on these reports.

A "good shift" was illustrated in the *Bureau Specialist* in 1936, which is from an unknown position and was reported as "showing on one stamp of a used pair."[8] French also illustrates this in his *Encyclopedia*, calling it a "strong" shifted transfer.

1½¢ Harding Rotary, Perf 10

Scott Number: 582
First Day of Issue: March 19, 1925
Perforation: 10
Scott Colors: Brown, dark brown
Press: Large rotary press
Plate Layout: 400 subjects, cut into panes of 100
Quantity Issued: Undetermined
Plate Numbers: Total of 37: lowest, 16825; highest, 18702

Philatelic Aspects and Varieties

First day of issue. This stamp was also issued on March 19, 1925, only at Washington, D.C. Released as it was on the same day as the flat-plate version, this stamp had little of its own identity. As with the flat-plate version, a good number of first-day covers were serviced, with no known cachets. First-day covers of the rotary stamp command a slight premium over the flat-plate version.

Shades. Ward noted in April 1925 that the brown shade of the rotary stamp differed from that of the flat-plate version, "taking on a grayish tinge."[9] When first listed in the 1926 edition of the *Specialized Catalogue*, its color was given only as deep brown. In the 1932 edition, brown was added as a minor shade. Johl, in his 1935 book, wrote that "this stamp was issued in a wide range of shades, the deep brown of the first printing being especially desirable."

Probably because of Johl's comment, Scott switched the shades around in the 1936 edition, making brown the major shade and deep brown the minor shade. However, in the 1938 edition, deep brown disappeared, and dark brown appeared in its place, as 582a. The small-letter listing was dropped in the 1979 edition, and today Scott continues to list brown as the major shade and dark brown as the minor shade.

Scott has never been entirely consistent or logical in assigning colors and shades, and this stamp proves the point. This stamp became 633 when the perforation gauge was gradually changed in 1927. Scott now lists that stamp with yellow brown as the major shade and deep brown — which disappeared in the 1938 catalog for 582 — as the minor shade.

Going back to Johl, he was no doubt correct in noting that this stamp appears in a wide range of shades. He added light yellow brown, yellow brown, deep yellow brown, pale brown and reddish brown.

Double paper. As with the two previous rotary-press stamps, this stamp was found on double paper where the webs of paper were joined. A double-paper listing went into the 1928 edition of the *Specialized Catalogue* and was for a time listed as 582b until this listing was dropped with the other double-paper listings in the 1946 edition.

Full sheets of 400. While the details of their appearance are not established, some full sheets of 400 subjects are known. These can only have come out of the Bureau or Post Office Department illegally through an employee, or more likely an official, or most likely as favor items. Vertical and horizontal pairs are known with full gutters between, but these are not errors. Scott noted the existence of these favor sheets for the first time in the 1940 edition of the *Specialized Catalogue* with the note: "No. 582 exists in full sheets of 400 subjects but was not regularly issued in that form."

Plate varieties. With so many plates made, we might expect some double transfers and other plate varieties, but much of the production of this stamp was in precanceled stamps, and this has consequently not been a well-studied stamp. No significant double transfers have been reported. Johl lists no plate varieties, and French lists only five, mostly scratches and corrosion marks.

1½¢ Harding Side Coil

Scott Number: 598
First Day of Issue: March 19, 1925
Perforation: 10 vertically
Scott Colors: Brown, deep brown
Press: Small rotary press
Plate Layout: 170 subjects, cut into coils
Quantity Issued: 2,146,673,000
Plate Numbers: Total of 62: lowest, 16828; highest, 19327

Philatelic Aspects and Varieties

First day of issue. This stamp was also released on March 19, 1925, only at Washington, D.C., on the same day as the flat-plate and rotary sheet stamps. As with the other varieties a good number of first-day covers were prepared and are valued lower than first-day covers of any of the other coils of these series.

Shades. As with the rotary version, this stamp was listed as deep brown when first listed in the 1926 edition of the *Specialized Catalogue*. As both these stamps were produced at the same time in the same plant and on the same type of press, we can assume that the same ink was used on at least the early printings.

As with the rotary version, Scott made brown the major shade and deep brown a minor shade in the 1935 *Specialized Catalogue*. In the case of the side coil, however, the deep brown shade has never disappeared from the Scott listings, and is given today as a minor shade. Thus we have in the current Scott *Specialized* a minor shade of dark brown for the rotary sheet stamp and deep brown for the end coil.

Johl, as usual, found many more names for what he saw, adding to the Scott shades yellow brown, deep yellow brown and reddish brown.

Coil varieties. As with the other rotary-press coils, joint-line pairs and stamps showing splices, cores and coil leaders exist. See Chapter 7.

Plate varieties. Scott lists no plate varieties on this stamp. Johl lists none, and French lists only a few minor varieties, no double transfers and only one example of a gripper crack, on 19323-17. This again demonstrates that this is largely an unstudied stamp, which was acknowledged by James Obrig in 1938, when he called it a "poor neglected" stamp. "Maybe it has not been in such good graces insofar as plate varieties are concerned," he posed, "because it was rather extensively precanceled."[10] This is no doubt the correct interpretation.

Of the total quantity of 2,146,673,000, more than half, or 1,222,120,000 were precanceled.

1½¢ Harding Flat-Plate Imperforate

Scott Number: 576
First Day of Issue: April 4, 1925
Perforation: Imperforate
Scott Colors: Yellow brown, pale yellow brown, brown
Press: Flat-plate press
Plate Layout: 400 subjects, uncut
Quantity Issued: Not determined
Plate Numbers: Total of 40 reported: lowest, 16829; highest, 16982
Scott Varities: Double transfer

Philatelic Aspects and Varieties

Like the other imperforates of this series, the practical reason for its issue was to supply the Mail-o-Meter company with stamp material with which to make the privately perforated coils used in its affixing machines.

Producing imperforate stamps was not difficult; in fact, it was easier than making perforated stamps, as sheets were merely taken from the flat-plate

The 1½¢ Harding

production before they were sent through the perforating machines. There was no separate press or production run for imperforates; it was simply a matter of packaging.

The same position varieties that exist on the other imperforates exist on this stamp as well. See Chapter 9.

First day of issue. This stamp was issued on April 4, 1925, only at Washington, D.C., at the Philatelic Stamp Agency. Several other stamps had the same first day of issue. These included the ½¢ Nathan Hale (551), the Lexington-Concord issue (617-19) and three rotary-press versions of the regular issue, the 4¢ (585), 5¢ (586) and 6¢ (587). Numerous first-day covers were serviced.

The large number of plate numbers that are found on this imperforate stamp are undoubtedly due more to collector demand at the Philatelic Stamp Agency than any representation of a large consumer or industrial demand.

Private perforations. Copies of this stamp used during the period of issue are more difficult to find than unused copies. Unused Schermack stamps, like the pair shown in Figure 85, were obtained by stamp dealers and are not uncommon. Most Schermack copies are locally precanceled "Chicago, Illinois" and are rather difficult to locate on cover. Used Schermack copies without this precancel are more difficult to find, and very few unprecanceled copies are known on cover. George Wagner, a Chicago collector, has shown this author a cover with an unprecanceled copy postmarked with a third-class Chicago postmark, carrying the corner card of Lord & Thomas Advertising. Ward also reported a use of this stamp by the Olsen Rug Company of Chicago.[11]

Figure 85. A pair of imperforate stamps with Schermack Type III perforations. Used copies on cover are scarcer than unused stamps.

Shades. When first listed in the 1926 edition of the *Specialized Catalogue*, the major shade was yellow brown, with pale yellow brown and brown as minor shades. Brown was listed as 576a in editions of the *Specialized Catalogue* from 1935 to 1978. The current catalog lists the same shades as the 1926 catalog, so there seems to be some consistency with this stamp, if not with others. Johl added dark yellow brown and reddish brown.

Double transfer. This listing is based on the double-transfer listing for the perforated flat-plate stamp (see above), since plate 16872 — the one reported with the numerous shifted transfers — also exists as an imperforate sheet.

233

1½¢ Harding End Coil

Scott Number:	605
First Day of Issue:	May 9, 1925
Perforation:	10 horizontally
Scott Colors:	Yellow brown, brown
Press:	Small rotary press
Plate Layout:	150 subjects, cut into coils
Quantity Issued:	25,389,000
Plate Numbers:	17027, 17028

Philatelic Aspects and Varieties

First day of issue. This stamp was issued on May 9, 1925, only at Washington, D.C. Ward reported that "there was such a great demand from postmasters for this variety that the department did not have the opportunity to give advance notice to collectors. ..."[12] If there was a great demand for this stamp, it must have been short-lived, for the quantity produced was rather small.

Plates and plate layout. Only two of the eight plates prepared ever went to press, and this pair of plates only went to press twice. The quantity produced would make only 50,778 coils of 500. As with the 2¢ end coil, unused copies are not difficult to obtain, but copies used on cover during the period of issue are somewhat uncommon.

The two plates used had the plate number and star in the right margin next to stamp 10, rather than in the left margin next to stamp 141. No copies showing a portion of the plate number are presently known.

Shades. When first listed in the 1926 edition of the *Specialized Catalogue,* the color was given only as yellow brown. In the 1939 edition, brown was added as 605a. The small letter designation was removed in the 1978 edition. Johl noted that "there is little variation in the shades, the deep yellow brown of the first printing being the least common."

Notes

1. Michael Eidsness Jr. to W. Irving Glover, February 27, 1925. Smithsonian Institution Libraries, Post Office Department Manuscripts.
2. Press release, Post Office Department, March 9, 1925.
3. Press release, Post Office Department, March 13, 1925.
4. Philip H. Ward Jr., "Chronicle of New Issues and Varieties," *Mekeel's Weekly Stamp News*, Vol. 39, No. 25 (June 22, 1925), p. 334.

5. See for example, Post Office Department, *A Description of United States Postage Stamps* (Washington: Government Printing Office, 1937), p. 59.
6. Philip H. Ward Jr., "Chronicle of New Issues and Varieties," *Mekeel's Weekly Stamp News*, Vol. 39, No. 16 (April 20, 1925), p. 216.
7. *Collectors Club Philatelist*, July 1934.
8. F.E. Stanton, "Plate Varieties Committee," *Bureau Specialist*, Vol. 7, No. 12 (December 1936), pp. 162, 168.
9. Philip H. Ward Jr., "Chronicle of New Issues and Varieties," *Mekeel's Weekly Stamp News*, Vol. 39, No. 14 (April 6, 1925), p. 192.
10. James H. Obrig, "Plate Varieties," *Bureau Specialist*, Vol. 9, No. 9 (September 1938), p. 109.
11. Philip H. Ward Jr., "Chronicle of New Issues and Varieties," *Mekeel's Weekly Stamp News*, Vol. 39, No. 24 (June 15, 1925), p. 312.
12. Philip H. Ward Jr., "Chronicle of New Issues and Varieties," *Mekeel's Weekly Stamp News*, Vol. 39, No. 23 (June 8, 1925), p. 300.

United States Stamps 1922-26

Chapter 21

The ½¢ Hale

Nathan Hale

Scott Number:	551
First Day of Issue:	April 4, 1925
Perforation:	11
Scott Colors:	Olive brown, pale olive brown, deep olive brown
Designer:	Clair Aubrey Huston
Engravers:	John Eissler (vignette)
	E.M. Hall (frame and lettering of "Hale")
	J.C. Benzing (scrolls and ribbon)
	E.M. Weeks (numerals)
Press:	Flat plate
Plate Layout:	400 subjects, cut into panes of 100
Quantity Issued:	626,241,783
Plate Numbers:	Total of 49: lowest, 17017; highest, 17086
Scott Varieties:	Cap on fraction bar (plate 17041)

The Political Background

No one knows what Nathan Hale really looked like. Nor does anyone really know what he said before he was hanged by the British as a spy during the Revolutionary War. Nathan Hale, although a minor figure in the Revolution, became one of its legendary martyrs.

Yale College, Hale's alma mater, helped to make and preserve this legend. And it was the 150th anniversary of Hale's graduation from Yale that was the occasion, in 1923, for George Dudley Seymour to start his campaign to get Hale on a stamp. Seymour was not only a Yale alumnus, but an admirer of Hale. He had purchased Hale's birthplace in Coventry, Connecticut, and had turned it into both a summer home and a museum that charged admission.

Seymour suggested that Hale replace Benjamin Franklin on the 1¢ stamp, but the Post Office Department did not buy the idea. The sesquicentennial of Hale's graduation from Yale having passed, Seymour continued to lobby for a stamp for the 150th anniversary of Hale's death, which would fall on September 22, 1925. Congressman Schuyler Merritt, also a Yale alumnus and a Republican from Stamford, joined Seymour's campaign, and by August 1924, Postmaster General New was persuaded to take the idea seriously.

"At present the Department is giving consideration to the issuance of a series of postage stamps to celebrate the Sesquicentennial of the signing of the American Independence," New wrote to Seymour, "and it is my belief that some tribute should be paid to the heroes of that period. ..."[1]

As we shall see in later chapters, no coherent plan ever materialized in the Post Office Department for commemorating the sesquicentennial of the American Revolution. But the need for a ½¢ stamp for the new postal rates of 1925 provided the occasion for the Hale stamp.

The Subject and Design

Although we don't know what he looked like, Nathan Hale was a very real figure. He was born in Coventry, Connecticut, on June 6, 1755, the son of Deacon Richard Hale, and one of 12 children. He entered Yale College in 1769 and was graduated in 1773 at the age of 18. For two years he taught at East Haddam and New London, then joined the Connecticut regiment in 1775 and was commissioned a captain in the Continental Army in 1776.

Hale's singular act of bravery came later in that same year when General George Washington asked Hale's commander to select a man to penetrate the British lines in New York to provide information about the size and strength of the enemy forces. Hale was the only volunteer.

Hale was not trained in intelligence, nor did he know anything of codes or ciphers. He disguised himself as a Dutch schoolteacher, crossed the British lines and followed the British army to Manhattan, where he was captured on September 21, 1776. Although he may have been betrayed by his cousin, a British loyalist, his notes about the military forces and movements were in plain English, and he is reported to have admitted his mission. He was hanged as a spy the next day, without trial, under orders of British General William Howe.

"I only regret that I have but one life to lose for my country," Hale is supposed to have said when asked if he had any final words. A similar remark appeared in the play *Cato* by the British playwright Joseph Addison, written in 1713. Perhaps Hale was familiar with the play.

No life portrait of Hale is known, and it would be somewhat unusual for there to have been a painting of a relatively poor and quite young man. The source of the portrait on the stamp is a photograph of a clay model of a statue by

Bela Lyon Pratt. The statue was commissioned by Yale in 1898. In 1913 it was placed in front of Connecticut Hall, the dormitory in which Hale roomed while an undergraduate student. Pratt is believed to have used a young man of Hale's age for the model.

The life-size statue depicts Hale as he is about to be hanged. His ankles are bound with rope, and his hands are likewise bound behind him. His clothing is that of his schoolmaster's disguise. As one writer has described this depiction, "Pratt has pictured him in disheveled garments with shirt opened at the throat, and with head thrown back as if uttering the immortal farewell words."[2]

George Dudley Seymour had a copy of this statue erected in 1923 at the Hale homestead he had purchased as a summer home and museum. The photograph used for the stamp (shown in Figure 86) was provided to the Post Office Department by Seymour, who noted that it was "made in Mr. Pratt's studio in Boston from the design when in the clay."[3]

Figure 86. The photograph of the clay model of Bela Lyon Pratt's statue of Nathan Hale was used as the source artwork for the ½¢ stamp.

Philatelic Aspects and Varieties

The Post Office Department seems not to have thought of this denomination as immediately necessary. It is not mentioned in Michael Eidsness' memo of February 27 (see Chapter 20), and it was not mentioned in the first announcement of stamps for the new rate on March 9.

On the following day, March 10, a die was started. But it was not until March 13 that an announcement was issued stating, "The Department is preparing to issue a new ½-cent stamp which may be used with the 1-cent stamp to supply sufficient postage."[4] This same announcement also said that this new stamp would also be useful for making the new third-class rate on 1¢ stamped envelopes. No subject or color, however, was mentioned. A die proof was approved before the engraving was completely finished, and the die was completed and hardened on March 20.

First day of issue. This stamp was issued on April 4, 1925, at Washington, D.C., and at New Haven, Connecticut, the site of Yale University. The first reports that the ½¢ stamp would use Nathan Hale as the design seem to have come from the office of Congressman Schuyler Merritt of Connecticut, and *Mekeel's* reported the information by reprinting an article in the *Hartford Courant*, which noted, "It is not an expensive stamp but there is nothing better open for Nathan at this moment."[5]

The date was the same as the three values of the Lexington-Concord issue (see Chapter 23). A large number of first-day covers were prepared, due in part to the low denomination of the stamp. New Haven covers command a very slight premium over Washington, D.C., covers.

Most of the covers that were serviced were franked by blocks of four to pay the 2¢ letter rate, but at least two first-day postcards are also known, franked with pairs of the stamp to pay the 1¢ postcard rate. Figure 87 shows one of the postcards, published by the Edward F. Judd Co. of New Haven. It is a photographic reproduction of the Pratt statue at Yale, and is franked on the reverse with a pair of the Hale stamps, postmarked New Haven.

Figure 87. A postcard picturing the Hale statue at Yale was used to service this first-day cover from New Haven, Connecticut. The reverse has a pair of stamps paying the 1¢ postcard rate.

Criticism. Philip Ward was particularly unimpressed by this stamp and had lots to say about it. "It is my personal opinion," he began, "that this stamp is possibly the most unattractive one ever turned out by the United States Government, and seems to have nothing in its favor in either design, color or appropriateness of portrait. It seems rather unusual to present Nathan Hale on our current series when such dignitaries as Woodrow Wilson, Andrew Jackson, John Marshall, James Madison and others, who have done much for their country, are not represented."[6]

As might be expected, this started off a debate on the stamp's merits. Hugh McLellan wrote to Ward arguing that "Nathan Hale is an inspiration to the patriotism of American youth, and the selection of his portrait very appropri-

The ½¢ Hale

ate in this sesquicentennial year."[7] One person who agreed with Ward however noted that "Hale accomplished nothing!" and that it was an "inequality ... certainly plain to everyone" to place Hale in the company of such great leaders as Washington.[8]

The full-face portrait also attracted criticism. As one of Hale's New Haven supporters put it, the proportions of Hale's portrait were larger "than the portraits on the other denominations of this series, and perhaps it is to be regretted that it was not reduced somewhat more to add to its symmetry when grouped with the rest of the set."[9]

Scott did in fact group this stamp with the regular-issue stamps issued in 1922 and 1923, giving it the catalog number 551. It was issued more than two years after 552 and almost a year later than 616.

Shades. The Bureau called the ink color of this stamp sepia. When first listed in the 1926 edition of the Scott *Specialized Catalogue*, the major shade was given as olive brown, with pale olive brown and deep olive brown listed as minor shades. This listing continues to the present day. Ward noted that the stamps placed on sale in Washington on the first day "were in two very distinct shades, one light, and the other dark."[10] Johl added only dark olive brown.

Cap on fraction bar. Although a number of plate varieties are known on this stamp, this variety, which is a relief break, is the only one listed by Scott. This "cap" is a small relief break that appears in the left denomination oval, on the horizontal bar that separates the "1" and the "2" in the "½" fraction. It appears on the first five vertical columns on both the upper-left and lower-left panes of plate 17041. This was first illustrated by Beverly King, who credited its discovery to Alfred Benners of Birmingham, Alabama.

King, writing in *Scott's Monthly Journal* in 1933, determined that this plate was laid out from right to left, and that the relief was unbroken in the right panes. "But the five rows on the left hand panes are constant." He added that "this is an item that is worthy of listing, and we are doing so herewith."[11] It was indeed included in the 1934 edition of the *Specialized Catalogue*. The variety is shown in Figure 88.

Figure 88. The "cap on fraction bar" variety is caused by a relief break. The left fraction bar shows the variety. The right fraction bar is normal.

Plate crack. There is also a pretty dramatic plate crack on the upper-left pane of plate 17047, running to the right of stamps 77, 87 and 97. This was first reported and illustrated in the *Shift Hunter Letters*, which credited its discovery to Lester Brookman.[12] It is also illustrated in Johl.

Notes

1. Harry S. New to George Dudley Seymour, August 14, 1924. Smithsonian Institution Libraries, Post Office Department Manuscripts.

2. Gerald E. Richter, "The Genesis of the Nathan Hale ½¢," *American Stamp Digest* (August 1936), p. 18.

3. George Dudley Seymour, information sheet provided to the Post Office Department, 1924. Smithsonian Institution Libraries, Post Office Department Manuscripts.

4. Post Office Department press release, March 13, 1925.

5. Reprinted in *Mekeel's Weekly Stamp News*, March 30, 1925, p. 177.

6. Philip H. Ward Jr., "Chronicle of New Issues and Varieties," *Mekeel's Weekly Stamp News*, April 20, 1925, p. 216.

7. Quoted in Philip H. Ward Jr., "Chronicle of New Issues and Varieties," *Mekeel's Weekly Stamp News*, May 11, 1925, p. 252.

8. Calvert R. Stier, "Portraits on Recent U.S. Issues," *Mekeel's Weekly Stamp News*, May 18, 1925, p. 261.

9. Gerald E. Richter, *op. cit.*, p. 18.

10. Philip H. Ward Jr., "Chronicle of New Issues and Varieties," *Mekeel's Weekly Stamp News*.

11. Beverley S. King, "Notes on General Issues," *Scott's Monthly Journal*, Vol. 13, No. 11 (January 1933), p. 321.

12. C.W. Bedford, *Shift Hunter Letter No. 42*.

Chapter 22

Lexington-Concord Issue

The Political Background

As the 150th anniversary of the Revolutionary War approached, a number of organizations began preparing for the observance of local events. Requests for stamps — and usually series of stamps — began to escalate, and these seemed to be taken on a case-by-case basis.

Although the Post Office Department sometimes alluded to a plan for a series of stamps marking the sesquicentennial of American Independence, no organized series emerged. Hundreds of organizations and dozens of influential members of Congress clamored and bullied for their own interests. The Post Office failed to develop a coherent plan, and eventually Postmaster General Harry S. New and his staff began to look at stamp requests as a nuisance.

The Lexington-Concord issue was certainly a worthy project. British troops were first fired upon by colonial militias in these towns — and in those between Concord and Boston as well — on April 19, 1775. The bloodshed was too great for there to be any turning back, and the war that made America an independent country got under way there and then.

This was one of the few series of stamps during this period that was mandated by Congress. A bill introduced on May 9, 1924, by Congressman Robert Luce of Waltham, Massachusetts, sought to establish a Lexington-Concord Sesquicentennial Commission, and to direct the postmaster general "to issue a special series of postage stamps, in such denominations and of such designs as he may determine, commemorative of the one hundred and fiftieth anniversary of the Battle of Lexington and Concord and of the one hundred and fiftieth anniversary of such other major events of the Revolutionary War as he may deem appropriate."[1]

Passed by both houses of Congress, the bill was sent to Postmaster General New by Herbert M. Lord, the director of the Bureau of the Budget, for his comments. In his response, we have perhaps the best articulation of New's feeling about issuing commemorative stamps and the role that both he and Congress should play.

"There is no objection to the issuance of special stamps for this particular occasion," New began. "However, the Department is not in favor of legislation of this kind. In fact, it discourages such legislation. Naturally the postal service can have too many varieties of postage stamps. In order to prevent this condition from arising it is believed that the best interests of the Government and all concerned would be better served if the preparation and issuance of special stamps were left to the discretion of the Department where it is now placed by existing law rather than by following any other procedure."[2] In the future, New, a former member of the Senate, would discourage congressional legislation that mandated new stamps.

In this particular case, rather than accepting the broad mandate of the bill, which contemplated a series of stamps for all "major events of the Revolutionary War," New and his department eventually limited it to only stamps for Lexington and Concord. And as he and his staff would soon discover, even the little Massachusetts towns involved could not agree on what should be issued.

Each town had its own *Minuteman* statue, and each town wanted it to be depicted on a stamp. The Lexington statue was clearly the inferior of the two, but it depicted a local hero, Captain John Parker, the commander of the Lexington Provincial Company.

Concord, on the other hand, was the site of the more famous *Minuteman* statue by the noted sculptor Daniel Chester French. It did not depict any individual, but stood for the universal American farmer, who was ready to defend liberty on a moment's notice, leaving his coat on his plow and picking up his musket.

The first designs for this series were a 2¢ value depicting the Lexington *Minuteman* and a 5¢ value depicting the Concord *Minuteman* (see Figure 89). Although this would result in two stamps with essentially the same design, it clearly recognized the two towns.

But two, it seems were not enough. Several other congressmen wanted to get in on the act. Congressman John Jacob Rogers, for example, represented Pepperel, Massachusetts, the birthplace of Colonel John Prescott, the commander of the colonial forces at Bunker Hill, and Rogers wanted "a special issue of postage stamps bearing the likeness of Colonel Prescott."[3]

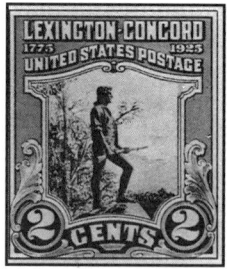

Figure 89. The two Minuteman *statues — at Lexington on the 2¢ value, and Concord on the 5¢ value — were the original subjects for what was originally intended to be a two-stamp issue.*

Secretary of War John W. Weeks had been appointed a member of the commission to oversee the observance of the sesquicentennial of Lexington and Concord, and from his correspondence we know that Paul Revere and John Hancock were also being considered as subjects, and that Weeks himself suggested "that the Paul Revere print be used."[4]

Depending on one's point of view, what saved the Post Office Department from having to issue an impossibly large series — or what killed a broad and coherent series on the Revolutionary War — was the pay-raise and postal-rate-increase bill of 1925.

By late January the Post Office Department realized that the stamps required for the new postal rates would be quite costly. "The issuance of commemorative stamps involves considerable additional expense," the Department wrote back to Congressman Rogers, "and as the [new law] does not provide an appropriation, the additional expense of such stamps as are issued prior to June 30, 1925, will of course have to be borne from the present appropriation for furnishing postage stamps."[5]

1¢ Washington at Cambridge

Scott Number: 617
First Day of Issue: April 4, 1925
Perforation: 11
Scott Colors: Deep green, green
Designer: Clair Aubrey Huston
Engravers: Frederick Pauling (vignette)
J.C. Benzing (frame)
E.M. Weeks (lettering and numerals)
Plate Layout: Flat plate; plates of 200 subjects, cut into panes of 50
Quantity Issued: 15,615,000
Plate Numbers: 16797, 16798, 16799, 16800

The Subject and Design

This stamp, some might be surprised to learn, does not relate to Lexington or Concord. The subject, labeled "Washington at Cambridge" depicts General George Washington taking command of the colonial forces on Cambridge Common on July 2, 1775, two and a half months after the skirmishes at Lexington and Concord.

Two other significant events of the Revolution had happened between the date of this scene and the date of Washington taking command of the army.

United States Stamps 1922-26

Fort Ticonderoga on Lake Champlain was captured by Ethan Allen and his troops on May 10, and the more important Battle of Bunker Hill was fought in Charlestown, Massachusetts, on June 17. Neither event was commemorated in this series.

That the Cambridge event was included was due to the intervention of Congressman Frederick W. Dallinger, of Cambridge, who was not only a member of the Lexington-Concord Sesquicentennial Commission, but was running for the Republican nomination for the U.S. Senate at the time. A dead elm tree also seems to have played a large part in the affair.

The famous Washington Elm, which had stood on Cambridge Common since about 1700, had over the years grown in legend as it shrunk in vitality. George Washington allegedly had stood under this elm as he took command of the Continental Army — the very scene that would be portrayed on the new stamp. The tree, over the years, lost many of its branches to age and rot. It was tarred and cemented and patched up many times, until October 26, 1923, when workmen attempting to saw off yet another dead limb accidentally knocked the tree over.

The loss of the tree just a few months short of the 150th anniversary of Washington's reputed appearance beneath it enhanced the tree's legend. Cambridge, grieving at its loss, planned a grand celebration for the sesquicentennial event on July 25, 1925. President Coolidge was even lined up as a speaker.

Congressman Dallinger was lobbying heavily for a stamp to promote the event, and Postmaster General New eventually caved in and expanded the Lexington-Concord issue to three stamps.

The reference artwork was provided by the Cambridge Public Library, which sent to the Post Office Department a "photoglyphic chart" of the design. This may be what we know today as a photostat. We know that the Post Office Department returned this "chart" to the librarian in Cambridge in March 1925, but apparently it has not been seen since.[6] Beverly King searched for the original artwork, but never was able to locate it, the librarian at Cambridge reporting that it was no longer in the library's possession.[7]

This author's search for the original artwork has been equally fruitless. The archivist at the library reported to me that he had "nothing on record" about this artwork or its return to the library.[8] Similarly, the Cambridge Historical Commission reports that "it does not resemble any image we have on file."[9]

The scene on the stamp clearly shows Washington standing under the elm as he reviews neatly uniformed troops drilling in what appears to be parade formation. There are several similar prints in existence, the first of which (Figure 90) seems to have been published in *Ballou's Pictorial*, a weekly newspaper published in Boston in 1855.

Twenty years later *The Diary of Dorothy Dudley* appeared. While purely fictitious, it helped establish the elm tree legend. For the date of July 3, 1775, Dudley's imagination records: "Today he formally took command under one of the grand old elms on the Common. It was a magnificent sight. The majestic figure of the General mounted upon his horse, beneath the wide-spreading branches of the partriarch tree; the multitude thronging the plain around, and

Figure 90. Published in 1855 in Ballou's Pictorial, *this illustration appears to be the first showing Washington taking command of the Continental Army under the fabled elm tree. The source illustration for the stamp has never been located.*

247

the houses filled with interested spectators of the scene, while the air rung with shouts of enthusiastic welcome as he drew his sword and thus declared himself the Commander-in-Chief of the Continental Army."[10]

This description was accepted as true by many other writers and illustrators, and Cambridge, of course, was eager to believe that the scene occurred at a spot that could be marked and commemorated with marble markers and bronze plaques. The stamp, when issued on April 4, 1925, helped not only to keep the elm-tree legend alive, but to sanction it.

A few months after the sesquicentennial ceremony was held, and the stamp issued, an amateur historian, Samuel Batchelder, read a lengthy paper before the Cambridge Historical Society debunking the Washington Elm tradition. Events could not have happened the way the tree's supporters believed, he argued. There were several reasons, not the least of which was that the men were much too busy to draw up in formation even if they knew how to do so.

"The paramount need," Batchelder argued, "was to strengthen defenses, and the army was strung out all the way from Malden to Roxbury, digging like beavers. To have assembled the army, or even a respectable portion of it, for a grand parade on Cambridge Common at that time would have been a risky business — rather like calling off the ditchers at a forest fire to attend a political rally."[11]

Rather, Batchelder stated, Washington spent the day traveling and inspecting the fortifications and defenses. He "took command" of the army by presenting his credentials to the other officers and taking over the headquarters order book.

Washington's leading biographer, James Thomas Flexner, also dismisses the scene on Cambridge Common as anything but actual. He writes: "The review with which the new Commander was said to have been greeted as he stood under 'the Washington Elm' is, although enshrined in the history books, pure legend. The army was not well enough trained to march in a review and would probably have greeted the Virginian with jeers not cheers."[12]

Flexner and other historians believe that Washington slipped inconspicuously into the encampment on the Sabbath. Another historian paints an equally dim scene: "Discipline was lax and officers were treated with little respect; drunkenness and malingering were common, provisions meagre ... the camps were filthy and perfunctorily guarded by sentries who frequently strolled away from their posts. ..."[13]

Had Washington found conditions to be as orderly as those depicted on the stamp, he would not have been so great a general, and the war might easily have been won earlier. Rather than proudly reviewing his new troops, the general's actions were quite contrary. He had eight officers court-martialed, one of whom he had whipped in front of his men. One of the first powers he

Lexington-Concord Issue

sought from the Continental Congress was the permission to hang deserters.

Philatelic Aspects and Varieties

First day of issue. This stamp was issued on April 4, 1925, at Washington, D.C., and at five Massachusetts cities and towns: Boston, Cambridge, Concord, Concord Junction and Lexington. There was adequate notification of this issue for first-day cover collectors and dealers to service covers, as the Post Office Department announced the issue on March 25.

While a few printed cachets are known, they are not pictorials. Several labels, depicting the *Minuteman* statues, both at Lexington and Concord, were used in preparing first-day covers. These covers command a higher price when the labels are tied to the covers by postmarks. At least two picture postcards relating to the locations were used to service first-day covers. One is of the First Parish Meeting House in Concord and the other is of Concord Bridge.

Shades. The Post Office Department described the color of this stamp as green. When this stamp was first listed in the 1926 edition of the Scott *Specialized Catalogue*, the major shade was given as dark green, and green was listed as a minor shade. This listing has been maintained ever since. Johl had no shades to add. A wide variation in shades on this stamp does not exist.

2¢ Birth of Liberty

Scott Number:	618
First Day of Issue:	April 4, 1925
Perforation:	11
Scott Colors:	Carmine rose; pale carmine rose
Designer:	Clair Aubrey Huston
Engravers:	Louis S. Schofield (vignette)
	J.C. Benzing (frame)
	E.M. Weeks (lettering and numerals)
Plate Layout:	Flat plate; plates of 200 subjects, cut into panes of 50.
Quantity Issued:	26,596,000
Plate Numbers:	16801, 16803, 16804, 16813, 16814, 16815, 16816, 17004

The Subject and Design

Once the Lexington *Minuteman* statue was ruled out as a subject, a scene of the battle was substituted. The matrix artwork was a painting by Henry Sandham, a Canadian-born artist, titled *The Dawn of Liberty* (see Figure 91). It was painted in Boston around 1885 and was acquired by the Lexington Historical Society in 1886. The original canvas is 10 x 6 feet. A print was provided to the Post Office Department by the Lexington Historical Society. The title under the stamp, "Birth of Liberty," is not the title of the painting.

Figure 91. Henry Sandham's painting, The Dawn of Liberty, *was the source artwork for the stamp. The stamp captions this as "Birth of Liberty."*

It shows a rather idealized scene of the battle, in which the Lexington men have formed a line to stop the advance of the uniformed British. The figure at the far right is Major John Pitcairn, mounted on a horse. During the actual skirmish, he was trying to keep his troops from firing, not ordering them to do so. As historian Robert Leckie has written of this affair, "Pitcairn swung his sword downward as the signal to cease fire." The figure in the foreground with his arm raised is Captain Jonas Parker of Lexington, who was also trying to keep his men from firing, not encouraging them to do so.

Who fired the first shot, we do not know, but the Lexington men were routed. The facts of this skirmish are that 10 Lexington men were killed and eight wounded. Only one British soldier was wounded, and there seems some doubt as to whether any of the Lexington men fired back at all. Although it would not make a very heroic painting, most of the Americans fled as the British fired and advanced.

A smaller detail from the same painting was used on a 10¢ stamp in 1975 (Scott 1563) to commemorate the 200th anniversary of the battles of Lexington and Concord.

The original model of the stamp was submitted without a title under the vignette. It was added by the Post Office Department when the model was approved.

Philatelic Aspects and Varieties

First day of issue. This stamp, with the two other denominations, was issued on April 4, 1925, at Washington, D.C., and five cities and towns in Massachusetts. See the comments under the 1¢ value above.

Shades. The Post Office Department described this stamp accurately as being printed in "red ink." When listed for the first time in the 1926 edition of the Scott *Specialized*, the major shade was given as carmine rose, and pale carmine rose was given as a minor shade. These same shades remain in the catalog today. Johl had no shades to add.

5¢ Minuteman Statue

Scott Number:	619
First Day of Issue:	April 4, 1925
Perforation:	11
Scott Colors:	Dark blue, blue
Designer:	Clair Aubrey Huston
Engravers:	J.C. Benzing (frame and vignette)
	E.M. Weeks (lettering and numerals)
Plate Layout:	Flat plate; plates of 200 subjects, cut into panes of 50.
Quantity Issued:	5,348,800
Plate Numbers:	16805, 16806, 16807, 16808
Varieties:	Line over head: 16807 LL 48

The Subject and Design

The central figure on the stamp is the *Minuteman*, a sculpture by Daniel Chester French erected in Concord, Massachusetts, as part of the celebration of the 100th anniversary of the first battle of the Revolutionary War.

French was only 25 years old when this sculpture was erected. It was his first commission, and its impact helped establish his career as America's unsurpassed sculptor of public monuments. His fame reached its high point in 1922, when his seated sculpture of Abraham Lincoln was dedicated in the Lincoln Memorial in Washington, D.C.

The *Minuteman* was always considered by Concord to be the most fitting subject for the stamp, but when the format was changed from an ordinary-sized stamp to a special-delivery-sized one, it left designer Clair Aubrey Huston with a problem: The aspect ratio of the vertical statue was not that of the horizontal stamp. To overcome it, he placed the figure between two Doric columns and added a tablet on either side. On these tablets he placed a few lines from Ralph Waldo Emerson's *Concord Hymn*, which had been composed in 1836:

"By the rude bridge that arched the flood,
Their flag to Aprils breeze unfurled,
Here once the embattled farmers stood,
And fired the shot heard 'round the world.' "

The first two lines were placed on the tablet at the left, while the third and fourth lines were placed on the tablet to the right. This was the wordiest U.S. stamp issued up to this time, and the first to contain lines of poetry.

The direct source for the artwork used on the stamp, interestingly enough, was a picture postcard of the statue, which was sent to the Post Office Department by the stamp's sponsors (see Figure 92). Emerson's *Hymn* is also lettered on the granite base for the bronze statue.

French's *Minuteman* was a powerful sculpture that captured both the heroic determination of the men at Concord and the image of the American citizen-soldier. The same view of the statue on this stamp was later used for postal savings stamps beginning in 1941 and for war savings stamps in 1942.

While the first shot of the

Figure 92. The postcard originally submitted as reference art for the stamp still exists in the Post Office Department's files.

Revolution may have been fired at Lexington, the first battle was really at the North Bridge in Concord on the same day. After routing the Lexington men, the British marched on to Concord to search for munitions and stores. As some of the British were destroying flour and dumping musket balls into the river, some members of the Concord Militia marched to the bridge. Their most immediate commander, Major Buttrick, did not order his men to hold their fire, but to deliver it. After the first volley from the Concord men, three British regulars fell dead, and four more were wounded.

This began the unruly British retreat as Minutemen from surrounding areas converged to snipe and harass their ranks. Of the 1,800 British who began the march, 273 were casualties. A war had begun.

The Philately

First day of issue. This stamp, with the two other denominations, was issued on April 4, 1925, at Washington, D.C., and five cities and towns in Massachusetts. See the comments under the 1¢ value above.

Shades. The Post Office Department gave the color of this stamp simply as blue. Scott, when it first listed this stamp in the 1926 edition of the *Specialized Catalogue*, gave the primary shade as dark blue, with blue as a minor shade. Johl had no additions. The four plates of this stamp only went to press once, and there should not be a wide variation in shades.

Line over head. Most illustrations of this variety, 26807 LL 48, make it appear that this line is rather heavy, as if the Minuteman were standing in front of a clothesline. But in actuality, this line is quite fine. This variety was first reported in 1931 by Max Johl, who described it as "a rather heavy scratch on the plate, as the line is much too regular to be a crack."[15]

George Sloane, however, probably had the best take on this variety, writing in 1932 that "the line is undoubtedly one of the many guidelines and rulings laid out on the steel plate in marking it off to indicate the proper position each stamp is to occupy when the subjects are transferred to the plate."[16]

As this stamp occurs over the bottom plate number, many copies were saved, either in plate blocks or as plate number singles.

Criticism. In general this set of stamps was well-received. John Luff, in particular, noted that "they have the merits of historical interest, striking pictures, fine engraving."[17] *Mekeel's* also noted in an editorial that the stamps are "excellent examples of engraving and the choice of subject is exceptionally good." However, the editorial went on to note, accurately, that on the 5¢ value, "it is a test of good vision to discern the inscription."[18]

The *American Philatelist* was perhaps more astute in its criticism that "the original drawings for the Lexington-Concord set were attractive, but what became of them when squeezed down ...?"[19]

Notes

1. House Joint Resolution 259, 68th Congress, 1st Session, May 9, 1924.

2. Harry S. New to Herbert M. Lord, January 14, 1925. Smithsonian Institution Libraries, Post Office Department Manuscripts.

3. John Jacob Rogers to Harry S. New, January 15, 1925. Smithsonian Institution Libraries, Post Office Department Manuscripts.

4. John W. Weeks to Harry S. New, January 29, 1925. Smithsonian Institution Libraries, Post Office Department Manuscripts.

5. Acting Third Assistant Postmaster General to John Jacob Rogers, January 21, 1925. Smithsonian Institution Libraries, Post Office Department Manuscripts.

6. W. Irving Glover to T. Harrison Cummings, Librarian, Cambridge Public Library, March 7, 1925. Smithsonian Institution Libraries, Post Office Department Manuscripts.

7. Johl, *Commemoratives*, p. 95.

8. Telephone conversation with Donald York, archivist, Cambridge Public Library, September 20, 1996.

9. Charles M. Sullivan, executive director, Cambridge Historical Commission, to the author, September 25, 1996.

10. Quoted in Samuel F. Batchelder, "The Washington Elm Tradition," *Proceedings* (Cambridge Historical Society, 1931), p. 50.

11. *Ibid*, p. 57.

12. James Thomas Flexner, *Washington: The Indispensable Man* (Boston: Little, Brown and Company, 1974), p. 66.

13. Christopher Hibbert, *Redcoats and Rebels: The American Revolution Through British Eyes* (New York: W.W. Norton & Company, 1990), p. 67.

14. Robert Leckie, *George Washington's War: The Saga of the American Revolution* (New York: Harper Collins, 1992), p. 110.

15. Max Johl, "Notes on General Issues," *Scott's Monthly Journal*, Vol. 11, No. 12 (February 1931), p. 376.

16. George Sloane, "1925 Lexington-Concord," *Stamps*, November 12, 1932, reprinted in *Sloane's Column* (Bureau Issues Association, 1961), p. 323.

17. John F. Luff, "Notes of the Month," *Scott's Monthly Journal*, Vol. 6, No. 3 (May 1925), p. 49.
18. "Editorial," *Mekeel's Weekly Stamp News*, Vol. 39, No. 16 (April 20, 1925), p. 214.
19. *American Philatelist* (May 1925).

United States Stamps 1922-26

Chapter 23

The Star Plates

The so-called star plates of the Series of 1922 came about as the result of an effort to improve the centering of perforations on flat-plate stamps and to prevent waste, since stamps that had perforations cutting into the design were usually rejected by the Post Office Department. One way to keep the perforations out of the design was to make the spaces between the stamps bigger, and that is just what the Bureau proposed.

Four experimental 2¢ plates were made in January 1925, with slightly wider spacing in the vertical margins than the usual .10 inch. These plates — 16505, 16506, 16507 and 16508 — did not, however, have any stars or other marginal markings to distinguish them. In February another set of four additional 2¢ plates were made with a spacing of about .11 inch in the vertical margins. These plates — 16656, 16657, 16658 and 16659 — also had no stars to distinguish that they were of the wider gauge.

Only the vertical margins were widened, for stamps in this format were printed on paper that had the grain running vertically, and the shrinkage, when the moistened stamp paper dried, was known to be greater across the grain than with it.

Figure 93 shows a block of the wide-spaced stamps compared with the earlier narrow-spaced stamps.

The experiment proved a success. While we do not have much documentation from the Bureau, Third Assistant PMG Glover wrote to BEP director Alvin Hall on March 23, 1925, stating that he had received letters on this subject earlier in the month and replied, "With reference to the design of a new postage stamp plate which will result in widening of the space between stamps, I have read with interest the advantage to your Bu-

Figure 93. The wider spacing of the vertical margins shows more clearly in multiples such as these. The top block is the wide gauge; the bottom block is narrow gauge. Plate 16758 is the only flat-plate sheet stamp marked with the small five-point star.

257

reau with respect to a greater reduced spoilage which now prevails due to improved perforation on sheets that have been printed with the larger margin."[1]

Soon the Bureau began a gradual changeover to wider-spaced stamp plates. These also required that a set of perforating machines be set to the wide-gauge plates. Because the narrow-gauge plates were still in use, stars were added to the margins of the wide-gauge plates as a signal to the operators of the perforating equipment. While the plate numbers alone might indicate whether a plate was wide-gauge or narrow-gauge, the stars provided a quicker indication of whether the stamps were to be sent through the perforator set for the narrow-gauge stamps or for the wide-gauge stamps. The stars no doubt saved time and prevented errors.

Three types of stars were used. A small five-point star was used only on one plate, 16758. A six-point star was used early on and then abandoned. A large five-point star eventually became the standard.

The stars appeared at first at the tops of most plates. Eventually, the layout was standardized with a large five-point star at the right side.

There seems to be no pattern to the use of the early stars, at least not where siderographers or plate finishers were concerned. All three types of stars were used at the same time on the early printings. The small five-point star was applied with the pantograph, the same device used to engrave the plate numbers. The six-point and large five-point stars were applied with a punch, as this was no doubt the faster method.

If we examine the "to press" dates of the early 2¢ star plates, we may find some reason for the three types of stars. Perhaps these were used to mark the four positions on the flat-plate press in an early experiment. For if we count no star at all as a type of marking, we get four types of star markings on the very early printings of the wide-gauge star plates.

Consider the following four 2¢ plates, which went to press for the first time on the same date:

Plate	Denom.	Star marking	First to press
16758	2¢	Small five-point star	04/20/25
16761	2¢	Six-point star	04/20/25
16762	2¢	No star, wide spacing	04/20/25
16764	2¢	Large five-point star	04/20/25

Perhaps the different star markings were used to indicate the alignment of the plate on the press, or some other variable such as the amount of moisture in the paper (although this would require four stacks of paper).

In any event we know that the small five-point star was used very early on and then eliminated. Similarly, the six-point star was eventually discontinued. Perhaps there was some use for these different marking devices that soon became unnecessary.

Giving some support to the theory that the different stars may initially have been used to mark the alignment of the plate on the press is the fact that the small five-point star seems to occur only on plates with short selvage on the top. This indicates that the plates were printed upside down in relation to the plates that show "full tops" or a large area of selvage at the top. Usually the plate printers turned the plates at some point to even out the wear, but I have never seen a small five-point star plate block with "full top" selvage.

Star Plates on Other Denominations

The 1¢ stamps were never printed from wide-gauge plates, with or without stars, as the bulk of the production for this value had already been taken over by the rotary press.

Stars seem to have been necessary only when narrow-gauge and wide-gauge stamps of the same value were in production at the same time, so although most of the other values of this series were eventually printed from wide-gauge plates, stars are found only on the 2¢, 12¢, 15¢, 20¢ and 13¢ values. (Star plates of the 13¢ value, which was not issued until January 1926, are treated in Chapter 32.)

The 8¢ stamp is a special category, as only a single plate went to press with a star — a six-point star at top. This plate went to press with three narrow-gauge plates, and although some examples with the plate number are known, none shows the star. It is discussed in more detail below.

There were no narrow-gauge plates produced for the ½¢, 1½¢, 13¢ or 17¢ stamp, as these values went into production after the decision had been made to adopt the wider gauge.

There are no wide-gauge plates of the $1, $2 or $5.

For stamps in the vertical format, which included the values from ½¢ to 15¢, it was the vertical margins that were .01 inch wider. For stamps in the horizontal format, which included the values from 17¢ to 50¢, it was the horizontal margins that were .01 inch wider.

The importance of and interest in the star plates has varied a bit over the years. G.W. Nowell-Usticke, the president of Stanley Gibbons Inc., of New York, wrote while this series of stamps was still current that "the chief interest lies in the star plates."[2] Max Johl, however, noted the existence of the star plates and the wider-gauge spacings, but commented that they "are interesting though too small to be worthy of separate catalog rating."[3]

For every value of this series, we can tell the spacing variety if we have the plate number. The *Durland Standard Plate Number Catalog* includes star-plate information on each value, and an excellent chart has been published in the *United States Specialist* by Wallace Cleland.[4]

2¢ Star Plates, Scott 554

Since the wide-gauge experiments began on this value, and because it was the most commonly used, there are more star-plate varieties of this denomination than any other.

Small five-point star. This variety is found only at the top-right position of plate 16758. The star is inverted and appears to the left of the plate number, F16758. This star is the same as the small star used on coil stamps of the same period and was applied to the plates using the pantograph. This star measures .16 inch wide from point to point.

Large five-point star at top. This star, which was applied using a hand punch, is often incomplete. It measures .25 inch wide from point to point. It appears at the top-right position of 37 different plates, and to the left of the plate number.

Large five-point star at side. This is the same star as above, and appears at the side plate position of the upper-right panes of 388 plates, below the plate number. This eventually became the standard star and the standard position.

Six-point star at top. This star measures .175 inch wide from point to point. Like the large five-point star it was applied with a hand punch and is sometimes incomplete. It appears at the top-right position of 11 plates and to the left of the plate number.

Six-point star at side. The six-point star appears only at the top-right position of plate 17196, below the plate number. It is the rarest and most valuable of the 2¢ star plates.

2¢ Star Plate, Scott 577

Large five-point star at side. The imperforate version of the 2¢ flat-plate stamp is also known with stars. Plate blocks are known with the large five- point star at the right of 48 plates. A five-point star also exists at the top of plate 17122, but no plate block from this position has come to light.

The Scott *Specialized Catalogue* differentiates between the narrow-gauge and wide-gauge plates in its listing of pairs of this stamp with Schermack Type III private perforations. While it lists these as "2mm" and "3mm" spacing, this is misleading, as the spacings were measured in hundredths of an inch. This spacing is more like .10 inch and .11 inch.

8¢ Star Plate, Scott 560

While the certified plate-proof sheets show that plate 16796 was laid out as a wide-gauge plate, with a six-point star at the top, no plate blocks are known that show this star in the selvage. Two plate number singles showing

16796 at the top are known. While four wide-gauge plates were made, only 16796 went to press, and it went to press with three other plates of the narrow gauge because no other narrow-gauge plate was available. Only 2,275 sheets from this plate were printed, and it is believed that "even this small number was probably further reduced by the poor centering that would result from running wide-gauge stock through perforators set for the narrow gauge of its mates."[5]

However, if the sheets were sorted by plate number, they could have been run through the correct perforator. This was not the only mixed-gauge printing, as there was a printing of the 12¢ value with two plates of each gauge.[6]

Figure 94. Plate 17418 shows the large five-point star at the upper-right position. Plate 17421 shows the six-point star at the upper-right position.

12¢ Star Plates, Scott 564

Large five-point star at side. This star appears at the upper-right position of four plates, below the plate number. The plates are 17418, 17419, 17420 and 18398 (see Figure 94).

Six-point star at side. This star appears only at the upper-right position of plate 17421, below the plate number. This is the highest-numbered plate for the six-point star (see Figure 94).

15¢ Star Plates, Scott 565

Large five-point star at side. This star appears at the upper-right position of eight plates, below the plate number.

20¢ Star Plates, Scott 567

This is the only horizontal-format stamp in the series to have star markings in the margins. Wide-gauge plates of this value have the wider spacing in the horizontal margins.

Large five-point star at side. This star appears at the upper-right position of 20 plates, below the plate number.

Notes

1. W. Irving Glover to Alvin W. Hall, March 23, 1925. Smithsonian Institution Libraries, Post Office Department Manuscripts.

2. G.W. Nowell-Usticke, *The Postage Stamps of the United States*, Volume 4 (New York: Stanley Gibbons Inc., 1938), p. 66.

3. Max G. Johl, *The United States Postage Stamps of the Twentieth Century*, Volume 3 (New York: H.L. Lindquist, 1935), p. 111.

4. W. Wallace Cleland, "Narrow and Wide Gauge Plates of the Fourth Bureau Issue," *United States Specialist*, Vol. 63, No. 7 (July 1992), p. 377.

5. Hugh M. Southgate, "The Narrow and Wide Gage Plates of Fourth Bureau Series," *Bureau Specialist*, Vol. 10, No. 1 (January 1939), p. 10.

6. W. Wallace Cleland, "Printing History of the Wide- and Narrow-Spaced Plates of the 1922 Series 8¢ and 12¢ Stamps," Part II, *United States Specialist*, Vol. 63, No. 4 (April 1992), p. 176.

Chapter 24

The Perforation 10 Rotaries

The success of the rotary press for the 1¢, 2¢ and 1½¢ denominations (see Chapters 11, 18, and 20) pointed to the day when the rotary press would take over the majority of stamp production at the Bureau of Engraving and Printing. By early 1925 this evolution was well under way. Star plates prepared for some of the flat-plate values of this series never went to press because flat-plate production was being rather quickly supplanted by the rotary-press production, at least for the 1¢ to 10¢ values.

As early as July 1924, the Post Office Department authorized the preparation of rotary plates for the 4¢, 5¢, 6¢ and 10¢ denominations "as it is now desired to conduct experiments with the production of the higher-denomination stamps by the rotary process."[1] Of these, only the 5¢ denomination went into production before 1925 — but only for precanceled stamps to help meet the Christmas rush. The first plates went to press on November 14.

The next stamp to go to press was the 4¢ denomination, on February 5, 1925, but again only for precanceled stamps. The 6¢ stamp, similarly, went to press on March 7 for precancels.

These three values, which had already appeared in precanceled form, were scheduled for release on April 4, in unused condition, with the new flat-plate ½¢ Hale. Officially, it seems, these rotary-press varieties were still considered somewhat experimental, and production was limited.

On April 8, 1925, Bureau director Alvin Hall called on W. Irving Glover at his office and made the case for the production of more stamps by the rotary press. While we have no information as to the specifics of this meeting, we can certainly imagine that Hall presented examples of the newly issued rotary-press stamps for inspection.

Glover, we know, answered by letter two days later, on April 10, stating, "For some time past the quality and finish of the postage stamps manufactured by the rotary presses in your Bureau have been greatly improved and it is believed that if stamps equal to the quality of those issued during that period are furnished, the public as a whole will be satisfied with the product."[2]

Furthermore, Glover authorized the production of all denominations up to the 10¢ value by the rotary press. At this point, however, the 1¢, 1½¢, 2¢, 4¢, 5¢ and 6¢ values had already been printed and issued. But not until another year had passed would all the values to the 10¢ stamp appear in rotary form.

(Note: Details on Scott 581, 582 and 583 have been treated in earlier chapters due to their earlier chronological appearance.)

United States Stamps 1922-26

3¢ Lincoln Rotary

Scott Number: 584
First Day of Issue: August 1, 1925
Perforation: 10
Scott Color: Violet
Press: Large rotary press
Plate Layout: 400 subjects cut into panes of 100
Plate Numbers: Total of 22: lowest, 17155; highest, 18446
Scott Varieties: None

Philatelic Aspects and Varieties

First day of issue. This stamp was issued in unused form on August 1, 1925, only at Washington, D.C. Although one of the lowest values, this stamp was issued rather late. As with most of the rotary values, this stamp was first released in precanceled form. The first plates went to press on June 22, 1925. There was sufficient notice to allow collectors and dealers to prepare first-day

Figure 95. Although first-day cover servicing was getting rather sophisticated by 1925, no printed cachets are known on the 3¢ value. This first-day cover pays the 2¢ letter rate and the 10¢ special delivery fee.

covers. Although printed cachets were being produced for some of the commemoratives that had been issued, none is known for this set of rotary-press regular issues. Most first-day covers of the period are rather plain. Figure 95 shows a block of four used to pay the 2¢ letter rate and 10¢ special delivery fee.

Most of the production of this stamp was used for precancels, and in unused condition it probably did not see more than about a year of use before it was replaced by the compound 11 x 10.5 perforation.

Shades. When first listed in the 1926 edition of the Scott *Specialized Catalogue*, the color was listed as violet, and it has not been changed. Johl added to this light violet, bright violet and deep violet.

Precancels. This stamp is known with 41 different Bureau precancels.

4¢ Martha Washington Rotary

Scott Number:	585
First Day of Issue:	April 4, 1925
Perforation:	10
Scott Colors:	Yellow brown, deep yellow brown
Press:	Large rotary press
Plate Layout:	400 subjects cut into panes of 100
Plate Numbers:	16079, 16080, 16660, 16661, 17436, 17437, 17739, 17760, 17761, 17989, 17990, 18365
Scott Varieties:	None

Philatelic Aspects and Varieties

First day of issue. This stamp was issued in unused form on April 4, 1925, only in Washington, D.C. One of the experimental values, this stamp was first issued in precanceled form. Philip Ward and Max Johl both cite early March 1925, and the Scott *Specialized* also gives "Mar 1925." However, the first two plates went to press on February 5, so perhaps the precancel release was even earlier.

In unused condition the stamp went on sale with several others at the Philatelic Stamp Agency. These included the 5¢ and 6¢ rotaries (see below) as well as the Lexington-Concord issue, and the 1½¢ Harding imperforate. We can imagine that with so many stamps issued on the same day, there must have been a good crowd of enthusiasts at the Washington Post Office that day.

Shades. When first listed in the 1926 edition of the *Specialized Catalogue*, the major shade was given as yellow brown with deep yellow brown as a minor shade. The listings have not changed. Johl noted that "one printing of this value resulted in a very dark brown which is entirely different than any other." This he listed as very dark brown. He also added pale brown, light brown, reddish brown, deep reddish brown and brown. This seems like a lot of shades for a stamp that was in production for only about two years.

Precancels. This stamp is known with 36 different Bureau precancels.

5¢ Roosevelt Rotary

Scott Number: 586
First Day of Issue: April 4, 1925
Perforation: 10
Scott Colors: Blue, deep blue
Press: Large rotary press
Plate Layout: 400 subjects cut into panes of 100
Plate Numbers: Total of 36: lowest, 16089; highest, 18850
Scott Varieties: Double transfer
a. Horizontal pair, imperf between

Philatelic Aspects and Varieties

First day of issue. This stamp was issued in unused form on April 4, 1925, only at Washington, D.C. Another of the experimental values, this stamp appeared in December 1924 in precanceled form during the Christmas rush. In unused form, it was released with other stamps on April 4 (see the 4¢ value above), and a relatively large number of first-day covers were serviced.

This stamp was in production for about two and a half years and is not as difficult to find with good centering as most of the other values.

Shades. When first listed in the 1926 edition, the color was given only as blue. In the 1927 edition deep blue was added as a minor shade. To these Johl added light blue and bright blue.

Double transfer. This listing went into the Scott *Specialized Catalogue* in the 1935 edition. It was no doubt based on the report of "the first shifted transfer on the 5¢ rotary" in *Shift Hunter Letter No. 67* in February 1934. This is a shift on the left side of the vignette, which also shows in the "Roo" of "Roosevelt" and the "Ce" of "Cents."

586a. Listed as a "horizontal pair, imperforate between," this variety is not well-documented. It was evidently reported first by Max Johl in *Stamps* in April 1935, when he noted, "The Uptown Stamp Company showed us a horizontal pair of the five cent rotary press perf 10 (586) which had no vertical perforations."[3] In Volume 3 of his *United States Postage Stamps of the 20th Century*," Johl lists this variety and notes, "one pair known."

The listing first went into the *Specialized Catalogue* in the 1936 edition as 586b (586a being a double-paper variety). It was not priced then, and it is not priced now. To the scanty information on this pair, the Stanley Gibbons publication, *The Postage Stamps of the United States,* notes that the pair "is precanceled Portland, Oregon."[4]

Precancels. This stamp is known with 38 different Bureau precancels.

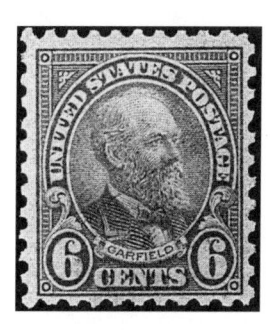

6¢ Garfield Rotary

Scott Number: 587
First Day of Issue: April 4, 1925
Perforation: 10
Scott Colors: Red orange, pale red orange
Press: Large rotary press
Plate Layout: 400 subjects cut into panes of 100
Plate Numbers: 16083, 16084, 17584, 17585, 17588, 17589, 17967, 17968, 18036, 18421
Scott Varieties: None

Philatelic Aspects and Varieties

First day of issue. This stamp was issued on April 4, 1925, only at Washington, D.C. Another of the experimental values, this value also appeared in precanceled form first. The March 1925 date given in the Scott *Specialized* is probably accurate, as the stamps could not have appeared earlier. The first plate went to press on March 7. It was released in unused form at the Philatelic Stamp Agency with several other stamps (see the 4¢ value above). A relatively large number of first-day covers were serviced.

Shades. When first listed in the 1926 edition of the *Specialized Catalogue*, the major shade was given as red orange with pale red orange as a minor shade. These remain the only shades listed today. To these Johl added only bright red orange.

Precancels. This stamp is known with 36 different Bureau precancels.

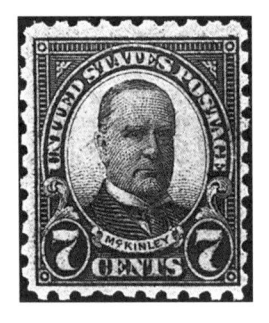

7¢ McKinley Rotary

Scott Number:	588
First Day of Issue:	May 29, 1926
Perforation:	10
Scott Color:	Black
Press:	Large rotary press
Plate Layout:	400 subjects cut into panes of 100
Plate Numbers:	17786, 17787, 17798, 17799, 18179, 18180, 18195, 18196
Scott Varieties:	None

Philatelic Aspects and Varieties

First day of issue. This stamp was issued on May 29, 1926, only at Washington, D.C. The 8¢ and 9¢ denominations were issued on the same date, which was also the date of issue of the Ericsson Memorial issue (see Chapter 36). This was a year later than most of the other rotary issues. Johl noted that these stamps were not produced until additional rotary presses had been installed at the Bureau. Chronologically, these three stamps were issued later

The Perforation 10 Rotaries

than the 13¢ Harrison (Scott 622) and the 17¢ Wilson (623), but since the values were expected, Scott numbers were reserved for them.

By this time, the collecting and servicing of first-day covers had become quite popular, and there is an ample supply of these covers.

Less than a year after this stamp appeared, the compound perforation was issued. In unused form, this stamp saw only 10 months of life. It is the least common of the entire perforation-10 set.

Shades. When first listed in the 1927 edition of the *Specialized Catalogue*, the color was given only as black. While this stamp seems to show little difference in shade, Johl was able to find a grayish black.

Precancels. This stamp is known with 18 different Bureau precancels.

8¢ Grant Rotary

Scott Number:	589
First Day of Issue:	May 29, 1926
Perforation:	10
Scott Colors:	Olive green, pale olive green
Press:	Large rotary press
Plate Layout:	400 subjects cut into panes of 100
Plate Numbers:	17816, 17817, 17832, 17833, 18189, 18190, 18775, 18777
Scott Varieties:	None

Philatelic Aspects and Varieties

First day of issue. This stamp was issued on May 29, 1926, only at Washington, D.C., with the 7¢ and 9¢ varieties (see the 7¢ value above). As with the other two stamps, this was rather late. Numerous first-day covers were serviced.

This stamp, too, saw a very short lifespan of 13 months before the perforation gauge was changed to 11 x 10.5.

Shades. When first listed in the 1927 edition of the *Specialized Catalogue*, the color was given only as olive green. In the 1932 edition, pale olive

269

United States Stamps 1922-26

green was added as a secondary shade. In addition Johl found olive yellow, olive bister and pale olive bister. This, too, is a lot of shades for a stamp with such a short lifetime, but there is clearly a lighter and darker shade of this stamp.

Precancels. This stamp is known with 18 different Bureau precancels.

9¢ Jefferson Rotary

Scott Number: 590
First Day of Issue: May 29, 1926
Perforation: 10
Scott Color: Rose
Press: Large rotary press
Plate Layout: 400 subjects cut into panes of 100
Plate Numbers: 17854, 17855, 18193, 18194
Scott Varieties: None

Figure 96. Issued in 1926, 10 months later than most of the other issues, the 7¢, 8¢ and 9¢ issues were released with little advance notice. Most first-day covers are quite plain. This one, serviced by Washington stamp dealer C.E. Nickles, is more colorful, with his printed corner card on an airmail envelope.

Philatelic Aspects and Varieties

First day of issue. This stamp was issued on May 29, 1926, only at Washington, D.C., on the same date as the 7¢ and 8¢ values (see the 7¢ value above). While first-day-cover servicing had gotten rather sophisticated by mid-1926, no printed cachets are known to have originated on covers of the 7¢, 8¢ or 9¢ rotaries. This was probably due in part to the short notice given and to the fact that these were not new designs. Figure 96 shows one of the more colorful first-day covers, on an airmail envelope, and with the corner card of Washington, D.C., dealer C.E. Nickles.

This stamp also had a rather short lifespan of just slightly less than 12 months in unused condition before the perforation gauge was changed to 11 x 10.5.

Shades. When this stamp was first listed in the 1927 edition of the *Specialized Catalogue*, the only color given was rose, and the Scott listing has not changed. Johl, however, noted that this stamp appeared in more shades than its flat-plate counterpart (for which Scott lists two shades). Johl found rose red, pale salmon, salmon and salmon red. This seems a lot of shades for four plates and a short lifespan, but we find some support for Johl's shades in the fact that plates 18193 and 18194 went to press five times each.

Precancels. This stamp is known with 13 different Bureau precancels. This is the least precanceled value of the series.

10¢ Monroe Rotary

Scott Number: 591
First Day of Issue: June 8, 1925
Perforation: 10
Scott Color: Orange
Press: Large rotary press
Plate Layout: 400 subjects cut into panes of 100
Plate Numbers: Total of 28: lowest 16107; highest 18623
Scott Varieties: None

Philatelic Aspects and Varieties

First day of issue. This stamp was issued on June 8, 1925, only at Washington, D.C. This was the highest value of the series that was initially authorized to be printed on the rotary presses and was always a value in high demand. Although Johl mentions that it was first issued in precanceled form, this does not seem to be true, as the first plates went to press on May 27, only a week before the stamp was issued in unused form.

Shades. As we noted with the flat-plate stamp, this is really a yellow stamp, although Scott calls it orange, and it was listed as such in the 1926 edition of the *Specialized Catalogue*. Johl also seems to have found a lot of red in this stamp, as he found orange yellow, yellow orange, deep yellow orange, and red orange. He noted that "one printing was in a red orange shade, somewhat similar to the six cent, and this is much more desirable than the others. ..."

Precancels. This stamp is known with 39 different Bureau precancels.

Notes

1. W. Irving Glover to Andrew Mellon, secretary of the treasury, July 24, 1924. Historical Resource Center, Bureau of Engraving and Printing.

2. W. Irving Glover to Alvin W. Hall, April 10, 1925. Historical Resource Center, Bureau of Engraving and Printing.

3. Max G. Johl, "Max G. Johl Replies on 20th Century U.S.," *Stamps*, Volume 11, No. 3 (April 20, 1935), p. 86.

4. G.W. Nowell-Usticke, editor, *The Postage Stamps of the United States: Issued During the Twentieth Century*, Volume IV: 1901 to 1937 (New York: Stanley Gibbons Inc., 1938), p. 71.

Chapter 25

The Special Handling Stamp

25¢ Special Handling

Scott Number:	QE4a
First Day of Issue:	April 11, 1925
Perforation:	11
Scott Color:	Deep green
Designer:	Clair Aubrey Huston
Engraver:	Edward M. Hall
Plate Layout:	Flat plate; plates of 200 cut into panes of 50
Quantity Issued:	Fewer than 23,800,000
Plate Numbers:	17095, 17096, 17097, 17098, 17099, 17101, 17102, 17103
Scott Varieties:	QE4, yellow green, "A" and second "T" of "STATES" joined at top (plate 17103)
	"A" and second "T" of "STATES" and "T" and "A" of "Post age" joined at top, (plate 17103)

The Subject and Design

Since this stamp was meant to signal a special service, its design was mostly functional. There was no portrait or scene, just the lettering in an arch and the denomination in a circle centered on the design. The background was a lathework design of the type used on currency and other securities.

The design and color were similar to the parcel post postage due stamps of 1912 that Bureau designer C. Aubrey Huston had also designed. These parcel post postage due stamps were discontinued in 1913 as being unnecessary.

The Political Background

In the Post Office Bill that paid for the pay raises of post office work-

273

ers (see Chapter 19), several postal rates were increased to make some classes and services pay more of their actual costs. The special handling stamp grew out of this attempt.

Parcel post, or fourth-class mail, although politically popular, particularly in rural areas, was not paying its way. As part of the new law, fourth-class mail was redefined as anything over eight ounces that was not included in first- or second-class mail. In addition to the existing rates, "an additional charge of 2 cents on each parcel" was levied, except on parcels collected on rural-delivery routes. This additional charge effectively raised the rate by 2¢ on each package.

Special handling was also added in the new law, and although it purports to offer an additional service, this in reality was another fee, as it was not optional on some types of packages.

While most live animals were considered unmailable matter, day-old chicks were among a very few "harmless live animals" that were permitted in the mail. Packages and crates of baby chicks could be sent as fourth-class matter, but these packages required special attention and quick delivery if the animals were to survive.

The special handling fee of 25¢ was instituted, according to the Post Office Department, for use on fourth-class mail matter to secure "the expeditious handling, accorded to mail of the first class."[1] However, the post office also noted that this "charge," not service, "applies to all parcels containing day-old chicks or baby alligators, which, because of their character, must be given special attention in handling, transportation, and delivery."[2]

Special delivery service was not included under the special handling fee.

This new fee went into effect on April 15, 1925. The stamps were made obsolete by a new rate structure in 1928. Although most stamps were not redeemable at post offices, an exception was made for the 25¢ special handling stamp. Customers could exchange them for the new values.

Clearly these stamps were not used only for shipping animals, as we find correspondence in the official files about redemption of stamps by such firms as the Ingersol-Rand Company and the Department of Highways of Pennsylvania.

At least 9,777 of the 25¢ stamps that had been returned were destroyed in December 1930.[3]

Philatelic Aspects and Varieties

There was obviously not a great demand for these stamps for mailing purposes. But since the stamps were put on sale at the Philatelic Stamp Agency, collectors had little difficulty obtaining unused examples and plate blocks.

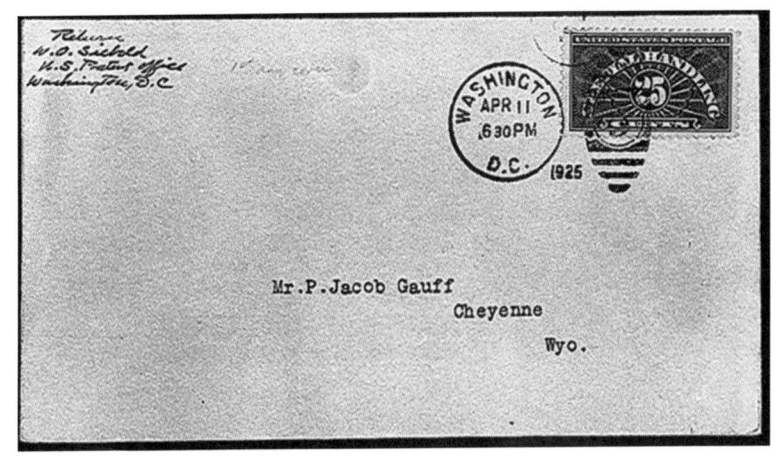

Figure 97. As a back-of-the-book stamp, there was not a great interest in the special handling stamp, and few first-day covers were serviced. This one has the corner card of William Siebold, an early first-day cover enthusiast. A 2¢ stamp, which pays the postage, is on the reverse side of the cover.

First day of issue. This stamp was issued on April 11, 1925, only at Washington, D.C. The date was the same as the new 15¢ special delivery stamp, which generated greater interest among collectors. A few first-day covers were serviced (see Figure 97).

Quantities and usage. Although a number of plates were laid out for this stamp, only eight went to press, and the records for the deliveries of these stamps seem to be much smaller than the number produced.

During the 1925 fiscal year, which ended on July 1, 1925, only 467 stamps were delivered to the Post Office Department, and this is probably the quantity delivered to the Philatelic Stamp Agency for first-day sale. In the following fiscal year, we find 1,583,033 stamps delivered.

While a number of first-day covers exist, commercial covers of the 25¢ value are relatively scarce. In ordinary use, these stamps would be affixed to boxes, crates or parcel tags, not to letters. So it seems that very few on-cover items were saved. The ordinary usage would be a single stamp per mailed article. There was no commercial need for pairs, blocks or other multiples.

This stamp became obsolete on July 1, 1928, when the rate was changed to 10¢ for packages up to two pounds, 15¢ for packages over two pounds but less than 10 pounds, and 20¢ for packages over 10 pounds.

No plates of the 25¢ value went to press after January 19, 1928, but stamps of this early 1928 printing are of a lighter yellow-green shade.

Cataloging. The Scott listings for these stamps do not always make sense and require some explanation. Scott also seems to have been confused about the dates at some points in its history.

Scott first listed this stamp in the 1926 edition of the *Specialized Catalogue* as 1463 and gave the color as deep green. In the 1932 edition, the yellow-green shade was listed for the first time as a separate catalog number, 1467.

In the 1938 edition, 1463 was eliminated entirely, and the deep-green shade was listed as 1467a, a subvariety of the yellow-green. This made for a seemingly simple album page layout, as the denominations now went in order, with the 10¢ value listed first, then the 15¢, 20¢ and 25¢. This, of course, tortures the true chronology.

In the 1940 edition, when Scott changed its numbering system, the listing for this stamp became QE4a, again as a subvariety of the yellow-green shade, which was listed as QE4. The listing remains thus to the present day.

In printing many of its albums, Scott also confused collectors by eliminating the space for the deep-green shade. My 1960 edition of Scott's *American Album*, for example, has a space for only QE4, with the date "1929." No wonder many collectors have trouble understanding this issue!

While the other values of the special handling stamps were later printed by the dry-printing method, this stamp was only printed by the "wet printing" method. There is no dry-printing variety.

Shades. The deep-green shade originally listed by Scott has been called blue green by a few writers, and this is somewhat descriptive of the early shade. This deep green that Scott now lists as a small-letter variety, QE4a, might well be dropped and simply listed as a shade, since Scott has dropped the small-letter listing for shades of other stamps of this period. Scott has taken the position that the most common shade should be the major shade regardless of the chronology. Deep green, however, is the original shade. Yellow green came later.

"A" and "T" of "States" joined. This variety, and the variety listed below, are relief breaks caused by a bit of metal that became dislodged as the designs were transferred onto plate 17103. Cloudy French has noted that "this relief break has been the subject of more erroneous reports than any other variety I can think of."[4] The relief break begins at 17103 UR 17 and progresses across and down the plate. Thus stamps from all four panes will show some varieties with this relief break. Gilbert Peakes sorted this out rather clearly in 1972, explaining that this break shows on 17103 UR 17-50, 17103 UL 21-50, and "it occurs on all the subjects of both lower panes."[5] This variety was first reported in *Mekeel's Weekly Stamp News* in January 1932, and Philip Ward, in a later column, quoted Bureau director Alvin W. Hall explaining: "A small piece of steel chipped out of the roll which made the letters 't' and 'a' appear as if they were connected or very close together."[6] The variety was listed by Scott for the first time in the 1934 edition of the *Specialized Catalogue*.

"A" and "T" of "STATES" joined and "T" and "A" of "POST-

AGE" joined. This is a further break on the same plate, which occurs only on the final five positions of the plate; that is, 17103 LR 46-50. These five positions will also show the relief break listed above. This variety was first listed in the 1938 edition of the *Specialized Catalogue*.

Notes

1. W. Irving Glover, "New Denomination 15-cent Special Delivery Stamp and 25-cent Special Handling Parcel Post Stamp, Issue of 1925," Post Office Department Announcement, April 8, 1925.

2. Post Office Department, *United States Official Postal Guide*, Vol. 5, No. 1 (July 1925), p. 13.

3. Third assistant postmaster general to chief inspector, Post Office Department, December 10, 1930. Smithsonian Institution Libraries, Post Office Department Manuscripts.

4. Loran C. French, *Encyclopedia of Plate Varieties on U.S. Bureau-Printed Postage Stamps* (Bureau Issues Association, 1979), p. 334.

5. Gilbert L. Peakes, "The Relief Breaks on the 25¢ Special Handling Stamp," *United States Specialist,* Vol. 43, No. 11 (November 1972), pp. 487-501.

6. Philip H. Ward Jr., *Mekeel's Weekly Stamp News*, March 28, 1932.

United States Stamps 1922-26

Chapter 26

The 15¢ Special Delivery

Motorcycle Special Delivery

Scott Number:	E13
First Day of Issue:	April 11, 1925
Perforation:	11
Scott Color:	Deep orange
Designer:	Clair Aubrey Huston
Engravers:	Louis S. Schofield (vignette and frame)
	E.M. Weeks (numerals and lettering "Fifteen Cents")
	E.M. Hall (other lettering)
Plate Layout:	Flat Plate; plates of 200 cut into panes of 50
Quantity Issued:	Greater than 17,205,233
Plate Numbers:	16833, 16834, 16835, 16836, 16857, 16858, 16859, 16860
Scott Varieties:	Double transfer

The Political Background

In an effort to get more mail to pay its own way, two new special delivery rates were put into effect on April 15 as part of the Postal Service Act of February 28, 1925.

Until this point, parcel post packages of any weight up to the 70-pound limit could be delivered for a 10¢ fee. The new rates were based on weight. Packages over two pounds, but less than 10 pounds would get special delivery service for 15¢ in addition to the regular postage. Packages over 10 pounds would get special delivery service for 20¢ in addition to the regular postage.

As this new rate was being proposed, Philip Ward wrote in favor of it, arguing that it was hardly fair for the special delivery messenger to get only 8¢ of a 10¢ fee to deliver "a bundle of several auto tires, or a bushel of peaches weighing 60 pounds."[1]

Under the new rate, the messenger would get 11¢ of the 15¢ fee, and 15¢ of the 20¢ fee.

The Subject and Design

This stamp was identical to the 10¢ (see Chapter 3) except for the denomination numerals and the "Fifteen Cents" below the vignette. On the day after the new rate was approved by the Senate, Michael Eidsness, the superintendent of the Division of Stamps, suggested that "in order to expedite the printing ... the present special-delivery stamp could ... be changed to the 15¢ denomination and printed in a different color."[2] This suggestion was acted upon.

The practice of changing the denomination of the original motorcycle design then became somewhat standard. New denominations of this stamp in 13¢ and 17¢ denominations were added in 1944. This was something of a tribute to the appeal and usefulness of the original design for the 10¢ stamp in 1922.

Philatelic Aspects and Varieties

First day of issue. This stamp was issued on April 11, 1925, only at Washington, D.C. This was the same date as the special handling stamp. There was ample notice for collectors and dealers to service first-day covers of this stamp, but as Henry Gobie has pointed out, "This is about the only time that this stamp should be found on a cover."[3] Most of the nonphilatelic usages of this stamp during its period of initial issue should be on parcels or on parcel tags.

In 1928, when the special delivery rates were revised and raised again, 15¢ became the rate for special delivery of fourth-class matter under two pounds, so this stamp saw some additional use. This same design and denomination was printed by the rotary press in 1931.

Double transfer. This listing first appeared in the second edition of the 1936 Scott *Specialized Catalogue*, and was no doubt based on a July 1935 report in *Stamps* magazine of a transfer that was "canted counterclockwise" on stamp 16836 UL 1. Scott does not list the position in its current catalog listing, but this is the only plate variety listed by French on this stamp.

Notes

1. Philip H. Ward Jr., "Chronicle of New Issues and Varieties," *Mekeel's Weekly Stamp News*, Vol. 38, No. 40 (October 6, 1924), p. 528.

2. Michael L. Eidsness Jr. to W. Irving Glover, February 27, 1925. Smithsonian Institution Libraries, Post Office Department Manuscripts.

3. Henry M. Gobie, *The Speedy: A History of United States Special Delivery Service* (self-published, 1976), p. 192.

Chapter 27

The ½¢ Due

Scott Number:	J68
First Day of Issue:	April 13, 1925
Perforation:	11
Color:	Dull red
Designer:	Clair Aubrey Huston
Engravers:	E.M. Weeks (numerals and lettering "Half Cent")
	S.B. Many and J. Kennedy (frame and other lettering from previous design)
Plate Layout:	Flat plate; plates of 400 cut into panes of 100
Quantity Issued:	32,563,000
Plate Numbers:	17127, 17128, 17129, 17130, 17131
Scott Varieties:	None

The Political Background

This stamp was something of an afterthought, as it was not contemplated in the original memo from Michael Eidsness on February 27, 1925, as to the number of new stamps and denominations that would be necessary for the rate change.

Where the orders for the other stamps needed for the new rates were all placed by March 13, we have no record of the ½¢ postage due being ordered before March 27, the date on which the model was approved. The die was started on the following day and completed and hardened on March 31. The first plate was certified on April 3, and the first plates went to press on the following day, April 4.

From what we can tell from the records, this was a rush job for the Bureau.

The Subject and Design

Already in existence was a series of postage due stamps, the design of which had not changed since 1894. Over the years the shades, watermarks and perforations had changed, but the design of what was known as the Series of 1894 was constant: a lathework background with a large number in the center.

The new ½¢ denomination was designed to conform to this series. The frame design and lathework were transferred from an existing die. New engraving was needed only for the numeral and the lettering of the denomination.

Philatelic Aspects and Varieties

First day of issue. While the date of issue of this stamp is given as April 13, there would seem to be no legitimate use of it until April 15, the date the rate went into effect. There was little advance word of the issue of this stamp. Philip Ward noted in his *Mekeel's* column of April 13 that "the Bureau … is preparing plates for a new ½¢ Postage Due stamp."[1]

Ward himself seems to have been the only person to act on this information and to have serviced first-day covers. With the help, no doubt, of the postmaster at his local Germantown Station in Philadelphia, Ward mailed himself a number of unsealed envelopes franked with a 1¢ stamp. The ½¢ postage due stamp was canceled with a circular datestamp (see Figure 98).

Usage. There was no difficulty in collecting the postage due for an even number of covers. But how did a letter carrier collect ½¢? Some covers are known with a ½¢ Hale postage stamp lightly attached as change.

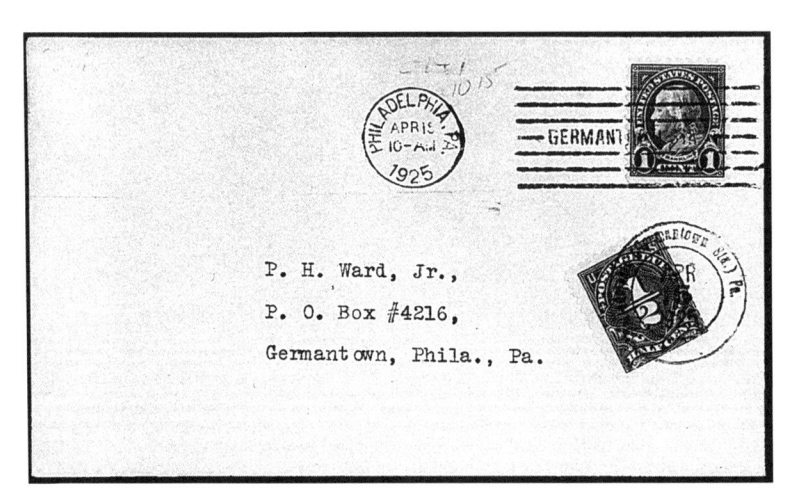

Figure 98. The only known first-day covers of this stamp were prepared by Philip Ward on covers that were inadequately franked on the day the rate went into effect.

The ½¢ Due

A new series of postage due stamps was issued in 1930, at which time this stamp was replaced. Thus it saw about six years of service.

Double transfer. Although not listed in Scott, this stamp is reported to have several plate varieties, including double transfers reported on 17130 LL 61 and 17130 LL 91.[2]

Notes

1. Philip H. Ward Jr., "Chronicle of New Issues and Varieties," *Mekeel's Weekly Stamp News*, Vol. 39, No. 15 (April 13, 1925), p. 197.
2. "Postage Due Varieties," *Bureau Specialist*, Vol. 17, No. 7 (July 1946), p. 164.

United States Stamps 1922-26

Chapter 28

The 20¢ Special Delivery

Post Office Truck

Scott Number: E14
First Day of Issue: April 25, 1925
Perforation: 11
Color: Black
Designer: Clair Aubrey Huston
Engravers: Louis Schofield (vignette and frame)
E.M. Weeks (numerals and lettering "Fifteen Cents")
E.M. Hall (other lettering)
Plate Layout: Flat plate; plates of 200 cut into panes of 50.
Quantity Issued: Fewer than 30,073,400
Plate Numbers: 17175, 17176, 17177, 17178, 17183, 17184, 17185, 17186, 17191, 17192, 17193, 17199, 17206, 17211, 17213, 17214
Scott Varieties: None

The Political Background

Like the 15¢ stamp, this issue was the result of the Postal Service Act of February 28, 1925. The 20¢ rate paid the special delivery fee for packages over 10 pounds. Although the rate went into effect on April 15, 10 days before the stamp was issued, the rate could easily be paid using two 10¢ stamps.

The messengers who delivered special delivery packages at this rate received 15¢ of this 20¢ fee.

The Subject and Design

The subject for the stamp was suggested by Michael L. Eidsness Jr., the superintendent of the Division of Stamps, who wrote that the same border

285

could be used as on the existing 10¢ special delivery stamp, "with the main subject being a parcel-post mail wagon, which would be symbolic of the service rendered."[1] While this suggestion was followed for the subject matter, a new border was also designed.

The stamp design is based on a photograph, which may have been taken for the purpose, as the scene seems somewhat posed (see Figure 99). However, there must not have been much of an attempt to use an up-to-date truck, as the photo and stamp design show what has been identified as "a Pierce Arrow mail truck, of a model certainly not made later than 1920, and perhaps not later than 1917."[2]

The truck has right-hand drive and is shown with a driver at the wheel with, according to the official description, "a carrier loading parcel-post packages for special delivery." The photograph was taken at the City Post Office in Washington, D.C. This was not only a handy location, but it also had the neoclassical architecture that fit in so well with the style of Bureau designer C. Aubrey Huston.

Huston modified the sketch only slightly, moving around a few of the architectural elements to be more balanced. The number of the truck in the photograph, however — 8246 — appears in the engraving on the issued stamp.

Philatelic Aspects and Varieties

First day of issue. This stamp was issued on April 25, 1925, only at

Figure 99. The source photograph for this stamp design may have been posed especially for the purpose. The truck has been identified as a Pierce Arrow with right-hand drive. The number of this truck, 8246, was also engraved on the stamp.

The 20¢ Special Delivery

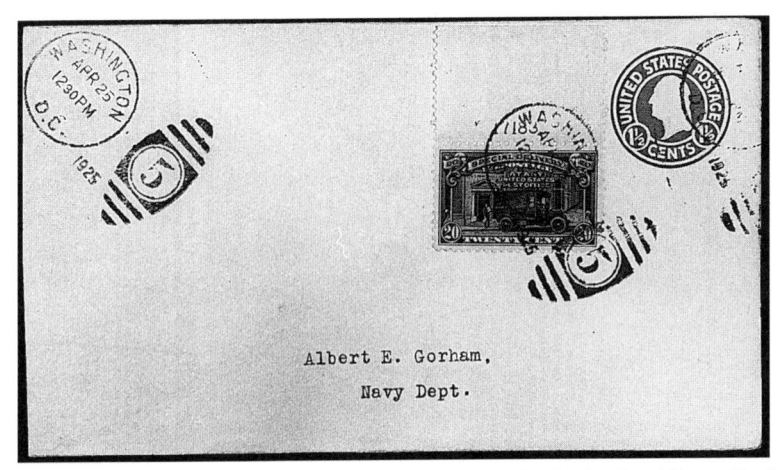

Figure 100. A first-day cover serviced by Washington, D.C., dealer Albert Gorham on a 1½¢ stamped envelope. The stamp is a plate number single of plate 17183.

Washington, D.C. As with most of the other stamps related to the 1925 rate change, there was adequate notice to allow for the servicing of first-day covers, and a fair number were produced (see Figure 100).

Usage. Like the 15¢ stamp issued 10 days earlier, this stamp was intended for use on packages. Domestic usages should be on parcel wrappers or tags. Unlike the 15¢ stamp, however, it also paid a letter rate for the special delivery or "Express" service to Canada, which was 20¢. Thus, nonphilatelic uses of this stamp at its time of issue can be found on cover.

In 1928, the special delivery rates were raised, making 20¢ the fee for parcels over 2 pounds but less than 10 pounds. Thus, this stamp received additional use on packages.

This stamp was not printed by the rotary press until 1951, when 20¢ became the special delivery rate for letters and other matter under 2 pounds. No doubt the 1920-ish truck must have seemed even more out of date then.

Notes

1. Michael L. Eidsness Jr. to W. Irving Glover, February 27, 1925. Smithsonian Institution Libraries, Post Office Department Manuscripts.
2. Stephen Rich, writing in *Weekly Philatelic Gossip* for October 1954 is credited with this description, in Henry Gobie, *The Speedy: A History of United States Special Delivery Service* (self-published, 1976) p. 193.

United States Stamps 1922-26

Chapter 29

The Norse-American Issue

The Political Background

As with the Huguenot-Walloon issue, there was no objection from Postmaster General Harry S. New to issuing this series. But the issue proved to be an expensive headache, and with very few exceptions, he and his department would oppose what they called "special issues" in the future. This stamp proved how troublesome and costly commemorative stamps could be.

The initial request for a stamp came from an organization calling itself the Norse-American Centennial. It wanted only a single stamp, showing the ship that brought the first Norwegian settlers to the United States. That ship, the *Restaurationen,* was to the Norwegian settlers what the *Mayflower* was to the Plymouth Rock pilgrims; only it sailed not in 1620 but in 1825, from Stavanger Harbor in Norway.

A centennial celebration was planned for the Minnesota State Fairgrounds in July 1925, and the job of lobbying for the stamp fell to the local congressman, Ole Kvale, a Norwegian-American and Independent Republican. Rather than just making a request to the postmaster general, Kvale filed a bill in Congress in May 1924, which like other legislation, was then referred to the proper congressional committee.

The committee chairman, Representative William Walton Griest, a Republican from Pennsylvania, forwarded the bill to Postmaster General New for his "consideration and recommendation."[1]

New's reaction is preserved in a note to Third Assistant W. Irving Glover. "We talked a little about the matter of this stamp," he wrote. "I have no objection to its issuance."[2] New wrote back to Congressman Griest the next day that "no objection will be interposed to the issuance of a postage stamp to commemorate the event. ..."[3]

During the year that followed, the single stamp request became a two-stamp issue. By December 13, Glover was writing to the editor of the Minneapolis *Tidende* that "no doubt two stamps will be issued. ..."[4] The 2¢ value would pay the standard letter rate, while a 5¢ value would pay the postage for an overseas letter to most countries, including Norway and the other Scandinavian countries. Unlike all previous commemoratives except for the Pan American issue of 1901, the stamps would be issued in two colors.

We do not know what role was played in these decisions by Michael Eidsness, the superintendent of the Division of Stamps, but Eidsness was himself of Norwegian descent and had usually been in favor of special issues.

Eidsness wrote in 1934, some nine years after the stamps were issued, that the two-color decision was something of an accident. He stated that the Bureau's designer, Clair Aubrey Huston, was "absent from duty" when the models for the stamps were presented to the Post Office Department, and that a "rookie" at the Bureau, "who was not entirely familiar with the standard method of submitting designs," presented models in two colors.[5]

This was in fact a departure from the norm. Usually models were submitted in black-and-white, stamp-sized photostats or photographs. The two-color models presented for the Norse-American issue were included on a single presentation board (Figure 101), which is still in the files of the Bureau.

According to Eidsness, these models "created a sensation" at the Post Office Department, and were "the most striking models ever offered by the Bureau."[6] Postmaster General New approved the models with his signature on January 12, 1925, and the stamps were then ordered to be printed in two colors.

There was probably no intention by the Bureau to have two different frame designs. The practice at the time was to use a single frame for all the denominations in a commemorative series, thus reducing the time and cost of engraving separate frames. But as presented, the two stamps each had a different frame design, and that is the way they were approved.

The issue also got other special treatment. Rather than being printed in sheets of 400, like most other stamps, the Norse-American stamps were laid out on 100-subject plates, like the $5 stamp of the regular issue. These sheets

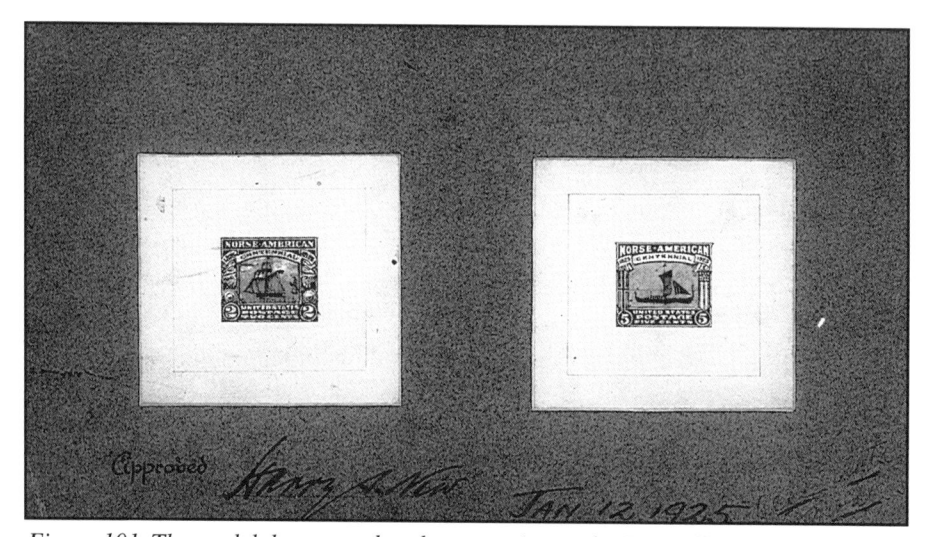

Figure 101. The model that caused such a sensation at the Post Office Department was submitted in two colors, with the stamps side by side. This was a departure from the usual procedure of submitting black-and-white models of single stamps.

would not be divided or cut into smaller panes for sale in post offices, and there would be no straight edges. These production decisions helped create a beautiful and well-produced set of stamps, but they would also cause embarrassment for the Post Office Department, which soon learned that it could not provide enough stamps to meet the demand.

Printing the stamps in two colors was a slow process. First the frames were produced in red or blue, then the sheets had to be dried before the vignettes were added in black in a second trip through the press. In addition, since the stamps were printed in small sheets of 100 (rather than the normal sheets of 400), it took a relatively long time to print large quantities.

2¢ Sloop Restaurationen

Scott Number:	620
First Day of Issue:	May 18, 1925
Perforation:	11
Scott Colors:	Carmine and black, deep carmine and black
Designer:	Clair Aubrey Huston
Engravers:	Edward J. Hein (vignette)
	W.B. Wells (frame)
	E.M. Hall (lettering)
Plate Layout:	Plates of 100 subjects, not cut into smaller panes
Quantity Issued:	9,104,983
Plate Numbers:	Vignette: 16687, 16688, 16689, 16690, 17353, 17355, 17356, 17379
	Frame: 16694, 16924, 16958, 16959
Varieties:	Black plate number omitted

The Subject and Design

Although the chief event commemorated was the centennial of the arrival of the ship *Restaurationen*, the sponsors of the stamp could find no reproduction of this ship. "There is no picture of *Restaurationen*," Gisle Bothne, the president of the Norse-American Centennial wrote to Congressman Kvale. "But a sister ship of practically the same dimensions, a sloop like *Restaurationen*, was built at the same time by the same people in the same place. There is a picture of this sister ship. This picture was brought from Norway last summer by Gunnar Malmin. ..."[7]

A picture of this unnamed ship had been reproduced in a Norwegian magazine, and a clipping was provided to the Post Office Department. This same clipping, which shows another ship in the background, was sent to the Bureau for reference for the stamp. It is shown in Figure 102.

It is interesting to note that in the official description of the stamp, the Post Office Department does not claim that the stamp illustrates the *Restaurationen*, but only that it "has for its central design a ship representing the sloop *Restaurationen*."[8]

Figure 102. The reference artwork for the 2¢ design was a clipping from a Norwegian magazine showing the sister ship of the Restaurationen.

The frame is somewhat elaborate, showing at both sides dragon heads and shields of the type that might be found on ancient Norse vessels.

Philatelic Aspects and Varieties

First day of issue. This stamp was issued, with the 5¢ value, on May 18, 1925. Many cities with large Norwegian-American populations requested to be first-day cities for the new stamps, and six were chosen in addition to Washington, D.C.: Benson, Northfield, Minneapolis and St. Paul, Minnesota; and Algona and Decorah, Iowa.

While most of the first-day covers that were serviced for this issue were without cachets, at least two individuals prepared covers on envelopes printed for the occasion. Albert Roessler, the New Jersey stamp dealer who was also a printer, prepared envelopes with a corner card that carried a text message about the stamps. Ernest Weschcke of St. Paul, Minnesota, also prepared special envelopes printed with the legends, "Norse-American Centennial" and "First Day Cover." (See Figure 103.)

Shortages. While there were apparently enough stamps to service first-day covers in each city, there was a shortage of stamps in most places for postal customers. Due to the complaints of Arch Coleman, the postmaster at Minneapolis, and Charles Moos, the postmaster at St. Paul, these two cities received a large percentage of the total press run.

The Post Office Department soon found itself deluged with requests. "Every day this office is receiving a large number of calls for Norse-Centennial stamps," the postmaster of Eau Clair, Wisconsin, wrote on May 22, in a letter typical of many others. "This community is populated largely by Scandinavians

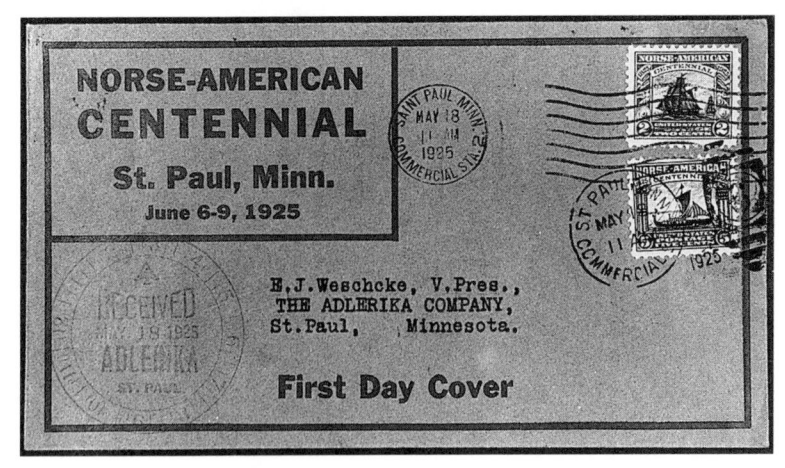

Figure 103. This is a combination first-day cover from St. Paul, Minnesota, on one of the few printed cacheted envelopes. It was serviced by Ernest J. Weschcke on a blue envelope with red printing.

and in as much as these stamps have received considerable publicity, they are very much in demand."[9]

Printing more stamps would have been possible, but in the case of the Norse-American issue, the costs were prohibitive. The Post Office Department learned that the stamps were costing 83¢ per thousand, or roughly 10 times more than ordinary stamps. In explaining why the costs were so high, the Bureau explained that "the order is comparatively small, that the cost of engraving new designs alone is over fifteen hundred dollars, that there are two plate printings, one being registered, and that there are only 100 stamps to the printed sheet."[10]

Congressman Kvale requested for months that more stamps be printed because of what he described, probably pretty accurately, as "dissatisfaction over the way in which the stamps have been circulated and distributed, until of late it has become an open criticism and near resentment."[11]

No second printing took place, however, and Eidsness later estimated that not more than 300 post offices ever received the Norse-American stamps, and some of those received "only one or two sheets each."[12]

Plate blocks. Because of the two-color printing, plate blocks of this stamp are usually saved as a block of eight stamps, showing two plate numbers at the top, one for the frame and one for the vignette. With eight vignette plates and four frame plates, there are 32 combinations of numbers, and all are known.

Shades. When first listed in the 1926 edition of the Scott *Specialized Catalogue*, the major shade was given as carmine and black, with deep carmine and black as a minor shade. Johl had no additions.

Black plate number omitted. This is a printing variety, rather than an error. It was caused when the vignette plate was not inked all the way to the edge of the plate, causing there to be no printing of the plate number.

5¢ Viking Ship

Scott Number:	621
First Day of Issue:	May 18, 1925
Perforation:	11
Scott Colors:	Dark blue and black
Designer:	Clair Aubrey Huston
Engravers:	J.C. Benzing (vignette and frame)
	E.M. Weeks (lettering)
Plate Layout:	Plates of 100 subjects, not cut into smaller panes
Quantity Issued:	1,900,983
Plate Numbers:	Vignette: 16927, 16928, 16929, 16957
	Frame: 16925, 16926, 16961, 16963

The Subject and Design

While we know a great deal about the source artwork of the design of this stamp, we do not know whose idea it was to include a Viking ship as one of the subjects of this series. There seems to have been no request for it by either the officials of the Norse-American Centennial or by the Post Office Department. It therefore seems likely that this was a suggestion by the Bureau.

The design purports to show what the Post Office Department described as "a Viking ship." This design was well-received initially, but in September 1925, a few months after the stamp was issued, Scott Stamp and Coin Company displayed a blow-up of the stamp in the window of its retail store at West 44th Street in New York City, with the caption, "Artist's Error."

Scott also took note of this error in its publication, *Scott's Monthly Journal*. "Examine the stamp with a magnifying glass," the article began. "You will find that the flag in question is … the Stars and Stripes of the United States of America. And it waves from a ship represented to be sailing about the year 1000 A.D. — centuries before our national emblem was officially adopted by resolution of Congress on June 14, 1777."

"Surely," the article went on, "this stamp carries one of the strangest

The Norse-American Issue

anachronistic designs in the history of philately."[13]

The Post Office Department, strangely, at first denied that this was an error. In answer to a letter, Michael Eidsness wrote, "From what I have been able to learn the flag in question is not the Stars and Stripes, but the intricate engraving appearing thereon would make it appear to some that this is a fact."[14]

However, a reader of the magazine identified the Viking craft as the same one that appeared in a photograph in the program of the World's Columbian Exposition of 1893 (see Figure 104). It was a reproduction of a Viking ship that had sailed from Norway to Newfoundland, then to Chicago by way of the St. Lawrence River and the Great Lakes. It was exhibited at the Norway Building of the exposition. The photograph in the program clearly showed an American flag in the bow and a Norwegian flag in the stern.

Figure 104. A photograph of the replica of the Viking ship from the program of the Columbian Exposition of 1893 was the reference artwork for the stamp. It proved that the flag on the stamp was an American flag.

Philatelic Aspects and Varieties

First day of issue. This stamp was issued on May 18, 1926, with the 2¢ value, at Washington, D.C., and six additional cities (see the 2¢ value above).

No inverts found. On the day after the stamp was issued, the *Newark News* apparently noted that an invert had been found, but none was ever produced. Ward wrote that "the Post Office was unusually careful in the issuing of these varieties, and not only the Bureau checked them up very carefully, but the Post Office had their own representative on the ground to see that no inverts got out."[15]

Plate blocks. As with the 2¢ value, the plate block of this stamp is usually collected in a block of eight showing two numbers at the top (see Figure 105). There were four frame plates and four vignette plates, making 16 combinations, all of which are known.

Plate varieties. While one writer studied several sheets of this stamp and found hat "it has so many extra lines, distinct and easily recognized, that your interest will not lag in the search for them,"[16] no double transfers or other significant plate varieties have been noted on this stamp, and Scott lists none.

295

Figure 105. The normal plate block format of both values of the Norse-American issue is a block of eight stamps with a center line and arrow, and two plate numbers. One plate number is for the black vignette, the other is for the colored frame.

Notes

1. William Walton Griest to Harry S. New, June 2, 1924. Smithsonian Institution Libraries, Post Office Department Manuscripts.

2. Harry S. New to W. Irving Glover, June 3, 1924. Smithsonian Institution Libraries, Post Office Department Manuscripts.

3. Harry S. New to William Walton Griest, June 4, 1924. Smithsonian Institution Libraries, Post Office Department Manuscripts.

4. W. Irving Glover to Carl G.O. Hansen, editor, Minneapolis *Tidende*, December 13, 1924. Smithsonian Institution Libraries, Post Office Department Manuscripts.

5. Michael L. Eidsness, "The Norse-American Commemorative," *Stamps*, Vol. 6, No. 11 (March 17, 1934), pp. 375-76.

6. *Ibid.,* p. 375.

7. Gisle Bothne, president, Norse-American Centennial to Representative Ole Kvale, January 5, 1924. Historical Resource Center, Bureau of Engraving and Printing.

8. Quoted from Post Office Department, *A Description of United States Postage Stamps* (Washington, D.C.: Government Printing Office, 1937), p. 61.

9. H.M. Johnson, postmaster, Eau Claire, Wisconsin, to W. Irving Glover, May 22, 1925. Smithsonian Institution Libraries, Post Office Department Manuscripts.

10. Alvin W. Hall to W. Irving Glover, May 16, 1925. Smithsonian Institution Libraries, Post Office Department Manuscripts.

11. O.J. Kvale to Robert S. Regar, January 8, 1926. Smithsonian Institution Libraries, Post Office Department Manuscripts.

12. Eidsness, *op. cit*, p. 376.

13. "Artist's Error," *Scott's Monthly Journal*, Vol. 6, No. 7 (September 1925), p. 161.

14. Michael L. Eidsness to J.J. Klemann Jr., November 4, 1926. Smithsonian Institution Libraries, Post Office Department Manuscripts.

15. Philip H. Ward Jr., "Washington Philatelic News," *Mekeel's Weekly Stamp News*, Vol. 39, No. 32 (August 10, 1925), p. 381.

16. Dr. S.G. Keller, "The Five-Cent 'Norse-American'," *American Philatelist*, Vol. 39, No. 3 (December 1925), pp. 135-40.

United States Stamps 1922-26

Chapter 30

Administrative Changes

Several important changes occurred in the Coolidge postal administration at the beginning of the 1926 fiscal year, which began on July 1, 1925. Paul Henderson, the second assistant postmaster general, left the Post Office Department to become general manager of National Air Transport, a fledgling but heavily financed air-carrier service that eventually became United Air Lines. The second assistant was responsible for transportation of mail, which included the rapidly growing airmail service. Henderson had been instrumental in building and lighting the highly successful Transcontinental Route (see Chapter 13) and he was an ideal candidate to run a new airline.

Airmail was not only the hot area of the Post Office Department, but it was about to get hotter as the government prepared to expand airmail by awarding contracts for new routes to private carriers.

With the administration's support, Congress had passed the Air Mail Act of 1925, often called the Kelly Bill for its chief sponsor, Republican Congressman Clyde Kelly of Pennsylvania. Signed by President Coolidge on February 2, it authorized the Post Office Department to contract with commercial carriers for domestic airmail.

While this meant that the Post Office Department would eventually get out of the business of operating airplanes and airports, it also meant that it would decide to a large extent how commercial aviation was going to be structured and financed in the United States.

Named to take Henderson's coveted spot as second assistant was W. Irving Glover, the third assistant who had been so active in stamp matters. Glover had conceived of the new issue of stamps in 1923 and had been a sympathetic ally of the Bureau for more efficient manufacturing by using the new rotary presses. To the philatelic press, he was the father of the Philatelic Stamp Agency, which had also become a moderate success, having reached sales of over $135,000 for the fiscal year that was ending.

Glover understood what we would now call public relations extremely well. He was responsive to stamp collectors and dealers, and had been a practicing politician before he was appointed to the position of third assistant. He seems to have been well-liked by philatelic writers. "This is a well earned promotion," Philip Ward wrote, "and Mr. Glover is the type of executive whom we would like to see reach the Postmaster Generalship."[1]

In an editorial, *Mekeel's* also noted, "It is perhaps needless to say that

Mr. Glover carries with him the best wishes of a host of collectors, and while they regret that to some extent they will lose his sponsorship, they rejoice in his promotion."[2]

The new job would put Glover on a very important stage at an opportune moment.

"With airline operators dependent upon the government for their very existence," one historian wrote, "the Postmaster General became the most powerful individual in civil aviation."[3] Glover, as second assistant, was very close to that seat of power. He took office on August 1, 1925. The deadline for bids for 12 new airmail routes was September 15, and the first five contracts were awarded on October 7.

Figure 106. W. Irving Glover (right), shortly after his promotion to second assistant postmaster general, confers with Postmaster General Harry S. New on airmail contracts.

What became known as "contract airmail," as we shall see in subsequent chapters, was responsible not only for the growth of airmail but for a number of new rates and the stamps to pay them. Figure 106 shows Glover, shortly after his promotion, discussing airmail contracts with Postmaster General New.

Replacing Glover as third assistant was Robert S. Regar, a career Post Office Department employee who had started as a personnel clerk in 1918 and had risen to the position of chief clerk in the postmaster general's office under Harry S. New. He was a Sunday school teacher by avocation and, while a competent administrator, lacked Glover's political skills and flair.

Passed over for the position of third assistant was Michael Eidsness, the superintendent of the Division of Stamps. At this time, the Philatelic Stamp Agency, which Eidsness supervised, was behind in orders and came under criticism that Glover clearly did not like. H.A. Mount, who had held the title of stamp agent since 1922 was replaced and moved into another department. Although Eidsness was not given the title, pay or authority, he soon filled Glover's role as spokesman for the department on stamp matters and became more visible to the collecting public than Regar ever did.

Glover, however, as second assistant, was not far away and not entirely removed from the world of philately, as the collecting of flight covers would soon become a new and popular aspect of the hobby. He maintained his interest in the new stamps that would be issued, especially airmail stamps. He would continue to be quoted often in the philatelic press, and he would attend the International Philatelic Exhibition in 1926 as a speaker.

Notes

1. Philip H. Ward Jr. "Chronicle of New Issues and Varieties," *Mekeel's Weekly Stamp News*, Vol. 39, No. 20 (July 20, 1925), p. 360.
2. "Editorial," *Mekeel's Weekly Stamp News*, Vol. 39, No 33 (August 17, 1925), p. 392.
3. Carrol V. Glines, *The Saga of the Air Mail* (New York: D. Van Nostrand Company Inc., 1968), p. 113.

United States Stamps 1922-26

Chapter 31

The 17¢ Wilson

Woodrow Wilson

Scott Number:	623
First Day of Issue:	December 28, 1925
Perforation:	11
Scott Colors:	Black, gray black
Designer:	Clair Aubrey Huston
Engravers:	John Eissler (vignette and ribbon)
	E.M. Hall (frame and lettering)
	J.C. Benzing (scrolls)
Plate Layout:	Flat plate; plates of 400 cut into panes of 100
Quantity Issued:	122,059,800
Plate Numbers:	18021, 18022, 18023, 18024, 18025, 18026, 18027, 18028
Scott Varieties:	None

The Political Background

Woodrow Wilson, the 28th president of the United States, died on February 3, 1924, at the age of 68. He had suffered a paralytic stroke in 1919, while president, and never fully recovered. While modern historians regard Wilson as one of the near-great presidents for leading America through World War I, his final years in office were marked largely by his failure to win ratification for the League of Nations plan that he so fervently hoped would assure world peace.

While Wilson, a Democrat, did not run for re-election to a third term in 1920, it was largely his policies and philosophy that were rejected when the voters chose the Republican candidate, Warren Harding, by a large margin.

Harding's death in office in August 1923, overshadowed the death of Wilson, which came only six months later. Although there was public grieving and ceremony, Wilson had been ill and away from the public stage for several years. As one modern historian has put it, "an old, urgent ghost was gone when Woodrow Wilson died."[1]

Although there were no doubt other suggestions for a stamp to honor the former president, Philip Ward, the Philadelphia dealer and stamp columnist for *Mekeel's*, was an admirer of Wilson and started his own campaign for the stamp in his column. He evidently wanted to be the first person to suggest the stamp, as he did it by telegram.

"On Sunday, February 3rd, Woodrow Wilson, who no doubt will rank as one of our greatest presidents, passed to the Great Beyond," he wrote in his column. "On the following morning I wired the President of the United States, the Postmaster General, and the Third Postmaster General as follows: 'A distinguished War President has given his life in the services of his country. Would not a Wilson Memorial Postage Stamp be a fitting tribute to his memory?' "[2]

Ward took up his crusade again a few weeks later, writing "The Postmaster General was almost swamped with letters from all over the country suggesting a Wilson Memorial Stamp as a fitting tribute to a great President. …" But Postmaster General New, Ward went on to report, "has decided that the time is not opportune for such an emission. In the first place the Harding stamp has just been issued under similar circumstances and is still current in many of the post-offices. To issue another stamp at this time would deflect from the Harding glory and then Mr. Wilson would not receive the honor to which he is entitled in copying something that had just been done."[3]

New, a former Republican senator who had opposed Wilson, his policies and his League of Nations treaty, was certainly not eager to issue a Wilson stamp. Ward's reporting that New felt it would "deflect from the Harding glory" is no doubt a candid assessment of the feelings inside the Post Office Department.

In addition, New had been a leading opponent of Wilson and his policies on several fronts. New had been the chairman of President Taft's re-election committee in 1912 when Taft lost to Wilson. As a Republican senator from Indiana, New was one of the leading opponents of the League of Nations and as a member of the Senate's powerful Committee on Foreign Relations, "he was able to deal President Wilson's League of Nations many body blows."[4] There were probably few men in Washington, D.C., at the time who had as much history opposing Woodrow Wilson as Harry S. New had.

For nearly a year, the issue seemed to rest. Ward resurrected it a year later, after a second stamp bearing Harding's portrait, the 1½¢ stamp of 1925 was announced. Although he was rarely critical of the Post Office Department on other matters, he was not happy to learn that Nathan Hale would get a stamp in the current series while more important figures were passed over. "It seems rather unusual," he wrote, "to present Nathan Hale on our current series when such dignitaries as Woodrow Wilson, Andrew Jackson, John Marshall, James Madison, and others, who have done much more for their country, are not represented."[5]

Among the nonphilatelic groups lobbying for the stamp was the Woodrow Wilson Foundation, which believed that a stamp should be issued for Wilson on December 28, the anniversary of his birth. On September 2, the foundation's president, Norman H. Davis, wrote to New with the stamp suggestion. When New's office replied that there was not sufficient time to issue a stamp by that date, Davis began a more public campaign that eventually enlisted President Coolidge as a supporter for the stamp.

"Honor should be paid the memory of Woodrow Wilson," Davis wrote in a letter to *The New York Times*, "our President who guided us during eight years of storm and stress such as no man ever faced, who laid down his life on the altar of sacrifice for what he believed to be the cause of the country and the world, and who called upon humanity to take the first step toward the abolishment of war, the greatest enemy mankind has ever known."[6]

By the end of September, President Coolidge let it be known that he, too, favored a stamp for Wilson, and this item also reached the newspapers. By this time, however, the Post Office Department had undergone the trauma of the Norse-American issue (see Chapter 29), which not only had been troublesome, but expensive. In late 1925, there was no enthusiasm in the Department for more special issues.

New and the Post Office Department answered the Wilson publicity with a somewhat harsh press release on September 30. It began: "The propaganda now being carried on by certain associations and individuals to commemorate the memory of the late President Woodrow Wilson by having his head placed on a United States postage stamp has made it appear that not only President Coolidge, but Postmaster General New is opposed to such action. Nothing could be further from the facts in the case."

This was not to say, however, that a stamp would be forthcoming in the immediate future. Instead, the release said that "in due time a stamp will be issued," and it quoted Postmaster General New as saying, "I thought it entirely fitting that the stamp should be issued but the time was not propitious."[7]

While obviously stung by the criticism that New did not want to issue a stamp for the Democrat Woodrow Wilson, the Department felt it was on firm ground with its position. There was no tradition of issuing stamps for former presidents so soon after their deaths.

Other than Harding and Wilson, Grover Cleveland was the most recently deceased president. Cleveland, a Democrat, had died in 1908, while Theodore Roosevelt, a Republican was president. No stamp was issued for him then, or during the Republican Taft administration. But during the eight years of the Wilson administration, no stamp was issued for Cleveland, either. It was not until the Harding administration that the 12¢ Cleveland stamp was issued on March 20, 1923. Similarly, the Wilson administration had not issued a stamp for Theodore Roosevelt, who died in January 1919.

While Davis and the Woodrow Wilson foundation kept up their lobbying effort for the stamp, Ward, who was of course familiar with the time it took to make engravings and plates, kept up his own campaign in the philatelic press. He did not buy the argument that there wasn't time to issue a Wilson stamp, as he knew how quickly the Post Office Department had acted in 1923 to get out the Harding stamp. He continued to hammer New and his administration for their partisanship, which he probably quite accurately knew to be the real cause for the decision not to issue a Wilson stamp on any firm schedule.

"We are told that the Post Office Department is resentful of charges that political bias has held up the issuing of the Wilson stamp," Ward wrote in early October, "but many of us are still of the opinion that Mr. Wilson's political faith has delayed his appearance upon the stamp."[8]

Ward also noted that he had had a telephone conversation "with Washington" on this matter. The person at the other end of the phone was no doubt Michael Eidsness, the superintendent of the Division of Stamps. Ward was advocating Wilson's portrait on a new value, either a 13¢ or 17¢, both of which would be useful under the new postal rates. Ward also went to Washington for the World Series between Washington and Pittsburgh, and may have called on Eidsness at that time as well.

We know that on October 16, Eidsness wrote a memo suggesting "that it would be of considerable advantage to the Department to adopt a 17¢ stamp, by reason of the fact that the Postal Service Bill provides for increased registration fees, which practically eliminates the 12-cent stamp for use on registered mail matter and requires 17¢ postage in lieu thereof."[9] The registry fee had been raised to 15¢, which with the 2¢ letter rate, called for 17¢ in stamps to mail the ordinary registered letter.

Shortly, Eidsness would also recommend a 13¢ stamp. This gave New a way out, for Wilson could be added as a subject in the ordinary series of stamps, rather than as a special or memorial issue.

Ward also continued to argue for the stamp in his column published on October 19, casting doubt on the truth of New's previous statement that there was not time enough to make new plates and engravings for a Wilson stamp in time for his birth anniversary. "I am afraid," Ward wrote, "that the general opinion of the philatelic public will continue to remain as heretofore, and the remarks of the Postmaster General are not sufficiently persuasive to lead us to believe that politics did not enter into the omission."[10]

A week later, Ward continued his push, this time suggesting a letter-writing campaign. "We want a Woodrow Wilson stamp," he wrote, "and if you feel the same way, address a communication to the President calling his attention that it is not the Department's intention of issuing a stamp showing Wilson until the occasion arises when further denomination is necessary. Tell him that you feel that he should be so honored without further delay."[11]

New finally gave in to the pressure, which was no doubt at this time being exerted by more powerful interests than Ward. By the second week in November, the order had been given for a Woodrow Wilson stamp, and the Bureau had completed a model, which was approved on November 12. Engraving of the new die was begun on the following day.

A victorious Ward reported on the front page of *Mekeel's* for November 23 that a new stamp would be issued. "It gives me great pleasure to be able to inform our readers that the Department has definitely decided to issue a new 17¢ stamp with a portrait of Woodrow Wilson," he wrote, and continued: "We started our efforts in behalf of such a stamp on the day that the late President died and we are glad to see that these efforts now bear fruit. We further believe that we were the first ones to suggest to the Postmaster General the desirability of a 17¢ stamp in this connection — calling his attention to the need for such a denomination."[12]

This procedure of denying a stamp, and then issuing one under pressure would soon become a pattern for the Department under Harry S. New. In the case of the Woodrow Wilson stamp, its advocates got exactly what they wanted: a stamp issued on December 28. New might have avoided a bushel of bad publicity by simply saying yes to the original request. But as we shall see, he became even more reluctant in the future to issue new stamps.

It may be interesting to note here that when Calvin Coolidge died on January 5, 1933, the Democratic administration of Franklin Roosevelt did not issue a stamp for him. It was not until five years later, as part of the Presidential series that depicted all deceased U.S. presidents, that Coolidge would appear on a stamp.

Today, the policy of the U.S. Postal Service is to issue no stamps honoring individuals until they have been deceased for 10 years. The one exception to that rule is for deceased U.S. presidents. "They may be honored with a memorial stamp on the first birth anniversary following death," says the guideline. That policy, interestingly, derives from the Woodrow Wilson stamp.

The Subject and Design

The photograph used on the Wilson stamp (Figure 107) was provided by Edith Bolling Wilson, his widow. It is different than the official portrait of Wilson that was engraved at the Bureau of Engraving and Printing by George F.C. Smillie in 1913 from a photograph taken by the Moffet Studio in Chicago.

Wilson served two terms as president, and the photograph used on the stamp is believed to have been taken during his second term. The frame of the stamp is the same as that on the other high values of the Series of 1922.

Wilson was by profession a scholar and historian. He had held only one political office before being elected president, and that was the governorship of New Jersey, which he held for only two years. His philosophy of government was that a president should be an active leader and reformer. During his first term, his successful legislative reforms included child labor laws, the income tax, anti-trust measures, and the Federal Reserve Act, which improved the government's control of the nation's money.

He succeeded in keeping the United States out of the European war during his first term, and was re-elected as a peace candidate in 1916. However, the country's sympathy with the Allied Powers and Germany's submarine warfare made neutrality unpopular. In 1917 Wilson led the United States into the war, "to make the world safe for democracy."

Figure 107. The photograph of Wilson used on the stamp was selected by his widow. It is believed to have been taken during his second term.

Congress gave him great emergency powers, and he emerged as a world leader. The Armistice of November 11, 1918, was negotiated on his famous Fourteen Points. He accepted the imperfect Versailles Treaty at the end of the war, believing it could be corrected by a world organization to be known as the League of Nations. But he suffered his greatest and most bitter defeat when Congress would not approve the League, which had already been ratified by the European powers.

It was on a speaking tour in support of the League in September 1919 that he suffered the paralytic stroke that left him an invalid for the remainder of his presidency.

Among Wilson's many biographers and students was Herbert Hoover, who had worked in European famine relief during the Wilson presidency and was secretary of commerce when the stamp was issued. A Republican who would succeed Coolidge to the presidency, Hoover wrote about Wilson in 1958, during his own retirement.

"For a moment at the time of the Armistice," Hoover noted, "Mr. Wilson rose to intellectual domination of most of the civilized world. With his courage and eloquence, he carried a message of hope for the independence of nations, the freedom of man and lasting peace. Never since his time has any man risen to the political and spiritual heights that came to him."[13]

Philatelic Aspects and Varieties

First day of issue. This stamp was issued on December 28, 1925. In addition to Washington, D.C., the stamp had a first day of issue at Staunton, Virginia, which was Wilson's birthplace; at New York City, the site of the Woodrow Wilson Foundation; and at Princeton, New Jersey, the site of Princeton University. Wilson had taught at Princeton, was made its president in 1902 and was elected governor of New Jersey in 1910.

First-day-cover collecting was becoming quite popular, and with this stamp we begin to see more elaborate cachets. Albert C. Roessler, the colorful dealer in Orange, New Jersey, prepared cacheted envelopes printed with a photograph of Wilson, and Charles E. Nickles, a Washington dealer, prepared three

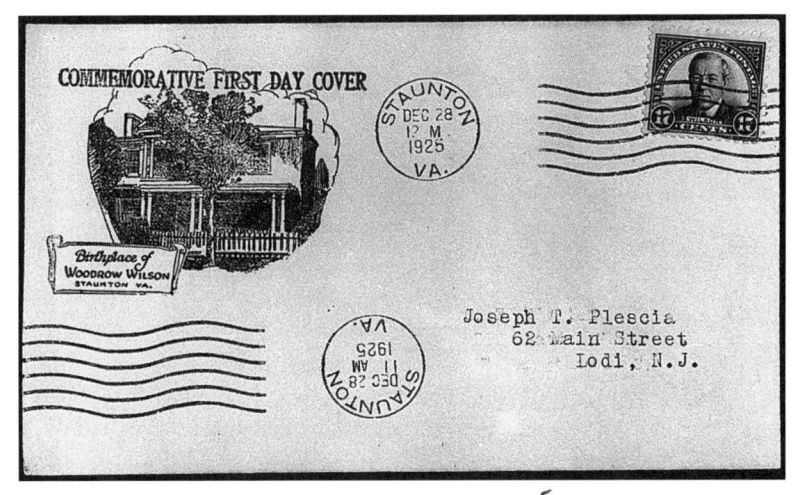

Figure 108. One of the very first pictorial cachets was serviced by the Washington, D.C., dealer C.E. Nickels. The postmaster at Staunton, Virginia, originally refused to cancel first-day covers until instructed to do so by the Post Office Department.

different illustrated cachets, showing Wilson's homes in Washington and Princeton, and his birthplace in Staunton, Virginia (see Figure 108).

The postmaster at Staunton was not very pleased to have had his office selected as a first-day city and had not yet received instructions from headquarters when he wrote to the Post Office Department on December 23, stating, "I have returned all [first-day-cover] requests to the writers with the suggestion that they write the Philatelic Agency, Washington, in order to secure this service." He went on to say that "all our regular employees will be extremely busy and certainly will not have time to look after this work."[14]

A telephone call from Washington straightened out the matter. The Staunton post office not only serviced the requests, but was instructed that all those that could not be mailed before the first-day date of December 28 "should be filled as though they were received before that date by turning back the canceling machine to the date of December 28."[15]

In the future, first-day post offices would get more elaborate instructions on servicing covers and, in most cases, with more advance notice.

Shades. When first listed in the 1927 edition of the Scott *Specialized Catalogue,* the primary shade was given as black, and gray black was listed as a secondary shade. Those same shades are listed today. Johl had no shades to add, noting that "it has practically no color variation."

Printed on both sides. A listing for this variety, as Scott 623a, first appeared in the 1932 edition of the *Specialized Catalogue* and seemed to be based on Ward's report in 1931 of "an oddity, namely a used copy of the current 17¢ Wilson, black, completely printed on the face with the whole corner ornament directly printed on the back."[16]

Johl took issue with this listing, writing: "The specialized catalog lists a variety 'Printed on both sides.' This would seem to indicate a stamp with full impression on both sides and as such, an extreme rarity. This however is not the case as the stamp in question has only a corner printed on the back and should only be ranked as a 'freak.' "[17]

The listing, however, was not removed from the *Specialized Catalogue* until the 1958 edition.

Notes

1. Elizabeth Stevenson, *Babbits and Bohemians: The American 1920s* (New York, The Macmillan Company, 1967) p. 114.
2. Philip H. Ward Jr., "Chronicle of New Issues and Varieties," *Mekeel's Weekly Stamp News,* Vol. 38, No. 7 (February 18, 1924), p. 106.
3. Philip H. Ward Jr., "Chronicle of New Issues and Varieties," *Mekeel's Weekly Stamp News,* Vol. 38, No. 10 (March 10, 1924), p. 144.
4. *Dictionary of American Biography*, Supplement 2, p. 486.
5. Philip H. Ward Jr., "Chronicle of New Issues and Varieties," *Mekeel's Weekly Stamp News,* Vol. 39, No. 16 (April 20, 1925), p. 216.
6. Quoted in Kent B. Stiles, "Of Topical Interest," *Scott's Monthly Journal*, Vol. 6, No. 8 (October 1925), p. 186.

7. Post Office Department, press release, September 20, 1925.
8. Philip H. Ward Jr., "Woodrow Wilson Stamp," *Mekeel's Weekly Stamp News*, Vol. 39, No. 41 (October 12, 1925), p. 473.
9. Michael L. Eidsness Jr., to Robert S. Regar, October 16, 1925. Smithsonian Institution Libraries, Post Office Department Manuscripts.
10. Philip H. Ward Jr., "Chronicle of New Issues and Varieties," *Mekeel's Weekly Stamp News*, Vol. 39, No. 42 (October 19, 1925), p. 504.
11. Philip H. Ward Jr., "Chronicle of New Issues and Varieties," *Mekeel's Weekly Stamp News*, Vol. 39, No. 43 (October 26, 1925), p. 516.
12. Philip H. Ward Jr., "Chronicle of New Issues and Varieties," *Mekeel's Weekly Stamp News*, Vol. 39, No. 47 (November 23, 1925), p. 564.
13. Herbert Hoover, *The Ordeal of Woodrow Wilson* (New York: McGraw-Hill Book Company, 1958), p. 300.
14. J.J. Kivlinghan, postmaster, Staunton, Virginia, to Robert S. Regar, December 23, 1925. Smithsonian Institution Libraries, Post Office Department Manuscripts.
15. Robert S. Regar to J.J. Kivlinghan, December 30, 1925. Smithsonian Institution Libraries, Post Office Department Manuscripts.
16. Philip H. Ward Jr., "Washington News," *Mekeel's Weekly Stamp News*, Vol. 45, No. 3 (January 19, 1931), p. 47.
17. Max J. Johl, *The United States Postage Stamps of the Twentieth Century*, Volume III (New York, H.L. Lindquist, 1935), p. 122.

Chapter 32

The 13¢ Harrison

Scott Number:	622
First Day of Issue:	January 11, 1926
Perforation:	11
Scott Colors:	Green, light green
Designer:	Clair Aubrey Huston
Engraver:	John Eissler (vignette)
	E.M. Hall (frame and lettering)
	J.C. Benzing (scrolls and ribbon)
Press:	Flate-plate press
Plate Layout:	Plates of 400 cut into panes of 100
Quantity Issued:	130,867,400
Plate Numbers:	18106, 18107, 18108, 18109, 18110, 18111, 18112, 18113, 18924, 19104, 19105, 19119, 19120, 19121, 19122
Scott Varieties:	None

The Political Background

This stamp may have been a salve to the postmaster general's irritation in issuing the Woodrow Wilson stamp (see Chapter 31). For just as Wilson was one of Harry S. New's political enemies, Benjamin Harrison was one of his heroes.

It is hard to determine exactly why a 13¢ stamp was necessary. Under the new parcel post rates, however, there was a 2¢ surcharge for most packages. This, combined with the 11¢ rate for parcels up to one pound sent to Zone 6, would make a 13¢ rate for many parcels. Heavy parcels sent locally and to Zone 1 and Zone 2 might also require 13¢ in franking. Parcel post zones were based on distance from the sending post office.

The new insurance-rate structure also seemed to create some demand

313

for the stamp, as it would pay the 3¢ postage rate for a two- to four-ounce third-class mailing plus the 10¢ insurance fee for an indemnity of $25 to $50.

On October 23, 1925, just a week after recommending a 17¢ stamp, superintendent Eidsness sent a memo to Third Assistant Postmaster General Robert S. Regar recommending a 13¢ stamp. "Since the enactment of the Postal Bill changing the postage rates," he wrote, "it has been found that a large demand has been made for the revival of the 13¢ stamp."[1]

Eidsness used the word "revival," as there had been a 13¢ denomination added to the Washington-Franklin series in January 1919 to cover the wartime 3¢ letter rate plus the 10¢ registry or special delivery fee. With the reduction of the letter rate to 2¢ six months later, this stamp saw little use. Large stocks were on hand at some post offices, and these, according to Eidsness, were being transferred to post offices "where large mail order houses conduct extensive business."

There had also been a 13¢ stamp in the Series of 1902. This stamp bore the portrait of Benjamin Harrison, the 23rd president, who had died on March 13, 1901. The first of the new stamps to be issued by the Theodore Roosevelt administration, this stamp was something of a memorial to Harrison.

Harrison, although born in Ohio, moved to Indianapolis, Indiana, at the age of 21, and made his legal and political career there. One of the other leading political families in Indianapolis was that of John Chalfant New, Harry New's father. The two Republican families were closely aligned politically, and President Harrison showed his regard for the senior New in 1889 by appointing him to the desirable position of consul general of the United States to London. Harry New was 30 years of age at this time and was just entering politics. At the age of 47, he was elected to the same Indiana seat in the U.S. Senate that Harrison had held from 1881 to 1887.

The idea of placing Harrison's portrait back on the 13¢ stamp undoubtedly came from Postmaster General New, and he even specified the portrait he wanted.

Models for the stamp were ordered from the Bureau on November 11 and were prepared within two days. In sending them for approval to New, Regar wrote: "Inasmuch as this is more or less a personal matter with you, I am enclosing, for your approval and return, a model of the proposed Benjamin Harrison 13¢ stamp. You will remember you told Mr. Eidsness and myself that you wanted the old portrait of Benjamin Harrison, or the same that was used on the 13¢ stamp of the 1902 issue."[2]

Two models were submitted, one with a smaller portrait of the same size used in 1902 and one with a portrait of the same size as that used for the other values of the series. The larger portrait was recommended by Regar and was approved by New on November 19.

The 13¢ Harrison

The Subject and Design

The matrix portrait from which the stamp is derived is a photograph taken by the firm of McHugh and Sherman (Figure 109), which is in the collection of the Prints and Photographs Division of the Library of Congress. The date and location are unknown, but this became the official portrait of Harrison and was engraved at the Bureau in 1891 during his presidency.

Benjamin Harrison was the grandson of William Henry Harrison, the ninth president of the United States and the son of John Scott Harrison, who served two terms in Congress.

He was elected to the presidency in 1888, defeating the Democratic incumbent Grover Cleveland. That campaign is known for Harrison's use of the "front porch" campaign, in which he stayed home and made speeches to visiting groups. Although he polled fewer popular votes than Cleveland, he won the electoral vote by a wide margin.

As president, he successfully pushed for the Sherman Anti-Trust Act, which outlawed business combinations that restrained trade, but he was accused of being cozy with the trusts when his administration failed to enforce it. He also supported the McKinley Tariff Act, which set high protective tariffs. He failed, however, to satisfy either the bosses or the reformers, and he is viewed by historians as one of the weakest of our presidents.

Figure 109. The source photograph for the Harrison stamp was taken by the firm of McHugh and Sherman. This became the official portrait of Harrison, and was also used on the 13¢ stamp of the 1902 series.

In 1892 he was renominated by the Republicans, but lost soundly in a rematch with Grover Cleveland due largely to a depressed economy.

Philatelic Aspects and Varieties

First day of issue. This stamp was issued on January 11, 1926, at Washington, D.C., and Indianapolis, Indiana. A large number of covers were serviced in both cities. Edward Worden, the wealthy New Jersey collector who had become a first-day cover enthusiast, had a number of covers — probably about 500 — serviced at North Bend, Ohio, Harrison's birthplace.

Worden sent one of these North Bend covers to Mrs. W. Irving Glover, the wife of the second assistant postmaster general, who had been reported to be a stamp collector. In an enclosed letter he wrote: "The Post Office Department made a slip (please don't tell your husband that I said so) in calling Indianapolis the home of Harrison and not including his birthplace, which was North Bend, Ohio."[3]

Worden went on to explain that he sent a representative there to service covers, and that these were the only ones mailed from North Bend that day.

While these were not official first-day covers, they have been recognized by Scott, and are listed and priced in the *Specialized Catalogue*. Jack Harvey has argued in favor of these: "They differ from other run of the mill 'unofficials' in at least two important respects. First there was a distinct historical relationship between North Bend and Harrison, the subject of the stamp. And secondly, the origin of these covers is authentically documented by Worden's letter to Mrs. Glover."[4]

Passing by North Bend as a first-day city was probably not a "slip" at all, since the town was small and the Post Office Department had just had an unpleasant experience with the postmaster in the small town of Staunton, Virginia, over the Wilson first-day covers (see Chapter 31). The Department was beginning to realize that first-day-cover collecting had grown so popular that designated post offices were being swamped with requests that they often had trouble filling in one day's time.

Worden also prepared several covers to which postal currency was affixed. No pictorial or printed cachets are known, probably because of the short notice that this stamp would be issued. At least one member of the U.S. Senate prepared covers with the corner card of the Committee on Military

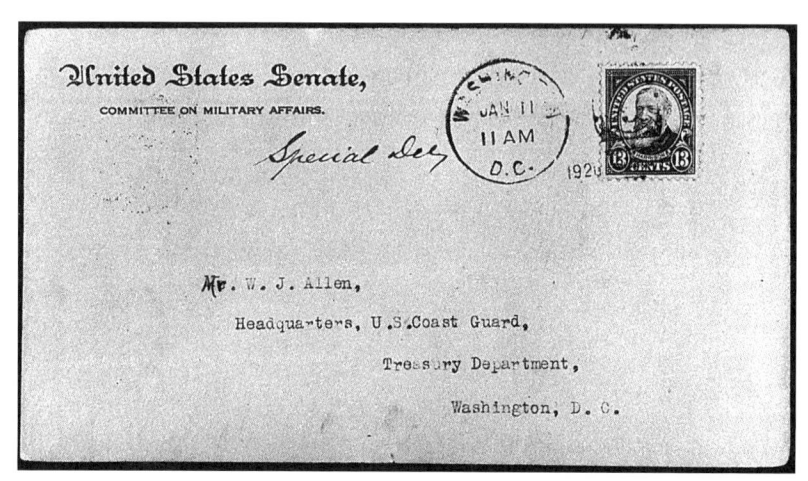

Figure 110. Few printed cachets are known. This one bears the corner card of a member of the United States Senate, in which Harrison served from 1881 to 1887.

Affairs (Figure 110).

Shades. When first listed in the 1927 edition of the *Specialized Catalogue*, the color was listed as blue green. It was changed to green in the 1935 edition, when light green was added as 622a. Today, the catalog lists green as the major shade, with light green as a secondary shade. Johl found quite a range of shades, including pale bluish green, light bluish green, bright bluish green, deep bright bluish green and dark bluish green.

Star plates. While all of the plates made for this stamp had the wider gauge spacing, two plates, 18109 and 18113, were marked with large five-point stars at the side. As there would have been no confusion about mixing these plates with narrow-gauge plates, it would seem that the stars were unnecessary. Star plate blocks are scarce, and 18113 has not been reported as being found by collectors.

Notes

1. Michael L. Eidsness Jr. to Robert S. Regar, October 23, 1925. Smithsonian Institution Libraries, Post Office Department Manuscripts.
2. Robert S. Regar to Harry S. New, November 13, 1925. Smithsonian Institution Libraries, Post Office Department Manuscripts.
3. This letter is reproduced in Jack V. Harvey, *First Day Covers of the Regular Postage Issue of 1922-1935*, Second Edition (American First Day Cover Society, 1985), p. 18.
4. Harvey, *ibid.*, p. 19.

United States Stamps 1922-26

Chapter 33

Contract Airmail

While the Wilson and Harrison stamps may have been slight diversions, the real focus of the Post Office Department in late 1925 and early 1926 was contract airmail, which established a number of new airmail routes to be run by private companies, most of them feeding into the government-run Transcontinental Route.

The eventual goal was to get the government out of the business of owning the routes and equipment while expanding airmail service to a wider part of the country. The so-called Kelly Bill (see Chapter 30) gave the authorization, but a great deal of work was left to the Post Office Department.

The Transcontinental Route made an almost straight line from San Francisco to New York. But mail from Los Angeles or Boston, for example, had to travel by train to San Francisco and New York, respectively, to connect with the route. Similarly, mail from St. Louis or Dallas had to travel by train to Chicago to hook up with the airmail route. The first new routes that were planned were feeders, mainly north and south, to connect with the Transcontinental.

Bids were requested for eight of 12 planned routes on July 15, 1925, and were to be kept sealed until September 15. On October 7, Postmaster General Harry S. New awarded contracts for five of the eight. The numbers for these contract airmail routes, or CAMs as they quickly became known, were assigned as follows:

CAM 1	Boston - New York	Colonial Air Transport
CAM 2	Chicago - St. Louis	Robertson Aircraft Corp.
CAM 3	Chicago - Dallas	National Air Transport
CAM 4	Los Angeles - Salt Lake City	Western Air Express
CAM 5	Elko - Pasco	Walter T. Varney

There were no awards for three other routes: Seattle-to-Los Angeles, Chicago-to-Birmingham, and Chicago-to-Minneapolis. New said in a prepared statement, "It would be a most unfortunate experiment to establish air mail lines upon a basis so insecure that their actual abandonment would be highly probable, if not actually certain."

But in making the five other awards, he predicted, "Upon the result of the enterprise this day entered upon depends the future of aerial transport in the United States."[1] History would show that he was correct.

The companies were given time to organize the routes, purchase equipment, and hire pilots and other personnel. But none of the first five firms cho-

Figure 111. This Stout 2A-T, named Maiden Dearborn IV, flew the first contract airmail from a snowy runway in Dearborn, Michigan, headed for Cleveland, Ohio. Ford Air Transport was the contractor.

sen to fly contract routes actually flew the first flight.

Henry Ford, of Ford Motor Company, had formed a company that had been flying freight for over a year between Detroit, Cleveland and Chicago, using planes designed by William S. Stout (see Figure 111). Ford had purchased Stout's fledgling aircraft company and was also manufacturing the metal-bodied planes. On January 7, 1926, Ford was awarded two airmail contracts for the cargo routes he was already flying. These were designated as follows:

| CAM 6 | Detroit - Cleveland | Ford Air Transport |
| CAM 7 | Detroit - Chicago | Ford Air Transport |

Within two weeks, two other awards were let:

| CAM 8 | Seattle - Los Angeles | Pacific Air Transport |
| CAM 9 | Chicago - Minneapolis | Charles Dickinson |

The Kelly Bill provided a rate structure of at least 10¢ per ounce that gave the contract mail carriers up to 80 percent of the airmail revenue they carried. The rates set by the Post Office Department in compliance with this law were given in an order of January 19, 1926. They would be 10¢ per ounce or fraction thereof on each route not exceeding 1,000 miles in length, 15¢ for routes exceeding 1,000 miles but not exceeding 1,500 miles, and 20¢ for routes over 1,500 miles.

In addition, mail traveling on the government's Transcontinental Route would be charged 5¢ per ounce for each of the three zones, rather than the previous 8¢ per ounce per zone (see Chapter 13).

Even before these rates went into effect, the Post Office Department saw trouble with them, and New, in his annual report for the 1925 fiscal year, recommended changes. "It will be observed that the existing legislation requires a careful check on each individual piece of airmail," he wrote. "All of this checking and calculating tends to slow down the handling of the mail, increases the chance of error, and incidentally will be expensive."[2]

As a remedy, New suggested that the legislation be amended to read, "The Postmaster General may in his discretion make contracts for the transportation of mail, including equipment, by aircraft at fixed rates per pound, under such regulations as he may prescribe."[3]

This would allow the mail simply to be weighed. Congress would give New the power to set these rates, but not before contract airmail began, with its complicated rates.

The First Contract Flights

On January 27, 1926, the Post Office Department announced that a new 10¢ airmail stamp would be issued and placed on sale on February 13. No contract airmail was being flown, and no first flight had been announced, but the location of the first day of sale gave away the news: The stamps would be placed on sale "at the post offices at Detroit and Dearborn, Mich.; Chicago, Ill.; Cleveland, Ohio; and Washington, D.C."

The first flight had to be on either CAM 6 or CAM 7, but in either case Ford Air Transport would fly the first flight, as it had the contracts for both routes. Not only was Ford ready to fly before any of the other carriers, but there was a sizable public-relations gain to having Ford make the first flight. It helped to signal to the public that the contracts were not being let to fly-by-night operators, but by well-financed and well-run firms. This was not always the case, but Ford was a fine example of the kind of carrier that the Department wanted to see involved. As historian William Leary has put it, "Ford, after all, was the symbol of the prosperity of the 1920s."[4]

For the first contract flight on February 13, 1926, Henry Ford, his son Edsel and the governor of Michigan were among the dignitaries gathered on a snow-covered field in Dearborn. The first plane to take off was a Stout 2-AT with a single Liberty 400 engine. It left Dearborn with mail for Cleveland, on CAM 6 about 10:30 a.m. W. Irving Glover, the second assistant postmaster general, represented the Post Office Department. In a relay, the first mail bag was passed "like a fast double play in baseball,"[5] from the Fords to the governor, to the postmaster of Detroit, to Glover, who placed it in the plane. Just before the plane took off, Henry Ford handed the pilot a letter addressed to his friend, Thomas Edison, for delivery in Orange, New Jersey.

A second plane, headed to Chicago on CAM 7, took off at 1:37 p.m. Thus inaugural flights were flown on both routes on the same day. These two routes shortened the time that mail would reach Detroit from both the east and the west. A large number of philatelic covers were carried on these initial flights.

The next route to be flown, on April 1, was CAM 10, which had been established between Miami and Jacksonville by Florida Airways. This route was unique in that it did not link up with the Transcontinental, and it was discontinued after a few months for lack of revenue. It was then reorganized by September with Macon, Georgia, as the northern terminus.

CAM 5 was inaugurated on April 6, over some of the roughest terrain anywhere, between Elko, Nevada, and Pasco, Washington. Walter Varney had been the only person to bid on this route, and some thought he was crazy for doing so. While the inaugural Pasco-to-Elko flight got through a storm that day with difficulty, the Elko-to-Pasco flight was interrupted by bad weather that forced pilot Franklin Rose to put his plane down in the mountains. He is reported to have hiked with his mail bag for 10 miles until he found a farm, then "borrowed a horse and rode to the nearest phone thirty miles away."[6] His mail was delayed three days. After that flight, Varney was allowed to shut down the route for two months to make adjustments.

The inaugural flight of CAM 9, on the Chicago-Minneapolis route inaugurated on June 7, ended in the fatal crash of pilot Elmer Partridge just after takeoff. Charlie Dickinson, the contractor, lost four of his five planes in the first three months and surrendered the route on October 1.

Despite the difficulties with some of the early flights, contract airmail proved a success. Most of the contractors were well-organized and well-financed. National Air Transport, which had hired Paul Henderson away from the Post Office Department, had raised over $10 million and purchased 10 new Curtiss Carrier Pigeon planes, hailed as the largest order yet placed for commercial aircraft, in preparation for flying the Chicago-to-Dallas route it had been awarded.

The goal of the Post Office Department under both presidents Harding and Coolidge was to get the government out of the air transport business and to have airmail carried by private enterprise, just as private railroads and steamship companies carried surface mail.

With solid firms like Ford Air Transport and National Air Transport involved in airmail, the day would not be far off when New could get the Post Office Department out of the air transportation business. Mid-1926, however, was not yet that time, and the Post Office Department continued to build its service even as it hoped to turn it over to others. In May 1926, the Post Office Department made an order for 40 Douglas M4 biplanes to replace its aging De Havilland DH-4s. The Douglas M4, popular with pilots, could carry 1,000 pounds of mail, and had a number of improvements, including brakes.

Notes

1. Quoted in Thomas J. O'Sullivan and Karl B. Weber, *History of the United States Pioneer and Government-Operated Air Mail Service, 1910-*

1928 (American Air Mail Society, 1973), p. 165.

2. Harry S. New, *Annual Report of the Postmaster General* (Washington: Government Printing Office, 1925), pp. 32-33.
3. *Ibid.,* p. 77.
4. William M. Leary, *Aerial Pioneers The U.S. Air Mail Service, 1918-1927* (Washington: Smithsonian Institution Press, 1985), p. 224.
5. "The Air Mail," *American Philatelist*, Vol. 39, No. 7 (April 1926), p. 467.
6. Donald B. Holmes, *Air Mail: An Illustrated History, 1793-1981* (New York: Clarkson N. Potter Inc., 1981), p. 149.

United States Stamps 1922-26

Chapter 34

The Map Airmails

While we think of the Map airmails as a series of three stamps, they were issued one at a time, over a period of 11 months. They were, however, issued in the order of their denominations, that is, the 10¢ value was issued first, then the 15¢ value and lastly the 20¢ value.

The three stamps have the same vignette and frame. Only the colors and numerals vary according to the denomination.

These were the first U.S. stamps to carry the words "Air Mail," and they were the first airmail stamps to be issued in the distinctive, elongated size, which was $1^{84}/_{100}$ inches wide by $^{75}/_{100}$ inches tall.

The name used by the Bureau for these stamps was "Series of 1926, Air Mail Service," but the stamps have become known by collectors as the Map airmails.

While most stamps in this book, including the first of the Map airmails, are listed in their actual chronology, the three Map airmails are treated as a group, placing the 15¢ and 20¢ stamps out of their proper chronology.

10¢ Map Airmail

Scott Number: C7
First Day of Issue: February 13, 1926
Perforation: 11
Scott Colors: Dark blue, light blue
Designer: Clair Aubrey Huston
Engravers: J.C. Benzing (vignette and frame)
E.M. Hall (lettering and numerals)
Plate Layout: Flat plate; plates of 200 cut into panes of 50.
Quantity Issued: 42,092,800
Plate Numbers: 18246, 18247, 18248, 18249, 18250, 18903, 18904, 18905
Scott Varieties: Double transfer (18246 UL 11)

325

United States Stamps 1922-26

The Political Background

As described in the previous chapter, the legislation providing for contract airmail specified that the rate for airmail matter flown on a contract basis would be not less than 10¢ per ounce. This stamp was requested in early January, and a model was approved on January 16, 1926.

There had actually been a need for a 10¢ airmail stamp for several months, as that was the rate for letters flying on night airmail service between New York and Chicago since July 1, 1925. We know, however, that Postmaster General Harry S. New wanted more authority to change the airmail rates so that contract airmail would be less complicated than it became (see Chapter 33). He requested this authority in November 1925, but it would be more than a year before he would get it from Congress. It seems logical that the Department put off the order for airmail stamps until the last minute in the hope that the rates might be changed.

The new 10¢ stamp would pay the complete rate for the contract part of the airmail service, but most airmail also flew on some part of the government route. The rate per zone was 5¢ in addition to the contract rate of 10¢. Thus, a letter of less than one ounce flying from Los Angeles to Boston in late 1926 would fly on CAM 4 from Los Angeles to Salt Lake City for 10¢, then it would fly over three government zones to New York for an additional 15¢ (5¢ per zone) and finally it would fly from New York to Boston on CAM 1 for another 10¢, making a total of 35¢. Figure 112 shows a cover that flew this route for 25¢ two weeks before CAM 1 became operational.

Figure 112. There were no airmail stamps to pay every possible contract rate. This cover, mailed on June 15, 1926, flew from Los Angeles to Salt Lake on CAM 4 for 10¢, then over three government routes at 5¢ each for a total of 25¢. If it had been posted two weeks later, it could have flown on CAM 1 from New York to Boston for another 10¢. CAM 1 was not flown until July 1.

The Map Airmails

An issue of stamps to pay all of the possible CAM plus government-route combinations would have required denominations of 5¢, 10¢, 15¢, 20¢, 25¢, 30¢ and 35¢. This complicated rate structure existed only from February 15, 1926, to February 1, 1927, when a uniform rate of 10¢ per half ounce regardless of distance was instituted and the zone system eliminated.

The Subject and Design

The model for this stamp (Figure 113) was rather unusual, as there was no larger working model. The illustration for the stamp was done in the same size as the actual stamp. This was an unusual practice at the Bureau. The reason for this is not known.

The design shows two airplanes, clearly De Havilland DH-4s, at either end of a map of the United States that shows the country's mountains and system of rivers. Perhaps it might have been more appropriate to show airways rather than waterways. The Bureau records state that the model was prepared from a map "submitted by the Geological Survey" and that "the central design represents a relief map of the United States showing some of the rivers and mountain ranges." On each side of the stamp is "an airplane in flight, one traveling east and the other toward the west."[1]

Figure 113. The model for the 10¢ Map airmail is unusual as it was drawn in stamp size. Usually a larger "working model" was made and reduced to stamp size for presentation.

This was not a stamp everyone loved. John Luff in particular disliked it. Here are his comments not long after the stamp was issued:

"Had a medal been offered for a homely and ill-balanced design, it would be awarded without hesitation to our new airmail stamp. The various features are out of proportion. The two aeroplanes occupy as much space as the distorted map and the letters of the inscription are so large that some of them have to be supported by brackets, at least we can see no other excuse for those alleged ornaments."[2]

Philip Ward, on the other hand, had this to say:

"Personally, I think the stamp one of the most striking that we have issued and its size immediately attracts the attention of the postal clerk. The large figures indicate its value and I believe that with this new stamp available that the air mail service is likely to be more satisfactory."[3]

Neither of these critics mentioned that the planes depicted on the stamps, the old reliable DH-4s, were growing obsolete. As mentioned in the previous chapter, new aircraft were quickly replacing the De Havillands, both among the contractors and at the Post Office Department.

The stamp was issued to correspond with the first contract airmail service, which was flown with metal Stout AT-2 planes, not with the fabric and wood DH-4s.

Philatelic Aspects and Varieties

First day of issue. The stamp was placed on sale on February 13 at Washington, DC.; Dearborn, Michigan; Detroit, Michigan; Cleveland, Ohio; and Chicago, Illinois. This was two days before the first contract flights. There seem to have been no cacheted covers prepared for this stamp. First-day covers from Cleveland and Dearborn are less common than those from the other cities.

With the flights on CAM 6 and CAM 7 on February 15, a new facet of collecting was created. The Post Office Department prepared rubber-stamped cachets for this flight and many more to follow. These first flights, however, did not necessarily carry this stamp. Some covers were prepared with this stamp (and others) canceled on the first day, February 13, and held for the first flights on February 15; thus they carry both the first-day cancellation and the first-flight cachet (see Figure 114).

Shades. When this stamp was first listed in the 1927 edition of the Scott *Specialized Catalogue*, it was listed as dark blue, and that was the only shade listed until the 1940 edition, when light blue was added as a secondary shade. The current catalog lists the same two shades. Johl added blue, bright blue and deep blue.

Double transfer. This was discovered by Frederick R. McAlpin, but

Figure 114. A combination first-day and first-flight cover. It was canceled in Cleveland, Ohio, on the first day of issue on February 13, 1926, and held for the inaugural flight of CAM 6 on February 15.

The Map Airmails

initially reported incorrectly by Philip Ward as being a variety of the Lindbergh airmail stamp of 1927, rather than this stamp, but "quite distinct."[4] The position was accurately described as 18246 UL 11. It shows a downward doubling on the right side of the stamp, which is most apparent in the bottom frameline and the tail of the right airplane (see Figure 115).

Figure 115. The double transfer at 18246 UL 11 is most easily seen in the stabilizer wing and the bottom frameline.

A double transfer was listed in the 1932 edition of the Scott *Specialized Catalogue*, but the position 18246 UL 11 was not included until the 1937 edition.

15¢ Map Airmail

Scott Number:	C8
First Day of Issue:	September 18, 1926
Perforation:	11
Scott Colors:	Olive brown, light brown
Designer:	Clair Aubrey Huston
Engravers:	J.C. Benzing (vignette and frame)
	E.M. Hall (lettering)
	F. Lamasure (numerals)
Plate Layout:	Flat plate; plates of 200 cut into panes of 50.
Quantity Issued:	15,597,307
Plate Numbers:	18745, 18746, 18747, 18748
Scott Varieties:	None

The Political Background

The original Post Office Department order of January 19, 1926, set the rates for contract airmail as 10¢ per ounce or fraction thereof on routes not exceeding 1,000 miles, 15¢ on routes exceeding 1,000 miles but not exceeding

1,500 miles, and 20¢ for routes over 1,500 miles.

Of the routes awarded in 1926, only one, CAM 8 from Seattle to Los Angeles, was more than 1,000 miles in length, and it was not flown until September 15. Essentially, the 15¢ stamp was issued to pay the rate on this route. However, as described above, many airmail covers required 15¢ postage, as that was the rate for a letter flying on a CAM route (for 10¢) and over one zone of the government Transcontinental Route (for 5¢ per zone).

The die for this stamp was begun in January, at roughly the same time as the 10¢ stamp, but it was put on hold for some time, no doubt because the Post Office Department was seeking legislation to change and simplify the complicated rate structure.

With the awarding of the Seattle-to-Los Angeles route on September 1, the 15¢ stamp was ordered, and the die that had been begun on January 28 was completed, approved and hardened on September 8. The first plates were completed and certified on September 14, but there was no time to print and package the stamps before the first flight on September 15.

Since the rates were changed in February 1927 to 10¢ for the first half ounce and 10¢ for each additional half ounce, there was no further need for an airmail stamp of the 15¢ denomination. It saw use for less than four months.

Philatelic Aspects and Varieties

First day of issue. Because the stamp could not be ready for the first flight on CAM 9, only Washington, D.C., was a first-day city. With little advance announcement, there was little time for cachetmakers to print cacheted covers, but one is known with a printed cachet, and this is listed as the "earliest

Figure 116. A first-day cover serviced by Henry Hammelman was marked for airmail service, but the proper rate would have been 10¢ for night airmail. Hammelman covers can often be identified by their distinctive handwriting.

The Map Airmails

known cacheted airmail FDC."[5]

Some first-day collectors and servicers mailed their covers far enough away to receive airmail service. Figure 116 shows a first-day cover serviced by Henry Hammelman of Washington, D.C., and sent to Chicago by airmail.

Usage. On October 23, a few weeks after this stamp was issued, W. Irving Glover, the second assistant postmaster general, spoke at the banquet at the end of the International Philatelic Exhibition in New York, telling the crowd of collectors that the Post Office Department would soon be relinquishing the ownership of the Transcontinental Route and putting the route out for bids. Privately he also said that plans were being made for a uniform airmail rate. Philip Ward reported correctly that "present indications are that the rate will be fixed at ten cents per half ounce or fraction thereof."[6]

In November, Kent Stiles also reported that "the recently-issued 15¢ U.S. airmail stamp may prove to be a 'good buy' — for philatelists may shortly have to say 'Good Bye' to it in so far as its sale at post offices is concerned." Postmaster General New by this time had announced that his department would be seeking the uniform rate, and that "establishing such a rate would conceivably lead to the issuing of a 20¢ airmail stamps, and possibly a 30¢, while making the use of the new 15¢ no longer necessary."[7]

While collectors and dealers were able to put away sufficient numbers of unused stamps, copies on cover used correctly during this period are not common.

Shades. The Bureau of Engraving and Printing listed the ink color of this stamp as brown; the Post Office Department, in announcing it, described it as sepia; and Scott first listed it in the 1927 edition of the *Specialized Catalogue* as olive brown. In the 1940 edition light brown was added as a minor shade. Johl found the shades to be sepia and light sepia.

20¢ Map Airmail

Scott Number: C9
First Day of Issue: January 25, 1927
Perforation: 11
Scott Colors: Yellow green, green
Designer: Clair Aubrey Huston
Engravers: J.C. Benzing (vignette and frame)
E.M. Hall (lettering)
F. Lamasure (numerals)
Plate Layout: Flat plate; plates of 200 cut into panes of 50.
Quantity Issued: 17,616,350
Plate Numbers: 18890, 18891, 18892, 18893, 18894, 18897, 18898, 18899
Scott Varieties: None

The Political Background

Just as the 10¢ stamp of this value was tied to the new rate for contract airmail, the 20¢ stamp, issued just a little over 11 months later, was tied to what became known as the uniform airmail rate of 1927. On December 23, 1926, the Post Office Department issued an order, effective February 1, 1927, changing the airmail rate to 10¢ per half ounce, regardless of distance.

This new rate was responsible for light-weight airmail envelopes and light-weight stationery to keep letters below a half ounce, but much mail matter weighed over a half ounce, and thus the 20¢ stamp was deemed necessary.

In October, Irving Glover indicated that "the new rate would possibly go into effect at the time the transcontinental service was taken over by a private contractor or contractors,"[8] but this was not to be. The Post Office Department wanted a uniform airmail rate as soon as possible. It would be only another eight months, however, until the Transcontinental Route was fully turned over to private air carriers.

On February 1, 1927, the same day the new unified airmail rate went into effect, the 8¢, 16¢ and 24¢ airmail stamps of 1923 were withdrawn from sale. The 15¢ airmail stamp was to remain on sale only until supplies were exhausted.

There seems to have been some misunderstanding among philatelic writers about restrictions on this stamp. Johl wrote that "with this issue, air mail stamps were restricted to usage on air mail matter."[9] This was not true. The official announcement for the stamp said: "This stamp, and other air mail stamps, are lawfully valid for postage on any mail matter but their use should be restricted, as far as practicable, to matter to be dispatched by air mail, for which they are specifically intended."[10]

Kent Stiles noted that this wording was new, as he wrote, "It is not recalled that such word has gone forth to postmasters in the Post Office Department's previous official notices regarding the 10¢ and 15¢ values."[11]

The Map Airmails

The official notice for the 15¢ stamp noted that it was "for use primarily in connection with the contract air-mail service, but valid for all purposes for which postage stamps of the regular issue are used."[12] Similar language was used in the notice for the 10¢ stamp, but neither suggested that their use "should be restricted." The Post Office Department went to some effort to have these stamps designed in a long, horizontal format that would distinguish them from other stamps, and the wording in the announcement seems to have been intended to reinforce the distinction.

Philatelic Aspects and Varieties

First day of issue. In addition to Washington, D.C., New York City was also a first-day city, although there was no connection to New York with this stamp. This seems to have been an attempt to get the stamp distributed more widely and in time for the February 1 rate change, which came only six days after the stamp was issued. First-day covers from New York carry a slight premium over Washington covers (see Figure 117).

Shades. The Bureau and the Post Office Department gave the ink color of this stamp as green, but Scott listed it as yellow green when it first appeared in the 1928 edition of the *Specialized Catalogue*. Green was added as Scott C9a in the 1946 edition. These small-letter varieties for color shades were eliminated in the 1979 edition. Johl noted that "two distinct shades appeared," which he called yellow green and light bluish green.

Inverted Fs. On two plates, 18890 and 18892, the Fs indicating that the plate was ready for hardening are inverted and were placed at the bottom of

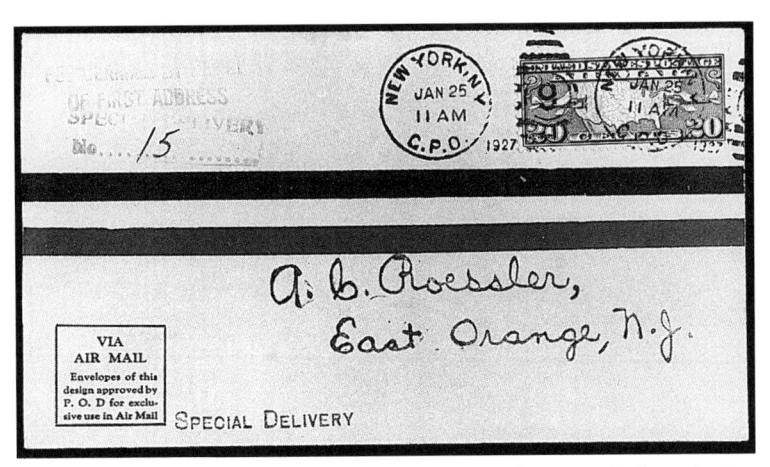

Figure 117. A first-day cover prepared by Albert Roessler, canceled on the first day of issue in New York, received no airmail service. The franking, however, provided more than enough for the 2¢ surface postage and the 10¢ special delivery fee.

333

the lower-left pane instead of at the usual position at the top of the upper-right pane. At some point, these inverted Fs were removed from the plates. Gilbert Peakes has done an extensive study of these plates, concluding that when the inverted F on plate 18892 was removed, it was punched into its proper location at the top right. But when the inverted F was removed from plate 18890, it was not punched into its proper location.[13]

Notes

1. "Stamp History," Card No. 445, Engraving Division, Bureau of Engraving and Printing.

2. John N. Luff, "Notes of the Month," *Scott's Monthly Journal*, Vol. 7, No. 2 (April 1926), p. 25.

3. Philip H. Ward Jr., "Chronicle of New Issues and Varieties", *Mekeel's Weekly Stamp News*, Vol. 40, No. 9 (March 1, 1926), p. 128.

4. Philip H. Ward Jr., Chronicle of New Issues and Varieties, *Mekeel's Weekly Stamp News*, Vol. 42, No. 21 (May 21, 1928), p. 342.

5. Michael A. Mellone, *Planty Photo Encyclopedia of Cacheted First Day Covers,* Volume 1 (Stewartsville, N.J.: F.D.C. Publishing Co., 1994), p. 107.

6. Philip H. Ward Jr., Chronicle of New Issues and Varieties, *Mekeel's Weekly Stamp News*, Vol. 40, No. 45 (November 8, 1926), p. 618

7. Kent B. Stiles, "Of Topical Interest," *Scott's Monthly Journal*, Vol. 7, No. 9 (November 1926), p. 278.

8. Ward, *op. cit., Mekeels*, Vol. 40, No. 45, p. 618.

9. Max G. Johl, *The United States Postage Stamps of the Twentieth Century*, Volume III (New York: H.L. Lindquist, 1935), p. 202

10. R.S. Regar, "New 20¢ Air Mail Stamp," [printed announcement] Government Printing Office.

11. Kent B. Stiles, "Of Topical Interest," *Scott's Monthly Journal*, Vol. 7, No. 12 (February 1927), p. 365.

12. R.S. Regar, "New 15¢ Air Mail Stamp," [printed announcement] Government Printing Office.

13. Gilbert L. Peakes, "A Study of the Inverted 'F' on 20¢ Air Mail Plates 18890 and 18892, *United States Specialist*, Vol. 43, No. 3 (March 1972), pp. 104-14.

Chapter 35

The Sesquicentennial Exposition Issue

2¢ Liberty Bell

Scott Number: 627
First Day of Issue: May 10, 1926
Perforation: 11
Scott Color: Carmine rose
Designer: Clair Aubrey Huston
Engravers: John Eissler (vignette and ornaments)
E.M. Hall, (frame and lettering)
Press: Flat-plate press
Plate Layout: Plates of 200 cut into panes of 50
Quantity Issued: 307,731,900
Plate Numbers: Total of 60: lowest, 18540; highest, 18613
Scott Varieties: Double transfer

The Political Background

This stamp was somewhat unusual for a commemorative issue at the time, as it was a single stamp rather than a series. Of the 14 commemorative issues up to 1926, 10 were multiple-stamp issues, and all three of the commemorative issues produced up to this time by the Harding-Coolidge postal administration had been multiple-stamp issues.

This stamp was similar, however, to seven other commemorative issues as it was issued to publicize an exposition. The sponsors of the Sesquicentennial International Exposition, planned for Philadelphia in 1926, began lobbying for a stamp in August 1923, when one of its officials began requesting information from the Post Office Department about the regulations governing the issuing of stamps. The Sesquicentennial Exhibition Association had al-

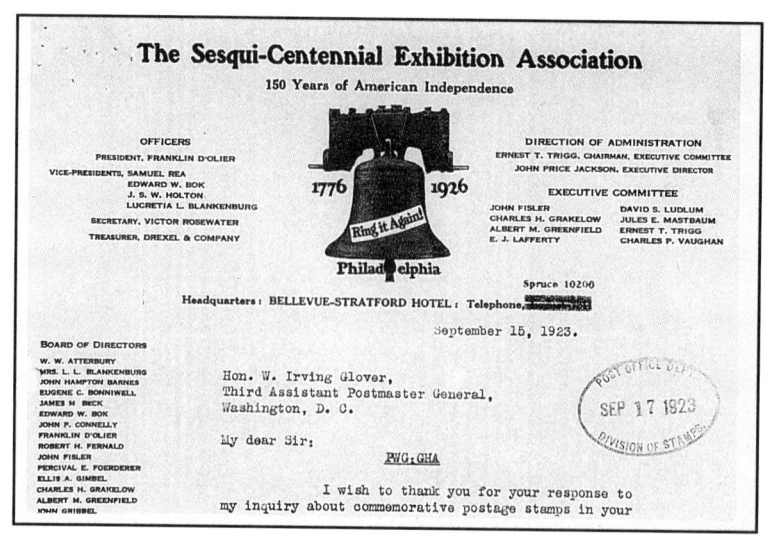

Figure 118. The letterhead on the original letter requesting the stamp featured the Liberty Bell. Did this give the Post Office Department an idea?

ready been established, with a large executive committee. It used on its letterhead stationery a large image of the Liberty Bell (see Figure 118).

By the following April, the association's secretary wrote to the postmaster general suggesting a "series of commemorative postage stamps that will emphasize the events attending the birth of the nation and re-enforce the lessons they should teach." For the subjects of these stamps, the group suggested, Carpenter's Hall, in which the first Continental Congress met; Independence Hall, where the members of the second Continental Congress met George Washington as general of the Army; the Liberty Bell; and, "for issue on their several appropriate dates ... portraits of notable signers of the Declaration, such as Jefferson, Franklin, Richard Henry Lee, John Hancock, John Adams, Robert Morris, Roger Sherman. ..."[1]

This of course, was a pretty ambitious issue of stamps. What is surprising in light of his later attitude is that Postmaster General Harry S. New, at this point in April 1924, actually liked the idea. He wrote to Third Assistant Glover: "Here is a suggestion that strikes me not unfavorably. Of course, not for its adoption in full but for something that will mark the event. Let's talk about it."[2]

On the same day, New replied to the exhibition association that "my first reaction is quite favorable to the adoption of a part of your program — at least to the extent of getting out something that will be appropriate, although your suggestions of subject are perhaps over-generous."[3]

Meanwhile, other suggestions were also received with suggestions for appropriate stamps to be issued to commemorate the 150th anniversary of the nation's independence. One suggestion from Washington State was a new pictorial series as follows:

 1¢   Boston Tea Party.
 2¢   Spirit of '76 (from picture of that name).
 3¢   Liberty Bell.
 4¢   Paul Revere's Ride.
 5¢   Minuteman at Lexington.
 8¢   Battle of Bunker Hill.
10¢   Washington Crossing the Delaware (from painting in New York Art Museum).
15¢   Signing of the Declaration of Independence.
20¢   Independence Hall.
25¢   Map of the 13 Original States.
50¢   Flag of the United States in 1776.
$1   Portrait of Washington between flags of 1776-1926.[4]

The writer at least had a plan for commemorating the sesquicentennial of the events of the American Revolution. The Post Office Department, unfortunately, did not, and ended up issuing stamps for events that had vocal support, rather than those that were necessarily of historical importance.

By the following year, the Department, although still planning some stamps for the sesquicentennial, had no firm plan. "While no definite steps have yet been taken to prepare a set of postage stamps to commemorate the 150th anniversary of the signing of the Declaration of Independence in 1926," Robert S. Regar replied to one of the suggestions for such a series, "it has been tentatively decided to issue special stamps. It cannot be stated at this time how many stamps it will be practicable to have, but undoubtedly a sufficient number will be issued to do justice to the important event which will be commemorated."[5]

These stamps, Regar noted, would probably not be printed in two colors as this particular writer proposed, for the Post Office Department had by this time been through the expensive and time-consuming difficulty of printing and distributing the bicolored Norse-American issue. "You can be assured that a like condition will be guarded against in connection with Sesqui-Centennial stamps. ..."[6]

By December of 1925, no decision had been reached, and there was no strong lobbying effort from the sponsors of the exposition. The original group had been reorganized near the end of 1924, and many of its members dropped out. One of them was Victor Rosewater, the original secretary of the association, who made the first list of "overgenerous" suggestions.

Writing on his own now, Rosewater argued strongly for a Liberty Bell stamp. "For doubtless good and sufficient reasons," he started, "consideration

337

of the Sesquicentennial stamps apparently has been held in abeyance." But, "inasmuch as the year 1926 is nearly here," he wanted to "recall and reinforce the suggestions already made so far as still practicable, and especially the issue of a stamp, in denomination most commonly used, bearing the likeness of the Liberty Bell, the most popular and most universally revered emblem of human freedom in all the world."[7] Rosewater went on to argue at some length for the use of the Liberty Bell, which had not previously been used on a stamp.

Once again, his letter seems to have struck a chord with Harry New, who wrote to his third assistant (Regar this time, as Glover had been promoted to second assistant): "Look over this Sesqui-Centennial stamp letter and we'll talk about it."[8]

They evidently did, and concluded that they were having a hard time figuring out who represented the planned exposition. But a few days later, New wrote back to Rosewater, "If your people have centered upon the design of the Liberty Bell, that will be approved by this Department and we might perhaps give you another, but under the circumstances, I don't think an issue of more than two can be reasonably expected."[9]

So we find that by the end of 1925, after having to issue stamps for a new postage bill and having an unpleasant budgetary experience with the Norse-American issue, the idea of large series of stamps for the sesquicentennial of the American Revolution had little or no support at the Post Office Department.

The government became a participant in the Philadelphia Exposition in 1925, and a National Sesquicentennial Exposition Commission was formed, with Secretary of State Frank Kellogg and Secretary of Commerce Herbert Hoover as members. Appointed as commissioner was Admiral Herman O. Stickney, who wrote to New on March 30, 1926, in an attempt to get the stamp issue resolved. "I understand that the Sesquicentennial Exhibition Association have had up the question of a special issue of United States postage stamps ..."[10] he wrote.

Robert Regar, the third assistant, and Michael Eidsness, the superintendent of the Division of Stamps, called on Admiral Stickney on April 14, and suggested to him that the Post Office Department issue only a single 2¢ stamp, depicting the Liberty Bell, but that this stamp be issued in a large quantity of 300 million. Stickney stated that the idea seemed fine to him, but that he would like to speak to Secretary Hoover "and get his views."[11]

Hoover, who now seems to have become the official authorizing the design, apparently had no objection. Stickney wanted the stamps to be on sale by May to publicize the exposition, which was to open on June 1.

The Bureau had little time to prepare a model, but as noted previously, a day or two was often all that was required. On April 20, a model was approved, with instructions that a supply be available for sale on May 10.

The Sesquicentennial Exposition Issue

The Subject and Design

The Liberty Bell was, ironically, cast in England in 1752, at the Whitechapel Foundry. The bell was commemorative in origin, as it was ordered in 1751 to mark the 50th anniversary of William Penn's 1701 Charter of Privileges, which spoke of religious freedom and the inclusion of ordinary citizens in enacting laws.

The speaker of the Pennsylvania Assembly, Isaac Norris, requested that a biblical verse be placed on the bell, and the words were cast in relief: "Proclaim LIBERTY throughout all the Land unto all the inhabitants thereof." This is from Leviticus 25:10. Also on the bell is the lettering "By Order of the Assembly of the Province of Pensylvania for the State House in Philada." Due to what we must believe was a typographical error, Pennsylvania is spelled wrong on the bell.

Not long after the bell arrived in Philadelphia it cracked, and it was recast by John Pass and John Stow, local craftsmen, who also put their own names on the bell. Centered on it, in larger letters than the inscription, are the words "Pass and Stow/Philada/MDCCLIII." They used metal from the original bell, which was 70 percent copper, 25 percent tin and small amounts of other metals. It weighs 2,080 pounds.

The bell, hung in the Pennsylvania State House, which later became known as Independence Hall, was rung many times, including July 8, 1776, when the Declaration of Independence was read publicly for the first time in Philadelphia. During the following years, 1777 and 1778, when the British occupied Philadelphia, it was removed to Allentown and hidden under the floor boards of the Zion Reformed Church. After the Revolutionary War, it was replaced in Independence Hall and rung annually on July 8 to observe the first reading of the Declaration.

According to tradition, the crack in the bell occurred on July 8, 1835, while also being tolled for the funeral of Supreme Court Justice John Marshall, but most histories of the bell note that the crack did not appear until 1846. According to the National Park Service, which now maintains the bell at the Liberty Bell Pavilion in Philadelphia, the bell was repaired once in 1846 "and rang for a George Washington birthday celebration, but the bell cracked again, and has not been rung since."[12]

The bell was not known as the Liberty Bell until the 1830s, when abolitionists adopted the bell as a symbol of their cause, saying that the cracked bell was an apt metaphor for a country that was fissured. After the Civil War, the bell traveled to several of the expositions publicized by previous stamps.

If not rung again, the bell was struck and sounded on April 6, 1917, when America declared war on Germany. This event may not have been far out of the minds of some Americans in 1926.

339

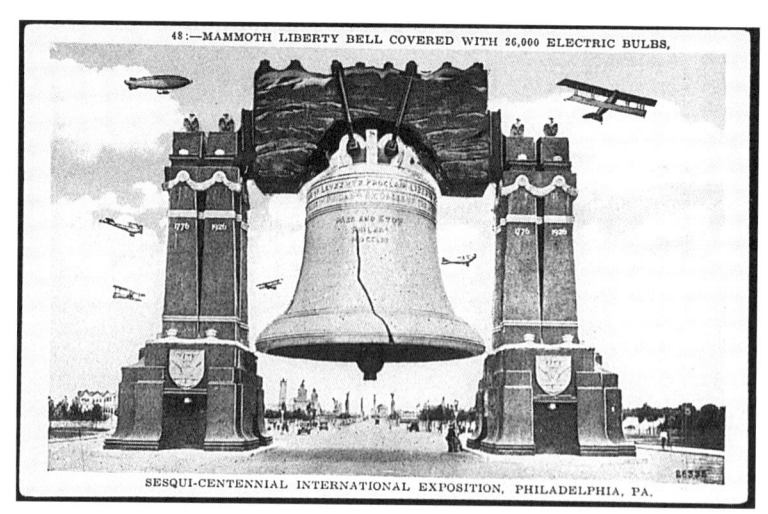

Figure 119. This postcard shows the giant illuminated Liberty Bell that formed the entrance to the Sesquicentennial Exhibition.

The source artwork for the bell that is depicted on the stamp was not a photograph of the Liberty Bell but of a giant replica of it that was placed over the main entrance to the exposition (see Figure 119). A part of the Westinghouse Electric exhibit, the "Mammoth Illuminated Liberty Bell" was covered with some 20,000 electric light bulbs. Many photographs of this bell were taken by John D. Cardinell, the "official photographer" of the exposition, and it is likely that one of his photographs, or perhaps one of his postcards, was used by the Bureau for making the model.

The pillars holding up the yoke of the bell, and the eagles on top of these, derive from the mammoth electrified bell, as do the shields on the base of the pillars. That this mammoth bell from the exposition was used on the stamp is perhaps fitting, for the stamp also carries the legend "Sesquicentennial Exposition."

This was one of Clair Huston's most striking stamp designs and an example of his mature style. He favored a neo-classical style and symmetrical designs. The acanthus leaves on either side of the stamp are typical elements and are similar to those he placed on the reverse of the $5 bill of 1928, which is still in use today.

Philatelic Aspects and Varieties

First day of issue. This stamp was issued on May 10, 1926, at Washington, D.C., Philadelphia, and Boston. As a commemorative issue, there was a great interest in first-day covers, and large numbers were serviced in all three cities. The bell was a well-known symbol that was easy to reproduce, and several printed cachets are known that reproduce the logotype of the exhibit, which also included the bell. Several picture postcards were also used in preparing first-day covers.

Criticism. Given that the sponsors of the exposition began asking for a stamp in 1923, it is ironic that Philip Ward criticized them for not asking for stamps soon enough to have a series of them printed. "It is unfortunate," he wrote, "that the Philadelphia Committee having the stamps in charge should so delay in taking the matter up with Washington that sufficient time was allowed to issue one stamp only."[13] If he only knew the truth!

Kent Stiles, however, who was constantly critical of countries that issued what he believed to be too many stamps, took the opposite approach. "The Post Office Department is to be congratulated," he wrote, "for restricting the new issue to a single adhesive. It had been reported in several philatelic journals that an extended series would appear."[14]

Mekeel's liked the stamp and editorialized that "the details of the workmanship of the stamp are handled fittingly so as to produce a whole that carries a message that stirs the American heart."[15]

As reported in the *American Philatelist*, however, the British critics were not so kind, reporting that one "takes the American Eagles on top the pillars supporting the bell to be newly hatched chickens and horrors, on the bottom of the pillars he claims to detect a crawling cockroach."[16]

First day and first flight. The first flight of Contract Air Mail Route No. 3, from Chicago to Dallas, was scheduled to be flown on May 12 by National Air Transport. Several postmasters on this route wrote to the Post Office Department noting that they had received requests from collectors for the new stamp on this flight. "Can you supply us with about 5000 and authorize their sale here on May 10th so that we may be able to meet this unusual demand," the postmaster of Moline, Illinois, inquired.[17]

In reply, Third Assistant PMG Regar wrote that "the Department will be glad to cooperate with you in this instance, and you are advised that a small supply of these stamps will be sent to you on May 10 for use on this initial flight." However, Regar was not authorizing a May 10 sale, as he continued, "Particular care should be exercised to see all envelopes and covers are canceled to show the actual date of mailing, and none is inadvertently canceled showing the first date of issue, May 10."[18]

However, some collectors were able to get covers canceled at the first-day cities on May 10, addressed them to cities on the new route, and marked them for airmail. These carry both the first-day cancels and the first-flight cachets (see Figure 120).

Shades. When first listed in the 1927 edition of the Scott *Specialized Catalogue*, the color was given as carmine rose, and only this shade is listed

Figure 120. A combination first-day and first-flight cover. It was canceled at Philadelphia on May 10 and mailed to Chicago for inclusion on the first flight of Contract Air Mail Route Number 3 from Chicago to Dallas.

today. To this, Johl added only dark carmine rose. The color of this stamp is pretty consistent for the large printing.

Double transfer. The plate and position for this variety seem to remain unknown. It was first reported by George Sloane in 1935, who credited D.J. Schoonmaker of Bethel, Connecticut, with the discovery. Sloane described this as "a very distinct double transfer" with the doubling showing mainly in the lettering at the top center of the stamp. He noted that the "AL" and "EXP" of "SESQUICENTENNIAL EXPOSITION" and the "ES" of "STATES" and "POS" of POSTAGE" were "somewhat doubled to the right." He added, "It is quite apparent without the use of a magnifier."[19]

Exposition cancels. Several special cancellations are known relating to the Sesquicentennial International Exposition. The Scott *Specialized Catalogue* lists a duplex handstamp as carrying a significant premium over the more common machine cancellations.

Part of the federal government's participation in the exposition was the operation of a "Model Post Office," which was described in a release from the first assistant postmaster general: "The office will be furnished with standard post office equipment, and mechanical conveyors and labor-saving devices will be in operation to show modern methods of handling mail in the larger post offices."[20] Ward, in helping to publicize this exhibit, wrote before it opened that "the service will be such that one can mail a picnic basket by parcel post after breakfast and receive it by noon-day."[21]

Canal Zone overprint. This is the only U.S. commemorative stamp to be overprinted for use by the Canal Zone. It was the policy of the Post Office

Department not to overprint commemoratives, but an exception was made after the stamp had been requested by the Canal Zone's purchasing officer in Washington, D.C. This exception was made, Third Assistant Regar wrote, "in view of the historical character of this stamp." But he advised the Canal Zone that "this should not be taken as a precedent in future requests for the surcharging of later issues of commemorative postage stamps."[22] The stamps, in a quantity of 300,000, were shipped to the Canal Zone on June 21 and were authorized for sale on July 4, a Sunday.

(This overprint is mentioned here because it was an exception to the usual policy. This book does not discuss the Canal Zone overprints of the regular issues, as that subject has been treated quite thoroughly in the excellent recent book, *Canal Zone Stamps*.[23])

Notes

1. Victor Rosewater, secretary, Sesquicentennial Exhibition Association, to Harry S. New, April 28, 1924. Smithsonian Institution Libraries, Post Office Department Manuscripts.

2. Harry S. New to W. Irving Glover, April 29, 1924. Smithsonian Institution Libraries, Post Office Department Manuscripts.

3. Harry S. New to Victor Rosewater, April 29, 1924. Smithsonian Institution Libraries, Post Office Department Manuscripts.

4. C.W. Urie to Harry S. New, September 1, 1924. Smithsonian Institution Libraries, Post Office Department Manuscripts.

5. Robert S. Regar to J.T.A. Hosbach, August 5, 1925. Smithsonian Institution Libraries, Post Office Department Manuscripts.

6. *Ibid.*

7. Victor Rosewater to Harry S. New, December 10, 1925. Smithsonian Institution Libraries, Post Office Department Manuscripts.

8. Harry S. New to Robert S. Regar, December 12, 1925. Smithsonian Institution Libraries, Post Office Department Manuscripts.

9. Harry S. New to Victor Rosewater, December 14, 1925. Smithsonian Institution Libraries, Post Office Department Manuscripts.

10. H.O. Stickney, commissioner, National Sesquicentennial Exposition, to Harry S. New, March 30, 1926. Smithsonian Institution Libraries, Post Office Department Manuscripts.

11. Robert S. Regar, memorandum, April 14, 1926. Smithsonian Institution

Libraries, Post Office Department Manuscripts.

12. National Park Service, "Liberty Bell," from the *Independence Hall National Historical Site* Internet site on the World Wide Web (www.libertynet.org as of 1/5/97).

13. Philip H. Ward Jr., "Washington Philatelic News," *Mekeel's Weekly Stamp News*, Vol. 40, No. 19 (May 10, 1926), p. 249.

14. Kent B. Stiles, "Of Topical Interest," *Scott's Monthly Journal*, Vol. 7, No. 3 (May 1926), p. 67.

15. "Editorial," *Mekeel's Weekly Stamp News*, Vol. 40, No. 21 (May 24, 1926), p. 278.

16. "New Issues of the United States," *American Philatelist*, Vol. 39, No. 11 (August 1926), p. 768.

17. George E. Carlson, postmaster, Moline, Illinois, to Robert S. Regar, April 29, 1926. Smithsonian Institution Libraries, Post Office Department Manuscripts.

18. Robert S. Regar to George E. Carlson, May 7, 1926. Smithsonian Institution Libraries, Post Office Department Manuscripts.

19. George Sloane, *Stamps*, May 11, 1935, reproduced in *Sloane's Column* (Bureau Issues Association: 1961), p. 323.

20. "Editorial," *Mekeel's Weekly Stamp News*, Vol. 40, No. 21 (May 24, 1926), p. 280

21. Philip H. Ward Jr., "Chronicle of New Issues and Varieties," *Mekeel's Weekly Stamp News*, Vol. 40, No. 23 (June 7, 1926), p. 304.

22. Robert S. Regar to A.L. Flint, general purchasing officer, Panama Canal, Washington, D.C., June 8, 1926. Smithsonian Institution Libraries, Post Office Department Manuscripts.

23. Gilbert N. Plass, Geoffrey Brewster and Richard H. Salz, *Canal Zone Stamps* (Canal Zone Study Group, 1986).

Chapter 36

The Ericsson Memorial Issue

Statue of John Ericsson

Scott Number:	628
First Day of Issue:	May 29, 1926
Perforation:	11
Color:	Gray lilac
Designer:	Clair Aubrey Huston
Engravers:	L.S. Schofield (vignette and frame)
	F. Lamasure (lettering and numerals)
Plate Layout:	Flat plate; plates of 200 cut into panes of 50.
Quantity Issued:	20,280,000
Plate Numbers:	18595, 18597, 18598, 18599, 18600, 18601, 18606, 18607
	18608, 18609, 18612, 18613
Scott Varieties:	None

The Political Background

After all of the reluctance to issue a Woodrow Wilson stamp, it seems a bit strange that Postmaster General Harry S. New would accede so readily to issuing a stamp for John Ericsson, a somewhat obscure American inventor.

There is very little correspondence in the Post Office Department file on this stamp. *Mekeel's* reported that the sponsors of the stamp, members of the Ericsson Memorial Committee, began thinking about a stamp in the summer of 1925, and that "the result of this movement was that Mr. Henry S. Henschen, treasurer of the Ericsson Memorial Committee, wired Congressman Carl R. Chindblom in regard to the stamp."[1]

345

It seems that most of the effort of the committee went to erecting a monument to John Ericsson, the Swedish-born inventor of the screw propeller and the designer of the iron-clad battleship *Monitor* during the Civil War. The committee was able to get an appropriation from Congress for $35,000 for a monument and a site near the newly dedicated Lincoln Memorial. Private donations added another $25,000 to the memorial fund.

Chindblom was more than just the congressman who was approached to ask for the stamp. He had been made the chairman of the John Ericsson Memorial Committee, which was a private organization. Congress had authorized a John Ericsson Memorial Commission to manage the funds. This commission was chaired by Senator Simeon Fess of Ohio, and had as a member Curtis Wilbur, the secretary of the Navy.

These politically powerful organizations had secured the attendance of the crown prince and princess of Sweden to the unveiling ceremony, and President Coolidge was to be the main speaker.

All of this was in place before Congressman Chindblom made his request for a stamp. In a letter to Postmaster General New, he noted that he had discussed the matter with Third Assistant Robert S. Regar, as New himself was in a Cabinet meeting when Chindblom called at the Post Office Department on April 20, five weeks before the statue was to be unveiled. "I shall try to see you tomorrow," Chindblom wrote.[2]

Within 24 hours, New and Chindblom had spoken, and New had agreed to a stamp. "I confirm what I have said to you personally since your letter was written," New wrote on April 21, "that the Department is preparing to issue a five-cent stamp of appropriate design."[3]

Congressman Chindblom and Senator Fess were both Republicans who were active in party affairs and national conventions. Whether this made any difference, we cannot tell, but it is worth noting that the suggestion to issue this stamp was met with less initial resistance than almost any other commemorative stamp of New's term as postmaster general.

The Subject and Design

It is the memorial to Ericsson, rather than Ericsson himself, that is the subject of this stamp, and the date of issue was connected to the monument's unveiling, not to an anniversary of Ericcson's birth or death. But John Ericsson, of course, was the person honored by the monument.

Most of the members of the Ericsson Memorial Committee were of Swedish descent, and Ericsson was to them a matter of ethnic pride. Born in the Swedish province of Vermland in 1803, Ericsson helped to plan a Swedish canal at the age of 14 and entered the Swedish army at the age of 17, where he was trained in surveying. In 1826 he moved to London, and over the next 12

The Ericsson Memorial Issue

years patented a number of inventions, the most important of which, in 1836, was the screw propeller, which is still the main form of marine propulsion. Steam vessels had previously been propelled mainly by paddlewheels.

After emigrating to the United States in 1839, he designed the *Princeton*, the first naval warship with a propeller and engines placed below the waterline. Ericsson became a U.S. citizen in 1848, and by the time the Civil War broke out, he was developing a ship with a revolving gun turret. The first of these became the famous *Monitor*, which was launched on January 30, 1862. The *Monitor* was a revolutionary ship that changed the architecture of naval war vessels into the 20th century. The celebrated battle between the *Monitor* and the iron-clad Confederate vessel, the *Merrimack* (actually renamed the *Virginia*), ended in a draw but began a new era in naval warfare.

Given Ericsson's fame as a naval engineer we might have expected his monument to have been a little more nautical in design, but the sculptor who was chosen, James Earle Fraser, chose an allegorical theme instead. On the white marble memorial, Ericsson is depicted as a seated figure in a chair. Dominating the sculpture are three standing figures representing Vision, Labor and Adventure (see Figure 121). It is the figure of Vision that faces in the same direction as Ericsson, and it is this standing allegorical figure, rather than the seated Ericsson, that dominates the stamp.

Figure 121. The Ericsson Memorial at Potomac Park in Washington, D.C., not long after it was completed. The allegorical figure of Vision rises above the seated Ericsson.

James Earle Fraser had been a student of the great American sculptor Augustus Saint-Gaudens, and had by this time garnered a great deal of fame. His 1915 bronze titled *End of the Trail* depicted an exhausted American Indian hunched over his tired horse and has become one of the most recognized sculptures of the American West. Fraser had previously designed the Buffalo nickel, and he would go on to sculpt, in 1931, the two large figures on either side of the steps of the Supreme Court.

Bureau designer Clair Aubrey Huston was provided with a small plaster model of the Ericsson Memorial, and prepared the stamp models from this. A model in the normal horizontal format was rejected, no doubt because Huston had sort of taken the sculpture apart and put two of the three standing figures on either side of the stamp, with Ericsson seated in the center (see Figure 122).

347

Figure. 122. One model for the stamp shows Ericsson in the center, with allegorical figures on each side. This was a sort of dismantling of the monument and was rejected.

His model in a vertical format was accepted. This was somewhat revolutionary on its own, for no U.S. postage stamp had ever before been issued in this "tall" format.

As originally prepared, the model for the stamp showed no trees in the background. However, Huston painted these in directly on the stamp-sized model, using a slightly lightened black ink. In the official description of the stamp, these are called "darkly silhouetted evergreens," which are set against "a dark sky."

Ericsson's Swedish heritage was also highlighted on the stamp, by a shield of Sweden in one corner and that of the United States in the other.

The style of the sculpture, in the contemporary Beaux-Arts mode, was somewhat different than the neo-classical style of designer Huston. Dominated by a modern sculpture with a bare-breasted central figure, tall in format, and in an unusual color, this stamp was different. *Mekeel's* commented on its appearance in an editorial: "The invariable remark that greets it from collecting lips is to the effect that the stamps bear the ear-marks or rather, atmosphere, of a foreign creation; and it is not to be denied that it carries old-world suggestions."[4]

Philatelic Aspects and Varieties

First day of issue. This stamp was issued on May 29, 1926, at Washington D.C., New York, Chicago and Minneapolis. These were all cities with large Swedish-American populations. Chicago was, in addition, the headquarters city of the Ericsson Memorial Committee. New York may have been chosen in part because the 5¢ denomination was used primarily on mail to foreign destinations.

With about two-weeks prior notice that this stamp would be issued, there was ample time for collectors to prepare first-day covers, and a relatively large number were serviced in all four cities. A handful of printed cachets are known, but it seems that no pictorial cachets were prepared. This may have been due not only to the short lead time, but also to the fact that no artwork for

The Ericsson Memorial Issue

the memorial was released in anticipation of the unveiling of the sculpture. In addition, Ericsson was not a well-known figure, and photographs or engravings of his portraits were not common.

However, the Rotnem Stamp Company got around this problem and alluded to Ericsson's Civil War connections by servicing a number of covers on old Civil War patriotic envelopes. These are in a smaller size than ordinary envelopes, and vary in design. Figure 123 shows one of these Rotnem first-day covers.

A glut. Initially ordered in a quantity of 15 million copies, the quantity was increased to 20 million on May 25, just four days before the first day of sale. This proved unnecessary, as the Post Office Department soon found that it had a glut of stamps on hand. The 5¢ denomination was not in as great demand as a 2¢ stamp would have been, and business users always seemed to shy away from commemorative stamps.

During the October following the issue date, Regar's office was sort of shoving the stamps down the throats of postmasters, telling them that they would be furnished the Ericsson stamps instead of the ordinary 5¢ stamps they had ordered. "Your cooperation in disposing of as many of these stamps as possible is desired," he explained, "and the Christmas mailings should afford a splendid opportunity of disposing of a considerable quantity."[5] At least 34 cities were supplied Ericsson stamps that they had not ordered.

Shades. The Bureau of Engraving and Printing specified the ink of this stamp as blue, the Post Office Department described it as purplish blue. When first listed in the 1927 edition of the Scott *Specialized Catalogue*, the shade was given as gray lilac.

Figure 123. First-day covers serviced by the Rotnem Stamp Co. of Minneapolis alluded to Ericsson's Civil War connection by using Civil War-era patriotic envelopes.

There was considerable discussion of the color of this stamp, as it was certainly different than the blue required by the Universal Postal Union for stamps paying the overseas rate to member countries.

In the discussion of the color, one collector argued this stamp was "truly an innovation" and that color charts showed it to be most accurately described as dark blue violet.[6]

Johl, who always seemed to have something to say about shades, found in addition deep gray lilac and purplish gray. He wrote, "The color used is different than that of any five cent stamp of the twentieth century." He also noted that "there was little true variation in the shade of this stamp, although exposure to the sun tended to fade out the purple and copies have been seen in a very light blue with no touch of the purple."[7]

Notes

1. "Editorial," *Mekeel's Weekly Stamp News*, Vol. 40, No. 26 (June 28, 1926), p. 338.

2. Carl R. Chindblom to Harry S. New, April 20, 1926. Smithsonian Institution Libraries, Post Office Department Manuscripts.

3. Harry S. New to Carl R. Chindblom, April 21, 1926. Smithsonian Institution Libraries, Post Office Department Manuscripts.

4. "Editorial," *Mekeel's Weekly Stamp News*, Vol. 40, No. 24 (June 24, 1926), p. 314.

5. Robert S. Regar to postmasters in 34 cities, October 27, 1927. Smithsonian Institution Libraries, Post Office Department Manuscripts.

6. Frank L. Applegate, "It's Dark Blue Violet," *American Philatelist*, Vol. 39, No. 11 (August 1926), p. 778.

7. Max G. Johl, *The Commemorative Stamps of the Twentieth Century*, Volume I (New York: H.L. Lindquist, 1947), p. 108.

Chapter 37

The 1½¢ Rotary Imperforate

Warren Harding

Scott Number: 631
First Day of Issue: August 27, 1926
Perforation: None
Scott Colors: Yellow brown, light brown
Press: Large rotary press
Plate Layout: Sheets of 400 subjects
Quantity Issued: 2,226,000
Plate Numbers: 18360, 18413
Scott Varieties: Without gum-breaker ridges

The Political Background

This stamp came about by mistake, as it was produced to fill a requisition for imperforate stamps for the Chicago post office. The customer for these imperforate stamps was the Pitney-Bowes Postage Meter Company, which had purchased the Mail-o-Meter Company in 1924. While most of the Mail-o-Meter affixing machines had been converted to use government coils, those in the Chicago area still used the privately perforated coils we know as Schermack Type III perforations.

The Mail-o-Meter's perforating equipment was set up to apply its proprietary rectangular perforations to imperforate sheets that had been printed on the flat-plate press, or at least had the same plate layout. The imperforate rotary-press sheets that were supplied had wide gutters rather than guidelines, and these imperforate sheets could not be perforated on the Mail-o-Meter equipment without massive waste. The sheets were therefore returned to the post office and were eventually replaced with sheets printed on the flat-plate press.

George Howard, the great specialist in private perforations, has noted that the imperforate sheets supplied to the Chicago post office would have been available not only to Pitney-Bowes, but to anyone who wanted to buy them. Most of the imperforate sheets were returned by the Chicago post office to the Bureau of Engraving and Printing, but Howard reported that "it is my understanding that not all of the 1½¢ rotary imperf sheets were returned to the Bureau."[1]

Howard went on to say that "nothing would have been easier than for the Bureau to perforate the returned sheets and ship them to post offices in panes of 100 along with the rest of the issue." This may not be quite true, as the perforator set up for these rotary-press stamps used rolls or webs of paper, not individual sheets. For the Bureau to perforate the rotary sheets on the flatbed perforators, it would have had to have set up a special configuration to accommodate the gutters — exactly the same situation that Pitney-Bowes found cumbersome.

Howard believed the stamps were sent to the Philatelic Stamp Agency because it was known that one or more sheets may not have been returned, and "knowing full well the philatelic value of the outstanding sheet or sheets they protected collectors by turning the entire issue over to the Philatelic Agency."[2]

On August 27, 1926, the stamps went on sale at the agency without any comment that they had been produced by mistake.

Philip Ward, in fact, reported that the imperforate variety of the 1¢ and 2¢ rotaries "will be issued in similar condition,"[3] but of course they were not, as there was no practical reason to issue them.

Philatelic Aspects and Varieties

This was the first and only rotary sheet stamp to be issued in imperforate form. Not only did it show the rotary plate layout clearly, but it provided collecting varieties that were similar to but different than the 400-subject flat-plate imperforate sheets. Rather than a centerline block, there was a cross gutter block (see Figure 124). Instead of arrow blocks at the top and bottom, there were gutter blocks showing short dashes. Instead of guideline pairs, there were pairs and blocks with vertical or horizontal gutters between.

The rotary stamps can be told from the flat-plate stamps by their size, as plates were curved in a vertical direction,

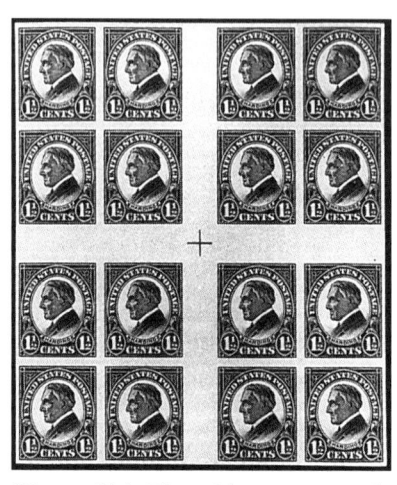

Figure 124. The wide gutters made these sheets unacceptable for private perforating, but the full sheets of 400 created new collecting varieties like this cross gutter block of 16.

The 1½¢ Rotary Imperforate

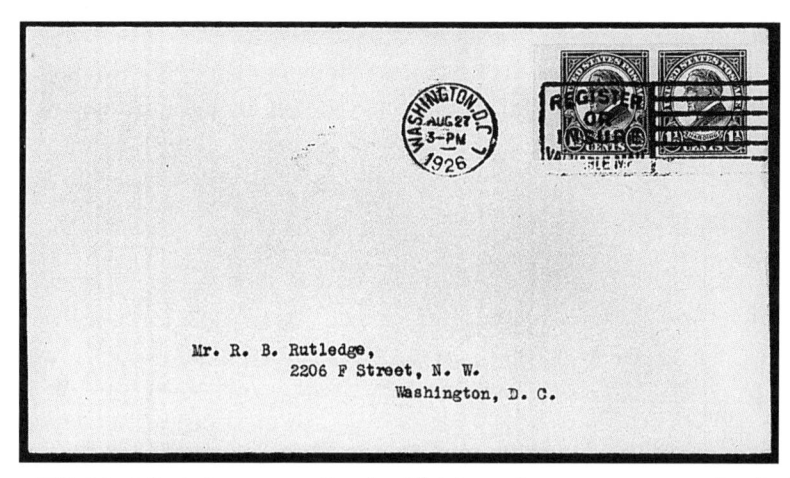

Figure 125. Most first-day covers for the 1½¢ imperforate stamp were franked with pairs. A cover franked with a single would be sent as third-class matter and would not ordinarily have received a datestamp.

making the rotary stamps taller than the flat-plate stamps.

First day of issue. This stamp was issued on August 27, 1926, only at Washington, D.C. Although there does not seem to have been much advance notice, first-day covers were serviced, primarily by Washington stamp dealer C.E. Nickles. Some of his covers show gutter blocks and other distinguishing features of this stamp. No printed cachets are known.

Some covers were serviced with single stamps, but these did not receive dated cancels, as third-class matter did not usually receive dated postmarks. The bulk of first-day covers are franked with pairs (see Figure 125).

Shades. When first listed in the 1928 edition of the Scott *Specialized Catalogue*, the color was given as yellow brown. Johl, too, found only this shade. In the 1935 edition, light brown was added as Scott 631a. The small-letter designation was removed in the 1979 edition, but the two shades remain in the catalog. Lewis Miers remarked in 1963, "It does seem strange that such a relatively small printing would have any shade varieties but nevertheless this is the case as the stamp does appear in several shades of brown."[4]

Without gum-breaker ridges. Most of the production of this stamp had gum breakers spaced so that about nine breaker ridges fell across two stamps. Some part of the production, however, had no gum breakers. Louis Fiset has reported that the variety without gum breakers was from the stock returned from Pitney-Bowes. "Since the stamps were produced for vending-machine use," he wrote, "there was little need to control for curl by applying gum breaker ridges. However, subsequent production to satisfy philatelic demand received breaker markings since that stock was intended for sale in pane and sheet form."[5] Sheets pulled from normal production to stock the Philatelic Stamp Agency from time to time would also help to explain why there are different shades.

That there were two varieties was first reported by Philip Ward in 1929.[6] The listing went into the *Specialized Catalogue* in the 1957 edition.

Notes

1. George Howard, "Vending and Affixing Machine Perforations," *United States Specialist*, Vol. 25, No. 6 (June 1954), p. 126.

2. *Ibid*.

3. Philip H. Ward Jr., "Chronicle of New Issues and Varieties," *Mekeel's Weekly Stamp News*, Vol. 40, No. 37 (September 13, 1926), p. 472.

4. Lewis A. Miers, "A Review of the Bureau Imperforates," *Bureau Specialist*, Vol. 34, No. 9 (September 1963), p. 289.

5. Louis Fiset, "Gum Breaker Experiments on BEP Definitives, 1919-31," *United States Specialist*, Vol. 60, No. 6 (June 1989), p. 283.

6. Philip H. Ward Jr., "Washington Letter," *Mekeel's Weekly Stamp News*, Vol. 43, No. 48 (December 2, 1929), p. 728.

Chapter 38

The First Rotary Booklet Stamps

Booklet Pane of Six

Scott Number: 583a
First Day of Issue: August 27, 1926
Perforation: 10
Scott Colors: Carmine, deep carmine
Press: Large rotary press
Plate Layout: Plates of 360 subjects, cut into panes of 6
Quantity Issued: Undetermined
Plate Numbers: 17450, 17451, 18550, 18551, 18662, 18663, 18695, 18696, 18697, 18698, 18705, 18706, 18708, 18710
Scott Varieties: None

The Political Background

There had been plans to produce booklet stamps on the rotary press as early as 1916, when plates were assigned for the same small rotary press that was used to print coils. These 153-subject plates, however, were never finished and thus never went to press.

But booklet stamps, first produced in 1900, had been growing rapidly in popularity. During the 1925 fiscal year, which ended on June 30, 1925, the Bureau of Engraving and Printing produced 690,668,040 booklet stamps in the 2¢ denomination and 155,473,200 booklet stamps in the 1¢ denomination, in a variety of booklets. As this was a substantial percentage of the production, it was logical that booklet stamps should eventually be produced on the rotary presses.

355

United States Stamps 1922-26

Two experimental plates, 17450 and 17451, were laid out in a 360-subject configuration that was nearly identical to the flat-plate layout. But instead of a single plate number at the top, these plates had a plate number in each of the four corners. The plates were certified on July 22, 1925, and went to press for the first time two days later on July 24. This was more than a year before the stamps were issued.

Two additional plates, 18550 and 18551, were certified on May 13, 1926. Unlike the first two plates, these did not have the flat-plate-style guidelines. Nor did any of the later 360-subject plates made for booklet stamps. These second two plates, however, varied slightly from the first two plates, as the spacing was slightly different, and these, too, were considered experimental.[1]

The output of both sets of experimental plates were made into two-pane booklets, so only these were available on August 27, 1926, when the first booklets were issued. The production from later plates was made into two-pane, four-pane and eight-pane booklets.

No comparable 1¢ booklet stamps were produced, as there were many unused 1¢ flat plates that had not yet gone to press. In addition, there was a diminished need for 1¢ stamps as the postcard rate had been raised to 2¢ in the rate increase of 1925. Nor was this booklet stamp ever paired with 1¢ stamps in combination booklets.

Philatelic Aspects and Varieties

This booklet stamp had a life of only about seven months, since the perforation gauge was changed for booklet stamps to 11 x 10.5 in February 1927. While the booklet panes are not scarce, they are not common. Full booklets, particularly in the eight-pane size, are quite scarce.

A tabular listing of the issued booklets follows:

Scott Booklet	Scott Stamp#	Panes	Face Value	Cover Design	Cover Stock	Cover Ink	Denom.
BK72	583a	2	24¢	Post Rider	Buff	Red	25¢
BK73	583a	4	48¢	Post Rider	Pink	Red	49¢
BK74	583a	8	96¢	Steamship	Blue	Red	97¢

Booklet pane positions. Since the first two plates were printed with guidelines, it seems that booklet panes should be available in all of the flat-plate booklet positions (see Chapter 10) with the exception of position D, the plate number position. However, only a single full pane with a guideline has been documented, and this is in position H, that is, with a guideline at the right[2] (see Figure 126.) At least three single stamps are known on cover with guidelines at the bottom, from position J panes.

The rarity of guideline copies is a bit puzzling. Richard Mast, a spe-

Figure 126. The only known pane of No. 583a showing a guideline. Three used single stamps have also been found, all with guidelines at the bottom.

cialist in this stamp, wrote that he searched for a pane of stamps with a guideline "for over thirty years without result."[3] In doing the arithmetic, he noted that with 31,895 impressions from the first two plates there should have been 446,530 panes with guidelines.

With only a single full pane known, it seems certain that no booklets with guideline panes were shipped to the Philatelic Stamp Agency. This would make sense if the shipment came from the second two plates. Perhaps the production from the first two plates was shipped to small towns where it was used up without notice.

When these booklets were first issued, it was believed that there would be subsequent printings from these first two plates, and this may explain why the booklet-pane collectors of the day did not search harder for these panes with guidelines at the time of issue. Hugh Southgate, a specialist in Bureau issues, reported that "plates 17450-51 were returned for rechroming 11 Sept. 1926, so that we may expect this ... pane to appear ... at some future date."[4] However, the plates were never put back to press.

Panes with plate numbers. With the plate numbers placed at the sides, the numbers were trimmed off in normal production. "Don't waste time hunting for any plate numbers," Philip Ward told his readers shortly after these booklets first appeared, "because the plate number is a thing of the past with the advent of the rotary work in booklets."[5]

But this did not prove true. As with coil stamps, plate numbers were occasionally found on booklet panes when the trimming was less than perfect. Panes with plate numbers, or partial plate numbers, are known for all of the plates used to print these panes except for 18695.

First day of issue. This booklet of stamps was issued on August 27, 1926, only at Washington, D.C. While there was little advance notice that these booklets were going to be issued, some collectors were no doubt watching for them, based on the plate number reports released by the Bureau. Ward reported in May that "it will be noted that two more plates of 360 subjects have been made for the booklets that are to be produced by the rotary press method."[6] This stamp also had the same first day of issue as Scott 631.

There were not many first-day covers prepared. The largest number was serviced by C.E. Nickles, who addressed most of them to Wm. Cornish.

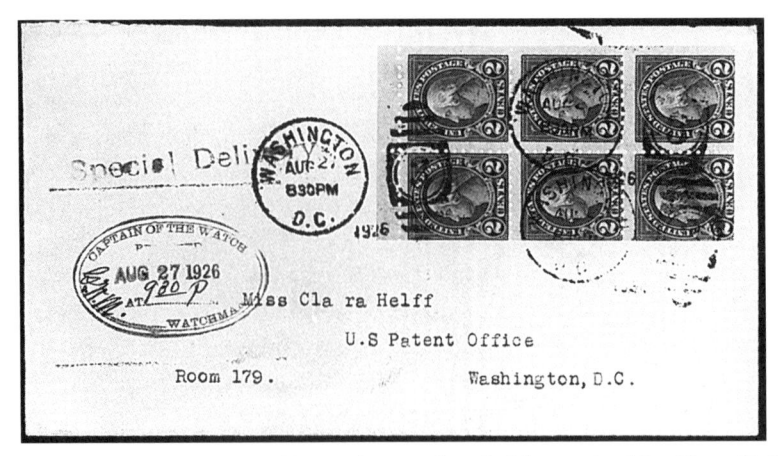

Figure 127. A first-day cover addressed to, and probably serviced by Clara Helff, one of the early first-day cover enthusiasts.

Albert Gorham also serviced a few covers bearing his printed corner card. Only a few others, like the one pictured in Figure 127, are known.

Notes

1. The spacing difference was in the gutters used to make the top margins or tabs of the booklets. As members of the Booklets and Booklet Panes Committee of the Bureau Issues Association reported in 1941, "The change in spacing of the stamps on the second set of plates will have to remain a matter of record only, in that it cannot be confirmed by comparisons of material." Oliver Williams, et al., "Booklets and Booklet Panes," *Bureau Specialist*, Vol. 12, No. 5 (May 1941), p. 115.

2. The story of this pane is told in Gary Griffith, "Guidelines on the First Rotary Press Booklet Panes," *United States Specialist*, Vol. 61, No. 12 (December 1990), pp. 657-61. See also "The Bristol Pane: Scott #583a with Guideline," *United States Specialist*, Vol. 64, No. 3 (March 1993), pp. 130-31.

3. Richard C. Mast, "Guide Lines on Rotary Press Perf 10 Booklet Panes," *United States Specialist*, Vol. 50, No. 7 (July 1979), p. 329.

4. Hugh Southgate, "Stamp Booklets of 1926," *Mekeel's Weekly Stamp News*, Vol. 41, No. 16 (April 18, 1927), p. 239.

5. Philip H. Ward Jr., "Chronicle of New Issues and Varieties," *Mekeel's Weekly Stamp News*, Vol. 41, No. 40 (October 4, 1926), p. 553.

6. Philip H. Ward Jr., "Chronicle of New Issues and Varieties," *Mekeel's Weekly Stamp News*, Vol. 41, No. 21 (May 24, 1926), p. 280.

Chapter 39

The Battle of White Plains Issue

Alexander Hamilton's Battery

Scott: 629
First Day of Issue: October 1926
Perforation: 11
Scott Color: Carmine rose
Designer: Clair Aubrey Huston
Engravers: John Eissler (vignette and ornaments)
H.I. Earle (frame, lettering, numerals)
Plate Layout: Flat plate; plates of 400 cut into panes of 100.
Quantity Issued: 40,639,485
Plate Numbers: 18765, 18766, 18767, 18768, 18769
Scott Varieties: a. Vertical pair, imperf between

The Political Background

Like many commemorative stamps of this period, this is one that Postmaster General Harry S. New did not want to issue. The proponents of the stamp were the town officials of White Plains, New York. In preparation for the 150th anniversary of a battle, or rather a skirmish, that took place there in 1776, they wanted Congress to pay for markers for the battlefield, and they wanted the Post Office Department to issue a commemorative stamp.

Help on both projects was solicited from the local congressman, Jonathan Mahew Wainwright, a highly decorated Army colonel who had seen action in France and Belgium during the war. Colonel Wainwright spoke to Postmaster General New about the stamp on March 29, and followed up with a letter arguing that the Battle of White Plains was "an event of sufficient importance to be commemorated with … a special stamp."[1]

New sent back the bad news on the following day. "I am well aware of the importance of this event in the War of the Revolution," he wrote, "but the

359

Department is very much restricted now in its postal issues because of lack of appropriated funds. ... As the matter now stands, I do not believe it will be possible to have a special stamp for the White Plains Anniversary."[2]

In the following few days, New received other letters arguing the merits of the stamp from the Rotary Club of White Plains and from the Westchester County Historical Society, which argued that "no more important battle of the Revolution was fought during the year 1776."[3]

This was certainly a stretch of history, for although the Continental forces under General George Washington did not have a great year in 1776, having spent most of it retreating, the Battle of Long Island in August was certainly the largest encounter, the Battle of Harlem Heights in September was the most heroic for the American troops, and Washington's crossing the Delaware River in December to capture Trenton was unquestionably the most successful and most important engagement that year. White Plains, in October, was merely one of the many small battles in the New York campaign.

The Post Office Department did not, however, argue about the importance of the battle. New turned over the matter to his third assistant, Robert S. Regar, who wrote to the historical society that "it would not be possible to have a White Plains stamp."[4]

The issue went public a few days later, when the local newspaper, *The Daily Reporter*, editorialized that the matter of a stamp was before the postmaster general. "The Battle of White Plains was one of the turning points of the Revolution," it said. "It is worthy of the Battle Stamp for which our citizens are petitioning the Federal government."[5]

This petitioning took the form of letters, 11 of them from prominent citizens of White Plains, which included judges, the county clerk, the secretary of the Westchester Hills Golf Club and the secretary of the Westchester County Automobile Dealers' Association. The letters from this distinguished group were forwarded to New by Congressman Wainwright, but New was unimpressed, and again had his third assistant reply.

"Inasmuch as conditions with reference to such a stamp have not changed since the Postmaster General wrote you on May 1st," Regar wrote back, "it is still considered impractical to provide a White Plains stamp."[6]

This, as one might imagine, did not sit well with the congressman. He soon enlisted the help of New York Senator James Wolcott Wadsworth Jr., a Republican who had served with New in the Senate for the five years from 1917 to 1921. Wadsworth asked New to meet with him and Congressman Wainwright, and New, of course, agreed to see them.

In preparation for the meeting, New asked his staff to provide him with information about his stamp budget. The response that came back was that it had been cut from $8,000,000 for the 1926 fiscal year to $7,500,000 for the

The Battle of White Plains Issue

1927 fiscal year. Since the event to be commemorated was in October, a White Plains stamp would be charged to the 1927 fiscal year budget, which would begin on July 1, 1926. Harvey Lovejoy, the deputy third assistant who prepared this budget memo, noted that "extreme care will have to be exercised to furnish stamped paper to the public in 1927 with the amount appropriated therefor."

The bills for producing the Liberty Bell stamp, which had just been issued, were fresh in Lovejoy's mind, and the stamps had cost 17¢ per thousand, more than double what the Department was paying for ordinary stamps. In presenting his figures, Lovejoy added his own argument against producing a commemorative stamp so early in a fiscal year that was bound to be tight. In his argument we find the reason why the White Plains stamp, when it was eventually issued, was in a small size.

"Owing to the size …," he wrote about commemorative stamps, "only 50 can be printed on a sheet, which makes more expense in handling. The ordinary stamps are printed 100 to a sheet. Furthermore, postmasters are required to account separately in their stamp accounts for special issues. I might also say that commemorative stamps, being of larger size than the ordinary stamps, are not desirable for the use of large mailers."[7]

While we don't have any minutes of the meeting between New and his congressional visitors, we do know the result. On July 2, New wrote to Congressman Wainwright telling him "I am very pleased to inform you that I have decided to authorize the issuance of such a commemorative stamp."[8]

The Subject and Design

In the same letter in which New announced the good news, he said "I will submit the models of postage stamps which you left at my office to the Bureau of Engraving and Printing."[9] Thus we know that Wainwright and Wadsworth brought artwork with them. These sketches (shown in Figure 128), which were recently located in the Post Office Department files at the Smithsonian's library at the National Postal Museum, are much more sophisticated than the sketches that Max Johl attributed to an artist named F.M. Farrar.[10] It may well be that when Johl's partner Beverly King attempted to collect the original sketches, he was able to find the cruder Farrar drawings in White Plains. He could not, of course, have collected these more sophisticated models, as they remained in the Post Office Department's files.

These newly found drawings are almost certainly the work of Edmund Ward, the same artist who painted the scene that was eventually used on the issued stamp. One of these drawings uses a frame design copied from the Trans-Mississippi issue of 1898. The vignette is a sketch of a detail from a painting by George Albert Harker depicting the battle scene and showing a field cannon being pulled up Chatterton's Hill, the site of the battle, by the American troops.

United States Stamps 1922-26

Figure 128. Two rough sketches for the White Plains issue were presented to the Post Office Department by a congressman and senator. One (left) uses a detail from the George Albert Harker painting of the battle as the vignette in a frame copied from the Trans-Mississippi issue of 1898. The other (right) shows a sketch very similar to the Ward illustration that was used on the issued stamp.

Accompanying this drawing was a photograph of Harker's painting, which had originally been done for a White Plains bank calendar.

The other scene was quite similar to the final painting used on the stamp, but it is in rougher form and the positions of the four figures are somewhat different.

Models for a stamp "in the size of the present special-delivery stamps" were requested from the Bureau on July 14. In requesting the models, "two models and a photograph submitted by Congressman Wainwright as suggestions of the design and subject"[11] were also sent to the Bureau.

Bureau artist C. Aubrey Huston prepared a model using the calendar painting as a vignette. This model, which is shown in Figure 129, created a rather crowded stamp that showed a uniformed officer, Captain Alexander Hamilton, at the head of the troops. It was Huston's standard procedure to draw frames but to use existing artwork for vignettes. It was rare for him to create a new illustration.

But before this model was submitted, one of the advocates of the White Plains stamp, Dr. Jason Samuel Parker, sent a finished painting by Edmund Ward of the sketch of the four figures around a cannon. Parker and several of his friends launched a campaign to use this artwork, rather than the Harker calendar painting on the stamp. Parker would later generate quite a bit of personal publicity about his role in

Figure 129. The first model of the stamp prepared by the Bureau used a larger detail from the Harker painting, showing the officer Alexander Hamilton urging his men forward.

Figure 130. After a painting by Edmund Ward was supplied, the Bureau provided two similar models in different sizes. Although the White Plains committee wanted the framelines removed, and the stamp printed in two colors, the Post Office Department chose the smaller model as submitted.

the advocacy and design of this stamp, which has found its way into philatelic literature but which is not entirely supported by the correspondence on file. His role in advocating the new design caused Congressman Wainwright to back off and in essence wash his hands of the matter. We find the Post Office Department corresponding with Parker on a few details.

The Bureau made two new models for the stamp (Figure 130), one in the special delivery size and one in the size of the issued stamp. Parker and his committee were sent the models, and he suggested changes.

"In preparing the models," he wrote, "it is the opinion of the Committee that if the border design is vignetted and made as simple as possible, without the scroll work and without the outer line, that the stamp will present a more striking and pleasing appearance."[12] Parker also wanted the stamp produced in two colors, and submitted a rough sketch showing these "improvements." This sketch is now listed as an essay for the stamp, and is listed by the Scott *Specialized Catalogue* as 629-E1. However, this sketch seems to have been derived from the Bureau model and was not a preliminary drawing for it. It is also worth noting that the Post Office Department did not take Parker's final advice, but issued the stamp in a single color, and with the outer border.

The title of the Ward painting used for this stamp was *Alexander Hamilton's Battery*, and the uniformed figure ramming the cannon on the right of the design represents Hamilton and has his facial features. However, the official Post Office Department announcement of the stamp made no reference at all to Hamilton, stating only that "the center vignette shows a gun crew in action, consisting of four men dressed in continental uniform, with cannon and ammunition. ..."

This may have been a reflection of the contemporary controversy that Hamilton was not commanding the field artillery at the battle scene. The Westchester Historical Society published a book in 1926 by Otto Hufeland, a

363

local historian who believed that Hamilton was elsewhere that day. "The artillery consisted of two guns from Alexander Hamilton's battery," Hufeland wrote, "but as his name does not appear in any of the contemporary accounts of the battle, it is probable that the guns were commanded by some subordinate officer whose name has not been recorded."[13]

Philatelic Aspects and Varieties

First day of issue. This stamp was unusual in that it did not have a first day of sale in Washington, D.C. The International Philatelic Exhibition opened on Saturday, October 16, in New York, and the stamp was sold there on the first-day date of October 18. Because of the number of dealers at the exhibition, and the easy access to the stamps, a large number of first-day covers were prepared, many with printed or rubber-stamped cachets.

The stamps also had a first day of sale at White Plains, New York, which was something of a town celebration.

Some of the covers canceled at the exhibition bear an October 16 date (see Figure 131), but only because of a mistake. The exhibition post office had been open on Saturday, "and when it opened on Monday morning, the clerk in charge canceled some letters before he discovered that he had overlooked changing the date."[14]

In White Plains, some 20,000 first-day covers were mailed by the post office there. The local newspaper reported, "To satisfy this demand the postmaster and members of his family worked for many hours placing stamps on self-addressed envelopes and enclosing in them the special letter allowed by Postmaster General New and prepared by the Chamber of Commerce."[15]

Figure 131. Some first-day covers bear an October 16 datestamp. This was caused by the clerk's failure to change the date on the canceler on Monday morning, October 18.

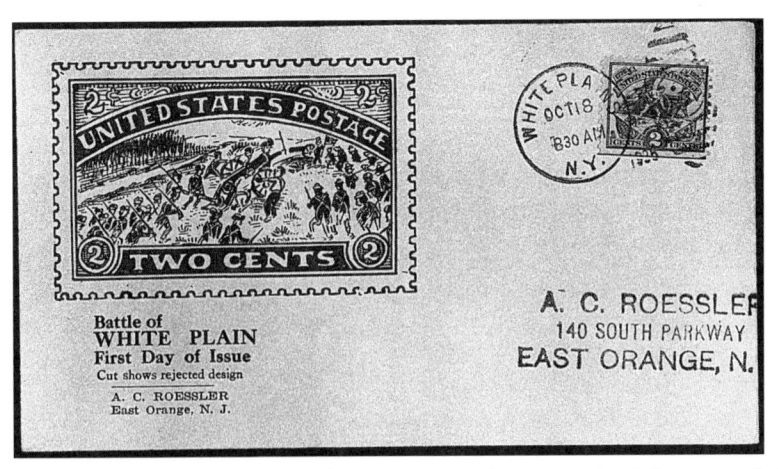

Figure 132. The first stamplike cachet by dealer Albert Roessler. The artwork, based on the Harker painting, was supplied by supporters of the stamp in White Plains, New York. The "Battle of White Plain" is a typographical error.

With this stamp we begin to see a multiplicity of printed cachets. This stamp in fact seems to be something of a demarcation between the relatively unadorned first-day covers that preceded it and the proliferation of fancy cachets that followed. For the first time we have artwork similar to that on the issued stamp used for a cachet. A print of the Ward painting, somewhat roughly reproduced on covers serviced by Otto Lampe, was no doubt supplied by the Chamber of Commerce. Jason Samuel Parker also serviced postcards with the Ward artwork.

Albert Roessler, the New Jersey stamp dealer and printer, prepared covers with, for the first time, a stamplike cachet (Figure 132). This was based on the Harker painting, and this artwork, too, must have been supplied to by the White Plains group.

The stamp was not available at the Philatelic Stamp Agency until October 28, and other covers were prepared from Washington on that date.

Shades. Both the Bureau and the Post Office Department described the color of this stamp as red. When first listed in the 1928 edition of the Scott *Specialized Catalogue*, the color was given as carmine rose, and it has remained thus. Johl found, in addition to this shade, light carmine rose.

Scott 629a. Vertical pair, imperforate between. Like many of the varieties of this period, this was first reported by Philip Ward. He credited the find to a Richard J. Schwartz, who found in Chicago a lower-left pane of 100 stamps from plate 18766. "One row of perforations is entirely missing — hence giving us 12 copies of the stamp unperforated horizontally, the balance of the sheet being of a freak nature showing a combination of vertical and diagonal perforations."[16]

Notes

1. Jonathan Mahew Wainwright to Harry S. New, March 30, 1926. Smithsonian Institution, Post Office Department Manuscript Collection.

2. Harry S. New to Jonathan Mahew Wainwright, March 31, 1926. Smithsonian Institution, Post Office Department Manuscript Collection.

3. Charles J. Dunlap, president, Westchester County Historical Society, April 19, 1926. Smithsonian Institution, Post Office Department Manuscript Collection.

4. Robert S. Regar to Charles J. Dunlap, April 24, 1926. Smithsonian Institution, Post Office Department Manuscript Collection.

5. "Editorial," *The Daily Reporter*, White Plains, New York, May 4, 1926.

6. Robert S. Regar to Jonathan Mahew Wainwright, May 8, 1926. Smithsonian Institution, Post Office Department Manuscript Collection.

7. Harvey Lovejoy to Harry S. New, May 15, 1926. Smithsonian Institution, Post Office Department Manuscript Collection.

8. Harry S. New to Jonathan Mahew Wainwright, July 2, 1926. Smithsonian Institution, Post Office Department Manuscript Collection.

9. *Ibid.*

10. See Max G. Johl, *The United States Commemorative Stamps of the Twentieth Century*, Volume 1 (New York: H.L. Lindquist, 1947), p. 109.

11. Robert S. Regar to Alvin W. Hall, July 14, 1926. Smithsonian Institution, Post Office Department Manuscript Collection.

12. Jason S. Parker to Robert S. Regar, August 19, 1926. Smithsonian Institution, Post Office Department Manuscript Collection.

13. Otto Hufeland, *Westchester County During the American Revolution: 1775-1783* (Westchester County Historical Society, 1926), p. 138.

14. Philip H. Ward Jr., "The New 2¢ White Plains Stamp," *Mekeel's Weekly Stamp News*, Vol. 40, No. 45 (November 8, 1926).

15. "A Remarkable Response," *The Daily Reporter* (White Plains, New York), October 19, 1926.

16. Philip H. Ward Jr., "Chronicle of New Issues and Varieties," *Mekeel's Weekly Stamp News*, Vol. 41, No. 5 (January 31, 1927), p. 74.

Chapter 40

The First U.S. Souvenir Sheet

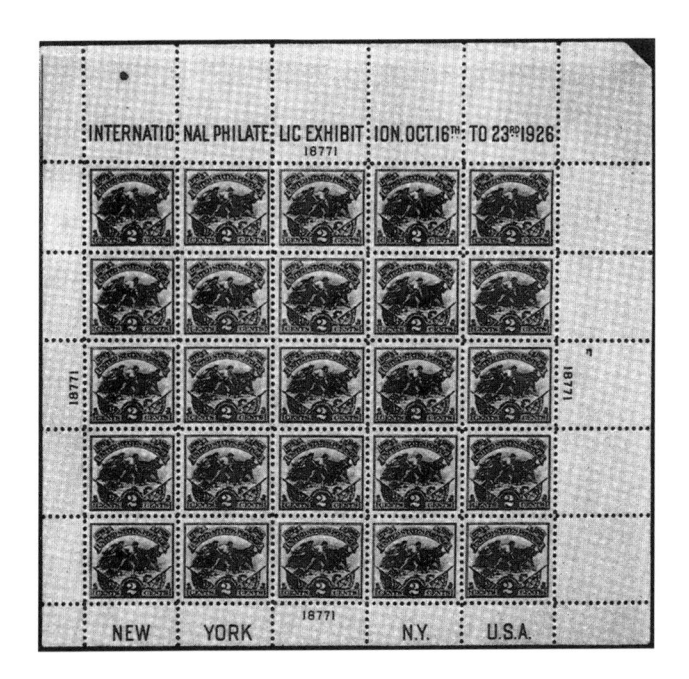

International Philatelic Exhibition Sheet

Scott Number: 630
First Day of Issue: October 18, 1926
Perforation: 11
Scott Color: carmine rose
Designer: Clair Aubrey Huston
Engravers: John Eissler (vignette and ornaments)
H.I. Earle (frame, lettering, numerals)
Press: Flat-plate press
Plate Layout: Plates of 100 cut into panes of 25
Quantity Issued: 107,398
Plate Numbers: 18770, 18771, 18773, 18774
Scott Varieties: Dot over first "S" of "STATES" 18774 LL 9 or 18773 LL 11

The Political Background

The first International Philatelic Exhibition was held in New York in 1913. The second, sponsored by the same group, the Association for Stamp

Exhibitions Inc., was planned for New York, in the city's Grand Central Palace, from October 16 to October 23, 1926. The Post Office Department, which had been friendly to collectors since the beginning of the Harding administration, made plans to participate in a major way.

Several personnel from the Department planned to attend, including Second Assistant PMG W. Irving Glover and Third Assistant PMG Robert S. Regar, both of whom agreed to speak at banquets. The Philatelic Stamp Agency arranged to set up a branch agency at the exhibition to sell unused U.S. issues, and the date of the release of the Battle of White Plains issue was also moved up to coincide with the first Monday of the show.

Who conceived the idea of a souvenir sheet is not known. According to Murray Bartels, a New York dealer and member of the show's executive committee, the Department at first planned to make up a small sheet of the current ordinary 2¢ stamps, as the idea of making a profit by selling large numbers of these sheets at the show was not lost on the Post Office Department. The 50¢ price probably seemed about right. In Bartels' telling, he was the person who convinced the Department to use the White Plains stamp instead of the regular issue. "Would it not be possible," he remembered asking Regar, "to issue this stamp a few days earlier, to prepare the small sheets of these instead of the regular 2¢ stamps?"[1]

On September 8, the Department sent an order to the Bureau for a 25-subject plate with special wording on all four sides. It also ordered 2,500,000 stamps "printed from the special 25-subject plate."[2]

This, of course, would require 100,000 impressions. We can imagine that the Bureau suggested instead that a 100-subject plate be used and that four panes of 25 be cut from sheets of 100. In any event, we know that it was 100-subject plates that were eventually laid out.

Four plates were used to print the sheets in advance of the exhibition. A fifth plate, 18772, was sent to the exhibition to be used with a hand-roller press to demonstrate stamp printing. A Bureau plate printer took 3,000 sheets of paper with him and printed White Plains souvenir sheets with 700 of them. These sheets, however, were not gummed or perforated. Nor were these sheets sold at the exhibition.

There was a rumor that these imperforate sheets were going to be acquired by an influential dealer and sold as a rare or special variety. But collector H.M. Konwiser, writing from the Collectors Club, took pains to scotch this plan if it indeed existed. He wrote to Harvey Lovejoy, the deputy third assistant: "If any stamp dealer, no matter how close he may claim to be 'to Washington' offers any of the White Plains stamps imperforate, I take it he will have received same in a manner not legitimate. A word from you to the proper men in the Post Office will avoid a philatelic scandal."[3]

On the following day, the Bureau received an order from the Department "to destroy not only the 700 printed sheets, but also the plate No. 18772."[4]

Not only were the printed sheets and the plate destroyed, but for good measure, it seems, the Bureau also destroyed the 2,300 sheets of blank paper.

Souvenir sheets from the other four plates that had not been sold at the exhibition were taken back to Washington and sold at the Philatelic Stamp Agency until the supply was exhausted. The souvenir sheet was not sold in post offices. Postmasters who tried to requisition them were told that they could only obtain them with "a personal order direct with the Philatelic Agency, which must of course, include a remittance to cover the value of the stamps together with return charges."[5]

Philatelic Aspects and Varieties

First day of issue. This sheet was first put on sale on October 18, 1926, only at the International Philatelic Exhibition in New York. Although many collectors and dealers at the show prepared first-day covers, it was cumbersome to attach a full pane of 25 to an envelope. A few servicers, notably Edward Worden of Millburn, New Jersey, did prepare covers with full panes. Many other covers were prepared with the top row of five stamps and the attached selvage and sent airmail (see Figure 133).

The White Plains sheet was not put on sale at the Philatelic Stamp Agency in Washington until October 28. Some covers with this date were serviced with Washington, D.C., cancellations, but these are not as desirable as those serviced from New York.

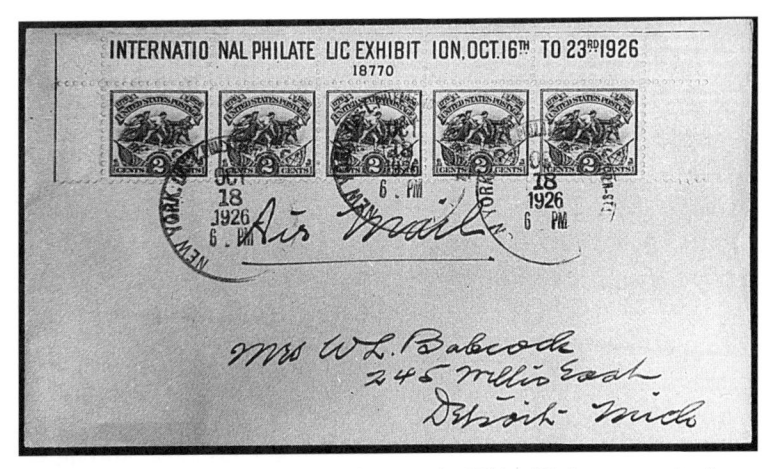

Figure 133. A strip of five stamps from the top of a White Plains souvenir sheet, mailed on the first day of issue, paid the 10¢ night airmail rate. The handstamp is from the International Philatelic Exhibition station.

Plate layout and plate number blocks. Since the individual stamps in the souvenir sheet are identical in design to the Battle of White Plains stamp, individual stamps from the souvenir sheet cannot be told from the ordinary panes of 100 unless they are accompanied by plate numbers, other marginal markings, selvage or plate varieties. Although plate blocks of six could be saved from the panes, this stamp is usually collected in a complete pane of 25 with the selvage attached.

As described above, the panes of 25 were printed from sheets of 100 subjects. One-inch gutters with guidelines ruled at their midpoints, separated the panes. Each pane of 25 carried four plate numbers, one on each side. The "F" marking was placed above the right plate number of the upper-right pane, not before the top-right number, which was its usual position.

Each of the four panes was inscribed at the top: "International Philatelic Exhibition, Oct. 16th To 23rd 1926" and "New York N.Y. U.S.A" at the bottom.

The stamps were perforated and the panes cut apart in the usual manner on the rotary perforators used for flat-plate stamps. This produced different sized panes depending on the position. Upper-left and upper-right panes should measure about 6³/16 inches wide by 5⁷/8 inches tall. Lower-left and lower-right panes are shorter and should measure about 6³/16 inches by 5³/8 inches.

Dot-over-S variety. This plate variety was reported almost immediately by Philip Ward, who noted a week after the stamps were sold: "My attention has been called to a slight variety on the southwest pane from plate 18774. On the ninth stamp directly above the "S" of "STATES" is a large dot."[6] It was probably caused by a defect in the plate, or more likely by damage to the plate. Because so many complete panes were saved, this position, 18774 LL 9, was an easy plate variety to find. On the same pane there is also another plate variety at position 3: a small line through the "C" of "CENTS."

The dot-over-S plate variety was listed in the 1928 edition of the Scott *Specialized Catalogue*, but under 629, as the souvenir sheet was not given its own catalog number until 1939.

The position of the dot-over-S variety was illustrated in a diagram by Max Adler in the *Collectors Club Philatelist* in 1928. Adler reported that mathematically there should be 6,712 sheets with this variety.[7] By the following year he was calling this variety "the well known large red dot."[8] This position, 18774 LL 9, is shown in Figure 134.

Figure 134. The dot-over-S plate variety is from position 18774 LL 9. This was the first to be listed, and is quite different than the variety Scott lists as 18773 LL 11.

In the same 1939 edition of the *Specialized Catalogue* that assigned Scott 630 to the pane of 25, an additional position was given for the dot-over-S: 18773 LL 11. This is not the same variety as 18774 LL 9. Although located over the "S" of "STATES," the dot is of a different form and, to some, not a dot at all and, to others, not really over the "S." Adler called this a "form of a hyphen."[9] Another writer, Adolph Weber, wrote in 1937 that "plate 18773 on the lower left pane also shows the dot on the 'S' of stamp Number 11 and not above it."[10]

Scarcity. This sheet, when first listed in the *Specialized Catalogue* for 1928 was given a catalog value of $1.50, or three times face. Nine years later *Mekeels* reported: "Collectors have only recently commenced to appreciate the relative scarcity of the small sheets. They are cataloged in Scott's *Specialized* at $5.50 and sell at auction from $4 to $7.25. Considering the number of small sheets printed, the fact that many were cut and used for postage, and, of greater importance, the fact that collectors insist on having the full sheet in their books, all make for greater scarcity. It can be safely assumed that this sheet will progressively increase in value."[11]

In 1959, Harry Weiss, in *Weekly Philatelic Gossip,* noted, "That White Plains sheet was not collected at all when it first came out — look at it now! Dealers are asking close to $50 for a souvenir sheet of this stamp now." The reason for the price escalation, in his opinion, was this: "Back in the early thirties, dealers had big stocks of them and could not sell them readily. They broke the sheets up and sold them as singles and blocks."[12]

Supply and demand is also an explanation. There were not a great number of this sheet to begin with: only 107,398. In addition to the sheets that were used for postage and broken up by dealers, these sheets also deteriorate in condition if not handled properly. The sheets separate at the perforations. The supply of complete sheets in fine to very fine condition will always be declining.

Notes

1. J. Murray Bartels, "Comments and Reminiscences," *Stamps*, Vol. 21, No. 13, p. 482.

2. Robert S. Regar to Andrew Mellon, September 6, 1926. Historical Resource Center, Bureau of Engraving and Printing.

3. H.M. Konwiser to Harvey Lovejoy, October 27, 1926. Smithsonian Institution Libraries, Post Office Department Manuscripts.

4. Robert S. Regar to Alvin W. Hall, October 28, 1926. Smithsonian Institution Libraries, Post Office Department Manuscripts.

5. Robert S. Regar to Postmaster, Woodstock, Vermont, October 30, 1926. Smithsonian Institution Libraries, Post Office Department Manuscripts.

6. Philip H. Ward Jr., "The New 2¢ White Plains Stamp," *Mekeel's Weekly Stamp News*, Vol. 40, No. 45 (November 8, 1926).

7. Max Adler, "The White Plains Exhibition Panes," *Collectors Club Philatelist*, Vol. 17, No. 1 (January 1928), p. 38.

8. Max Adler, "The White Plains Plates," *Weekly Philatelic Gossip*, November 30, 1929, p. 1126.

9. *Ibid.*

10. Adolph H. Weber, "White Plains Exhibition Sheets," *Mekeel's Weekly Stamp News*, Vol. 51, No. 30 (July 26, 1937), p. 442.

11. Electric Eye [pseud.], "White Plains Exhibition Sheets, No. 629B," *Mekeel's Weekly Stamp News*, Vol. 51, No. 27 (July 5, 1937), p. 411.

12. Harry Weiss, "The Inside Straight," *Weekly Philatelic Gossip*, Vol. 67, No. 23 (January 31, 1959), p. 549.

Epilogue

The last stamp to be issued in 1926 was experimental in nature. This was the 2¢ value of the Series of 1922 with compound perforations: 11 at the top and bottom, and 10.5 at the sides. It is the stamp we know as Scott 634.

Issued only at Washington, D.C., on December 10, 1926, it was not given much of an announcement, but several dealers were able to service large numbers of first-day covers. Albert Gorham, who prepared the cover shown in Figure 135, sent hundreds of them out to prospective customers with an insert stating that "it has not been previously publicly announced."

In this same insert, Gorham noted that upon this experimental stamp "will depend the future of all perforated rotary press stamps of all denominations."

This was not too much of an exaggeration. There had been complaints from the public about rotary-press stamps for some time. While the old problem with curling had been largely overcome, some of the new complaints were about the stamps' adhesive qualities, but a large number described difficulties in tearing the stamps apart. A thick paper was believed to be at the root of the problem.

"Most of the complaints now being received," the Post Office Department told the Bureau, were that "the paper is thick and heavy, making it difficult to separate the stamps at the perforations without tearing into the stamps."

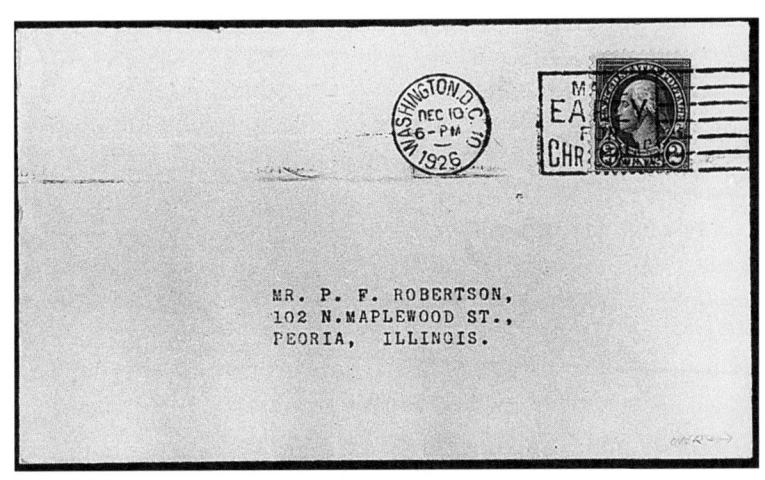

Figure 135. The last stamp of 1926 was experimental in nature and was also the beginning of a new group of stamps with compound perforations. First-day covers like this were mailed out in large numbers by some dealers.

An investigation into the thickness of the paper showed that it wasn't really much thicker than that of flat-plate stamps, about which no complaints were received. What was different were the perforations. Where the flat-plate stamps had 11-gauge perforations, the rotary-press stamps had 10-gauge perforations.

Thus with the rotary stamps there were fewer holes — and more paper — between the stamps. They were indeed harder to tear apart. But the 11-gauge perforation was believed to be too weak for the high-speed two-way perforator that was used to perforate rotary sheet stamps.

A compound gauge of 11 at the top and bottom, and 10.5 on the sides was found to work well at the Bureau. Only one of the two-way perforators was equipped with new pin and die wheels, but it was used to perforate some 20 million stamps that were sent to the New York post office as a test during the Christmas mailing rush.

The experimental supply performed well. The Bureau once again had come up with a solution to improve the acceptability of rotary-press stamps.

Within six months, all of the two-way perforators were refitted, and eventually all of the denominations of the Series of 1922, except for the dollar values, were given this new compound perforation.

No other value of the series was issued with these compound perforations in 1926, however. The other values up to the 10¢ appeared within seven months. The stamps we know with Scott numbers between 632 and 642 were issued between February 3 and July 27, 1927.

These are best treated as a group and will be covered in a subsequent volume on U.S. stamps issued from 1927 to 1932.

That volume will also continue the story of the stamps of the Coolidge and Hoover administrations and the political forces behind the decisions to issue them. Although Harry New would not be asked to stay on as postmaster general after Herbert Hoover was elected in 1928, most of the other Post Office Department executives stayed in place, including Second Assistant W. Irving Glover and the superintendent of stamps, Michael L. Eidsness Jr.

Only when the Democratic Party took over the White House in 1933, with the election of Franklin Delano Roosevelt, did the personnel and the policies change significantly.

The terms of the three Republican presidents of the 1920s — Harding, Coolidge and Hoover — make a logical period in which to group and study U.S. stamps. I have greatly enjoyed writing about the stamps issued from 1922 to 1926, and I am looking forward to continuing the story. I hope the readers of this book will also find that volume useful.

Photo Credits

Figure 91   Lexington Historical Society
Figure 100   Courtesy James T. McCusker
Figure 103   Courtesy James T. McCusker
Figure 116   Courtesy James T. McCusker
Figure 117   Courtesy James T. McCusker

Index

A

Addison, Joseph 238
Adler, Max 370, 371
Air Mail Act of 1925 299
Aircraft Production Board 165
Airmail service 4–6, 9, 159–170
    "Air Mail Service" markings 166
    Contract airmail 319–323, 326, 341
    First-flight covers 321–322, 341, 342
    Night flying 159–170, 326
    Reorganization 9, 299–300
    Test flights 163–164
    Transcontinental Route 4–6, 159–170, 299, 319–323, 330, 331, 332
    Map 160
Allen, Ethan 246
Allen, Frederick Lewis 221
Alvonis Company 72
American Bank Note Company 79
American Gas Accumulator Company 160
American Philatelic Society 3, 163, 166, 167
American Philatelist 20, 253, 341
American Revolution 238, 243, 244, 245, 251, 253, 337, 338, 359–360
American Stamp Journal 94
Anderson, Spencer 72
Andrus, B.L. 215
Arlington Memorial Amphitheatre 90–91

B

Babcock, W.L. 20, 69
Bacon, Henry 93
Baldwin, Marcus 38, 40, 88
Ballard, Orville 96
Ballou's Pictorial 246, 247
Bartels, Murray 368
Bartholdi, Frederic August 79, 97
Bartholdi's *Liberty Englightening the World* 26
Batchelder, Samuel 248
Battle of Bunker Hill 246
Battle of Lexington and Concord 243–255
Bedford, C.W. 89
Benners, Alfred 241
Benzing, Joachim C. 37, 38, 40, 80, 173, 227, 237, 245, 294, 303, 313, 325, 329, 332
The BIA Check List of the Postage Stamp Booklet Covers of the United States 143

Bierstadt, Edward 52, 53
Boers, Herman E. 66, 96, 98, 171, 172
Boone, Commander Joel T. 157
Boston Philatelic Society 71
Boston Public Library 71
Bothne, Gisle 291
Brady, Mathew 44, 57, 58, 65, 66
Brazer, Clarence 202
Brett, George 51
Brookman, Lester 187, 188, 241
"Buffalo Bill" 88
Bureau Issues Association 19, 37, 143
Bureau of Engraving and Printing 4, 9–14
    1922 10¢ motorcycle special delivery 16, 19
    1922 series 23–35, 37–105
    1923 Black Hardings 172–181
    1925 ½¢ Nathan Hale 241
    1925 17¢ Woodrow Wilson 307–308
    1926 1½¢ Harding rotary imperforate 352
    1926 White Plains issue 361
    Booklet stamps 355–358
    Coil waste 127–136
    Dry printing 276
    Engravers 11, 37
    Flat-plate booklets 143–149, 356
    Flat-plate press 4, 10–12, 37, 41, 107, 108, 128, 151, 193, 228, 257–262, 351
    Gumming 12
    Huguenot-Walloon issue 202–212
    Imperforates 137–141
    Intaglio printing 10–12
    Liberty Loan bonds scandal 9, 110, 111, 214
    Perforating 12–14
    Perforations, compound 373–374
    Perforators
        Flat-plate 116, 185
        One-way coil 116, 127
        Rotary 13, 37, 108, 112
        Two-way 154, 185
    Precancels .. 117, 119, 121, 122, 123, 124, 125, 151–152, 183, 263–272, 266
    Reorganization 9–14
    Rotary press 41, 107–113, 115–126, 127, 151–155, 193, 213–214
    Star plates 257–262
    Stickney press 107–113, 152, 183, 185, 193, 214
    Wet printing 276
    White Plains souvenir sheet 368–372
Bureau precancels ... 117, 119, 121, 122, 123, 124, 125, 151–152

376

Bureau Specialist 57, 61, 77, 86, 183, 229
Burleson, Albert 3, 4
Burr, David H. 42

C

Caffieri, Jean Jacques 39
Calvin, John.. 200
Cambridge Historical Commission 246, 248
Cambridge Public Library 246
Canal Zone overprint.. 342
Canal Zone Stamps 343
Cancellations, Sesquicentennial
    Exposition 342
Cassian, Brother 61–62, 172
Chalmers, Charles 84, 85
Chindblom, Carl R. 345, 346
Church, Frederic 85
Civil War 75, 339, 346, 349
Clark, Hugh 69
Cleland, Wallace 259
Cleveland, Grover 29, 30, 70–72,
                                        305, 306, 315
Coil stamps 37
    Coil waste 127–136, 185
    Endwise 107–108, 108, 193–197
    Sidewise 107, 193
Cole, Ezra 42, 43
Coleman, Arch 292
Collectors Club of New York 3, 54, 368
Collectors Club Philatelist 370
Collier, P.F., & Sons 135
Colonial Air Transport 319
Columbian Exposition of 1893 295
Committee on Foreign Relations 304
Committee on Military Affairs 316
Continental Bank Note Company 97
Coolidge, Calvin 157–158, 200, 221, 223, 246,
            299, 305, 307, 308, 322, 335, 346, 374
Corcoran Gallery of Art 85
Cornish, William 357
Coulter, W.A. 34, 81, 82
Courier Litho Co. 70
Covers
    Contract airmail 326, 342
    First-day
        1922 10¢ special delivery 18–19
        1922 series 37, 39, 44, 45, 50, 53,
                         56, 60, 63, 66, 67, 71, 76,
                80, 83, 86, 89, 92, 93, 95–96, 98
        1923 airmails 165–166, 167, 168–169
        1923 Black Hardings 171, 175–176, 177
        1923 imperforates 138–139
        1923-25 sidewise coils 118, 120,
                              122, 123, 124, 125
        1924 endwise coils 195–196
        1924 Huguenot-Walloon issue 204

Covers, first day (continued)
    1925 ½¢ Nathan Hale 240
    1925 ½¢ postage due 282
    1925 1½¢ Hardings 228, 230, 231, 234
    1925 2¢ Norse-American 292
    1925 15¢ special delivery 280
    1925 17¢ Woodrow Wilson 309
    1925 20¢ special delivery 286–287
    1925 25¢ special handling 275
    1925 Lexington-Concord 249, 253
    1925-26 rotaries, perf 10 264–269
    1926 1½¢ Harding rotary imperf 353
    1926 2¢ George Washington
        Compound perforations 373
    1926 2¢ Sesquicentennial
        Exposition 340–341
    1926 2¢ White Plains 364–365
    1926 5¢ Ericsson Memorial 348–349
    1926 13¢ Benjamin Harrison 315–316
    1926 airmails 328, 330–331, 333
    1926 booklets, rotary 357–358
    1926 White Plains souvenir sheet 369
    First-flight ... 321–322, 328, 330–331, 341, 342
    Patriotic 349
Crawford, Thomas 26, 97
Cromwell, Caroline Prentice 51
Crow, French 176
Curtiss Carrier Pigeon planes 322

D

Dallinger, Frederick W. 246
Daugherty, Harry 2, 221
Daughters of the American Revolution .. 199, 207,
                                            209, 210
Davis, John W. 158, 221
Davis, Norman H. 305, 306
Dawson, H.P. 165, 167, 202, 205, 206
de Aviles, Menendez 201
de Bry, Theodore 203, 208
de Coligny, Gaspard 200
De Havilland DH-4 .... 5, 160, 161–162, 165,
                               168–169, 322, 327, 328
de la Pierria, Albert 201
de Laudonniere, Rene Goulaine 201
Department of Highways of
    Pennsylvania 274
DeVoss, James T. 51
DeWitt, Henry C. 87
The Diary of Dorothy Dudley 246
Dickinson, Charles 320, 322
Dominican Republic special delivery stamp 18
Douglas M4 322
Durand, Asher 62
Durland, C.B. 86, 177
Durland Standard Plate Number
    Catalog 19, 37, 196, 259

377

Dutch West India Company 201

E

Earle, Howard I. 61, 97, 359, 367
Eastman, L.E. 68
Edict of Nantes 200
Edison, Thomas 321
Eidsness, Michael L. ... 17, 66, 176, 186, 215, 225, 226, 239, 280, 281, 285, 289–290, 293, 295, 300, 306, 314, 338, 374
Eissler, John 48, 49, 52, 53, 57, 58, 60, 65, 66, 70, 71, 96, 98, 168, 237, 303, 313, 335, 359, 367
Election of 1924 221–224
Ellis, F.L. 88
Emerson, Ralph Waldo 252
Ericsson, John 345–350
Ericsson Memorial Committee 345, 346, 348
Estabrook, William 173

F

Fairbanks, Ernest E. 134
Fakes
    1923 1¢ Benjamin Franklin coil waste, perf 11 x 10 133
    1923 1¢ Benjamin Franklin sheet rotary first-day cover 153
Fall, Albert 32, 82, 158
Farrar, F.M. 361
Federal Reserve Act 308
Ferry, Edward T. 61
Fess, Simeon 346
Fireman's Fund Insurance Company 82
Fiset, Louis 353
Fisher, Lawrence S. 153
Five Civilized Tribes 75
Flexner, James Thomas 248
Florida Airways 322
Ford Air Transport 320, 321, 322
Ford, Edsel 321
Ford, Henry 320, 321
Ford Motor Company 320
Fort Caroline National Memorial 209
Frampton, Ross 67
Franklin, Benjamin 23, 29, 30, 38, 39, 59, 62
Frazer, James Earle 347
French, Daniel Chester 244, 251, 252
French, Loran "Cloudy" 20, 43, 45, 48, 51, 57, 64, 77, 92, 96, 99, 121, 123, 124, 125, 148, 166, 195, 197, 205, 218, 229, 231, 232, 276, 280
Frost, George D. 96

G

Garfield, James 29, 30, 52, 55, 57, 65

General Electric 160
Geological Survey 327
Geronimo 75
Gibbons, Stanley 190, 259, 267
Gibbons, Stanley, catalog 60, 83, 184
Gill, De Lancey 73, 74
Glass, Carter 73
Glover, Anna 3, 16, 315, 316
Glover, Frances 80
Glover, W. Irving 2, 3, 4, 6, 15, 16, 17, 23, 24, 26, 27, 29, 30, 33, 45, 54, 62, 66, 74, 80, 91, 97, 108, 110, 115, 153, 158, 166, 171, 172, 178, 215, 225, 226, 257, 263, 289, 299, 300, 321, 331, 332, 336, 338, 368, 374
Gobie, Henry 280
Gorham, Albert 287, 358, 373
Grant, Ulysses S. 29, 30, 57–58, 62, 65
Greely & Benjamin 208
Griest, William Walton 289
Griscom-Russell 111
Grunin, Louis 86

H

Hale, Nathan 237–242
Hale, Richard 238
Hall, Alvin 257, 263, 276
Hall, Edward M. 15, 37, 38, 40, 43, 48, 52, 57, 59, 61, 65, 73, 78, 80, 87, 94, 95, 128, 167, 168, 173, 202, 205, 207, 227, 228, 237, 273, 279, 285, 291, 303, 313, 325, 329, 332, 335
Hamilton, Alexander 362
Hamilton's, Alexander, Battery 359, 363–364, 365
Hammelman, Henry 19, 123, 330
Hancock, John 244
Handbook of American Indians North of Mexico 74
Harding, George 176
Harding, Warren G. 1–7, 9, 16, 23, 32, 33, 44, 46, 49, 52, 57, 62, 65, 80, 82, 90, 108, 128, 157–158, 159, 161, 162, 171–181, 199, 221, 228, 303, 304, 305, 306, 322, 335, 368, 374
Harker, George Albert 361, 362, 365
Harlem Heights, Battle of 360
Harris & Ewing 49, 50
Harrison, Benjamin 57, 314
Harrison, William Henry 315
Hart, William J. 148, 217
Hartwell, E.F. 183
Harvey, Jack 123, 153, 217, 316
Hatton, William 72
Hayes, Rutherford B. 29, 30, 57, 65
Hayes, Scott R. 65, 66

Hays, Will 2, 4, 5, 6
Hein, Edward J. 63, 291
Helff, Clara 96, 358
Hendee Manufacturing Company 18
Henderson, Paul 159, 160, 163,
164, 299, 322
Hill, Louis A. 4, 17, 27, 34,
45, 66, 74, 82, 93, 111, 214
Hitchings, F.W. 176
Hollow Horn Bear 27, 74, 75
Hoover, Herbert 221, 308, 338, 374
Hoover, W.B. 188
Houdon, Jean-Antoine 38, 39, 40, 41
Howard, George 139, 351, 352
Howe, William 238
Hufeland, Otto 363, 364
Huguenots 200–201
Huston, Clair Aubrey 10, 15, 17, 18, 23,
24, 25, 26, 37, 58, 79, 97, 165, 166,
168, 173, 174, 202, 203, 205, 207, 208,
209, 227, 237, 245, 249, 252, 273, 279,
281, 285, 286, 290, 291, 294, 303, 313, 325,
329, 332, 335, 340, 345, 347, 348, 359, 362, 367

I

Indian Motorcycle Manufacturing Company 18
Ingersol-Rand Company 274
International Philatelic Exhibition, 1926 300,
331, 364, 367–372

J

Jackson, Andrew 240, 305
Jalabert, Charles 46
Jefferson, Thomas 29, 30, 59–60, 62
Johl, Max G. 20, 24, 39, 41, 42, 45, 47, 51, 53,
56, 58, 60, 63, 64, 71, 72, 76, 77, 78, 80, 83, 84,
86, 88, 91, 92, 118, 121, 122, 123, 124,
125, 128, 135, 139, 140, 147, 148, 152,
153, 154, 167, 169, 176, 178, 183, 184,
187, 190, 194, 195, 202, 204, 205, 206,
209, 210, 217, 218, 229, 230, 231, 232,
233, 234, 241, 249, 253, 259, 265, 266,
267, 268, 269, 271, 272, 293, 310, 317,
328, 331, 333, 342, 350, 353, 361, 365
Johnson, Hiram 81
Judd, Edward F., Co. 240

K

Kaslowski, Karl 196
Kauffmann, Leo C. 45, 47, 60
Kellogg, Frank 338
Kelly Bill 299, 319, 320
Kelly, Clyde 299
Kempf, Norman 119

Kennedy, J. 281
Kimble, Ralph 204, 210
King, Beverly 24, 169, 202,
208, 209, 241, 246, 361
Kirby, Wallace W. 214
Kiusalis, Richard 186, 188
Klein, Eugene 63, 64
Knight, Charles R. 88
Knight, Jack 159
Konwiser, H.M. 368
Konwiser, Samuel 176
Kuhn, Carolyn 43, 121, 196, 218
Kvale, Ole 289, 291, 293

L

LaFollette, Robert 221
Lamasure, Frank 70, 73, 329, 332, 345
Lamb, Martha J. 205, 206
Lampe, Otto 365
Laudonniere, Rene 207
League of Nations 62, 303, 304, 308
Levison, J.B. 82
Lewis and Clark 88
Lewis, Leslie 184
Lexington Provincial Company 244
Liberty Bell 336–344
Liberty Loan bonds scandal 9, 110, 111, 214
Library of Congress 65, 85, 175, 315
Lilly, Josiah K. 48, 69, 86
Lincoln, Abraham 29, 30, 44, 55, 57, 62, 252
Lincoln Memorial 92–93, 95, 174, 346
Linn, George 175
Long Island, Battle of 360
Longacre, James B. 62
Longworth, Nicholas 49
Lord & Thomas Advertising 233
Lord, Herbert 161, 243
Lovejoy, Harvey 361, 368
Luce, Robert 243
Luff, John 51, 64, 67, 91, 253, 327

M

Madden, Martin 159
Madison, James 240, 305
Maerz, A.J. 70
Magee, Joseph V. 160
Maiden Dearborn IV 320
Mail-o-Meter Company 137, 140, 232, 351–352
Malmin, Gunnar 292
Manning, Catherine 88
Many, S.B. 281
Markovits, Robert 19
Marshall, John 240, 305
Mast, Richard 356
Mayflower Pilgrims 199, 201, 289

379

McHugh and Sherman 315
McKinley Tariff Act 315
McKinley, William 29, 30, 49,
        55, 56, 57, 62, 65, 171
McLean, Edward 180
McLean, Emily B. 180
McLellan, Hugh 240
Mekeel's Weekly Stamp News 19, 148, 153, 162,
        190, 240, 253, 276,
        282, 299, 307, 341, 348, 371
Mellon, Andrew 9, 74, 108, 109, 111, 128, 221
Melville, Fred J. 72
Merritt, Schuyler 238, 240
Miers, Lewis 353
Mills, Clark 40, 41
Mills, F.P. 208
Minuteman statue 244, 249, 251–255
Moberly, Joe 188
Moffett Studio 174, 175, 307
Monroe Doctrine 61, 62
Monroe, James 61–62, 62
Morison, Samuel Eliot 201
Mount, Howard 171, 300
Multipost Company 115
Musin, A. 202
Myers, Edward E. 48, 55, 81, 84, 85, 90, 91

N

National Air Transport 299, 319, 322
National City Bank of Chicago 137
National Huguenot-Walloon New Netherland
        Commission 199, 202, 205, 208
National Sesquicentennial Exposition
        Commission 338
National Thrift Week 39
National Wholesale Liquor Dealers Association
        labels 79
New, Harry S. 32, 33, 82, 158, 160,
        161, 164, 176, 179, 199, 214, 215,
        221, 222, 225, 226, 238, 243, 244,
        246, 280, 289, 290, 300, 304, 305,
        307, 313, 319, 321, 326, 336, 338,
        345, 346, 359, 360, 361, 364, 374
New, John Chalfant 314
Niagara Falls 85–87
Nickles, C.E. 124, 270, 271, 309, 353, 357
Nieu Nederland 201, 202
Noble, Gilbert 152
Norris, Isaac 339
Norse-American Centennial 289, 294
Nowell-Usticke, G.W. 259

O

Obrig, James 232
Olsen Rug Company 233

Owen, Arthur 131, 132, 176, 184

P

Pacific Air Transport 320
Paddock, J.E. 75
Pan American Exposition 88
Parker, Charles 65
Parker, Jason Samuel 362, 363, 365
Parker, John 244
Partridge, Elmer 322
Pass, John 339
Pauling, Frederick ... 173, 174, 175, 207, 227, 245
Peakes, Gilbert 276
Penn, William 339
Perforations, private 137–138, 139, 233
        Schermack 137, 180, 233, 260, 351
Perrett, Geoffrey 221
Philadelphia Exposition 338
Philatelic Foundation 42, 51, 135, 191
Pitney-Bowes 351–352, 353
The Postage Stamps of the United States 267
Postal Service Bill 306
Pratt, Bela Lyon 239
Precancels
        Bureau 151–152, 183, 263
        Chicago 139
Prescott, Colonel John 244
Proofs, die 11, 16

Q

Quintard, George H. 50

R

Railway Mail Service 164
Rates, postal
        1925 rate change 221–224,
                225, 273–274, 285, 306
        Airmail 320–321, 326
                Contract 329–330, 332
                Night and day 162–163, 326, 369
        Domestic letter rate 39, 40, 76, 118, 163,
                173, 223, 240, 264, 265, 289, 306, 333
        Fourth-class 274
        Insurance rate 314
        Parcel post 274, 313
        Postcard 224
        Registry fee 306
        Special delivery 15, 196, 223, 225, 264,
                265, 279–280, 285–287, 333
        Special handling 223, 273–277
        Third-class 139, 225, 353
Regar, Robert 300, 314, 337,
        341, 343, 346, 349, 360, 368, 374
Republican National Committee 2

380

Restaurationen 289, 291–292
Revere, Paul 244
Ribaut, Jean 200, 201, 203, 207, 208, 209, 210
Rich, Steven 18
Richelieu, Cardinal 200
Robertson Aircraft Corp. 319
Rockwood, George 56
Roessler, Albert 292, 309, 333, 365
Rogers, John Jacob 244, 245
Rood, John R. 96
Roosevelt, Alice 50
Roosevelt, Edith 50
Roosevelt, Franklin D. 307
Roosevelt, Ted 50
Roosevelt, Theodore 1, 2, 23, 24, 26,
  29, 30, 49, 50, 55, 62, 75, 305, 306, 314
Rose, George Jr. 9
Rosewater, Victor 337, 338
Rotnem Stamp Company 349
Rubel, Charles 68
Rutstein, Leo 98

S

Saint-Gaudens, Augustus 347
Sawyer, Charles 157
Schenk, J.C. 48
Schermack perforations 137, 140, 180,
  233, 260, 351
Schiff, Jacques C. Jr. 69, 72
Schofield, Louis S. 15, 55, 56, 57, 58, 73,
  74, 78, 80, 81, 83, 87, 89, 90, 91, 92,
  93, 94, 95, 202, 249, 279, 285, 345
Schoonmaker, D.J. 342
Schwartz, Richard J. 365
Scott Specialized Catalogue of United States
  Stamps 19, 20, 39, 41,
  42, 45, 47, 48, 50, 51, 53, 54, 56, 58,
  60, 61, 63, 64, 66, 67, 68, 71, 76, 77,
  78, 80, 83, 86, 89, 90, 92, 94, 96, 98, 99,
  118, 120, 121, 122, 123, 124, 125, 128,
  130, 131, 140, 146, 147, 148, 154, 166,
  167, 169, 176, 178, 188, 189, 190, 194,
  195, 196, 197, 204, 206, 210, 217, 218,
  225, 229, 230, 231, 232, 233, 234, 241,
  249, 253, 260, 265, 266, 267, 268, 269,
  271, 272, 275–276, 280, 293, 310, 316,
  317, 328, 329, 331, 333, 341, 342,
  349, 353, 354, 363, 365, 370, 371
Scott Stamp & Coin 69, 91, 129, 294
Scott's American Album 276
Scott's Monthly Journal 41, 58, 62, 68, 83, 86,
  119, 121, 241, 294
Sesquicentennial Exhibition
  Association 335–336
Sesquicentennial International
  Exposition 335–344, 340

Seymour, George Dudley 237, 239
Shaughnessy, Edward H. 5, 6, 159, 161
Shaughnessy, Myrtle 6
Sherman Anti-Trust Act, ... 315
Shift Hunter Letter 48, 83, 84,
  89, 195, 196, 197, 241
Siebold, William O. 98, 196, 275
Sinkler, Wharton 51
Skinner, Charles 79
Sloane, George 42, 43, 53, 54, 72, 89, 130, 197,
  207, 210, 253, 342
Smillie, George F.C. 9, 10, 43, 44,
  59, 60, 61, 63, 73, 74, 307
Smith, R. Ostrander 10
Smithsonian Institution 73, 74, 78, 88, 98, 361
Soulman, George 217
Southgate, Hugh 42, 77, 78, 184, 357
Souvenir sheet, first U.S. 367–372
Sperry Gyroscope 160
Stamp Lover 121
Stamps 72, 122, 169, 197, 267, 280
Star plates. *See* United States stamps: 1922 star
  plates
Statue of Freedom 97–98
Statue of Liberty 78–80, 97
Stevenson, John 24, 25
Stickney, Benjamin 9, 107, 108, 109, 110, 111,
  112, 113, 214, 216
Stickney, Herman O. 338
Stiles, Kent 331, 332, 341
Stoudt, John Baer 202, 203, 208
Stout, William S. 320
Stout 2A-T 320, 321
Stow, John 339
Stuart, Gilbert 46, 59–60
Sullivan, Mark 171

T

Taft, William Howard 1, 123, 304, 305
Teapot Dome oil-lease scandal 32, 221
Thorp, Prescott Holden 135
Tilden, Samuel J. 65
Transcontinental Route. *See* Airmail service:
  Transcontinental Route

U

Underwood & Underwood 85
United Air Lines 299
United States Capitol 95, 97
United States Post Office
  Department 1, 2, 3, 5, 6, 9, 19, 24, 25,
  26, 27, 30, 32, 34, 38, 39, 41, 44, 45, 46, 49,
  50, 53, 56, 58, 60, 61, 62, 63, 66, 71, 75,
  80, 82, 83, 89, 92, 94, 96, 97, 98, 107, 108,
  109, 110, 111, 112, 127, 128, 138, 147, 148,

381

U.S. Post Office Department (continued)
151, 157, 158, 161, 162, 166, 167, 168, 171, 172, 173, 174, 175, 177, 178, 187, 206, 208, 209, 213, 214, 222, 224, 225, 226, 228, 229, 230, 238, 239, 243, 244, 245, 246, 249, 252, 253, 257, 263, 290, 292, 293, 294, 295, 299, 306–311, 316, 319, 320, 326, 330, 331, 336, 337, 346, 349, 359, 360, 361, 362, 363, 368, 373–374
Division of Stamps 17, 176, 186, 215, 225, 280, 285, 289–290, 300, 306
Philatelic Stamp Agency 4, 6, 16, 17, 45, 47, 60, 120, 129, 133, 134, 137–138, 139, 140, 153, 168, 171, 176, 177, 179, 194, 195, 217, 233, 266, 268, 274, 275, 299, 309, 352, 353, 357, 365, 368, 369

United States Postage Stamps of the
20th Century 267
United States Postal Service
  Stamp policy 307
United States Specialist 188, 259
United States stamps
  1894 issue 23
  1898 Trans-Mississippi issue 361, 362
  1901 Pan American issue 289
  1902 issue 29, 44, 46, 60, 315
  1904 Louisiana Purchase 55, 60, 61, 63
  1908 special delivery 10
  1911 registry stamps 4
  1912 parcel post postage dues 273
  1913 2¢ parcel post 16, 17
  1913 5¢ Panama-Pacific 81
  1918 airmail invert 64
  1918 airmail issue 4
  1919 Victory issue 4
  1920 Pilgrim Tercentenary issue 4, 199
  1922 1¢ Washington-Franklin,
    rotary 183, 185
    Kansas City, Mo., precancel ... 183–184, 186
  1922 13¢ star plates 259
  1922 2¢ Black Harding 171–181
  1922 motorcycle special delivery 15–21, 23, 26, 280, 286
    Colors and shades 20
    Design 17–18
    Double transfer 15, 20
    First-day covers 18–19
    Plate layout 19–20
    Plate number blocks 19
    Small-letter variety 19
    Star plates 257–262
  1922-25 series 1–2, 37–105, 113, 128, 227
    Golden Gate stamp 34
    Models 24–26, 26–28
    Planning 23–35
    Plate layout 38
    Plate number blocks 38

1922-25 series (continued)
  Politics 28–32
  Yosemite stamp 33–34
  ½¢ Nathan Hale 37, 233, 237–242, 304
    Cap on fraction bar 241
    First day of issue 239–240
    Plate crack 241
    Shades 241
  1¢ Benjamin Franklin 23, 38–39, 151, 177, 183, 238
    Double transfer 39, 48
    First day of issue 39
    Plate varieties 39
    Shades 39
  1¢ Benjamin Franklin coil waste,
    perf 11 x 10 132–133
    Earliest use 132–133
    Fakes 133
    Imperforate at bottom 133
    Plate numbers 133
    Quantity issued 133
  1¢ Benjamin Franklin coil waste,
    perf 11 x 11 133–136
    Earliest use 135
    Fakes 135
    Scarcity 134–135
  1¢ Benjamin Franklin imperf 138–139
    Chicago precancel 139
    First day of issue 138–139
    Scarcity 139
    Schermack perforations 139
  1¢ Benjamin Franklin sheet
    rotary 151–155
    Double paper 154
    Earliest usage 153
    Perforation and division 154
    Plate layout 153
    Shades 154
  1¢ Benjamin Franklin sheet rotary,
    perf 11 .... 187–189, 191, 263
    Kansas City precancel 187, 188
    Rarity 189
    Size 189
  1¢ Benjamin Franklin side coil 118-119
    Bureau precancels 119
    Double transfer 118
    First day of issue 118
    Gripper cracks 118, 119
    Joint line pair 118
    Plate numbers 118–119
    Shades 118
  1¢ Benjamin Franklin
    booklet pane 147–148, 148
    Double transfer 147
    First day of issue 147
    Plate varieties 147
    Shades 147

382

1922-25 series (continued)
  1¢ Benjamin Franklin end coil 194–195
    First day of issue 194, 195
    joint line pair 194, 195
    Plate numbers 194–195
    Plate varieties 195
    Shades 194
  1½¢ Warren G. Harding ... 37, 225–235, 304
  1½¢ Warren G. Harding end coil 234
    First day of issue 234
    Plates and plate layout 234
    Shades 234
  1½¢ Warren G. Harding flat plate 226,
                                             227–229
    Double transfer 227, 229, 233
    First day of issue 228–229, 230, 231
    Shades 229, 230
  1½¢ Warren G. Harding flat plate
    imperforate 227, 232-233, 266
    Double transfer 232, 233
    First day of issue 233
    Perforations, private 233
    Shades 233
  1½¢ Harding rotary, perf 10 ... 226, 229, 263
    Double paper 230
    First day of issue 230, 231
    Plate varieties 230–231
    Shades 230, 231
    Sheets of 400 230
  1½¢ Harding rotary imperforate 351–354
    First day of issue 353
    Shades 353
    Without gum-breaker ridges 353–354
  1½¢ Harding side coil 231–232
    Coil varieties 232
    First day of issue 231
    Plate varieties 232
    Shades 231
  2¢ George Washington 11, 23, 40–43,
                                                172, 177
    Double transfer 42–43
    First day of issue 41, 47
    Shades 41
    Star plates 257-259, 260
    Varieties 40, 41–42, 45
  2¢ George Washington booklet pane 148
    Double transfer 148
    First day of issue 148
    Plate varieties 148
    Shades 148
  2¢ George Washington booklet stamps,
    rotary 355–358
    Booklet pane positions 356–357
    First day of issue 357–358
    Plate numbers 357

1922-25 series (continued)
  2¢ George Washington coil waste,
    perf 11 x 10 129-130
    Earliest use 129
    Imperforate at bottom 130
    Plate numbers 130
    Quantity issued 129–130
    Recut in eye 129, 130
  2¢ George Washington coil waste,
    perf 11 x 11 131–132
    Earliest use 131–132
    Plate numbers 132
    Recut in eye 132
  2¢ George Washington compound
    perforations 373–374
  2¢ George Washington end coil 195–197
    Cracked plate 195, 196
    First day of issue 195–196
    Gripper cracks 197
    Joint line pair 195, 196
    Plate numbers 196
    Plate varieties 196–197
    Shades 196
  2¢ George Washington imperforate 140
    First day of use 140
    Schermack perforations 140
  2¢ George Washington rotary,
    perf 10 213–219
    Double paper 218
    Earliest-documented cover 217
    First day of issue 217
    Plate layout 217–218
    Plate varieties 218
    Shades 217
  2¢ George Washington side coil 115,
                                               119-121
    Bureau precancels 121
    Double transfer 119, 121
    First day of issue 118, 120, 122
    Gripper cracks 119, 121
    Joint line pair 119
    Plate numbers 121
    Plate varieties 121
    Shades 120–121
  3¢ Abraham Lincoln 43–45, 89
    First day of issue 44
    Plate blocks 45
    Shades 45
  3¢ Abraham Lincoln coil 122
    Bureau precancels 122
    Cracked plate 122
    First day of issue 122, 124
    Joint line pair 122
    Plate numbers 122
    Shades 122

1922-25 series (continued)
   3¢ Abraham Lincoln rotary 264–265
      First day of issue 264–265
      Shades 265
   4¢ Martha Washington 45
      First day of issue 47
      Shades 47, 94, 229
      Varieties 46, 47–48
   4¢ Martha Washington coil 123
      Bureau precancels 123
      First day of issue 123
      Gripper cracks 123
      Joint line pair 123
      Plate numbers 123
      Shades 123
   4¢ Martha Washington rotary 265
      First day of issue 265–266, 268
      Precancels 266
      Shades 266
   5¢ Theodore Roosevelt 4, 23, 48–51
      Double transfer 49, 51
      First day of issue 50
      Shades 50, 76
      Varieties 49, 50–51
   5¢ Theodore Roosevelt coil 124
      Bureau precancels 124
      First day of issue 124
      Joint line pairs 124
      Plate numbers 124
      Plate varieties 124
      Shades 124
   5¢ Theodore Roosevelt rotary 266–267
      Double transfer 266, 267
      First day of issue 266–267
      Horizontal pair, imperf between . 266, 267
      Precancels 267
      Shades 267
   6¢ James A. Garfield 51
      Double transfer 52, 53-54
      First day of issue 53, 56
      Shades 53
   6¢ James A. Garfield rotary 267–268
      First day of issue 268
      Precancels 268
      Shades 268
   7¢ William McKinley 55–57, 174
      Double transfer 55
      First day of issue 56, 76, 83
      Plate varieties 56–57
      Shades 56
   7¢ William McKinley rotary 268–269
      First day of issue 268–269, 270, 271
      Precancels 269
      Shades 269
   8¢ Ulysses S. Grant 57–59
      Double transfer 57, 58–59
      First day of issue 58, 76, 83

1922-25 series
   8¢ Ulysses S. Grant (continued)
      Plate varieties 58–59
      Shades 58
      Star-plate varieties 59, 260
   8¢ Ulysses S. Grant rotary 268-270
      First day of issue 268-269, 270, 271
      Precancels 270
      Shades 269–270
   9¢ Thomas Jefferson 47, 59–61
      Double transfer 59, 61
      First day of issue 60
      Plate varieties 61
      Shades 60
   9¢ Thomas Jefferson rotary 268-271
      First day of issue 268-269, 270, 271
      Precancels 271
      Shades 271
   10¢ James Monroe 47, 53, 61
      First day of issue 63
      Perforation varieties 61, 63–64
      Plate varieties 64
      Shades 63
   10¢ James Monroe rotary 271–272
      First day of issue 272
      Shades 272
   10¢ James Monroe sidewise coil 108, 125
      Bureau precancels 125
      First day of issue 124, 125
      Joint line pair 125
      Plate numbers 125
      Plate varieties 125
      Shades 125
   11¢ Rutherford B. Hayes 30, 32, 50, 65
      First day of issue 66, 67
      Perforation varieties 65, 68–69
      Plate markings 69–70
      Shades 66–67
   12¢ Grover Cleveland 70
      Double transfer 70, 72
      First day of issue 71, 89, 95
      Perforation varieties 70, 72
      Plate varieties 72
      Shades 71–72
      Star plates 259, 261
   13¢ Benjamin Harrison 313–317, 319
      First day of issue 315–316
      Shades 317
      Star plates 317
   14¢ American Indian 73–78, 87
      Double transfer 73, 77
      First day of issue 75, 83
      Plate varieties 76–78
      Relief breaks 76–77
      Shades 76
      Wide-spacing variety 77–78

1922-25 series (continued)
- 15¢ Statue of Liberty 78–80, 97
  - First day of issue 80, 85, 86, 92
  - Shades 80
  - Star plates 78, 80, 259, 261
- 20¢ Golden Gate 33-34, 80, 81
  - Double transfer 81, 83–84
  - First day of issue 83
  - Plate varieties 83–84
  - Perforation varieties 81, 83
  - Shades 83
  - Star-plate varieties 81, 259, 261
- 25¢ Niagara Falls 84–87
  - Bridge Over Falls 86–87
  - Double transfer 84, 86
  - First day of issue 76, 80, 85–86, 92
  - Perforation varieties 84, 86
  - Shades 86
- 30¢ Buffalo 71, 87–90
  - Double transfer 87, 89–90
  - First day of issue 89, 95
  - Shades 89
- 50¢ Arlington Amphitheater .. 29, 90–92, 92
  - First day of issue 80, 85, 92
  - Plate varieties 92
  - Shades 92
- $1 Lincoln Memorial 92–94, 95
  - Double transfers 92, 94
  - First day of issue 93
  - Plate layout 93–94, 96
  - Plate number blocks 93–94
  - Shades 94
- $2 U.S. Capitol 71, 94–96
  - First day of issue 89, 95–96
  - Plate layout 96
  - Plate number blocks 96
  - Plate varieties 96
  - Shades 76, 96
- $5 America 28, 29, 33, 96–97, 290
  - First day of issue 89, 95, 98
  - Plate layout 98
  - Plate number blocks 98
  - Plate number, missing 99
  - Plate varieties 99
  - Shades 98–99
- 1923 airmail stamps 162–170
  - 8¢ 162–163, 165–166, 167
    - Double transfer 165, 166
    - First-day covers 163, 165–166
    - Shades 166
  - 16¢ 166–167
    - Double transfer 167
    - First day of issue 167
    - Shades 167
  - 24¢ 168–169
    - Double transfer 168, 169

1923 airmail stamps
- 24¢ (continued)
  - First day of issue 168–169
  - Shades 169
- 1923 2¢ Black Hardings 199, 225, 226
  - Flat plate 173, 177, 189
    - Double transfer 173, 176
    - First day of issue 175–176
    - Imperforate error 176–177
    - Perforation varieties 176
    - Shades 176
  - Imperforate 179–180
    - First day of issue 180
    - Position pieces 180
    - Schermack perforations 180
  - Rotary 177, 183, 263
    - Complaints 178
    - Double paper 178
    - First day of issue 177
    - Full vertical gutter
      between 177, 178–179
    - Plate markings 178
  - Rotary perf 11 .... 190–191, 217
    - Rarity 191
    - Size 191
- 1923 imperforates 137–141
- 1924 Huguenot-Walloon issue 199–212
  - Models 203
  - 1¢ 199, 201–205, 206, 289
    - Double transfer 202, 204–205
    - First day of issue 204
    - Shades 204
  - 2¢ 200, 205–207, 209
    - Damaged transfer 207
    - Double transfer 205, 206–207
    - First day of issue 206
    - Shades 206
  - 5¢ 200, 207–209
    - Broken circle 207, 210–211
    - First day of issue 210
    - Plate varieties 206
    - Shades 210
- 1924-26 rotaries, perf 10 213
- 1925 ½¢ postage due 281–283, 285
  - Double transfer 283
  - First day of issue 282
  - Usage 282–283
- 1925 15¢ special delivery 279–280, 287
  - Double transfer 279, 280
  - First day of issue 280
- 1925 17¢ Wilson 303–311, 313, 319, 345
  - First day of issue 309
  - Printed both sides 310
  - Shades 310
- 1925 Lexington-Concord 225, 233, 240,
  243–255, 266

385

1925 Lexington-Concord (continued)
 1¢ 245–249
  First day of issue 249
  Shades 249
 2¢ 249–251
  First day of issue 253
  Line over head 253
  Shades 253
 5¢ 253
1925 Norse-American issue 289–297, 337
 2¢ 291–293
  First day of issue 292
  Plate blocks 293, 295
  Plate number omitted 293–294
  Shades 293
  Shortages 292–293
 5¢ 294–295
  First day of issue 295
  Invert 295
  Plate blocks 295, 296
  Plate varieties 295
1925 20¢ special delivery 285–287
 First day of issue 286–287
 Usage 287
1925 25¢ special handling 273–277
 Cataloging 275–276
 First day of issue 275
 Quantities 275
 Relief breaks 273, 276–277
 Shades 276
 Usage 275
1925-26 rotaries, perf 10 263–272
1926 2¢ Battle of White Plains 359–366
 Designs and models 362–364
 First day of issue 364–365
 Shades 365
 Souvenir sheet 367–372
 Vertical pair, imperf between 359, 365
1926 2¢ Sesquicentennial issue .. 335–344, 361
 Canal Zone overprint 342–343
 Criticism 341
 Double transfer 335, 342
 First day of issue 340–341, 342
 Shades 341–342
1926 5¢ John Ericsson
 First day of issue 268, 348-349
 Quantity issued 349
 Shades 349–350
1926 International Philatelic Exhibition
 souvenir sheet 367–372
 Dot over the "S" 367, 370–371
 First day of issue 369
 Imperforate sheets 368
 Plate layout 370
 Plate number blocks 370
 Scarcity 371

1926 Map airmails 325–334
 10¢ 325–329, 332, 333
  Double transfer 328–329
  First day of issue 328
  Shades 328
 15¢ Map airmails 325, 329–331
  First day of issue 330–331
  Shades 331
  Usage 331
 20¢ Map airmails 325, 331–334
  First day of issue 333
  Inverted Fs 333–334
  Shades 3331926
Coil waste 127–136
Coils
 Bureau precancels 117
 Endwise 107–108, 193–197
 Rotary-press 107–113, 115–126
 Sidewise 107, 115–126, 128
 Splices 117
Flat-plate booklets 143–149
 Booklet construction 145–147
 Booklet pane positions 145
 Panes 147
 Paper grain 147
Flat-plate sheet 115, 130, 151, 257–262
Fractional stamps 223, 225–235
Rotary sheet 107–113, 373–374
 Peforation problems 108–109
Sheet rotary rarities 183–192
Sheet rotary stamps 151–155
Souvenir sheet, first
 Souvenir sheet 367–372
Washington-Franklin series 1, 30, 38, 39, 40,
 42, 44, 52, 53, 57, 59, 76, 107, 108, 109,
 127, 128, 143, 151, 174, 177, 183, 194, 314
Scott numbers
 12 59
 205 52
 216 52
 224 52
 256 52
 304 44
 305 52
 310 60
 324 60
 325 61
 399 81
 473 42
 497 108
 498e 143
 542 .... 108, 151, 177
 543 .... 151, 177
 544 .... 183, 184, 185
 545 128
 546 128
 551 .... 233, 237–242

386

Scott numbers (continued)
Scott #	Pages
552	38, 241
552a	143, 147–148
553	227, 227–229
554	40–43, 259, 260
554a	41, 42
554b	41–42
554c	43, 143, 148
554d	42, 51, 64
555	43–45
556	45–48
556a	47–48
556b	48
557	48–51
557a	50
557b	50–51
557c	51
558	51
559	55–57
560	57–59, 259, 260–261
561	59–61
562	61
562a	63–64
562b	64
562c	64
563	65
563a	68
563b	68
563c	68
563d	68
564	70, 259, 261
564a	72
564b	72
565	73–78, 259, 261
566	78–80
567	81, 259, 261
568	42, 84–87
568b	86
569	87–90
570	90–92
571	92–94
571a	94
572	94–96
573	96–97
573a	98
575	138–139
576	232–233
577	140, 259, 260
578	132–133
579	129–131, 131, 132
581	151–155, 177, 178, 217, 263
582	227, 229, 263
583	213–219, 263
583a	218, 355–358
584	264–265
585	233, 265
586	233, 266

Scott numbers (continued)
Scott #	Pages
586a	267
587	233, 267–268
588	268–269
589	269–270
590	270
591	271–272
594	133–136
595	131–132
596	184, 185, 187–189
597	118–119
598	227, 231–232
599	119
599A	121
600	122
601	123
602	124
603	125
604	194–195
605	234
606	195–197
610	171–181, 227
610a	176
611	171–181, 227
612	171–181, 191, 217, 227
613	184, 185, 190–191, 227
614	201–205
615	205–207
616	207–209, 241
617-19	233, 243–255
620	291–294
621	294–295
622	269, 313–317
623	269
623a	310
627	335–344
628	345–350
629	359–366
629a	365
630	367–372
631	351–354
634	373–374
BK57	143–144
BK66	144
BK67	144
BK68	143, 144
BK69	145
BK70	145
BK71	144–147
BK72	356–358
BK73	356–358
BK74	356–358
C3a	64
C4	162–163, 165–166
C5	166–167
C6	168–169
C7	325–329

387

Scott numbers (continued)
C8 329–331
C9 332–334
C9a 333
E12 15–21
E12a 19, 20
E13 279–280
E14 285–287
J68 281–283
QE4 273
QE4a 273–277
U481 .... 227, 228

The United States Postage Stamps of the Twentieth Century 24
United States Treasury Department 109, 112, 115, 128
Universal Machine Co. 111
Universal Postal Union 49, 173, 350
Unknown Soldier's tomb 90, 91, 92
Uptown Stamp Company 135, 267

V

Vanderlyn, John 62
Varieties
 Broken circle
  1924 5¢ Hugenot-Walloon 207, 210–211
 Cracked plate
  1923 3¢ Abraham Lincoln 122
  1924 1¢ end coil 195
  1924 2¢ end coil 195, 196
  1925 ½¢ Nathan Hale 241
 Damaged transfer
  1924 2¢ Hugenot-Walloon 207
 Dot over "S"
  International Philatelic Exhibition souvenir sheet 367, 370–371
 Double paper
  1924 2¢ George Washington rotary, perf 10 218
  1925 1½¢ Harding rotary, perf 10 230
 Double transfers
  1922 motorcycle special delivery 15, 20
  1922 series 38, 39, 40, 42–43, 46, 48, 49, 51, 52, 54, 55, 57, 58-59, 61, 70, 72, 73, 77, 81, 83–84, 86, 87, 89–90, 92, 94
  1923 1¢ Benjamin Franklin coil 118, 119
  1923 2¢ Black Harding, flat plate .. 173, 176
  1923 2¢ George Washington coil ... 119, 121
  1923 8¢ airmail 165, 166
  1923 16¢ airmail 167
  1923 24¢ airmail 168, 169
  1924 1¢ Franklin booklet pane 147
  1924 2¢ Washington booklet pane 148
  1924 Hugenot-Walloon 202, 204, 205
  1925 ½¢ postage due 283
  1925 1½¢ Harding flat plate .. 227, 229, 233

Varieties
 Double transfers (continued)
  1925 1½¢ Harding flat-plate imperf 232
  1925 5¢ Theodore Roosevelt rotary 266, 267
  1925 15¢ special delivery 279, 280
  1926 2¢ Sesquicentennial 335, 342
 Gripper cracks
  1923 1¢ Benjamin Franklin coil 118, 119
  1923 2¢ George Washington coil ... 119, 121
  1923 4¢ Martha Washington coil 123
 Joint line pairs
  1923 1¢ Benjamin Franklin coil 118
  1923 2¢ George Washington coil 119
  1923 2¢ George Washington coil waste, perf 11 x 10 130
  1923 3¢ Abraham Lincoln coil 122
  1923 4¢ Martha Washington coil 123
  1923 5¢ Theodore Roosevelt coil 124
  1923 10¢ James Monroe coil 125
  1924 1¢ end coil 194, 195
  1924 2¢ end coil 196
 Perforation varieties
  1922 series 40, 41–42, 46, 47-48, 49, 50-51, 61, 63–64, 65, 68–69, 72, 81, 83, 84, 86
  1923 1¢ Benjamin Franklin coil waste, perf 11 x 10 133
  1923 2¢ Black Harding, flat plate 176
  1923 2¢ George Washington coil waste, perf 11 x 10 130
  1925 5¢ Thedore Roosevelt rotary 266, 267
  1926 2¢ Battle of White Plains 359, 365
 Plate number omitted
  1925 2¢ Norse-American 291, 293–294
 Plate varieties
  1922 series 53-54, 56-57, 58-59, 61, 64, 72, 83-84
  1924 2¢ George Washington rotary, perf 10 218
  1924 Huguenot-Walloons 206–207
  1925 ½¢ Nathan Hale 237, 241
  1925 1½¢ Harding rotary, perf 10 .. 230–231
  1925 1½¢ Harding side coil 232
 Printed both sides
  1925 17¢ Woodrow Wilson 310
 Recut in eye
  1923 2¢ George Washington coil waste, perf 11 x 10 .... 129, 130
  1923 2¢ George Washington coil waste, perf 11 x 11 .... 131, 132
 Relief breaks
  1922 14¢ American Indian 76–77
  1925 25¢ special handling 273, 276–277
 Small letter
  1922 motorcycle special delivery 19

Varieties (continued)
　Star plates 77, 140
　1922 series 40, 59, 78, 80, 81
　Triple transfer
　　1922 1¢ Franklin 39
Varney, Walter T. 319, 322
Versailles Treaty 308

W

Wadsworth, James Wolcott Jr. 360, 361
Wagner, George 153, 233
Wainwright, Jonathan Mahew 359, 360, 361, 362, 363
Walloons 200–201, 202, 205–206
Ward, Edmund 361, 362, 363, 365
Ward, Philip 3, 4, 19, 42, 49, 50, 53, 63, 64, 65, 87, 120, 123, 131, 134, 138, 140, 148, 153, 162, 167, 169, 176, 178, 186, 203, 204, 217, 229, 230, 234, 240, 241, 265, 276, 279, 282, 304, 306, 307, 329, 331, 341, 342, 352, 354, 357, 365, 370
Washington Elm 246, 247
Washington, George 1, 23, 29, 30, 40, 59, 62, 172, 238, 241, 245, 246, 247, 336, 360
Washington, Martha 29, 30, 46, 62
Washington Post 180
Weber, Adolph 371
Weber, Karl 161

Weekly Philatelic Gossip 371
Weeks, Edward M. 15, 45, 65, 70, 165, 227, 237, 245, 249, 279, 281, 285, 294
Weeks, John W. 244
Weiss, Larry 371
Wells, William B. 57, 92, 291
Weschcke, Ernest 292, 293
Westchester County Historical Society 360, 363
Western Air Express 319
Westinghouse Electric 340
White Plains, Battle of 359–366
Whittaker, Harold F. 138
Wilbur, Curtis 346
Wilmeth, James 9, 109, 110, 111, 127, 128
Wilson, Edith Bolling 307
Wilson, Woodrow 1, 4, 10, 23, 49, 62, 73, 75, 159, 240, 303–311, 319
Wilson, Woodrow, Foundation 309
Wittenauer, George 56
Worden, Edward C. 19, 93, 96, 98, 124, 315, 316, 369
Work, Hubert 6, 15, 16, 26, 32–33, 34, 45, 82, 157, 221
Wulson, Max 135

Y

Yale University 237–238
Yosemite National Park 81, 82

389

About the Author

Gary Griffith has collected United States stamps since childhood, and specializes in the stamps of the Series of 1922. His competitive exhibit, "The 2¢ Washington 1922," has won 10 gold medals at national competitions and was included in the American Philatelic Society's "Champion of Champions" competition in 1991.

He is a former editor of the *United States Specialist*, and has contributed to a number of general interest and specialized stamp publications, including *Essay-Proof Journal, Linn's Stamp News, Stamp Collector, First Days* and *Scott's Stamp Monthly*.

A former television reporter and producer, he lives in Washington D.C., where he has been the bureau chief for Hearst Broadcasting since 1989.